QUIZ MASTER

500 NEW

QUIZZES

Published by Collins
An imprint of HarperCollins Publishers
Westerhill Road
Bishopbriggs
Glasgow G64 2QT

HarperCollins Publishers
1st Floor, Watermarque Building, Ringsend Road, Dublin 4, Ireland

First Edition 2019

10 9 8 7 6 5 4

ISBN 978-0-00-834820-5

Typeset by Puzzler Media

Printed and bound by CPI Group (UK) Ltd, Croydon, CR0 4YY

If you would like to comment on any aspect of this book, please contact us at the above address or online.
E-mail: puzzles@harpercollins.co.uk

Introduction

What makes a good quiz? A witty and amusing host and a choice of interesting categories are good places to start.

You could combine the hosting talents of Alexander Armstrong and Jeremy Paxman but you need a great set of questions too.

That's where *Collins Quiz Master* comes in. We've taken the hassle out of creating the perfect quiz by providing 10,000 questions on all manner of subjects in an easy-to-use format.

There's something on offer for everyone, too, from easy questions for those taking their first tentative steps from quizzing base camp right up to super-tricky testers for those experienced trivia travellers heading for the highest peaks of general knowledge.

Let's get going.

The quizzes

The book is divided into two parts, each with 250 quizzes. Half of the quizzes are based on themes ranging from biology to buildings, geography to golf, nature to numbers and a whole host of subjects in between. The rest of the quizzes are pot luck and contain a little bit of everything.

The quizzes in each part of the book are grouped together depending on how tricky we think they are. The easy ones come first, followed by medium and finally hard.

Easy

With a wide range of themes on offer in our easy section, you're bound to find some questions and quizzes easy and others a bit harder. It's not all straightforward in this section though: watch out for a few themes that aren't quite as obvious as the title suggests. Quiz 251 marks the start of the second easy section.

Medium

You'll get a good general knowledge workout when you tackle our medium quizzes. Classic themes that appeared in the easy section are repeated here, but you'll most likely need some extra thinking time to complete the quizzes at this level. The second medium section starts at Quiz 401.

Hard

You'll really need to work those little grey cells when you venture into our hard quiz section, so set aside plenty of time. An enthusiast's knowledge would be a definite advantage on some of the themed quizzes. When you've toiled your way through the first section, the second hard section begins at Quiz 476.

The answers

Each quiz header tells you where the answers are printed. They're mostly just a couple of pages away, for example the answers to Quiz 1 appear at the bottom of Quiz 3. The exceptions are the last two quizzes in each part of the book, which appear at the bottom of the first two quizzes in that part.

Running a quiz

When you're running a quiz night, there's a great sense of satisfaction to be had in doing a job well, and a little bit of effort beforehand will go a long way to making sure that your quiz goes without a hitch.

❖ Plan: consider how many questions you want to ask in the time available, making sure you leave enough thinking time between questions. Once you've done that, pick a good range of subjects so that there's something for everyone.

❖ Rehearse: Go through all the questions you're going to be asking beforehand, checking any potentially tricky pronunciations and making sure your timings work. Note down all the questions (notes look better in a quiz environment than reading from a book) and answers. Every effort has been made to ensure that all the answers in *Collins Quiz Master* are correct. Despite our best endeavours, mistakes may still appear. If you see an answer you're not sure is right, or if you think there's more than one possible answer, then do check.

❖ Paper and writing implements: make sure you prepare enough sheets of paper for everyone to write on, including scrap paper, and have plenty of pens to hand for those who need them.

❖ Prizes: everyone likes a prize. No matter how small, it's best to have one on offer.

Good luck! We hope you enjoy *Collins Quiz Master*.

Contents

Easy Quizzes

Easy Quizzes

251. Pot Luck
252. Gold and Silver
253. Pot Luck
254. Television
255. Pot Luck
256. Sport
257. Pot Luck
258. Literature
259. Pot Luck
260. Occupations
261. Pot Luck
262. The UK
263. Pot Luck
264. Phil and Friends
265. Pot Luck
266. Flowers
267. Pot Luck
268. Art
269. Pot Luck
270. Food and Drink
271. Pot Luck
272. Wolves
273. Pot Luck
274. Geography
275. Pot Luck
276. Sweet Things
277. Pot Luck
278. Also Known As
279. Pot Luck
280. Politics
281. Pot Luck
282. Words
283. Pot Luck
284. Angry
285. Pot Luck
286. Rock Music
287. Pot Luck
288. Duos
289. Pot Luck
290. Science
291. Pot Luck
292. Playing Cards

293. Pot Luck
294. Film
295. Pot Luck
296. LP
297. Pot Luck
298. Animal Idioms
299. Pot Luck
300. Inventions and Initiatives
301. Pot Luck
302. Quiz Shows
303. Pot Luck
304. Months
305. Pot Luck
306. Ball Sports
307. Pot Luck
308. Children's Literature
309. Pot Luck
310. Plan B
311. Pot Luck
312. Europe
313. Pot Luck
314. Science Fiction
315. Pot Luck
316. History
317. Pot Luck
318. Pop Music
319. Pot Luck
320. Comedy
321. Pot Luck
322. Silly
323. Pot Luck
324. Leisure
325. Pot Luck
326. In the End
327. Pot Luck
328. Rugby League
329. Pot Luck
330. Technology
331. Pot Luck
332. Rain
333. Pot Luck
334. Colours

335. Pot Luck
336. Planet Earth
337. Pot Luck
338. Life Begins
339. Pot Luck
340. Classical Music
341. Pot Luck
342. Seaside
343. Pot Luck
344. Numbers
345. Pot Luck
346. US Sitcoms
347. Pot Luck
348. Unhappy
349. Pot Luck
350. Luxury
351. Pot Luck
352. 1990s Television
353. Pot Luck
354. Dance
355. Pot Luck
356. High Time
357. Pot Luck
358. Biopics
359. Pot Luck
360. Music
361. Pot Luck
362. Picture Perfect
363. Pot Luck
364. Cartoon Characters
365. Pot Luck
366. Organisations
367. Pot Luck
368. Spooky
369. Pot Luck
370. Africa
371. Pot Luck
372. Rock and Roll
373. Pot Luck
374. Buildings and Structures
375. Pot Luck
376. Film in Numbers
377. Pot Luck

1. Castle Drogo lies in which English county?

2. John Willoughby is a character in which Jane Austen novel?

3. Which former UK Prime Minister wrote the 2007 book *More Than a Game: The Story of Cricket's Early Years*?

4. Dave Lister is a leading character in which TV sitcom?

5. How is Gordon Sumner better known?

6. Old Trafford is located in which city?

7. What does a thermometer measure?

8. Iridology concerns which part of the human body?

9. What number is represented by the Roman numerals LXXI?

10. How many stars feature on the flag of Chile?

11. In which year was the requirement to display tax discs on vehicles in the UK abolished?

12. Julie Hesmondhalgh played Hayley Cropper in which long-running series?

13. Q is a famous magazine about what subject?

14. What do the initials OECD stand for?

15. The central part of a daffodil shares its name with which musical instrument?

16. During which year did the WWI Battle of Amiens take place?

17. Which two doctors presented the 2019 series *Twinstitute*?

18. What is sold in a French *patisserie*?

19. In which country was Che Guevara born?

20. Who had a hit with Queen on the single *Under Pressure*?

Easy

Medium

Hard

Answers to QUIZ 249 – Pot Luck

1	*The Inbetweeners*	11	Montpellier
2	St Wolfgang	12	Cubism
3	Cornflower	13	Algeria
4	Horsefly	14	1769
5	Evan Dando	15	490
6	Danish	16	Oleg the Seer
7	Nosebleed	17	Cloudberry
8	46	18	Abe Mitchell
9	The Solomon Islands	19	Penelope Fitzgerald
10	*Brother Bear*	20	Bertha von Suttner

Easy

1. What fruit combines with egg in the Greek dish avgolemono?
2. What are soba and udon types of?
3. Which type of pasta is shaped like a corkscrew?
4. Which alcoholic drink's name means "water of life" in Gaelic?
5. The Greek dish tzatziki consists of which fruit in yogurt?
6. What colour is a Chantenay?
7. Wontons are meat-filled dumplings as part of which country's cuisine?
8. How many "eyes" does a coconut have?
9. Clementine is a hybrid variety of which fruit?
10. A samosa is typically served as what course of a meal?
11. The Mexican liqueur Kahlu'a has what flavour?
12. Bisque is what type of dish?
13. The raw fish dish of sashimi comes from which country?
14. What colour is the Sangiovese grape?
15. From which country does the beetroot dish Borscht originate?
16. The Waldorf salad was named after a hotel in which US city?
17. What are the bunches in which bananas are grown known as?
18. The name of which Italian cheese means "recooked"?
19. What fruit was fed to sailors to fend off scurvy due to its high Vitamin C content?
20. The lagers Grolsch® and Heineken® both come from which country?

Medium

Hard

Answers to QUIZ 250 – Television

1	*Seven of One*	11	*Black Books*
2	Suzanne Ross	12	1971
3	Howard Goodall	13	Brian Protheroe
4	Essex	14	Bette Davis and Joan Crawford
5	*The Valleys*	15	As a weather forecaster
6	*Bless This House*	16	*Timewasters*
7	Magnus Martinsson	17	*All Together Now*
8	*Bread*	18	Alan Partridge
9	Jenny Seagrove	19	*Yes, Minister*
10	2002	20	*Bounty Hunters*

1 Which motor company manufactures the Kona vehicle?

2 The Beatles hailed from which English city?

3 In the story of the nativity, how many wise men visited the infant Jesus?

4 In which Irish city is Trinity College, home of the *Book of Kells*?

5 Which actor wrote the 1999 memoir *With Nails*?

6 Which of these is the correct spelling of the fitness aid: dumm-bell, dumb-ell or dumb-bell?

7 Li is the symbol for which element?

8 Where in the human body is the premolar?

9 Brussels sprouts belong to which group of plants?

10 Which type of bird shares its name with one of Batman's arch-enemies?

11 In the French comic strip, Asterix is a member of what tribe?

12 Proverbially, what does a bad workman always blame?

13 In which Olympic sport would you find competitors wearing a "slider shoe"?

14 *Mambo Italiano* was a major 1950s US hit for which female singer?

15 On which continent is the country of Ghana?

16 Which birth sign would you be, if born on December 1?

17 Professor Robert Langdon is the creation of which author?

18 What took place at Bethel, New York, in August 1969?

19 The TV series *Noel's House Party* was set in which fictional village?

20 Which actor finished second in the Le Mans 24-hour race in 1979?

Easy

Medium

Hard

Answers to QUIZ 1 – Pot Luck

1	Devon	11	2014
2	*Sense and Sensibility*	12	*Coronation Street*
3	Sir John Major	13	Music
4	*Red Dwarf*	14	Organisation for Economic Co-operation and Development
5	Sting		
6	Manchester	15	Trumpet
7	Temperature	16	1918
8	Eye	17	Chris and Xand van Tulleken
9	71	18	Cakes and pastries
10	One	19	Argentina
		20	David Bowie

1. How many monarchs reigned in the House of Hanover?
2. Which king reigned in the United Kingdom during WWI?
3. Mary, Queen of Scots, was Queen Consort of which other country from 1559 to 1560?
4. How many feathers are there in the crest of the Prince of Wales?
5. What relation was Mary Tudor to Edward VI?
6. The royal motto *Dieu et mon droit* (God and my Right) is taken from which language?
7. How old was Queen Elizabeth I when she became Queen of England?
8. How many wives did Henry VIII have?
9. Who became King of England following the Battle of Hastings?
10. Who was the first monarch to stay at Balmoral Castle?
11. Which of Queen Elizabeth II's children was made Earl of Wessex in 1999?
12. Which king was played by Colin Firth in *The King's Speech*?
13. Charles I became king of England, Scotland and Ireland in what decade?
14. How many kings of Scotland were called David?
15. Edward VIII briefly reigned in which year?
16. In the Wars of the Roses, what colour was the York Rose?
17. Who was King of England directly before Henry VIII?
18. In 1987, what title was given to Princess Anne?
19. Which of Queen Elizabeth II's grandchildren was born first?
20. What was the original name of Buckingham Palace?

Easy

Medium

Hard

Answers to QUIZ 2 – Food and Drink

1	Lemon	11	Coffee
2	Noodles	12	(Shellfish) soup
3	Fusilli	13	Japan
4	Whisky	14	Red
5	Cucumber	15	Russia
6	Orange	16	New York City
7	China	17	Hands
8	Three	18	Ricotta
9	Orange	19	Lime
10	Starter	20	The Netherlands

QUIZ 5 – Pot Luck

ANSWERS ON PAGE 7

1   What part of the body would be examined by an audiologist?

2   In which decade was the RAF aerobatic team the Red Arrows formed?

3   Malala Yousafzai, co-recipient of the 2014 Nobel Peace Prize, was born in which country?

4   *Dawn of the Dinosaurs* (2009) was a sequel to which animated film?

5   In athletics, are races run clockwise or anti-clockwise?

6   Who presents the TV series *My Million Pound Menu*?

7   What word can mean both a fish and a place for a bird to stand?

8   Wembley Stadium is located in which English city?

9   What nationality was the author Richmal Crompton?

10 The city of Aachen is in which country?

11 Which Scottish river gives its name to a type of cargo ship known as a "puffer"?

12 *Being and Nothingness* (1943) is a famous work by which philosopher?

13 Who has been appointed Europe's Ryder Cup captain for 2020?

14 What is the common name given to the winged fruit of the ash tree known as a samara?

15 Who won the 2019 film BAFTA for Best Supporting Actress?

16 In which country were Oldsmobile cars manufactured?

17 How many UK parliamentary constituencies were there in 2019?

18 What type of animal is a bandicoot?

19 During which war did Wilfred Owen write his famous war poems?

20 In which ocean do the Galapagos islands lie?

Easy

Medium

Hard

Answers to QUIZ 3 – Pot Luck

1	Hyundai	11	Gauls
2	Liverpool	12	His tools
3	Three	13	Curling
4	Dublin	14	Rosemary Clooney
5	Richard E Grant	15	Africa
6	Dumb-bell	16	Sagittarius
7	Lithium	17	Dan Brown
8	In the mouth	18	The Woodstock festival
9	Cabbage	19	Crinkley Bottom
10	Penguin	20	Paul Newman

Easy

1   How many terms did George Washington serve as President of the USA?

2   In what year was Prohibition first enforced in the USA?

3   What do Americans call a chemist's shop?

4   The Strip is a famous area in which Nevada city?

5   New Mexico, Texas, California and which other state border Mexico?

6   What statement was adopted on July 4, 1776?

7   What term is given to a large area of flat, grassy land in North America?

8   On which island is Wall Street located?

9   In what year did George W Bush become President of the USA?

10 Which American state lies closest to the old Soviet Union?

11 What name is given to the annual championship match of the National Football League?

12 What are "Hershey's Kisses"?

13 Wiliam Penn founded which US state?

Medium

14 Is the US Open tennis championship played on clay, grass or a hard court?

15 How many US states are bigger by area than Rhode Island?

16 Of what is Yosemite an example?

17 Columbia University is located in which city?

18 Which city has been selected to host the Olympic Games for a second time in 2028?

19 Which state is nicknamed "The Bayou State"?

20 In what decade was the first Academy Awards ceremony held?

Hard

Answers to QUIZ 4 – Royalty

1	Six	11	Prince Edward
2	George V	12	George VI
3	France	13	1620s (1625)
4	Three	14	Two
5	Half-sister	15	1936
6	French	16	White
7	25	17	Henry VII
8	Six	18	Princess Royal
9	William I (William the Conqueror)	19	Peter Phillips
10	Queen Victoria	20	Buckingham House

1 In which country is the football trophy the Copa del Rey contested?

2 On which Beatles album does the song *Michelle* appear?

3 What does the German phrase *auf weidersehen* mean?

4 *Fingal's Cave* is a work by which composer?

5 What colour is the Teletubby Tinky Winky?

6 Which luxury car brand features a trident on its logo?

7 The Charnock Richard services are on which English motorway?

8 Which late 15th-century Italian artist sketched designs for a parachute and a form of helicopter?

9 In Roman mythology, Diana is equivalent to which Greek goddess?

10 Keith Richards is a founder member and guitarist with which British band?

11 What is a Red Dwarf?

12 As at the end of 2010, which company had overtaken McDonald's to become the largest restaurant chain in the world?

13 Which *Dad's Army* character was associated with the phrase "Do you think that's wise?"

14 What, in relation to motoring, is the DVSA?

15 The 1964 film *Zulu* was set in which century?

16 What number shirt does a scrum-half wear in Rugby Union?

17 Who wrote "All animals are equal, but some are more equal than others"?

18 The D'Oyly Carte Opera Company performed the works of which musical twosome?

19 What term is given to a period of time, often four hours, when a ship's crew is on duty?

20 What colour is bilirubin, a major ingredient of bile?

Easy

Medium

Hard

Answers to QUIZ 5 – Pot Luck

1	Ears	11	Clyde
2	1960s (1964)	12	Jean-Paul Sartre
3	Pakistan	13	Padraig Harrington
4	*Ice Age*	14	Key
5	Anti-clockwise	15	Rachel Weisz (*The Favourite*)
6	Fred Sirieix	16	USA
7	Perch	17	650
8	London	18	Marsupial
9	English	19	WWI
10	Germany	20	Pacific Ocean

Easy

1 "The Golden Bear" is the nickname of which retired golfer?

2 Who in 1969 became the first British player to win The Open in 18 years?

3 How is a score of one over par referred to on any given hole?

4 The Belfry course is in which country?

5 Which was the only championship of the four majors that Tom Watson failed to win?

6 What nationality is Jean van de Velde, best known for his last hole failure at the 1999 Open?

7 Which former president was awarded the PGA Lifetime Achievement award in 2009?

8 Which author famously said "Golf is a good walk spoiled"?

9 In which European country did the 2018 Ryder Cup take place?

10 Adam Scott became the first man of which nationality to win the Masters in 2013?

Medium

11 What is the name given to the nervous twitching caused by tension when putting?

12 What is a "wedge"?

13 What term is given as a measure of a golfer's playing ability?

14 Which golfer is known as "The Big Easy"?

15 Which club is usually used on the green?

16 Top women's golfer Ariya Jutanugarn is from which country?

17 What do golfers traditionally shout as a warning to those close to the flight of a golf ball?

18 What nationality was the golfer Gary Player?

19 How many holes are typically played on a tournament golf course?

20 US golfer Davis Love has what number after his name?

Hard

Answers to QUIZ 6 – The USA

1	Two	11	Super Bowl
2	1920 (until 1933)	12	Chocolate sweets
3	A drugstore	13	Pennsylvania
4	Las Vegas	14	Hard court
5	Arizona	15	49
6	The Declaration of Independence	16	National Park
7	Prairie	17	New York City
8	Manhattan	18	Los Angeles
9	2001	19	Louisiana
10	Alaska	20	1920s (1929)

1 The Muslim festival of Eid traditionally lasts for how many days?

2 What nationality was fashion designer Karl Lagerfeld?

3 What does the musical term *poco a poco* mean?

4 Proverbially, how is a fair exchange described?

5 Where in the body is the macula?

6 Which stroke is performed in the second leg of a medley swimming race?

7 The binary number 101 has what decimal equivalent?

8 Which fictional detective was introduced in the novel *The Mysterious Affair at Styles*?

9 Waitrose & Partners is part of which retail group?

10 What date is Hallowe'en?

11 Elijah Wood voices Mumble in which 2006 animated film?

12 Which country is known as the Pays-Bas in French?

13 What is the three-letter code for Frankfurt airport?

14 What word can mean both a type of drum and to entrap?

15 Which two metals lend their names to species of birch?

16 Which 1980s TV series featured the characters of David Addison and Maddie Hayes?

17 Who had a 1998 hit with *Millennium*?

18 What characteristic is exhibited by someone who is parsimonious?

19 What name is given to the main body of an aeroplane?

20 Which 1978 film had the tag line "Just when you thought it was safe to go back in the water"?

Easy

Medium

Hard

Answers to QUIZ 7 – Pot Luck

1	Spain	11	(An old, relatively cool) star
2	*Rubber Soul*	12	Subway
3	Goodbye	13	Sergeant Wilson
4	Mendelssohn	14	Driver and Vehicle Standards Agency
5	Purple	15	19th century (1879)
6	Maserati	16	Nine
7	M6	17	George Orwell (in *Animal Farm*)
8	Leonardo da Vinci	18	Gilbert and Sullivan
9	Artemis	19	Watch
10	The Rolling Stones	20	Yellow

1   The columns of the periodic table are known by what name?

2   On which planet does a day last longer than 243 Earth days?

3   What is the largest muscle in the body?

4   Cu is which chemical element's symbol?

5   Where in the body would you find the uvula?

6   What is the sixth planet from the Sun?

7   "Argentine" relates to which metal?

8   Which parts of a cell are usually referred to as "X" and "Y"?

9   String theory is a branch of which science?

10 What is meant by the term "geocentric"?

11 Christiaan Barnard performed the first successful transplant of which human organ?

12 Caliban is a moon that orbits which planet?

13 What is the second-most abundant element in the human body?

14 The Apollo 11 mission lasted a total of how many days?

15 Helium, neon, argon and krypton are all which type of element?

16 Werner Heisenberg, recipient of the Nobel Prize in Physics in 1932, was of what nationality?

17 NASA was founded in what decade?

18 What term is used to describe a space void of air?

19 What is the SI unit of length?

20 Where are the two triceps muscles to be found?

Answers to QUIZ 8 – Golf

1	Jack Nicklaus	11	Yips
2	Tony Jacklin	12	A club (for playing short lob shots)
3	Bogey	13	Handicap
4	England	14	Ernie Els
5	US PGA	15	Putter
6	French	16	Thailand
7	George HW Bush	17	Fore!
8	Mark Twain	18	South African
9	France	19	18
10	Australian	20	III

1 *Strangers in the Night* (1966) and *My Way* (1969) were hits for which singer?

2 Damsons belong to which family?

3 In which century did Catherine the Great rule Russia?

4 The radio code word for which letter of the alphabet is also the word for a river-mouth?

5 What does the process of depilation do?

6 In March 2019, which celebrity became the world's youngest billionaire?

7 What is the maximum score with three darts?

8 What term is given to a group of sheep?

9 The 2018 TV series *Trust* centred on the kidnapping of the grandson of which US businessman?

10 What colour was the *Thunderbirds* car which had the number plate FAB 1?

11 Who wrote the play on which the 1994 film *The Madness of King George* was based?

12 Julian Assange took refuge in which nation's London embassy from 2012 to 2019?

13 In relation to metal, for what does the "S" stand in EPNS?

14 Which sign of the zodiac is represented by the Ram?

15 What two words that sound the same but are spelt differently mean "convent member" and "zero"?

16 How many notes are there in a pentatonic scale?

17 Who provided the voice for Bugs Bunny and Yosemite Sam, amongst many others?

18 What is taffeta?

19 What two liquids were mixed to create the sailor's drink grog?

20 Which comedian published the book *Revolution* in 2014?

Answers to QUIZ 9 – Pot Luck

1	Four	11	*Happy Feet*
2	German	12	The Netherlands
3	Little by little, slowly	13	FRA
4	No robbery	14	Snare
5	In the eye	15	Silver and copper
6	Backstroke	16	*Moonlighting*
7	Five	17	Robbie Williams
8	Hercule Poirot	18	Mean with money
9	John Lewis Partnership	19	Fuselage
10	October 31	20	*Jaws 2*

Easy

Medium

Hard

Easy

Medium

Hard

1   What name did Tom Hanks give to the volleyball in the 2000 film *Cast Away*?

2   The 2018 film *All is True* was directed by and starred which actor as William Shakespeare?

3   Who directed the 1993 film *The Remains of the Day*?

4   *The Dam Busters* is set during which war?

5   Which classic 1959 British film is based on a novel by John Braine?

6   David Oyelowo played which famous world figure in the 2014 film *Selma*?

7   What word completes the title of the 2009 Disney film *The Princess and the ___*?

8   Which film won the Best Picture Oscar at the 2019 Academy Awards ceremony?

9   In 2013 Leonardo DiCaprio played the lead role in what literary adaption?

10 *Jack* and *The Rainmaker* were 1990s films directed by whom?

11 In what year was *Dr No*, the first Bond film, released?

12 Truly Scrumptious is a character from which 1968 film?

13 Film-maker Christopher Nolan rebooted what superhero franchise in the 21st century?

14 Ang Lee directed a version of which classic Jane Austen work in 1995?

15 In which country is *The Inbetweeners 2* set?

16 Who directed the 1991 film *The Commitments*?

17 *Lost In Translation* is set in which Asian city?

18 Marlin is the leading character in which 2003 film?

19 Who played Phileas Fogg in the 1956 film *Around the World in 80 days*?

20 In which year was the first Harry Potter film released?

Answers to QUIZ 10 – Science

1	Groups	11	Heart
2	Venus	12	Uranus
3	Gluteus maximus	13	Carbon
4	Copper	14	Eight
5	Throat	15	Inert gas (or noble gas)
6	Saturn	16	German
7	Silver	17	1950s (1958)
8	Chromosomes	18	Vacuum
9	Physics	19	Metre
10	Having the Earth at the centre	20	Upper arms

1. Where would you be eating a meal if you were *al fresco*?
2. In *Only Fools and Horses*, what name did Del give to his son?
3. What type of creature is a small mountain ringlet?
4. Which animation studio created the character of Yogi Bear?
5. Haematology is associated with which constituent of the body?
6. Who wrote the fable of *The Boy Who Cried Wolf*?
7. What is the usual short form of the word "perambulator"?
8. Fontina cheese originated in which country?
9. The Blue Planet is the name often given to which planet?
10. The Inca Empire was located mostly in which modern-day country?
11. Who wrote the 1941 novel *Frenchman's Creek*?
12. Which size of paper measures 297 mm by 420 mm?
13. For what did the "E" stand in the initials of the wartime organisation ENSA?
14. How many players are there in a handball team?
15. How does something that is soporific make you feel?
16. In which country did the Charolais breed of cattle originate?
17. Which island's name means "rich port" in Spanish?
18. What is the name of Rula Lenska's *Coronation Street* character?
19. The ship the *Mary Rose* can be seen in which UK city?
20. What does "Gospel" mean?

Easy

Medium

Hard

Answers to QUIZ 11 – Pot Luck

1	Frank Sinatra	11	Alan Bennett
2	Plum	12	Ecuador
3	18th century (1762-96)	13	Silver
4	Delta	14	Aries
5	Removes hair	15	None and nun
6	Kylie Jenner	16	Five
7	180	17	Mel Blanc
8	Flock	18	(A smooth woven) fabric
9	Jean Paul Getty	19	Rum and water
10	Pink	20	Russell Brand

1   *Writing's on the Wall* was the theme song to which James Bond film?

2   In which film did Wallace and Gromit run a business called "Anti-Pesto"?

3   Which cocktail combines vodka, Galliano and orange juice?

4   Who portrayed William Wallace in the 1995 film *Braveheart*?

5   In which country was tennis champion Ken Rosewall born?

6   Which Asian country is famous for its Great Wall?

7   Walloons come from which European country?

8   What insect is said to be "on the wall" in a style of documentary making?

9   Which Swedish detective did Sir Kenneth Branagh portray on television from 2008 to 2015?

10   Bodmin Moor is in which county?

11   Which national rugby union team is nicknamed "The Wallabies"?

12   What is the term for a system that prevents unauthorised access to a computer?

13   Proverbially, what do walls have?

14   In which two colours do Millwall FC traditionally play?

15   The Blackwall Tunnel links the London borough of Tower Hamlets with which other borough?

16   Who released the 1978 album *The Wall*?

17   In the poem by Robert Louis Stevenson, what "shines on thieves on the garden wall"?

18   Which *MasterChef* judge is also a presenter on *Inside the Factory*?

19   What was the nickname of the American Civil War general Thomas Jackson?

20   *Walls Come Tumbling Down* was a 1985 hit for which band?

Answers to QUIZ 12 – Film

1	Wilson	11	1962
2	Sir Kenneth Branagh	12	*Chitty Chitty Bang Bang*
3	James Ivory	13	Batman
4	WWII	14	*Sense and Sensibility*
5	*Room at the Top*	15	Australia
6	Martin Luther King	16	Alan Parker
7	Frog	17	Tokyo
8	*Green Book*	18	*Finding Nemo*
9	*The Great Gatsby*	19	David Niven
10	Francis Ford Coppola	20	2001

1   The temporal lobe lies in which part of the human body?

2   *Uncle Vanya* is a 19th-century play by which dramatist?

3   What is the name of the Swedish activist who initiated the school strikes against climate change in 2018?

4   *21* is a Brit Award Best Album winner by which singer?

5   Seborrheic dermatitis affects which part of the body?

6   In the nursery rhyme, where was Simple Simon going when he met the pieman?

7   The Graham Hill Bend and Sheene Curve are points on which motor-racing circuit?

8   John Alderton and Joan Sanderson appeared in which TV series first shown in 1968?

9   What colour is Woodstock in the *Peanuts* cartoon strip?

10   What word for a long narrow pillow is an anagram of "lobster"?

11   How many stars are there on the Subaru automobile logo?

12   What is the English translation of the *Palais de Papes*, a historical building situated in Avignon?

13   The name of which dance translates to "double step"?

14   What was *The African Queen* in the title of the 1951 film?

15   The French horn belongs to which section of the orchestra?

16   A scullery is an annex to what type of room?

17   Whose garden does Peter Rabbit stray into in the Beatrix Potter tales?

18   What word can mean both an area from where stone is removed and a creature's prey?

19   What shape is the head of an Allen key?

20   The *EastEnders* character nicknamed "Cruella Stella" died on her wedding day on which she was set to marry whom?

Easy

Medium

Hard

Answers to QUIZ 13 – Pot Luck

1	Outdoors	11	Dame Daphne du Maurier
2	Damien	12	A3
3	A butterfly	13	Entertainments (National Service Association)
4	Hanna-Barbera	14	Seven
5	Blood	15	Sleepy
6	Aesop	16	France
7	Pram	17	Puerto Rico
8	Italy	18	Claudia Colby
9	Earth	19	Portsmouth
10	Peru	20	Good news

1 Who had a hit in 1992 with *To Be With You?*

2 Boyz II Men released *One Sweet Day* with which female star?

3 *I Wish It Would Rain Down* was a 1990 hit for which musician?

4 Which band released the 1994 album *Voodoo Lounge?*

5 Geri Halliwell (now Horner) was known as which "Spice"?

6 *You're Still The One* was the first UK top ten hit for which US singer?

7 *Escapade* was a hit for which member of the Jacksons?

8 In the title of the Ace of Base song, what was *All That She Wants?*

9 Liam Gallagher was a member of which 1990s band?

10 Who released the album *Automatic for the People?*

11 The boy band Five were formed in which country?

12 "My loneliness is killing me" is a line from which no.1 of the 1990s?

13 Who had an international hit in 1996 with *Don't Speak?*

14 *Jagged Little Pill* was an album by which singer?

15 Which band toured with the "Zoo TV Tour" in 1992-93?

16 *Never Forget* was a 1995 hit for which band?

17 Who composed the music for the 1994 musical *Copacabana?*

18 "Every night in my dreams, I see you, I feel you" are the opening lyrics to which 1997 song?

19 Who wrote the 1990 Sinead O'Connor hit *Nothing Compares 2 U?*

20 Will Smith sang about what city in 1998?

Answers to QUIZ 14 – Wall to Wall

1	*Spectre*	11	Australia
2	*The Curse of the Were-Rabbit*	12	Firewall
3	Harvey Wallbanger	13	Ears
4	Mel Gibson	14	Blue and white
5	Australia	15	Greenwich
6	China	16	Pink Floyd
7	Belgium	17	The Moon
8	Fly	18	Gregg Wallace
9	Kurt Wallander	19	Stonewall
10	Cornwall	20	The Style Council

1 Which baseball legend's nicknames included "The Sultan of Swat"?

2 Which emperor's attempts to invade Britain in 55 BC were ruined by bad weather?

3 How many raindrops are there on the Met Office symbol for light rain?

4 Although pronounced differently, what word can mean both "to blow hard" and a self-service meal?

5 A short sequel to which film was written in aid of Comic Relief in 2019?

6 Which Secretary to the Admiralty (d.1703) was most famous for his diary?

7 In which country was the fashion designer Jean Muir born?

8 Which variety of pasta has a name that means "little worms"?

9 The daughter of which *Inspector Morse* actor plays journalist Dorothea Frazil in the TV series *Endeavour*?

10 Bird, clear and smash are terms used in what indoor sport?

11 What number is represented by the Roman numerals XXXV?

12 In Greek mythology, who killed the Minotaur?

13 The Royal Mausoleum at Frogmore is in which county?

14 What may be 14 in London, 10 in New York or 42 in Paris?

15 A quarterback is a position in which sport?

16 What type of vehicle was manufactured by the British company de Havilland?

17 In the name of the MOBO awards, for what does the "B" stand?

18 *Forever After* is the fourth film in which series?

19 A short sleep might be referred to as how many winks?

20 Which composer was mentioned in the title of a 1950s Chuck Berry hit?

Easy

Medium

Hard

Answers to QUIZ 15 – Pot Luck

1	The brain	11	Six
2	Anton Chekhov	12	Palace of the Popes
3	Greta Thunberg	13	Paso doble
4	Adele	14	A boat
5	The skin	15	Brass
6	To the fair	16	A kitchen
7	Brands Hatch	17	Mr McGregor's
8	*Please Sir!*	18	Quarry
9	Yellow	19	Hexagonal
10	Bolster	20	Phil Mitchell

1   How many wishes does the Genie grant to Aladdin when emerging from the magic lamp?

2   What is the name of the wizard who visits Frodo at the start of *The Lord of the Rings*?

3   *The Magician's Nephew* is the sixth in which series of seven novels?

4   Who wrote the 1988 novel *Wyrd Sisters*, which featured the witches Granny Weatherwax, Nanny Ogg and Magrat Garlick?

5   Who composed the opera *The Magic Flute*?

6   What was the name of the snail in *The Magic Roundabout*?

7   In what year was the Beatles film *Magical Mystery Tour* released?

8   Which famous songwriting duo wrote *Magic Moments*?

9   How were Cher, Michelle Pfeiffer and Susan Sarandon known in the title of a 1987 film?

10 Which two actors co-starred as magicians in the 2006 film *The Prestige*?

11 Who plays the title role in the *Magic Mike* films?

12 Magic Johnson is a retired professional in which sport?

13 What word beginning with "a" is used by magicians when performing tricks?

14 Roy Wood was the lead singer with which glam rock band?

15 Who played Dorothy in the 1939 film *The Wizard of Oz*?

16 Who was the pinball wizard in the rock opera by The Who?

17 In the Harry Potter books and films, what is the name of the shop in Diagon Alley that sells wands?

18 What is the usual time known as "the witching hour"?

19 In which year did Queen have a hit with *A Kind of Magic*?

20 What colour is the fairy in the 1940 Disney film *Pinocchio*?

Answers to QUIZ 16 – 1990s Music

1	Mr Big	11	England
2	Mariah Carey	12	*Baby One More Time*
3	Phil Collins	13	No Doubt
4	The Rolling Stones	14	Alanis Morissette
5	Ginger	15	U2
6	Shania Twain	16	Take That
7	Janet	17	Barry Manilow
8	Another Baby	18	*My Heart Will Go On* (Celine Dion)
9	Oasis	19	Prince
10	REM	20	*Miami*

QUIZ 19 – Pot Luck

ANSWERS ON PAGE 21

1   In which county is the coastal town of Lowestoft?

2   *Food Glorious Food* is a song from which musical?

3   What term is given to a pressurised can?

4   What was the first name of Russian inventor Pavlov, famous for "Pavlov's Dog"?

5   How many points is the pink ball worth in snooker?

6   In which city are the headquarters of NATO?

7   How many stripes are there on the Irish flag?

8   The rose is the national symbol of which country?

9   What word, meaning a low pressure belt of surface winds at the equator, can also relate to a bout of sadness?

10 The BCG vaccine is used in the prevention of which disease?

11 Hajj is a pilgrimage in which religion?

12 In relation to published work, for what do the initials PLR stand?

13 What is the term for a vote cast by a representative, rather than the person voting?

14 Who had a hit with *This Used to be my Playground* (1992)?

15 Who composed the 1945 work *The Young Person's Guide to the Orchestra*?

16 The Michael family and the Siddiqui family appear on which reality TV show?

17 What is the first name of the character played by Julia Roberts in *Notting Hill*?

18 Which Hollywood actor starred in the 2019 series *Wild Bill*?

19 In the abbreviation for the voluntary organisation the RNLI, for what does the "L" stand?

20 A lepidopterist studies what kind of creatures?

Easy

Medium

Hard

Answers to QUIZ 17 – Pot Luck

1	Babe Ruth	11	35
2	Julius Caesar	12	Theseus
3	One	13	Berkshire
4	Buffet	14	Dress size
5	*Four Weddings and a Funeral*	15	American football
6	Samuel Pepys	16	Aeroplanes
7	England	17	Black
8	Vermicelli	18	*Shrek*
9	John Thaw (Abigail Thaw)	19	Forty
10	Badminton	20	Beethoven (*Roll Over Beethoven*)

Easy

1   Samantha Jones was a character in which US TV series first shown in 1998?

2   In *The Simpsons*, what are the names of Ned Flanders' sons?

3   In the 1960s and 1990s series *Flipper*, what type of creature was the title character?

4   *Brookside* was set in which UK city?

5   How many contestants take part in *The Chase*?

6   Who played the title role in the 2018 series *Bodyguard*?

7   Where was the John Simm thriller *Strangers* largely set?

8   In which sitcom would you find a character called Arnold J Rimmer?

9   Which celebrity won the 2019 series of *Dancing on Ice*?

10 Who created *The X Factor*?

Medium

11 Suzannah Lipscomb presents programmes on which general subject?

12 What is the name of Fred Thursday's daughter in *Endeavour*?

13 Which channel broadcast the 2019 series of *The Bachelor UK*?

14 *Blackadder II* was set during the reign of which monarch?

15 The sitcom *Derry Girls* is set in which country of the UK?

16 Who created the sitcom *Only Fools and Horses*?

17 Which 1980s series took its two-word title from the radio code words for J and B?

18 Abbey Clancy won which reality show in 2013?

19 The character of Villanelle, played by Jodie Comer, appears in which series?

20 Graham Crowden and Stephanie Cole starred in which 1990s sitcom?

Hard

Answers to QUIZ 18 – Magic

1	Three	11	Channing Tatum
2	Gandalf	12	Basketball
3	The Chronicles of Narnia	13	Abracadabra
4	Sir Terry Pratchett	14	Wizzard
5	Mozart	15	Judy Garland
6	Brian	16	Tommy
7	1967	17	Ollivanders
8	Burt Bacharach and Hal David	18	Midnight
9	*The Witches of Eastwick*	19	1986
10	Hugh Jackman and Christian Bale	20	Blue

ANSWERS ON PAGE 23

1   What is a dingle?

2   Dame Judi Dench played Laura Dalton in which 1980s sitcom?

3   What was the subtitle of the 2018 sequel to *Jurassic World*?

4   Which vegetable has a variety called sugar snap?

5   What is the nickname of Catherine Shipton's character in the TV series *Casualty*?

6   The 1889 novel *Three Men in a Boat* was set on which river?

7   Who wrote, directed and starred in the 1936 film *Modern Times*?

8   Reg Dwight is the real name of which celebrity?

9   The phrase "paper tiger", used to describe something not as threatening as it seems, originated in which country?

10   Which of the following was UK Prime Minister first: David Lloyd George, Herbert Asquith or Stanley Baldwin, all subsequently made Earls?

11   Who captained England during the 2013 Ashes series?

12   The Lilac Fairy and Carabosse are two characters in which Tchaikovsky ballet?

13   The UN Security Council was founded with how many permanent members?

14   Which six-letter word of German origin beginning with "k" describes something considered to be showy and in bad taste?

15   What colour is a bilberry?

16   The Rio Grande flows across Mexico and which other country?

17   What relation was Fidel Castro to Raúl Castro?

18   How many books are there in the Torah?

19   What type of instrument is a zither?

20   Which horse won the 2019 Grand National?

Easy

Medium

Hard

Answers to QUIZ 19 – Pot Luck

1	Suffolk	11	Islam
2	*Oliver!*	12	Public Lending Rights
3	Aerosol	13	Proxy vote
4	Ivan	14	Madonna
5	Six	15	Benjamin Britten (Baron Britten)
6	Brussels	16	*Gogglebox*
7	Three (green, white and orange)	17	Anna (Scott)
8	England	18	Rob Lowe
9	Doldrums	19	Lifeboat
10	Tuberculosis	20	Butterflies and moths

QUIZ 22 – M

Easy

1   Which 2019 M. Night Shyamalan film is a sequel to both *Unbreakable* (2000) and *Split* (2016)?

2   What number is represented by the Roman numerals MM?

3   Which band recorded the 1993 song *Mmm Mmm Mmm Mmm*?

4   In the 2015 Bond film *Spectre*, who played M?

5   Which word represents the letter M in the radio phonetic alphabet?

6   Which English city has postcodes that start with a single letter M?

7   How many centimetres are there in a metre?

8   On a standard keyboard, which letter is to the left of M?

9   The department store chain H&M was founded in which country in 1947?

10 The letter M is in which position in the alphabet?

Medium

11 What does M indicate in a report of a cricket match?

12 Which French mode of address is abbreviated to M?

13 Which American rock band recorded the 1997 song *MMMBop*?

14 In the company name HMV, for what does the "M" stand?

15 Who played the MC in the 1972 film *Cabaret*?

16 In which decade did M People have a hit with *Moving On Up*?

17 What do the letters MG stand for in the name of the former car company?

18 What is the full name of the food additive usually referred to as MSG?

19 On a mobile phone with number keys, the M appears on which number?

20 Which Booker T and the MG's single reached the UK top ten in 1979, 18 years after its original release?

Hard

Answers to QUIZ 20 – Television

1	*Sex and the City*	11	History
2	Rod and Todd	12	Joan
3	Dolphin	13	Channel 5
4	Liverpool	14	Elizabeth I
5	Four	15	Northern Ireland
6	Richard Madden	16	John Sullivan
7	Hong Kong	17	*Juliet Bravo*
8	*Red Dwarf*	18	*Strictly Come Dancing*
9	James Jordan	19	*Killing Eve*
10	Simon Cowell	20	*Waiting For God*

QUIZ 23 – Pot Luck

ANSWERS ON PAGE 25

1 Which former French international footballer was sacked as manager of Monaco in January 2019 after only three months in the job?

2 Which size of paper measures 105 by 148 mm?

3 How many senses do humans have?

4 Alan Bradley was killed by what mode of transport in a 1989 episode of *Coronation Street*?

5 A Hawaiian pizza usually includes which fruit as a topping?

6 Brownsea Island lies in which English county?

7 The magazine *Mojo* is about what subject?

8 According to the proverb, what is as good as a wink to a blind horse?

9 Enchiladas originated in which country?

10 What is the title of the poem by Wilfred Owen that begins "What passing-bells for these who die as cattle"?

11 *Disco Inferno* and *Manhattan Skyline* feature on which 1977 film sound track?

12 Which aftershave was famously advertised to the sound of *O Fortuna* from *Carmina Burana*?

13 Which yellowish-orange colour is an anagram of "chore"?

14 On a standard Monopoly™ board, how many properties are dark blue?

15 Which one of the seven deadly sins is another word for laziness?

16 Who was the 40th President of the USA?

17 How many protons are present in hydrogen?

18 Pentecost is celebrated seven Sundays after which event?

19 Who would perform an *entrechat*?

20 How many knights are on the board at the start of a game of chess?

Answers to QUIZ 21 – Pot Luck

1	A deep wooded hollow or valley	11	Sir Alastair Cook
2	*A Fine Romance*	12	*The Sleeping Beauty*
3	*Fallen Kingdom*	13	Five (China, France, Soviet Union, USA, UK)
4	Pea	14	Kitsch
5	Duffy	15	Blue
6	River Thames	16	The USA
7	Sir Charlie Chaplin	17	Brother
8	Sir Elton John	18	Five (the Pentateuch)
9	China	19	Stringed instrument
10	Herbert Asquith (First Earl of Oxford and Asquith)	20	Tiger Roll

23

Easy

1   What is the capital city of the Australian state of Queensland?

2   Mecca lies in which country?

3   The flag of China contains how many stars?

4   Which mountain range is the greatest in length, the Andes or the Urals?

5   What is the Italian name for Turin, after which a Ford car was named?

6   Beachy Head lies above which body of water?

7   The city of Haarlem is in which European country?

8   What is the capital of Sicily?

9   In which country is Jasper National Park?

10 At only 115 square miles, the Maldives is the smallest country in which continent?

11 How many main islands make up Japan?

12 What is the largest city in France?

13 Sacramento is the capital of which US state?

14 Babylonia is a historical region in which modern day country?

Medium

15 In which county is the seaside town of Felixstowe?

16 Swazi is a native language on which continent?

17 Is County Wexford in the north-west or the south-east of Ireland?

18 What do the names of Interlaken in Switzerland and Interlagos in Brazil mean in English?

19 In which city does the busiest airport in Germany lie?

20 Which is the second largest country in the world by area?

Hard

Answers to QUIZ 22 – M

1	*Glass*	11	Maiden over
2	2000	12	Monsieur
3	Crash Test Dummies	13	Hanson
4	Ralph Fiennes	14	Master's (His Master's Voice)
5	Mike	15	Joel Grey
6	Manchester	16	1990s (1993)
7	100	17	Morris Garages
8	N	18	Monosodium glutamate
9	Sweden	19	6
10	13th	20	*Green Onions*

ANSWERS ON PAGE 27

1   Which Spice Girl joined the judging panel on the 2014 UK series of *The X Factor*?

2   Scientists revealed the first ever photograph of what astronomical feature in April 2019?

3   The *St Matthew Passion* (1727) is a work by which composer?

4   Who was the female star in the TV series *Gimme Gimme Gimme*?

5   Boxing's Klitschko brothers come from which country?

6   Which film won the Oscar for Best Picture first, *Chariots of Fire* or *Terms of Endearment*?

7   What name is given to the needle of a vinyl record-player?

8   The name of which South American city means "River of January" in English?

9   Which TV presenter married rower Helen Glover in 2016?

10 In which ballet does Clara travel to the Land of Sweets?

11 What is an infant seal called?

12 What type of vehicle is a wain?

13 What did Robert Burns describe as a "Wee, sleekit, cowrin, tim'rous beastie" in a 1785 poem?

14 Which unit of energy sounds the same as the word for a precious stone?

15 Rabbis are figures of authority in which religion?

16 Which chocolate bar shares its name with money that is offered as a reward?

17 Who had a hit in 1985 with *That's What Friends Are For*?

18 How many incisor teeth does a human usually have?

19 In what key is a piece of music that has a key signature of no sharps or flats?

20 Was the Anglo-Saxon kingdom of Wessex in the north or the south of England?

Answers to QUIZ 23 – Pot Luck

1	Thierry Henry	11	*Saturday Night Fever*
2	A6	12	Old Spice
3	Five (sight, hearing , taste, smell, touch)	13	Ochre
4	Tram	14	Two (Mayfair and Park Lane)
5	Pineapple	15	Sloth
6	Dorset	16	Ronald Reagan
7	(Popular) music	17	One
8	A nod	18	Easter Sunday
9	Mexico	19	A ballet dancer
10	*Anthem for Doomed Youth*	20	Four

QUIZ 26 – Art

1   Who painted the 1874 work *The Dance Class*, depicting a ballet performance?

2   Roy Lichtenstein belonged to which artistic school?

3   What part of his body did Van Gogh famously mutilate?

4   The Scottish National Art Gallery lies in which city?

5   The Roman remains of Fishbourne Palace is noted for what art form on its floors?

6   Which term for a colour can also refer to an outcry?

7   Art Nouveau became popular in which century?

8   In which Italian city is the Bargello Museum located?

9   Which artist created *Girl with Balloon*, which famously shredded itself after being sold at auction in 2018?

10 "Throwing" is a process used by which type of artist?

11 The Metropolitan Museum of Art lies in which American city?

12 How is the painting *La Gioconda* better known?

13 The Medici family were the patrons of which High Renaissance artist?

14 What name accompanies Winsor in the making of art materials?

15 What nationality was the sculptor Auguste Rodin?

16 In which London art gallery would you find the Turbine Hall?

17 Cadmium, Indian and Naples can precede which colour in the name of pigments?

18 The Bloomsbury Group originated in which country?

19 In which European city is the Musée d'Orsay?

20 Tracey Emin was born in which decade?

1   What name is given to a young male horse?

2   Which was invented first, the television or the video recorder?

3   Which Greek letter shares its name with a river-mouth?

4   Which pale colour is an anagram of "cure"?

5   In what form are tulips planted?

6   Which public school did actor Dominic West attend?

7   Which of these spellings is correct: disipline, dissiplin or discipline?

8   Moeen Ali plays cricket for which country?

9   According to the nursery rhyme, what is Monday's child?

10 Which country has the international car registration letter B?

11 *Don't Bring Me Down* was a 1979 hit for which group?

12 Which French term describing a free hand, translates as "white card"?

13 Which country won the Six Nations trophy in 2019?

14 The town of Andover is in which English county?

15 Which mythical creature appears on the flag of Bhutan?

16 Which word meaning "contorted" can also describe an amused expression?

17 In which European country is the city of Vichy?

18 How many British Classic horse races are there?

19 Who succeeded Michael Foot as leader of the Labour Party?

20 In which decade did Westlife have their first UK no.1?

Easy

Medium

Hard

Answers to QUIZ 25 – Pot Luck

1	Mel B	11	Pup
2	A black hole	12	A cart or wagon
3	Johann Sebastian Bach	13	A mouse
4	Kathy Burke	14	Joule (jewel)
5	Ukraine	15	Judaism
6	*Chariots of Fire*	16	Bounty
7	Stylus	17	Dionne Warwick
8	Rio de Janeiro	18	Eight
9	Steve Backshall	19	C
10	*The Nutcracker*	20	The South

Easy

1   *Boléro* (1928) was an orchestral piece by which composer?

2   How many instruments play a cadenza?

3   In what century did Johannes Brahms live?

4   The 1914 piece *The Lark Ascending* was written by which English composer?

5   *Lied* is the German word for what?

6   Nigel Kennedy is famed for playing which instrument?

7   Which German-born composer became a British subject in 1727?

8   What does the Italian term *adagio* mean?

9   Sir Simon Rattle and Herbert Von Karajan have both been conductors for the Philharmonic Orchestra in which city?

10 The Salzburg Festival is associated with which composer?

11 What is the nickname of Beethoven's fifth symphony?

12 What nationality was the composer Carl Orff?

Medium

13 How is an *a cappella* song performed?

14 *The March of the Toreadors* comes from an opera by which composer?

15 In which country was Franz Schubert born?

16 Modulation involves the change of what?

17 Who composed the operas *La Traviata* and *Rigoletto*?

18 A word describing music for a small number of players shares its name with which old-fashioned name for part of a house?

19 How many reeds does an oboe have?

20 Which phrase used in classical music literally means "beautiful song"?

Hard

Answers to QUIZ 26 – Art

1	Edgar Degas	11	New York
2	Pop art	12	*The Mona Lisa*
3	His ear	13	Michelangelo
4	Edinburgh	14	Newton
5	Mosaics	15	French
6	Hue	16	Tate Modern
7	19th century (1890s)	17	Yellow
8	Florence	18	England
9	Banksy	19	Paris
10	A potter	20	1960s (1963)

ANSWERS ON PAGE 31

1 What number is represented by the Roman numerals XIX?

2 What piece of kitchen equipment is also a word meaning to harshly criticise?

3 David Beckham began his professional playing career with which club?

4 What is the internet country code for Australia?

5 What name is given to the lowest-level seating area in a theatre?

6 King or Queen of the Jungle is the title given to the winner of which TV show?

7 The name of what geometrical shape is an anagram of "pathogen"?

8 In a medley swimming race, which stroke is performed on the first leg?

9 What foodstuff is Parmigiano-Reggiano?

10 In which European country is the city of Potsdam?

11 Which duo had hits in the 1970s with *Only Yesterday* and *Yesterday Once More*?

12 On a standard keyboard, which letter is immediately to the right of W?

13 What was the title of Frankie Goes to Hollywood's third UK no.1?

14 The viola is found in which section of the orchestra?

15 JLS came second to which winner of *The X Factor*?

16 What is the term for one below par for a hole in golf?

17 What was the title of Shakin' Stevens' first UK no.1?

18 *Mansfield Park* (1814) was a novel by which author?

19 In relation to flying, for what do the initials CAA stand?

20 The newspaper *Pravda* is published in which country?

Easy

Medium

Hard

Answers to QUIZ 27 – Pot Luck

1	Colt	11	The Electric Light Orchestra
2	Television	12	*Carte blanche*
3	Delta	13	Wales
4	Ecru	14	Hampshire
5	Bulbs	15	A dragon
6	Eton College	16	Wry
7	Discipline	17	France
8	England	18	Five
9	Fair of face	19	Neil Kinnock (Baron Kinnock)
10	Belgium	20	1990s (1999)

Easy

1 The U-Bahn is the name of the underground rail system in which European city?

2 The town of Lymington is linked to which island by a ferry route?

3 In which decade was the Highway Code introduced in the UK?

4 The Eurostar service transferred from Waterloo to which other London terminal in 2007?

5 Which Prime Minister officially opened the M25 in 1986?

6 How is America's National Railroad Passenger Corporation better known?

7 What type of transport would use a VTOL system?

8 A museum at Crich in Derbyshire is dedicated to what type of vehicle?

9 In which century was the New York subway opened?

10 From which London station does the Stansted Express depart?

11 The travelcard in use in London is named after which marine creature?

12 In which city is Australia's busiest airport?

13 What type of ship is the PS *Waverley*?

14 In what decade did safety helmets become compulsory in the UK for moped and motorcycle riders?

15 What is a disabled parking permit commonly called in the UK?

16 Termini and Trastevere are railway stations in which European capital city?

17 For what do the initials MOT stand in the car safety check?

18 What colour is the main text on the Alitalia airline logo?

19 The Cardiff Gate services are on which motorway?

20 For what do the initials ABTA stand?

Medium

Hard

Answers to QUIZ 28 – Classical Music

1	Maurice Ravel	11	The Fate
2	One	12	German
3	19th century (1833-97)	13	Without accompaniment
4	Ralph Vaughan Williams	14	Bizet (*Carmen*)
5	Song	15	Austria
6	Violin	16	Key
7	Handel	17	Verdi
8	Slowly	18	Chamber
9	Berlin	19	Two
10	Mozart	20	*Bel canto*

1   Who directed the film *Trainspotting*?

2   Which band had a 1966 hit with *Paint it Black*?

3   How many ridings of Yorkshire were there?

4   Dennis Rodman was a famous name in which sport?

5   Which of Judy Garland's daughters was born first, Liza or Lorna?

6   In which section of the orchestra would you find a marimba?

7   *Ambridge Extra* was a spin-off from which popular soap opera?

8   What type of creature is Patrick in the TV series *SpongeBob SquarePants*?

9   How many consonants are there in the alphabet?

10 What is the meaning of the place name Terra Nova?

11 Which actor won the Best Actor Oscar first, Gene Hackman or John Wayne?

12 Massachusetts is on which coast of the USA?

13 The term "arabesque" refers to one leg raised behind and what, extended?

14 What is the French word for "four"?

15 Chicory is part of which family of plants?

16 What type of creature is Horton in the Dr Seuss stories?

17 Which item of kitchen equipment shares its name with a stringed instrument?

18 The Wash is an inlet of which sea?

19 Mark Ramprakash won which reality TV show in 2006?

20 What is the name of the long projections on a wind turbine?

Easy

Medium

Hard

Answers to QUIZ 29 – Pot Luck

1	19	11	The Carpenters
2	Pan	12	E
3	Manchester United	13	*The Power of Love*
4	.au	14	Strings
5	Stalls	15	Alexandra Burke
6	*I'm a Celebrity...*	16	Birdie
7	Heptagon	17	*This Ole House*
8	Butterfly	18	Jane Austen
9	Cheese (Italian)	19	Civil Aviation Authority
10	Germany	20	Russia

1. In the nursery rhyme *Little Boy Blue*, where was the boy who looks after the sheep found asleep?

2. What could Jack Sprat not eat?

3. Where was Little Jack Horner eating his Christmas pie?

4. As well as the master and the little boy, who else was expecting a bag of wool in *Baa Baa Black Sheep*?

5. What did Doctor Foster step in when he went to Gloucester?

6. What drink is mentioned in *Polly Put the Kettle On*?

7. Where did Tom the Piper's Son go crying?

8. To where did the little lamb follow Mary?

9. What was the maid doing in *Sing a Song of Sixpence*?

10. Where were the men in the tub in *Rub-a-dub-dub*?

11. How many men did the Grand Old Duke of York march up and down a hill?

12. What was Little Tommy Tucker going to be given for his supper?

13. Who punished the Knave of Hearts for stealing the tarts?

14. What creature did Pussy Cat frighten on visiting the Queen?

15. In *Hickory Dickory Dock*, what time did the clock strike?

16. What colour hair did Bobby Shafto have?

17. What type of cake is mentioned in *The Lion and the Unicorn*?

18. In the traditional rhyme, which child is "full of grace"?

19. What did Jack and Jill go up the hill to fetch?

20. Which animal laughed in the rhyme *Hey Diddle Diddle*?

Answers to QUIZ 30 – Getting Around

1	Berlin	11	Oyster
2	Isle of Wight	12	Sydney
3	1930s (1931)	13	Paddle steamer
4	St Pancras	14	1970s (1973)
5	Baroness Margaret Thatcher	15	Blue Badge
6	Amtrak	16	Rome
7	Aircraft (Vertical Take-Off and Landing)	17	Ministry of Transport
8	Tram	18	Green
9	20th century (1904)	19	M4
10	Liverpool Street	20	Association of British Travel Agents

1 What word can mean both "to put in hock" and a chess piece?

2 The Zeppelin was what type of transport?

3 What is an osteospermum?

4 Which actor played the title character's love interest in the 1989 film *Shirley Valentine*?

5 The River Exe flows through which two counties?

6 Otology is associated with which part of the body?

7 According to the nursery rhyme, on which day of the week did Solomon Grundy take ill?

8 In which year did Björn Borg win his first Wimbledon singles title?

9 Leah and Rachel were wives of which Old Testament figure?

10 Who starred in the TV series *The Fall and Rise of Reginald Perrin*?

11 Mike Atherton captained the English national team in which sport?

12 How many children were there in the TV series *The Waltons*?

13 The Battle of Lewes Road in 1926 took place near to which British city?

14 *Hakuna Matata* is a song from which Disney film?

15 *How Can We Be Lovers* was a 1990 hit for which singer?

16 In which country is the IT security firm Kaspersky based?

17 Cranberries originated on which continent?

18 Whom did Henry VIII marry first, Anne Boleyn or Anne of Cleves?

19 Is someone described as "taciturn" a chatty person or an uncommunicative person?

20 In which year did the first Tour de Yorkshire cycle race take place?

Easy
Medium
Hard

Answers to QUIZ 31 – Pot Luck

1	Danny Boyle	11	John Wayne (1969)
2	The Rolling Stones	12	East coast
3	Three (North, East and West)	13	Arm
4	Basketball	14	*Quatre*
5	Liza (Minnelli)	15	Daisy family
6	Percussion	16	Elephant
7	*The Archers*	17	Mandolin
8	A starfish	18	North Sea
9	21	19	*Strictly Come Dancing*
10	New land	20	Blades

Easy

1 How many inches are there in a hand?

2 A cube has how many faces?

3 How many cents are there in a dime?

4 What number is represented by the Roman numerals CII?

5 Proverbially, how many lives does a cat have?

6 How many inches are there in three yards?

7 How many squares are there on a chessboard?

8 All angles in a triangle add up to what number?

9 How many gods are worshipped in a monotheistic religion?

10 How many furlongs are there in a mile?

11 A "ton" refers to how many monetary pounds?

12 How many degrees are there in quarter of a circle?

13 Before decimalisation, how many pence were there in a pound?

14 How many metres are there in five kilometres?

Medium

15 What is the cube root of eight?

16 How many legs does a quadruped have?

17 How many squares are there on each side of a Scrabble® board?

18 What is the French word for "ten"?

19 What number would a hooker wear in a game of rugby union?

20 The tetrarchy system was based around the rule of how many people?

Hard

Answers to QUIZ 32 – Nursery Rhymes

1	Under a haystack	11	10,000
2	Fat	12	Brown bread and butter
3	Sat in a corner	13	The King of Hearts
4	The dame	14	A little mouse
5	A puddle	15	One
6	Tea	16	Yellow
7	Down the street	17	Plum cake
8	School	18	Tuesday's child
9	Hanging out the clothes	19	A pail of water
10	Out to sea	20	The little dog

ANSWERS ON PAGE 37

1   Produced from 1955 until 1976, what was a Sunbeam Rapier?

2   Does an anion have a positive or a negative charge?

3   Which city lies further north, Aberdeen or Dundee?

4   In Japan, what type of drink is matcha?

5   Are the stripes on the German flag horizontal or vertical?

6   Proverbially, what is an Englishman's home?

7   What is the first event in a triathlon?

8   In which decade was the Apple record label founded?

9   Michele Dotrice played Betty, wife of Frank, in which TV series?

10 What type of creature is a speckled wood?

11 For which team did Lewis Hamilton win the 2015 F1 World Championship?

12 *The Ladykillers* is set in which city?

13 What part of a kettle shares its name with the general term for a chemical substance?

14 What is the highest council tax band in England?

15 Which musical features the Save-a-Soul mission?

16 Rum and Eigg are part of which group of islands?

17 How many pillars of Islam are there?

18 What was the first name of the founder of the Butlin's camps?

19 The town of Sittingbourne is located in which English county?

20 In which sitcom does Linda Robson play Tracey Stubbs?

Easy

Medium

Hard

Answers to QUIZ 33 – Pot Luck

1	Pawn	11	Cricket
2	Airship	12	Seven
3	A flower (of the aster family)	13	Brighton and Hove
4	Tom Conti	14	*The Lion King*
5	Devon and Somerset	15	Michael Bolton
6	Ear	16	Russia
7	Thursday	17	North America
8	1976	18	Anne Boleyn
9	Jacob	19	Uncommunicative
10	Leonard Rossiter	20	2015

Easy

1 Blue is the colour associated with which UK political party?

2 The band Blue reformed in 2011 to represent the UK in which competition?

3 In the nursery rhyme *Little Boy Blue*, where is the sheep?

4 What type of creature is a bluebottle?

5 Which heritage line runs from East Grinstead to Sheffield Park in Sussex?

6 The 1972 film *Lady Sings the Blues* was about which US singer?

7 Which national flag appears on a Blue Ensign?

8 Which aid to mobile communication is named after a 10th-century Scandinavian king?

9 "Boys in blue" is a nickname of people in which profession?

10 Which former German state lends its name to a dark blue pigment?

Medium

11 "Letters I've written, never meaning to send" is a line from which Moody Blues hit?

12 What type of food is Danish Blue?

13 Which singer starred in the 1961 film *Blue Hawaii*?

14 *Blue Monday* was a 1983 hit for which group?

15 What type of creature is a British Blue?

16 Blue and which other colour are used to describe the two main tributaries of the River Nile?

17 *Don't Fear the Reaper* was a 1976 single by which band?

18 Lesley Judd and Simon Groom are amongst former presenters of which children's TV series?

19 The blue jay is native to which continent?

20 In the type of music known as "R&B", "B" stands for "Blues". For what does the "R" stand?

Hard

Answers to QUIZ 34 – Numbers

1	Four	11	100
2	Six	12	90
3	Ten	13	240
4	102	14	5000
5	Nine	15	Two
6	108	16	Four
7	64	17	15
8	180 (degrees)	18	Dix
9	One	19	2
10	Eight	20	Four

1   The term "vascular" refers to which part of the human body?

2   What name is given to the piece of turf gouged out by a golf club making a stroke?

3   The D-Day invasion of Normandy occurred in which year?

4   What two types of bread were the lion and the unicorn given in the nursery rhyme?

5   Who had a 1983 hit with *Baby Jane?*

6   Cathy and Claire answered problems in which girls' magazine, first published in 1964?

7   What word can mean both a wall-mounted item and a build-up on teeth?

8   What type of vegetable is a Maris Piper?

9   The town of Thetford lies in which English county?

10   "There must be some kind of way outta here" is a lyric from which song?

11   Which UK fashion house is most noted for its trench coats?

12   In 1964, which group recorded the original version of *Under the Boardwalk?*

13   What is the capital of Sweden?

14   The River Ribble flows through North Yorkshire and which other county?

15   Which causes the build-up of limescale, hard water or soft water?

16   Which human rights organisation's logo features a candle in barbed wire on a yellow background?

17   *Four Weddings and a Funeral* was released in which decade?

18   What is the term for someone who studies animals?

19   In the title of a 1973 single by Sir Elton John, *Saturday Night* was *Alright* for what activity?

20   Who asked the questions on *The Weakest Link?*

Easy

Medium

Hard

Answers to QUIZ 35 – Pot Luck

1	A car	11	Mercedes
2	Negative	12	London
3	Aberdeen	13	Element
4	(Green) tea	14	Band H
5	Horizontal	15	*Guys and Dolls*
6	His castle	16	Inner Hebrides
7	Swimming	17	Five
8	1960s (1968)	18	Billy (William)
9	*Some Mothers Do 'Ave 'Em*	19	Kent
10	A butterfly	20	*Birds of a Feather*

Easy

1   For which 2008 film was Kathryn Bigelow the first woman to win the Best Director Oscar?

2   Saoirse Ronan's breakthrough role was as a precocious teenager in which 2007 film?

3   Who played the role of Jake Sully in the 2009 film Avatar?

4   In which 2007 film does the character called Anton Chigurh pursue Josh Brolin's character Llewelyn Moss?

5   What was Daniel Craig's first James Bond film?

6   Julia Roberts portrayed which real life character in 2000?

7   In 300, Leonidas is king of where?

8   *Oil!* by Upton Sinclair was the basis for which 2007 film?

9   *Walk the Line* is a biography of which singer?

10 For which film did Hilary Swank receive her second Best Actress Oscar?

11 Which role was specifically written for Uma Thurman by Quentin Tarantino?

12 Who played Alfred the butler in *Batman Begins*?

Medium

13 "In the face of an enemy, in the Heart of One Man, Lies the Soul of a Warrior" was a tag line from which 2003 film?

14 Which film won the Academy Award for Best Picture in 2006?

15 In which 2008 film did Leonardo DiCaprio and Kate Winslet play Frank and April Wheeler?

16 In the Sacha Baron Cohen film, Borat was from which country?

17 Who played *Juno* in the film of the same name?

18 Who wrote and directed the 2004 mystery *The Village*?

19 In which year was *Harry Potter and the Philosopher's Stone* released?

20 Who starred alongside Jake Gyllenhaal in *Brokeback Mountain*?

Hard

Answers to QUIZ 36 – Blue

1	Conservative Party	11	*Nights in White Satin*
2	Eurovision Song Contest	12	Cheese
3	In the meadow	13	Elvis Presley
4	Fly	14	New Order
5	The Bluebell Railway	15	Cat
6	Billie Holiday	16	White
7	Union Jack	17	Blue Öyster Cult
8	Bluetooth	18	*Blue Peter*
9	Police	19	North America
10	Prussia (Prussian blue)	20	Rhythm

1 In which decade did Clement Attlee (First Earl Attlee of Walthamstow) become Prime Minister of the UK?

2 Who captained England during the 2005 Ashes series?

3 What industry did the main characters in *The Full Monty* formerly work in?

4 In Italian cuisine, what is *pomodoro*?

5 Which character in *The Simpsons* has been voiced by both Jodie Foster and James Earl Jones?

6 Typically, how many judges preside at a boxing match?

7 On which Oasis album is the track *Don't Look Back in Anger*?

8 Off which motorway is the city of Gloucester?

9 What name is given to a baby shark?

10 In which decade did the Tamagotchi™ toy go on sale?

11 What is the fourth sign of the zodiac?

12 What is the correct spelling of the word meaning "present", currant or current?

13 At what time were the teddy bears to be taken home in the song *The Teddy Bears' Picnic*?

14 What word can refer to both a written piece of music and a total of points?

15 What product did "eight out of ten owners say their cats preferred" in a marketing campaign?

16 Dunstable lies in which English county?

17 Which chemical element is named after the Greek god of the Sun?

18 What are meze?

19 *The Ride of the Valkyries* was composed by whom?

20 What is the main vitamin found in a carrot?

Answers to QUIZ 37 – Pot Luck

1	Blood vessels	11	Burberry
2	Divot	12	The Drifters
3	1944 (June 6)	13	Stockholm
4	White and brown	14	Lancashire
5	Sir Rod Stewart	15	Hard water
6	*Jackie*	16	Amnesty International
7	Plaque	17	1990s (1994)
8	Potato	18	Zoologist
9	Norfolk	19	*Fighting*
10	*All Along the Watchtower* (Bob Dylan)	20	Anne Robinson

Easy

Medium

Hard

Easy

Medium

Hard

1   West Ham United retired the number six shirt in 2008 as a mark of respect for which player?

2   In which country did curling originate?

3   Who won his fifth Formula One World Championship title in 2018?

4   How many overs does each team play in a game of one-day cricket?

5   In 1903, Maurice Garin became the first winner of which cycle race?

6   In what year did the Soviet Union boycott the Summer Olympics?

7   Which snooker player won the 2019 Masters tournament?

8   What colour is the home jersey of the Irish rugby union team?

9   Which team won the 2018 Ryder Cup?

10 How many points is a field or drop goal worth in rugby league?

11 How many feet above the floor is the centre of the net in a game of badminton?

12 Which tennis player won his record-breaking seventh Australian Open in 2019?

13 Which three-letter abbreviation denotes the international governing body of cricket?

14 What nationality is the golfer Robert Karlsson?

15 In which winter sport would a competitor execute a salchow?

16 Who won the 2018 BBC Sports Personality of the Year award?

17 In the first modern Olympics in 1896, what colour medals were given to the winning competitors?

18 Villa Park is a football venue in which UK city?

19 How many points is the yellow ball worth in snooker?

20 What was the cause of a six-day shut down of horse racing in February 2019?

Answers to QUIZ 38 – Film 2000

1	*The Hurt Locker*	11	The Bride in the *Kill Bill* films
2	*Atonement*	12	Sir Michael Caine
3	Sam Worthington	13	*The Last Samurai*
4	*No Country for Old Men*	14	*Crash*
5	*Casino Royale* (2006)	15	*Revolutionary Road*
6	Erin Brockovich	16	Kazakhstan
7	Sparta	17	Ellen Page
8	*There Will Be Blood*	18	M Night Shyamalan
9	Johnny Cash	19	2001
10	*Million Dollar Baby*	20	Heath Ledger

1   What two-word Latin term means "of sound mind"?

2   Mollie Sugden played Mrs Slocombe in which UK sitcom?

3   The Strait of Gibraltar lies between the Atlantic Ocean and which other major body of water?

4   Which film marked Gary Oldman's debut as a writer?

5   In which sport might you use a foil or a sabre?

6   What would you store in a dosette box?

7   What colour is the engine Henry in the stories by Reverend W Awdry?

8   How many islands make up the Aran Islands?

9   The town of Wadebridge lies in which English county?

10 What is the English translation of the colour *café au lait*?

11 Which group sang the theme song to the ITV series *Robin of Sherwood*?

12 Brothers Joe and Fred Davis were world champions in which sport?

13 Which verb can mean both "to eat your food quickly" and "to run"?

14 What is a penstemon?

15 In which year did Steven Gerard make his debut for the England national football team?

16 Marzipan is made from which nut?

17 Who was elected US president first, William McKinley or William Taft?

18 Which chemical element has the symbol Br?

19 The Hoover Dam lies on which American river?

20 Who directed the 1990 film *Life is Sweet*?

Easy

Medium

Hard

Answers to QUIZ 39 – Pot Luck

1	1940s (1945)	11	Cancer
2	Michael Vaughan	12	Current
3	They were steel workers	13	Six o'clock
4	Tomato	14	Score
5	Maggie	15	Whiskas
6	Three	16	Bedfordshire
7	(What's the Story) Morning Glory	17	Helium (Helios)
8	M5	18	Appetisers (in the Middle East)
9	Pup	19	Wagner
10	1990s (1996)	20	Vitamin A

1   United Airlines operates from which nation?

2   In which country is Cancun Airport located?

3   Where is the airline Cathay Pacific based?

4   Stelios Haji-Ioannou famously founded which budget airline?

5   Fort Lauderdale-Hollywood International Airport lies in which US state?

6   Iberia is an airline from which nation?

7   In the name of the airline known as BA, for what does the "B" stand?

8   Aeroflot is based in which city?

9   What is the three-letter carrier code for American Airlines?

10 A Coruña Airport can be found in which country?

11 The airport in Salzburg is named after which composer?

12 Lech Walesa Airport serves which Polish city?

13 Olympic Airlines is the national carrier of which country?

14 In which county is London Luton Airport?

15 LaGuardia Airport is found in which US State?

16 Aer Lingus is the national airline of which country?

17 Which airline has "the Spirit of Australia" on its logo?

18 Which carrier is known as the Royal Dutch Airline?

19 In which European capital city is Ryanair based?

20 In which country would you find the airport with the code AMS?

Answers to QUIZ 40 – Sport

1	Bobby Moore	11	Five feet
2	Scotland	12	Novak Djokovic
3	Lewis Hamilton	13	ICC
4	50	14	Swedish
5	Tour de France	15	Ice skating
6	1984	16	Geraint Thomas
7	Judd Trump	17	Silver
8	Green	18	Birmingham
9	Europe	19	Two
10	One	20	Equine flu

1 Alex James and Dave Rowntree are members of which band?

2 Barry Grant was a notorious character in which British soap?

3 Who wrote the play *A Song at Twilight* (1966)?

4 Japan co-hosted the 2002 FIFA World Cup with which other nation?

5 Kym Marsh first found fame on which reality show?

6 Bury and Wigan are boroughs in which metropolitan county?

7 What four words follow "Age shall not weary them" in *For the Fallen* by Laurence Binyon?

8 Which Ben Stiller film was subtitled *The Legend of Ron Burgundy*?

9 On which continent is the country of Cambodia?

10 What is the more common name given to somnambulism?

11 The Calgary Flames compete in which sport?

12 To what did the Ecology Party change its name in 1985?

13 What substance gives carrots their orange colour?

14 Gascony is a region of which European country?

15 What infringement does a tennis player commit if they step over the baseline before hitting the ball in a serve?

16 A scallion is a name for a member of which family of vegetables?

17 What North American plant, blown across the ground by the wind, symbolises a deserted area?

18 In the song associated with Frank Sinatra, which US city is "My kind of town"?

19 What shape is a honeycomb in a beehive?

20 What is the internet country code for Canada?

Answers to QUIZ 41 – Pot Luck

1	*Compos mentis*	11	Clannad
2	*Are You Being Served?*	12	Snooker
3	The Mediterranean Sea	13	Bolt
4	*Nil By Mouth*	14	(A flowering) plant
5	Fencing	15	2000
6	Pills	16	Almond
7	Green	17	William McKinley
8	Three	18	Bromine
9	Cornwall	19	Colorado River
10	Coffee with milk	20	Mike Leigh

Easy

1   What word beginning with "y" is a term for an unsophisticated country person?

2   The word "defenestration" describes the act of throwing something or somebody through what?

3   What word for "flattery" takes its name from an Irish castle?

4   What general word for a pastime is also the name of a bird of prey?

5   Proverbially, you should strike when what is hot?

6   Which Latin phrase, often used about superheroes, means "second self"?

7   What is the name for the white of an egg?

8   What term is given to the art or science of flying?

9   Does "brevity" mean long or short duration?

10 Which word meaning "to talk constantly" can also be applied to the noise of a small dog?

11 What does an entomophobe fear?

12 Which is the correct spelling of this commonly misspelled word: concious, connsious or conscious?

Medium

13 In Cockney rhyming slang, what is a "dicky bird"?

14 Used to describe an afternoon performance, what time of day does the word matinee actually relate to in French?

15 What term is given to either the shortest or longest day of the year?

16 From the Latin for "ship", what term denotes the main part of a church?

17 What type of animal is described as ovine?

18 How is the word "and" defined in grammatical terms?

19 What eight-letter word beginning with "v" describes a person of no fixed abode?

20 What is the term for a word that means the opposite of another?

Hard

Answers to QUIZ 42 – Up in the Air

1	USA	11	Mozart
2	Mexico	12	Gdansk
3	Hong Kong	13	Greece
4	easyJet	14	Bedfordshire
5	Florida	15	New York
6	Spain	16	Republic of Ireland
7	British	17	Qantas
8	Moscow	18	KLM
9	AAL	19	Dublin
10	Spain	20	The Netherlands

1   What name links the main characters in the 1966 film *Born Free* and the 2013 film *Frozen*?

2   What is the more common name for dyspepsia?

3   The name of which Greek god means "a brief sleep" when read backwards?

4   Which former athlete was appointed president of the International Association of Athletics Federations in 2015?

5   Gorden Kaye played the leading character in which sitcom?

6   In which English county is Doncaster Racecourse?

7   As at the start of 2019, how many cities were there in Devon?

8   Which Irish town is it a long way to in the title of a music-hall song?

9   "Turn off your mind, relax and float downstream" are the opening words to which Beatles song?

10   What nationality was pioneer aviator Amy Johnson?

11   Which company manufactures the "Gear" fitness trackers?

12   Which monarch reigned earlier, Charles I or Mary I?

13   In which TV series did Idris Elba play the character of Stringer Bell?

14   Which word for a harbour can also mean "take something away"?

15   Morgan Le Fay is a character in which legend?

16   In relation to the energy in food, for what do the initials GI stand?

17   Conversions are worth how many points in rugby union?

18   Which city is fringed by the Cheshire Plain?

19   What word completes the title of a 1985 Stephen Frears film: *My Beautiful ___*?

20   Which part of the body do you bend to genuflect?

Answers to QUIZ 43 – Pot Luck

1	Blur	11	Ice hockey
2	*Brookside*	12	The Green Party
3	Sir Noël Coward	13	Carotene
4	South Korea	14	France
5	*Popstars*	15	Foot fault
6	Greater Manchester	16	Onion
7	Nor the years condemn	17	Tumbleweed
8	*Anchorman*	18	Chicago
9	Asia	19	Hexagonal
10	Sleepwalking	20	.ca

Easy

1   In the name of the US TV channel ABC, for what does the "C" stand?

2   What three-letter word is used to describe an archaeological excavation?

3   What do the letters SPF stand for in relation to skincare?

4   For what is "Met" short in the name of the London police force?

5   Which Conservative MP is often referred to as IDS?

6   What was the three-letter nickname of the 36th president of the USA?

7   Which muscles are often described as "abs"?

8   JPR Williams (b.1949) represented Wales in which sport?

9   *NME* is a famous magazine about what subject?

10 For what does the "J" stand in the name of JRR Tolkien?

11 Members of the NUT trade union work in what profession?

12 Which organ of the body is checked in an ECG test?

13 What three-letter term is given to the fourth note of a scale?

14 In which county is the River Fal?

Medium

15 What "gift" is an eloquent person said to have?

16 What was the title of the 1991 TV series created by Alan Bleasdale that starred Robert Lindsay as a city council leader?

17 Hoy belongs to which island group?

18 Who played Hercule Poirot in the 2018 TV adaptation of *The ABC Murders*?

19 For what are the companies DPD and UPS known?

20 What do the letters SAT stand for in relation to the National Curriculum?

Hard

Answers to QUIZ 44 – Words

1	Yokel	11	Insects
2	Window	12	Conscious
3	Blarney	13	Word
4	Hobby	14	Morning
5	The iron	15	Solstice
6	Alter ego	16	Nave
7	Albumen	17	Sheep
8	Aviation	18	Conjunction
9	Short duration	19	Vagabond
10	Yap	20	Antonym

1 The 1963 film *Tom Jones* was based on a novel by which writer?

2 Which of these is the correct spelling: maneuvre, manoeuvre or manuvere?

3 The Ebor Handicap is a flat race held in which city?

4 What animal is an exhausted person compared to?

5 On which river does the city of Durham lie?

6 Semillon is a type of which fruit?

7 Which TV doctor published the 2018 diet book *The Fast 800*?

8 Francois Pienaar captained which rugby union team to victory in the 1995 World Cup?

9 What word means the ability of an object to float?

10 Bernard Butler and Brett Anderson were original members of which rock band?

11 Michael McIntyre was a judge on the fifth series of which reality show?

12 How long does Ramadan last?

13 Mauritius lies in which ocean?

14 What is vetch?

15 Matt Tebbutt presents TV programmes on what subject?

16 In which decade did Ann Jones win eight Grand Slam tennis championships?

17 A podiatrist is concerned with what part of the body?

18 Induction loop systems, present in many public buildings, are designed to be used with what type of device?

19 What word can mean "eager", "intense" or "to lament"?

20 What type of creature is a Manx shearwater?

Easy

Medium

Hard

Easy

1 Duane Eddy was noted for playing which instrument?

2 Who had an international hit in 2005 with the song *Dakota*?

3 *La Bamba* was the biggest hit for which US singer?

4 In 1984 which Bruce Springsteen song was the first to win him a Grammy?

5 Whose first single (2009) was entitled *Mama Do*?

6 Simon Le Bon is the lead singer with which band?

7 Which singer was born in Tupelo, Mississippi on January 8, 1935?

8 The Blackhearts were the backing group of which singer?

9 What was the name of the Spice Girls' first album?

10 In 2014, who became the first British female solo artist to have five UK no.1 singles?

Medium

11 Whose seventh studio album was entitled *Ray of Light*?

12 Who topped the UK singles charts in 2019 with *7 Rings*?

13 *More Than Words* was a 1991 hit for which rock band?

14 Which 2004 song by U2 shares its title with that of a 1958 Alfred Hitchcock film?

15 ABBA was formed in which country?

16 What was the title of Billie Myers' 1998 hit?

17 *Reet Petite* was a 1986-7 posthumous hit for which singer?

18 What was the title of the first UK top ten single for the band James?

19 *Sheer Heart Attack* was an album released by which British band?

20 Justin Hawkins was the lead singer with which 2000s band?

Hard

1 How often does golf's Ryder Cup take place?

2 Who was the last king of Scotland?

3 On which river does Hereford lie?

4 What is a schism?

5 How many darts does a player throw on each turn?

6 Which film was released first, *The Sound of Music* or *Cabaret*?

7 In which country did avocados originate?

8 Which member of the Monty Python team directed the 1985 film *Brazil*?

9 What would you make of a molehill if you were prone to exaggerating?

10 Leah Totton and Alana Spencer have both been winners on which reality show?

11 In the name of the WWI military organisation the BEF, for what did the "F" stand?

12 Who played Joe Friday in the 1987 film *Dragnet*?

13 What word for a female waterbird is also the name of a writing implement?

14 Mrs Danvers is the housekeeper at which fictional house in a 1938 novel?

15 What was the first name of Bert Kwouk's character in the Inspector Clouseau films?

16 Which future UK Prime Minister was Education Secretary from 1970 to 1974?

17 Which group had a hit in 1978 with *Fantasy*?

18 Dan Biggar plays international rugby union for which country?

19 Nurse Ratched is a character in which Oscar-winning 1975 film?

20 What is the singular of "criteria"?

Answers to QUIZ 47 – Pot Luck

1	Henry Fielding	11	*Britain's Got Talent*
2	Manoeuvre	12	29 or 30 days
3	York	13	Indian Ocean
4	Dog (dog-tired)	14	A wild plant
5	River Wear	15	Food
6	Grape	16	1960s
7	Dr Michael Mosley	17	Feet
8	South Africa	18	Hearing aid
9	Buoyancy	19	Keen
10	Suede	20	A bird (seabird)

ANSWERS ON PAGE 52

1   Which institution is known by the initials GOSH?

2   In which year was the position of Mayor of London created?

3   What was the name of the gorilla who was a famous resident of London Zoo until his death in 1978?

4   Which Channel 4 TV series is filmed in the Paternoster Chop House?

5   The Royal Albert Hall was opened in what century?

6   Which area of London precedes "Village" to form the name of a Bohemian area of New York?

7   In which year did London introduce congestion charging?

8   The west London area of Chiswick lies in which borough?

9   Why did Big Ben begin a prolonged silence in August 2017?

10 The Shard is in which borough of London?

11 The postcode N1C covers the area around which main line station?

12 In which building did the future Queen Elizabeth II marry Prince Philip?

13 Which mainline train station is the main London terminus for trains from the West Country?

14 What is the name of the concert hall on the River Thames that was opened in 1951?

15 The Sainsbury Wing is part of which art gallery?

16 Kensington Gardens sit in the Royal Borough of Kensington and Chelsea and which other borough?

17 What is the current name of the structure formerly known as the Post Office Tower?

18 What is the national dialling code for London?

19 London cadets in which branch of the emergency services train at Hendon College?

20 Which building on London's South Bank was once used to store stock cubes?

Answers to QUIZ 48 – Pop Music

1	Guitar	11	Madonna
2	Stereophonics	12	Ariana Grande
3	Ritchie Valens	13	*Extreme*
4	*Dancing in the Dark*	14	*Vertigo*
5	Pixie Lott	15	Sweden
6	Duran Duran	16	*Kiss the Rain*
7	Elvis Presley	17	Jackie Wilson
8	Joan Jett	18	*Sit Down*
9	*Spice*	19	Queen
10	Cheryl	20	The Darkness

1   Who directed the film *The English Patient*?

2   What word can mean a deep crack in rock or a small crack in a tooth?

3   Johan Cruyff played for which country's national team in the 1970s?

4   Where would you find your conjunctiva?

5   In what century did Elizabeth I become Queen of England?

6   Which English town is famous for its concrete cows?

7   What term is given to the coloured nutritional labels on food products?

8   What is the term given to an unusually high-pitched singing voice produced by a man?

9   Bridge Street, Turpin Road and George Street are locations in which long-running series?

10 What is the main vitamin in an orange?

11 What word can mean both a baseball player and a mixture with which to make pancakes?

12 Who wrote the 1845 poem *Home Thoughts from Abroad*?

13 In which winter sport might a power play occur?

14 Which 1939 musical film features the characters of Aunty Em and Uncle Henry?

15 How many hurdles are jumped in 400m hurdles races?

16 What, according to the proverb, is procrastination?

17 The technology firm Huawei is based in which country?

18 Kielder Forest lies in which county?

19 Which fish is proverbially said to be slippery?

20 Who was sacked as UK Defence Secretary in May 2019?

Answers to QUIZ 49 – Pot Luck

1	Every two years	11	Force
2	James VI	12	Dan Aykroyd
3	River Wye	13	Pen
4	A separation or disruption (especially religions)	14	Manderley (*Rebecca*)
5	Three	15	Cato
6	*The Sound of Music* (1965)	16	Baroness Margaret Thatcher
7	Mexico	17	Earth, Wind & Fire
8	Terry Gilliam	18	Wales
9	A mountain	19	*One Flew Over the Cuckoo's Nest*
10	*The Apprentice*	20	Criterion

1   The plant periwinkle has what colour flowers?

2   What type of creature is a nightjar?

3   In which southern Welsh county are the Preseli Hills?

4   What are grouped together to form a coppice?

5   Which has the most number of legs, four spiders or five beetles?

6   What is bladderwrack?

7   A promontory is a high area of land bordering what?

8   Which river is the longer, the Amazon or the Yangtze?

9   Where is the Sun always positioned when you look at a rainbow?

10   Hound Tor lies in which National Park?

11   What name is given to birds' early-morning singing?

12   Which tree has been affected in recent years by a "dieback" disease?

13   A brimstone butterfly has what colour wings on the top surface?

14   What term is given to the natural environment of a plant or animal?

15   What part of a plant is referred to as "foliage"?

16   The Larsen Ice Shelf lies in which continent?

17   What term is given to a very heavy snowstorm accompanied by strong winds?

18   The jackal is a member of which family of animals?

19   Grayling is the name of a type of butterfly and which other creature?

20   What is the more common name of the plant *nepeta*, referencing its effect on a particular type of animal?

Answers to QUIZ 50 – London

1	Great Ormond Street Hospital	11	King's Cross
2	2000	12	Westminster Abbey
3	Guy	13	Paddington
4	*First Dates*	14	Royal Festival Hall
5	19th century (1871)	15	National Gallery
6	Greenwich	16	City of Westminster
7	2003	17	The BT Tower
8	Hounslow	18	020
9	Stopped for renovation work	19	Police
10	Southwark	20	The OXO Tower

QUIZ 53 – Pot Luck

1   The Cinque Terre lies on the Ligurian coastline in which country?

2   How many players are on the pitch for one team in an American Football match?

3   In which decade was *TV-am* first broadcast?

4   What number is represented by the Roman numerals CC?

5   Which city lies further south, Derry or Newry?

6   What word can mean both part of a chair and a weapon?

7   Greece joined WWI in which year?

8   Bill Owen played a leading role in which long-running UK sitcom?

9   What term is given to a punishment imposed by a church authority?

10 The radio code words for which two letters of the alphabet are types of dances?

11 The video game series *Top Spin* features what sport?

12 In the 1989 Disney film, what colour are the Little Mermaid's fins?

13 Complete the opening line of a famous Wordsworth poem "I wander'd lonely as a ___"?

14 Which country has the international car registration letter CDN?

15 The jackfruit originated on which continent?

16 Daisy Goodwin created which regal TV series, first broadcast in 2016?

17 A sexton works in what type of building?

18 How many subjects are covered by a book known as a monograph?

19 Which process of improving posture is named after its creator (d.1955)?

20 Which novel by Joseph Heller was adapted for TV in 2019?

Easy

Medium

Hard

Answers to QUIZ 51 – Pot Luck

1	Anthony Minghella	11	Batter
2	Fissure	12	Robert Browning
3	The Netherlands	13	Ice hockey
4	In the eyes	14	*The Wizard of Oz*
5	16th century (1558)	15	Ten
6	Milton Keynes	16	The thief of time
7	Traffic-light system	17	China
8	Falsetto	18	Northumberland
9	*EastEnders*	19	Eel
10	Vitamin C	20	Gavin Williamson

Easy

1 What did the MPs who left the Labour and Conservatives parties in February 2019 originally call their new collective?

2 In what year did David Lloyd George (First Earl of Dwyfor) become UK Prime Minister?

3 How many different UK Prime Ministers were there in the 1970s?

4 How old was Ronald Reagan when he was inaugurated as US President?

5 Which party won a landslide victory in the 1945 UK General Election?

6 In what year of the 1960s did Sir Winston Churchill die?

7 Leo Varadkar was elected to which position in 2017?

8 In which city is the headquarters of the Scottish Parliament?

9 The Central Committee administer which political party?

10 What relation is Jeb Bush to George W Bush?

11 Glasnost and Perestroika were key policies of which leader?

Medium

12 Which much-talked-about term during the Brexit negotiations is also a term used in baseball and rounders?

13 Who was Prime Minister of the UK during the Falklands War?

14 Walter Mondale was the vice president to which US President?

15 In 2011, who became the leader of North Korea?

16 What title is given to the ceremonial head of state in Japan?

17 Who was French President first, Georges Pompidou or Charles De Gaulle?

18 Who was appointed to the post of Foreign Secretary in 2018 following Boris Johnson's resignation?

19 In a vote in the UK parliament, to which side do the "ayes" go?

20 Who became president of the European Council in 2014?

Hard

Answers to QUIZ 52 – Natural World

1	Blue	11	The dawn chorus
2	A bird	12	The ash tree
3	Pembrokeshire	13	Yellow
4	Trees	14	Habitat
5	Four spiders (32)	15	The leaves
6	Seaweed	16	Antarctica
7	Water	17	Blizzard
8	The Amazon	18	Dogs
9	Behind you	19	A fish
10	Dartmoor	20	Catmint or catnip

ANSWERS ON PAGE 57

1   The Scott Monument lies in which city?

2   "Never made it as a wise man I couldn't cut it as a poor man stealing" is a lyric from which song?

3   What is the seventh colour of the rainbow?

4   How many first-class county cricket clubs are there in England and Wales?

5   What is the name of the lower chamber of the US Congress?

6   In which city was *The Liver Birds* set?

7   Which happened first: the dissolution of Parliament by Charles I or the Gunpowder Plot?

8   Which is the correct spelling of an outline of events: cenario, scenario or senario?

9   The Great Red Storm is a feature of which planet?

10 What word can mean both a power source and a large store of weapons?

11 In the netball position WA, for what does the "A" stand?

12 In which decade did Pink Floyd release the album *The Final Cut*?

13 For what do the letters HP stand in the name of the computer company?

14 Heath Ledger played which Batman villain in a 2008 film?

15 The Camargue region lies in which European country?

16 What is the main colour of the coat worn by Chelsea Pensioners?

17 Which part of the body might be described as "gimlet"?

18 In darts, how many points is the bull worth?

19 In which Jane Austen adaptation did Alan Rickman play Colonel Christopher Brandon?

20 Which film won the Outstanding British Film award at the 2019 BAFTAs?

Easy

Medium

Hard

Answers to QUIZ 53 – Pot Luck

1	Italy	11	Tennis
2	11	12	Green (bluish-green)
3	1980s (1983)	13	Cloud
4	200	14	Canada
5	Newry	15	Asia
6	Arm	16	*Victoria*
7	1917	17	A church
8	*Last of the Summer Wine* (Compo)	18	One
9	Penance	19	Alexander Technique
10	F and T (Foxtrot and Tango)	20	*Catch-22*

ANSWERS ON PAGE 58

1   In which decade did Metro Bank launch in the UK?

2   What name was given to September 16, 1992 in the UK for financially-related reasons?

3   In relation to money, for what do the initials CPI stand?

4   Who released the 1976 single *Money, Money, Money*?

5   Proverbially, what coin will always turn up?

6   In 2000, Paul Lewis became the main presenter of which radio finance programme?

7   Who was Chancellor of the Exchequer immediately before Philip Hammond?

8   How many different pictures of Queen Elizabeth II featured on the £1 coin between 1983 and 2000?

9   What does the "A" stand for in the term ATM?

10 Royal Bank of Scotland has its headquarters in which city?

11 Arthur Fowler stole Christmas Club money in *EastEnders* to pay for whose wedding?

12 In use from the 1970s until the 1990s, what type of financial product was Access?

13 Which financial company bought Northern Rock in 2012?

14 What denomination was the first polymer banknote issued by the Bank of England?

15 Which financial journalist and TV presenter founded the website moneysavingexpert.com?

16 The piece of eight was an old coin from which country?

17 In 1982, which was the first bank to reintroduce Saturday opening?

18 Which bank collapsed in 1995 after fraudulent activity by trader Nick Leeson?

19 In which decade was the Sunday Trading Act passed, allowing more shops to trade on that day?

20 As at May 2019, what was the cost of a standard first class stamp in the UK?

Answers to QUIZ 54 – Politics

1	The Independent Group	11	Gorbachev
2	1916	12	Backstop
3	Four	13	(Baroness) Margaret Thatcher
4	69	14	Jimmy Carter
5	The Labour Party	15	Kim Jong-un
6	1965	16	Emperor
7	Taoiseach (Prime Minister of Ireland)	17	Charles De Gaulle
8	Edinburgh	18	Jeremy Hunt
9	The Communist Party	19	The right
10	Brother	20	Donald Tusk

1   In which decade was the first Formula 1 race held?

2   What does the German word *schnell* mean in English?

3   Which James Bond film was released first, *Goldfinger* or *Thunderball*?

4   In which year did the driving test change to include following instructions from a satnav?

5   What number *Love Potion* featured in the title of a 1950s song?

6   Which philosopher said that "Hell is other people"?

7   Which city featured in the title of the second *Home Alone* film?

8   In which century did composer Dmitri Shostakovich live?

9   "When shall we three meet again?" is the opening line of which Shakespeare play?

10 In which sport is the pitch called a gridiron?

11 Which is the largest of the Isles of Scilly?

12 In which winter sport do competitors travel lying down face first?

13 Which group featured in the 1964 film *A Hard Day's Night*?

14 Swaledale lies in which National Park?

15 *Love Really Hurts Without You* was a 1976 hit for which singer?

16 Which thin pastry is traditionally used in Greek cooking?

17 Proverbially, what area of water is referred to as calm?

18 In which country was the company Airbnb founded?

19 Mycoprotein is derived from which type of group of plants?

20 In *Beauty and The Beast*, what is Lumière?

Answers to QUIZ 55 – Pot Luck

1	Edinburgh	11	Attack (wing attack)
2	*How You Remind Me* (Nickelback)	12	1980s (1983)
3	Violet	13	Hewlett-Packard
4	18	14	The Joker (*The Dark Knight*)
5	House of Representatives	15	France
6	Liverpool	16	Red
7	The Gunpowder Plot (1605)	17	The eyes
8	Scenario	18	50
9	Jupiter	19	*Sense and Sensibility*
10	Battery	20	*The Favourite*

1   Who was the famous love of Marc Antony in Roman times?

2   How did the Romans refer to "the mass" of the people?

3   What was the name of the supreme advisory body to the magistrate in Roman times?

4   On what date did the Ides of March take place?

5   What was a hippodrome?

6   Watling Street was a Roman route in which country?

7   Of what was Victoria the Roman Goddess?

8   On which Roman hill were the imperial palaces built?

9   In which county can the remains of the Vindolanda fort be seen?

10   Mancunium was the Roman name for which English city?

11   Who famously crossed the Rubicon in 49 BC?

12   How many Roman soldiers were originally in a century?

13   Which Roman items would have been made with tesserae?

14   The Roman numerals CD are equivalent to what number?

15   What was the official colour of Roman Emperors?

16   The remains of what type of Roman building can be seen at Lullingstone in Kent?

17   What tribe of people sacked Rome in AD 410?

18   Who led the Carthaginian expeditions against Rome?

19   Of what was Somnus the Roman God?

20   Albion was the Roman name for which country?

Answers to QUIZ 56 – Money

1	2010s (2010)	11	Michelle (his daughter)
2	Black Wednesday	12	Credit card
3	Consumer Price Index	13	Virgin Money
4	ABBA	14	£5
5	A bad penny	15	Martin Lewis
6	*Money Box*	16	Spain
7	George Osborne	17	Barclays Bank
8	Three	18	Barings Bank
9	Automated	19	1990s (1994)
10	Edinburgh	20	70p

1 What was the name of the hotel in the 2014 film starring Ralph Fiennes?

2 What is the occupation of someone who collects and maintains historical records?

3 Which desert covers the greatest area in square miles, the Gobi Desert or the Sahara Desert?

4 Jockey Frankie Dettori is which nationality?

5 In which decade was the film *Brassed Off* released?

6 Bradford is situated just on the edge of which range of hills?

7 Which 1980s sitcom featured Anton Rogers and Julia McKenzie as William and Hester Fields?

8 According to the proverb, what was never won by faint heart?

9 What word can mean both a fish and an old style bladed weapon?

10 What system of signalling uses red and yellow flags at sea and blue and white on land?

11 From which language do we get the word *contretemps*?

12 What was the name of the fort in the children's series *Camberwick Green*?

13 In which decade was the Sir Alfred Hitchcock film *Spellbound* released?

14 What is the maximum number of players in a game of croquet?

15 In which county is the town of Bromsgrove?

16 What word can mean both a small drinking vessel and a sporting trophy?

17 Where in a room would you find a lintel?

18 "The Lord is My Shepherd" is a traditional bingo call for which number?

19 On a standard keyboard, which letter is immediately to the left of D?

20 What sauce is traditionally served with roast pork?

Easy

Medium

Hard

Answers to QUIZ 57 – Pot Luck

1 1950s (1950)
2 Quick or fast
3 *Goldfinger* (1964)
4 2017
5 9
6 Jean-Paul Sartre
7 New York
8 20th century (1906-75)
9 *Macbeth*
10 American Football

11 St Mary's
12 Skeleton
13 The Beatles
14 Yorkshire Dales
15 Billy Ocean
16 Filo pastry
17 Millpond
18 USA (San Francisco)
19 Fungi
20 Candlestick

Easy

1   Anakin Skywalker turns into which villain?

2   In which film does Luke discover Leia is his sister?

3   Daisy Ridley played which character in *The Force Awakens*?

4   How many feet tall is Chewbacca?

5   Ewan McGregor plays which character in the series?

6   Which film is Episode 2 of the series?

7   Natalie Portman appeared in how many *Star Wars* films?

8   R2D2 was played by whom?

9   Luke Skywalker was trained by which two characters?

10   Who composed the original *Star Wars* music?

Medium

11   Which young *Star Wars* character did Alden Ehrenreich play in a 2018 film?

12   What is the surname of Kylo in *The Force Awakens*?

13   What is the name of the heavily armoured space station featured in the series?

14   Darth Maul first appeared in which film?

15   Who is frozen at the end of *The Empire Strikes Back*?

16   How many Star Wars films were released before *The Phantom Menace*?

17   Hayden Christensen made his debut in which film?

18   Which character's face was partly based on that of Albert Einstein?

19   Jabba the Hutt first appeared in which film?

20   Carrie Fisher first appeared in which *Star Wars* film?

Hard

Answers to QUIZ 58 – The Romans

1	Cleopatra	11	Julius Caesar
2	Plebeians or Plebs	12	100
3	The Senate	13	Mosaics
4	March 15	14	400
5	Sports stadium (involving horses)	15	Purple
6	England	16	Villa
7	Victory	17	Visigoths
8	The Palatine Hill	18	Hannibal
9	Northumberland	19	Sleep
10	Manchester	20	England

1 Amanda Holden has been a judge on which reality show since its first series?

2 Thomas Savery (d.1715) developed the first commercial pumping device powered by which form of energy?

3 What word can mean both rubbish and a group of young animals born at the same time?

4 Which ballet features a battle between gingerbread men soldiers and a Mouse King?

5 What name is given to the area under a church?

6 What is a pea-souper?

7 Ben Price plays which character in *Coronation Street*?

8 Jonathan Edwards was the first triple jumper to achieve what distance?

9 Which of these cities is closest to the Welsh border, Hereford or Gloucester?

10 In athletics, into what do sprinters place their feet while waiting for the race to begin?

11 Starring Gary Cooper and Grace Kelly, what type of film is the 1952 Oscar-winning *High Noon*?

12 Which book of the Old Testament recounts Sarah's pregnancy with Isaac?

13 Who votes for the winner of the Man of Steel Award?

14 Which group's hits include *Emotional Rescue* and *Undercover of the Night*?

15 In relation to personal banking, for what do the initials TSB stand?

16 Lancia vehicles are manufactured in which country?

17 In which county is Worksop?

18 Which section of the army is specifically trained to use large guns?

19 Rattan furniture is made from a plant native to which continent?

20 What name is given to the person in charge of exhibits at a gallery or museum?

Answers to QUIZ 59 – Pot Luck

1	*The Grand Budapest Hotel*	11	French
2	Archivist	12	Pippin Fort
3	Sahara Desert	13	1940s (1945)
4	Italian	14	Four
5	1990s (1996)	15	Worcestershire
6	Pennines	16	Cup
7	*Fresh Fields*	17	Above a door or window
8	Fair lady	18	23
9	Pike	19	S
10	Semaphore	20	Apple sauce

1   *Don't Rain on My Parade* is a song from which musical?

2   What two-word French term appears on labels for air mail?

3   Lucy Pargeter plays Chas Dingle in which TV series?

4   Which medieval Parisian building experienced a devastating fire in April 2019?

5   An incident with the particle accelerator at STAR Labs featured in which TV superhero series?

6   What is the name of the sport that involves being lifted into the air while wearing a parachute?

7   Banned in the UK, for what is the substance paraquat used?

8   Who wrote *The Pardoner's Tale*?

9   What is a pariah?

10   The famous road Park Lane is in which borough of London?

11   On a road sign reading P&R, the "P" stands for Park. For what does the "R" stand?

12   How many chambers are there in the UK parliament?

13   What ingredient is used in a dish described as *parmigiana*?

14   In which country is Mount Parnassus?

15   From what is parquet flooring made?

16   A parr is a young fish of what species?

17   George Parr was a fictional character on which comedy show?

18   Which former chat-show host is known as "Parky"?

19   The country of Paraguay lies on which continent?

20   For which football club did Ray Parlour play from 1992 to 2004?

Answers to QUIZ 60 – Star Wars

1	Darth Vader	11	Han Solo
2	*Return of the Jedi*	12	Ren
3	Rey	13	Death Star
4	Eight feet	14	*The Phantom Menace*
5	Obi Wan Kenobi	15	Han Solo
6	*Attack of the Clones*	16	Three
7	Three	17	*Attack of the Clones*
8	Kenny Baker	18	Yoda
9	Obi Wan and Yoda	19	*Return of the Jedi*
10	John Williams	20	*A New Hope* (originally *Star Wars*)

1 Which 1980 boxing film tells the tale of Jake LaMotta?

2 What type of bend in a road shares its name with a tress-holding item?

3 In which decade was *The Big Breakfast* first broadcast?

4 On which motorway are the Cherwell Valley services?

5 Is Caerphilly cheese a hard or soft cheese?

6 The name of what type of formal garden is taken from the French for "on earth"?

7 The village of Godshill, noted for its model village, lies on which island?

8 "Caught in a landslide, no escape from reality" is a line from which song, first released in 1975?

9 What is the purpose of a damper in a piano?

10 Which is the correct spelling of the word meaning "funny": humerus, humorous, or humourous?

11 What name is given to a store of munitions?

12 Whereabouts would you find a metatarsal bone?

13 Who was the Shadow Chancellor of the Exchequer from 2011 to 2015?

14 Since which year have young people in the UK been required to continue in training or education until the age of 18?

15 Who managed the England national men's football team from 2006 to 2007?

16 What is the occupation of a member of the professional body RICS?

17 Who conceived and presents *The South Bank Show*?

18 What do Beanz Meanz in the famous advertising slogan?

19 The International Date Line runs through which ocean?

20 In cookery, what measure is abbreviated to "tbsp"?

Answers to QUIZ 61 – Pot Luck

1	*Britain's Got Talent*	11	A western
2	Steam	12	Genesis
3	Litter	13	Fellow players
4	*The Nutcracker*	14	The Rolling Stones
5	Crypt	15	Trustee Savings Bank
6	Dense fog	16	Italy
7	Nick Tilsley	17	Nottinghamshire
8	18m	18	Artillery
9	Hereford	19	Asia
10	Starting blocks	20	Curator

1 In which TV series did the character Nora Batty appear?

2 Alan B'Stard was the lead character in which series?

3 'Allo, 'Allo! was set during which war?

4 Audrey fforbes-Hamilton was a leading character in which sitcom?

5 Who wrote the 1978-83 sitcom *Butterflies*?

6 Caroline Aherne and Craig Cash co-wrote which sitcom that began in the late 1990s?

7 Chigwell is the setting for which show?

8 Chris O'Dowd and Richard Ayoade played central characters in which sitcom, first broadcast in 2006?

9 Who wrote *One Foot in the Grave*?

10 Dougal McGuire was a character in which show?

11 Harry Enfield co-starred with Martin Clunes in the first series of which sitcom, aired in 1992?

12 *George and Mildred* was a spin-off from which show?

13 *Gourmet Night* is a famous episode of which sitcom?

14 Gus Hedges and George Dent were central characters in which series?

15 In which county was *The Vicar of Dibley* set?

16 Who starred as Patrick Glover in *Father, Dear Father*?

17 Brenda Furlong was the leading character in which series?

18 Who played the son in the series *Steptoe and Son*?

19 In which series did James Bolam first play Terry Collier?

20 What was the first name of Mr Brittas in *The Brittas Empire*?

Answers to QUIZ 62 – Par for the Course

1	*Funny Girl*	11	Ride
2	*Par avion*	12	Two (House of Commons and House of Lords)
3	*Emmerdale*	13	Parmesan cheese
4	Notre-Dame de Paris	14	Greece
5	*The Flash*	15	Wood
6	Parascending	16	Salmon
7	Weedkiller	17	*Bremner, Bird and Fortune*
8	Geoffrey Chaucer	18	Sir Michael Parkinson
9	A social outcast	19	South America
10	Westminster	20	Arsenal FC

1. What was the profession of Hippocrates?

2. What sport is being played when England play Australia for the Ashes?

3. Mike the landlord and Boycie the car dealer featured in which sitcom?

4. Which North African mountain range shares its name with a figure from Greek mythology?

5. Which is the correct spelling of a word meaning unusual: unacustommed, unaccustomed or unnaccustomed?

6. In *Toy Story 2*, what was the name of the horse?

7. In which English county is the 2,000 Guineas Stakes run?

8. Which Premier League football team has a mascot named Gunnersaurus?

9. What word meaning "join" is also the name of a UK cash machine network?

10. *Bring it All Back* (1999) was the first hit for which group?

11. Bannockburn, scene of a famous battle, lies immediately south-east of which Scottish city?

12. Bondi Beach lies in which Australian state?

13. Who wrote the spoof soap opera *Acorn Antiques*?

14. Grange-over-Sands is a town in which county?

15. "Nothing is so good it lasts eternally" are the opening words to which 1984 song?

16. The transit of which planet across the Sun last took place in 2004 and will not occur again until 2117?

17. Which fairy-tale character did Lily Collins play in the 2012 fantasy adventure film *Mirror Mirror*?

18. The River Plate forms part of the border between Uruguay and which other country?

19. For which 1972 film did Al Pacino win his first Best Supporting Actor Oscar nomination?

20. What kind of fruit is a muscat?

Answers to QUIZ 63 – Pot Luck

1	*Raging Bull*	11	Arsenal
2	Hairpin	12	On the foot
3	1990s (1992)	13	Ed Balls
4	M40	14	2011
5	Hard cheese	15	Steve McClaren
6	Parterre	16	Surveyor
7	Isle of Wight	17	Melvyn Bragg (Baron Bragg)
8	*Bohemian Rhapsody*	18	Heinz
9	Reduce sound	19	Pacific Ocean
10	Humorous	20	Tablespoon

1 Kylie Minogue was a coach on which UK talent show in 2014?

2 *Max and Paddy's Road to Nowhere* was a spin-off from which show?

3 What did the company Miners sell?

4 Who is best known for playing Max Branning in *EastEnders*?

5 The city of Minneapolis is in which US state?

6 Who played Charlie Edwards in the TV series *Hotel Babylon*?

7 Minestrone soup originated in which country?

8 The Circus Maximus stadium is located in which European city?

9 Minorca lies in which group of islands?

10 In which TV series did Maxine Peake play QC Martha Costello?

11 Minnie the Minx appears in which children's comic?

12 What silver item did Maxwell possess in the title of a Beatles song?

13 *I Could Be So Good For You* was the theme song to which TV series?

14 Who played *Max* in the 2015 film *Mad Max: Fury Road*?

15 Mina Harker and Renfield are characters in which 1897 novel?

16 In which 2000 film did Russell Crowe play the character of Maximus?

17 Ming the Merciless is an enemy of which hero?

18 Maxim's restaurant, known for its art nouveau décor, is in which French city?

19 Who played Mork in the TV series *Mork and Mindy*?

20 Which London museum has a cinema showing IMAX films?

Answers to QUIZ 64 – British Sitcoms

1	Last of the Summer Wine	11	Men Behaving Badly
2	The New Statesman	12	Man About the House
3	WWII	13	Fawlty Towers
4	To the Manor Born	14	Drop the Dead Donkey
5	Carla Lane	15	Oxfordshire
6	The Royle Family	16	Patrick Cargill
7	Birds of a Feather	17	dinnerladies
8	The IT Crowd	18	Harry H Corbett
9	David Renwick	19	The Likely Lads
10	Father Ted	20	Gordon

1   According to the nursery rhyme, what was the colour of the nutmeg on *My Little Nut Tree*?

2   Gremolata is a savoury garnish of chopped parsley, garlic and which fruit?

3   Who replaced Jon Pertwee as the star of *Doctor Who*?

4   In which decade did McDonalds open its first outlet in Moscow?

5   Which leader was born first: Alexander the Great or Hannibal?

6   What part of the body is affected by diphtheria?

7   Camber Sands lies in which southern county of England?

8   Which comedian and actor played radio DJ Adrian Cronauer in the 1987 film *Good Morning, Vietnam*?

9   Which golf club shares its name with an item of computer software?

10 What French word does an audience call to encourage a performer to continue at the end of a show?

11 Which athletics road race is run over a distance of 42.195 kilometres?

12 *A Brief Inquiry into Online Relationships* won British Album of the Year at the 2019 Brit Awards for which band?

13 Which newsreader was the original host of the game show *Treasure Hunt*?

14 What word can mean both a regular action and a nun or monk's clothing?

15 What name is given to a communal dining hall in an educational or religious establishment?

16 In which decade did *The Thin Blue Line* first air on TV?

17 In the name RAF, for what does the "R" stand?

18 Who hosted the 2019 game show *Small Fortune*?

19 Which comedian swam the length of the River Thames for Comic Relief in 2011?

20 The third part of which film trilogy, starring Michael J Fox, is set in the Wild West?

Easy

Medium

Hard

Answers to QUIZ 65 – Pot Luck

1	Physician	11	Stirling
2	Cricket	12	New South Wales
3	*Only Fools and Horses*	13	Victoria Wood
4	Atlas Mountains	14	Cumbria
5	Unaccustomed	15	*I Know Him So Well*
6	Bullseye	16	Venus
7	Suffolk (Newmarket)	17	Snow White
8	Arsenal FC	18	Argentina
9	Link	19	*The Godfather*
10	S Club 7	20	Grape

Easy

1   What is the marsupium on a kangaroo more commonly called?

2   Does a fennec fox have noticeably large ears or noticeably small ears?

3   An orange tip is what type of creature?

4   What term is given to the skin on the back of a cobra's neck when it is spread out?

5   The Tibetan ox has what shorter name?

6   What colour is a male mallard's head?

7   What on a fish may be pectoral or ventral?

8   From which country does the Dobermann Pinscher originate?

9   What is a young penguin called?

10   What name is given to a cow that has not yet had a calf?

11   Which Chinese dog is noted for its thick coat and blue-black tongue?

12   Howler and proboscis are species of which creature?

13   Which word can follow "collared", "rock" and "turtle" in the name of birds?

14   What colour fur does the mountain hare have in summer?

15   "Storey" is an anagram of which creature's name?

16   What term is given to a group of antelopes?

17   What obvious feature do monkeys have that apes do not?

18   In what do stag beetle larvae live?

19   What colour is an Arctic fox?

20   What is the world's largest land predator?

Medium

Hard

Answers to QUIZ 66 – Min and Max

1	*The Voice UK*	11	*The Beano*
2	*Peter Kay's Phoenix Nights*	12	Hammer
3	Make-up	13	*Minder*
4	Jake Wood	14	Tom Hardy
5	Minnesota	15	*Dracula*
6	Max Beesley	16	*Gladiator*
7	Italy	17	*Flash Gordon*
8	Rome	18	Paris
9	Balearic Islands	19	Robin Williams
10	*Silk*	20	Science Museum

ANSWERS ON PAGE 71

1   Which Russian leader met Pope John Paul II at the Vatican in 1989?

2   Proverbially, what can you not get out of a stone?

3   Which of Henry VIII's wives had the same name as the actress who starred in the TV series *Dr Quinn, Medicine Woman*?

4   Does Harwich lie on the east coast or the west coast of England?

5   What is "Westie" short for in the name of the dog breed?

6   Camelot Group introduced which event to the UK in 1994?

7   What name is given to an area given over to the growing of fruit trees?

8   Which comedian co-starred with Eric Idle in the 1990 film *Nuns on the Run*?

9   The Frisian Islands lie off the coast of which European country?

10 What name is given to phrases such as "Red leather yellow leather" and "The Leith police dismisseth us"?

11 The fortified town of San Gimignano can be found in which European country?

12 Chablis wine is made in which region of France?

13 Part of the London district of Westminster, St John's Wood underground station is on which line?

14 What was the first name of the famous 18th-century furniture maker Chippendale?

15 Peru and Colombia are the only two countries to share a border with which other South American country?

16 Who was the UK Foreign Secretary from 2007 to 2010?

17 Which "wise" creatures are associated with the phrase "See no evil, hear no evil, speak no evil?"

18 In equestrian sport, a three-day event usually consists of dressage, cross country and which other event?

19 Which British actor played the monk Silas in the 2006 film *The Da Vinci Code*?

20 Which Beatles song has the opening lines "In the town where I was born, lived a man who sailed to sea"?

Easy

Medium

Hard

---

1 What word completes this famous quote from *As You Like It:* "All the world's a ___"?

2 Which play features the Montagues and the Capulets?

3 In *The Taming of the Shrew*, what relation is Petruchio to Katherina?

4 Mustardseed appears in which play?

5 Lorenzo and Jessica form a couple in which play?

6 What item of furniture did Shakespeare famously leave to his wife?

7 Which play ends at the Battle of Bosworth Field?

8 In terms of number of lines, which is the longest of Shakespeare's plays?

9 What colour stockings does Malvolio get tricked into wearing in *Twelfth Night*?

10 Puck is the servant to which character?

11 In which play would you find Mistress Page and Mistress Ford?

12 How many daughters does King Lear have?

13 The Battle of Agincourt is the central part of which play?

14 Desdemona is the wife of which leading character?

15 What relation is Malcolm to Duncan in *Macbeth*?

16 *Henry VI* is written in how many parts?

17 After which Roman emperor did Shakespeare name a play?

18 What word completes the name that Shakespeare is often given: the Bard of ___?

19 In *The Tempest*, what is the name of Prospero's daughter?

20 How many "Ages of Man" are mentioned in *As You Like It*?

Answers to QUIZ 68 – Animal World

1	Pouch	11	Chow
2	Noticeably large ears	12	Monkey
3	A butterfly	13	Dove
4	Hood	14	Brown
5	Yak	15	Oyster
6	Green	16	Herd
7	Fins	17	Tails
8	Germany	18	Decaying wood
9	Chick	19	White
10	Heifer	20	Polar bear

1   What seven-letter word beginning with "o" is descriptive of a bad sign?

2   Which comedy film series starring Steve Guttenberg featured the tall character of Moses Hightower?

3   Who reigned earliest, Charles I, Elizabeth I or James I?

4   The *New Horizons* probe flew past which body of the solar system in 2015?

5   Which word meaning uncommunicative is an anagram of "nett rice"?

6   What is the SI unit of mass?

7   In what decade did Disney release *Snow White and the Seven Dwarfs*?

8   Which of these cities is most easterly, Aberdeen or Ipswich?

9   Which animals take part in the game of flyball?

10 What word can mean both a narrow valley and a channel beside a bowling alley?

11 Crathes Castle lies in which Scottish county?

12 In what century did The War of the Spanish Succession take place?

13 Amy Childs found fame on which reality show?

14 How many Australian states have a cardinal point of the compass in their name?

15 *There are Worse Things I Could Do* is a song from which musical film?

16 Who played Philip Marlowe in the 1946 film *The Big Sleep*?

17 What word can mean both to eat too much and a deep narrow valley?

18 In which English county is the town of Crediton?

19 Which of The Wombles shares his name with a Russian city?

20 Who captained Argentina in the 1986 FIFA World Cup?

Easy

Medium

Hard

Answers to QUIZ 69 – Pot Luck

1	Mikhail Gorbachev	11	Italy
2	Blood	12	Burgundy
3	Jane Seymour	13	Jubilee Line
4	East coast	14	Thomas
5	West Highland terrier	15	Ecuador
6	National Lottery	16	David Miliband
7	Orchard	17	Monkeys
8	Robbie Coltrane	18	Showjumping
9	The Netherlands	19	Paul Bettany
10	Tongue-twisters	20	*Yellow Submarine*

1   *Pas de trois* is a dance for how many people?

2   Which form of dance is featured in the 1948 film *The Red Shoes*?

3   *You Should Be Dancing* was a 1976 hit for which group?

4   The terminology of ballet is generally derived from which language?

5   What is the title of the Irving Berlin song that begins "There may be trouble ahead"?

6   Who released the 1972 single *Tiny Dancer*?

7   In which century did the Turkey Trot become popular?

8   From which country does the samba originate?

9   *Dance With Me Tonight* was a 2011 hit for which singer?

10 How many veils were involved in Salome's dance in the Bible?

11 Who partnered Ann Widdecombe when she appeared on the eighth series of *Strictly Come Dancing*?

12 How many basic foot positions exist in classical ballet?

13 The eightsome reel is a traditional dance associated with which country?

14 Who had a 2008 hit with *Just Dance*?

15 Who composed the music for *The Nutcracker*?

16 What is the name for a traditional Gaelic evening of song and dance?

17 In which UK city is the Sadler's Wells dance theatre?

18 What is the name for the person who provides the instructions at a barn dance?

19 Who had chart success in 1961 with *Let's Twist Again*?

20 Ice dance forms a part of which winter sport?

Answers to QUIZ 70 – Shakespeare

1	Stage	11	*The Merry Wives of Windsor*
2	*Romeo and Juliet*	12	Three
3	Husband	13	*Henry V*
4	*A Midsummer Night's Dream*	14	Othello
5	*The Merchant of Venice*	15	Son
6	His second best bed	16	Three
7	*Richard III*	17	*Julius Caesar*
8	*Hamlet*	18	Avon
9	Yellow	19	Miranda
10	Oberon	20	Seven

1 How is the Volkswagen Type 1 more usually referred to?

2 What is meant by the French term *de trop*?

3 What was Blackadder's first name in the TV series?

4 For what were tally sticks used?

5 Which style of trousers shares its name with something made illegally?

6 Which emperor is known for fiddling while Rome burned?

7 From which country was the *White Heather Club* TV variety show broadcast?

8 What is the married surname of the athlete Jessica who won heptathlon gold at the 2012 London Olympics?

9 In which county are the water gardens of Studley Park?

10 Which Premier League football team has had Vicarage Road as its home ground since 1922?

11 Huguenot is a railway station in which borough of New York City?

12 Which actor and comedian starred in the 2005 film *The 40-Year-Old Virgin*?

13 Which country has land borders with Myanmar (Burma), Laos, Cambodia and Malaysia?

14 Which chemical element has the symbol P?

15 In which month do Australia and New Zealand celebrate Anzac Day?

16 What word can mean both a paper-perforating device and a mix of drinks?

17 Parcelforce is a subsidiary of which company?

18 Which snooker player is nicknamed "The Wizard of Wishaw"?

19 What was the name of the organisation that owned the majority of the British rail infrastructure between 1994 and 2002?

20 The name of which US state completes the title of the 1984 film *The Hotel ___*, which starred Jodie Foster and Beau Bridges?

Answers to QUIZ 71 – Pot Luck

1	Ominous	11	Aberdeenshire
2	*Police Academy*	12	18th century (1701-14)
3	Elizabeth I	13	*The Only Way is Essex*
4	Pluto	14	Four (New South Wales, Northern Territory,
5	Reticent		South Australia, Western Australia)
6	Kilogram	15	*Grease*
7	1930s	16	Humphrey Bogart
8	Ipswich	17	Gorge
9	Dogs	18	Devon
10	Gully	19	Tomsk
		20	Diego Maradona

1. Who provides the voice of Apu in *The Simpsons*?

2. The Jungfrau is in which Swiss range of mountains?

3. In the Bible, who was Esau's father?

4. Subaru is a car manufacturer from which country?

5. Justin Trudeau became Prime Minister of which country in 2015?

6. The term "cru" is used to grade what type of drink?

7. Corfu lies in which sea?

8. What type of food is served as pilau in India?

9. The country of Guinea-Bissau is on the west coast of which continent?

10. Oahu is an island in which US state?

11. Part of the traditional Highland dress, what is a skean-dhu?

12. What flavour is the liqueur Cointreau®?

13. The shih-tzu dog originated in which country?

14. A sou was a former coin in which European country?

15. What type of bird is a marabou?

16. What is "flu" short for?

17. The term "ecru" is usually applied to which unbleached material?

18. What is the plural of the word "tableau"?

19. What type of creature is a gnu?

20. The defence system of ju-jitsu originated in which country?

Answers to QUIZ 72 – Dance

1	Three	11	Anton du Beke
2	Ballet	12	Five
3	The Bee Gees	13	Scotland
4	French	14	Lady Gaga
5	*Let's Face the Music and Dance*	15	Tchaikovsky
6	Sir Elton John	16	*Ceilidh*
7	20th century (1900s)	17	London
8	Brazil	18	Caller
9	Olly Murs	19	Chubby Checker
10	Seven	20	Figure skating

Easy

1. On which instrument is a nocturne usually played?

2. Which Hollywood star played the role of security guard Larry Daley in the 2006 film *Night at the Museum* and its sequels?

3. In which century did the poet Tennyson live and die?

4. What does the "H" stand for in the sporting abbreviation NHL?

5. Which Radio 5 presenter joined the *Newsnight* team of presenters in 2019?

6. Which leader was born first, Charlemagne or Julius Caesar?

7. Manufactured in the 1950s, what type of vehicle is a Green Goddess?

8. Which disease is known as "pink eye"?

9. In which decade did the satirical magazine *Punch* cease publication after over 150 years?

10. If you are working hard, what are you said to be burning at both ends?

11. What star sign is someone whose birthday is on October 1?

12. Who won the 2019 Football Writer's Association Men's Player of the Year award?

13. Which country invaded Kuwait in 1991?

14. The town of Yeovil is in which English county?

15. Who was Home Secretary from 1993 to 1997?

16. What was the name of Sir Anthony Hopkins' character in the film *The Silence of the Lambs*?

17. In which country was former tennis champion John Newcombe born?

18. What five-letter verb beginning with "w" means to exercise power or a weapon?

19. Brooke Vincent plays which character in *Coronation Street*?

20. What name is given to the part of a chimney above roof level?

Medium

Hard

Answers to QUIZ 73 – Pot Luck

1	Volkswagen Beetle	11	Staten Island
2	Too much	12	Steve Carell
3	Edmund	13	Thailand
4	Recording numbers or quantities	14	Phosphorus
5	Bootleg	15	April (25th)
6	Nero	16	Punch
7	Scotland	17	Royal Mail Group
8	Ennis-Hill	18	John Higgins
9	North Yorkshire	19	Railtrack
10	Watford FC	20	*New Hampshire*

Easy

1 Which south of England football club played home games at The Dell until 2001?

2 What nationality is former England football manager Fabio Capello?

3 For which football club did goalkeeper Bob Wilson (b.1941) play from 1963 until his retirement in 1974?

4 Ibrox Stadium is situated in which Scottish city?

5 Which football team plays its home games at Goodison Park?

6 In which country did the vuvuzela feature prominently in the 2010 FIFA World Cup finals?

7 The Bernebéu Stadium is home to which football club?

8 Which club retired the no.14 shirt in 2007 to honour Johan Cruyff?

9 Anderlecht are a team from which European country?

10 Which Spanish team did Liverpool FC beat in the 2019 Champion's League semi-final?

Medium

11 Which Scottish club plays home games in green and white hooped shirts?

12 Carlos Tevez signed for which Italian club in 2013?

13 Which football club won the 2019 Championship?

14 Clarence Seedorf played international games for which country?

15 In a 4-4-2 team arrangement, how many defenders are there?

16 Who became manager of Manchester United immediately after Sir Alex Ferguson?

17 As at 2019, how many times has Mexico hosted the FIFA World Cup?

18 Which team won the 2019 women's FA Cup?

19 Which club won seven consecutive Greek titles between 1997 and 2003 and again between 2011 and 2017?

20 What term is given to the combined goals of both matches in a competition that has a home and away game in each round?

Hard

Answers to QUIZ 74 – U-End

1	Hank Azaria	11	Dagger
2	(Bernese) Alps	12	Orange
3	Isaac	13	China
4	Japan	14	France
5	Canada	15	A stork
6	Wine	16	Influenza
7	Ionian Sea	17	Linen
8	Rice	18	Tableaux
9	Africa	19	Antelope
10	Hawaii	20	Japan

1 Which former US tennis player became known for a "You cannot be serious!" outburst in a 1981 match?

2 Where is a kippah worn?

3 What is the name of Kellie Bright's character in *EastEnders*?

4 What colour is the bullseye on a standard dartboard?

5 The beer Sol originated in which country?

6 How many doors does a coupé car have?

7 For what do the initials OTT stand when used as an adjective?

8 In Cockney rhyming slang, what is "Rosie Lee"?

9 The Colorado River rises in which mountain range?

10 Who released the 1982 single *Don't Pay the Ferryman*?

11 Who was Archbishop of Canterbury from 1991 to 2002?

12 In 2003, Felix Baumgartner became the first person to skydive across which stretch of water?

13 Roker is a seaside resort in which English city?

14 Where in the body is the occipital bone?

15 In 2019, who was named as the US Ryder Cup captain for 2020?

16 Up to the reign of Elizabeth II, how many English kings were called William?

17 In the initials of the trade union RMT, for what does the "M" stand?

18 Which US president was nicknamed "Dubya"?

19 In which decade was the pet passport introduced in the UK?

20 *I'm So Excited* and *Jump (For My Love)* were 1980s hits for which US group?

Easy

Medium

Hard

1. How many judges do competitors sing in front of in *All Together Now*?

2. Who won the 2018 series of *Britain's Got Talent*?

3. The winners of which sporting series include Joe McElderry and Joey Essex?

4. Which professional dancer partnered 2018 *Strictly Come Dancing* winner Stacey Dooley?

5. Who replaced Claudia Winkleman as host of *The Great British Sewing Bee* for the 2019 series?

6. Which Channel 4 reality TV competition involves fugitives trying to evade capture?

7. Ryan Seacrest was the host of which long-running US talent show, first broadcast in 2002?

8. Who co-presented the first series of *The Big Family Cooking Showdown* with Nadiya Hussain?

9. What was the name of the all-round sports competition that was first broadcast on the BBC in 1973?

10. The first series of *The X Factor* was won by which singer?

11. What was the title of Sonia's 1993 Eurovision UK entry?

12. Which competition did Rahul Mandal win in 2018?

13. What was the English name of the programme *Jeux Sans Frontières*?

14. Jane Devonshire and Simon Wood are former winners of which competition?

15. Who was Ulrika Jonsson's original co-presenter on *Gladiators*?

16. In which iconic building was the 2019 *Great British Menu* banquet held?

17. Which *Glee* actor was a dance captain on the 2019 series *The Greatest Dancer*?

18. In which series were One True Voice beaten by Girls Aloud?

19. Which 2018 Channel 5 competition was won by Aberdeen Model Railway Club?

20. In which year was *The Voice UK* first shown on ITV?

Answers to QUIZ 76 – Football

1	Southampton FC	11	Celtic
2	Italian	12	Juventus
3	Arsenal FC	13	Norwich City FC
4	Glasgow	14	The Netherlands
5	Everton FC	15	Four
6	South Africa	16	David Moyes
7	Real Madrid	17	Twice (1970 and 1986)
8	Ajax	18	Manchester City
9	Belgium	19	Olympiacos
10	Barcelona	20	Aggregate score

1 What type of creature is a siskin?

2 What number is represented by the Roman numerals XXIV?

3 "The higher you build your barriers the taller I become" is a lyric from which song?

4 Until 2003, what service was obtained by dialling 192 on a telephone?

5 Which singer is known by the nickname "The Boss"?

6 The island of Hispaniola is the second-largest island in which body of water?

7 What is the collective name for domestic fowl such as ducks or chickens?

8 What colour is a Belisha beacon?

9 Which is the next prime number after 17?

10 As at 2019, how many times has the USA hosted the Summer Olympic Games?

11 What do you do, if you give someone the cold shoulder?

12 Carmel McQueen was a long-serving character in which soap?

13 What is said to be the lowest form of wit?

14 What is the term for a period of rest to recover from an illness?

15 Which former England football manager was associated with the phrase "Do I not like that"?

16 As at 2019, which Scandinavian country was not a member of the European Union?

17 Which beer was advertised in the 1970s with the phrase "works wonders"?

18 The province of Phuket is part of which country?

19 In which English county is the town of Boston?

20 What colour are the flowers of a celandine?

Answers to QUIZ 77 – Pot Luck

1	John McEnroe	11	George Carey (Baron Carey of Clifton)
2	On the head	12	English Channel
3	Linda Carter	13	Sunderland
4	Red	14	In the skull
5	Mexico	15	Steve Stricker
6	Two	16	Four
7	Over the top	17	Maritime
8	Tea	18	George W Bush
9	Rocky Mountains	19	2000s (2001)
10	Chris de Burgh	20	The Pointer Sisters

1   What name is given to a camouflaged structure from which to watch birds?

2   In what type of building does Eleanor Rigby pick up the rice, in a Beatles song?

3   What type of structure is the Temperate House in Kew Gardens?

4   Which north-east England cathedral is the home of the Shrine of St Cuthbert?

5   What name is given to the covered area around a square in a cathedral or monastery?

6   Kenilworth Castle is situated in which county?

7   In which country was architect Robert Adam born in 1728?

8   What accompanied "wattle" as an old building material?

9   The video for Britney Spear's *Baby One More Time* is mainly set where?

10   What is a mausoleum?

11   In which US state is the John F Kennedy Space Center?

12   Which Agatha Christie sleuth featured in a full-length novel for the first time in *Murder at the Vicarage*?

13   In which century was the Royal Observatory at Greenwich built?

14   What term is given to the building next to a cricket pitch?

15   What type of dwelling derives its name from the French for "small house"?

16   In the UK, what grade is given to listed buildings of exceptional interest?

17   In the fable of the Three Little Pigs, of what material did the third pig build his house?

18   What collective name is given to the buildings in which soldiers live, as well as the group of soldiers themselves?

19   In the story of the nativity, in which type of building was Jesus born?

20   Where do Laura and Alec first meet in the film *Brief Encounter*?

Answers to QUIZ 78 – Television Competitions

1   100
2   Lost Voice Guy
3   *The Jump*
4   Kevin Clifton
5   Joe Lycett
6   *Hunted*
7   *American Idol*
8   Zoë Ball
9   *Superstars*
10   Steve Brookstein
11   *Better the Devil You Know*
12   *The Great British Bake Off*
13   *It's a Knockout*
14   *MasterChef*
15   John Fashanu
16   Abbey Road Studios
17   Matthew Morrison
18   *Popstars: the Rivals*
19   *The Great Model Railway Challenge*
20   2017

1   Beth Tweddle won which reality TV show in 2013?

2   How much does a job cost if it is carried out *ex gratia*?

3   Which is the next prime number after 47?

4   Which former *Neighbours* actor appeared in the film *The Hurt Locker* as Staff Sergeant Matthew Thompson?

5   What does "velocity" mean?

6   At which racecourse is the Irish Grand National run?

7   By what name is Vitamin B3 also known?

8   Who wrote and starred in the TV series *Fleabag*?

9   In 2008, *Viva la Vida* became the first single by which band to top the UK charts?

10 Which European nationality can be put before "auction", "courage" and "double" to make phrases?

11 Which of these cities lies further west, Derby or Lichfield?

12 Who starred in the original 1927 film *The Jazz Singer*?

13 Stroud is in which English county?

14 Who sang about *Marlene on the Wall* in 1985?

15 What description is given to the result of a vote in which all voters opt for the same choice?

16 Malta lies in which sea?

17 Which animal's milk is used to make Roquefort cheese?

18 Whitehaven lies on the coast of which county?

19 What hairstyle takes its name from its resemblance to furrows in a ploughed field?

20 What is the name of Amanda Henderson's character in the TV series *Casualty*?

Answers to QUIZ 79 – Pot Luck

1	A bird	11	Snub them
2	24	12	*Hollyoaks*
3	*(Something Inside) So Strong* (Labi Siffre)	13	Sarcasm
4	Directory enquiries	14	Convalescence
5	Bruce Springsteen	15	Graham Taylor
6	Caribbean	16	Norway
7	Poultry	17	Double Diamond
8	Amber or orange	18	Thailand
9	19	19	Lincolnshire
10	Four	20	Yellow

1 In which city does Gucci have its headquarters?

2 What is the first name of Cara Delevingne's elder sister, also a model?

3 Who took over the Versace label after the death of Gianni Versace?

4 In which country was the fashion magazine *Harper's Bazaar* founded?

5 "Bless my cotton socks, I'm in the news" is the opening line of which 1981 song?

6 What is a tabard?

7 Barbara Hulanicki founded which fashion label?

8 What did the shop Freeman, Hardy and Willis sell?

9 Who recorded the 1979 song *Forever in Blue Jeans*?

10 The Dr Scholl's® brand is concerned with what part of the body?

11 What does the word *faux* mean?

12 *Sharp Dressed Man* was a 1983 song by which US band?

13 Which items of clothing, usually worn by dancers, became popular in the 1980s as a result of the films *Fame* and *Flashdance*?

14 Who was Queen Elizabeth II's official dressmaker from 1952 to 1989?

15 Fashion designer Jean-Paul Gaultier was born in which country?

16 Which style of shoe was particularly popular with glam rock bands in the 1970s?

17 What term is given to civilian dress, when worn by a member of the armed services?

18 Which item of leisurewear derives its name from an atoll in the Pacific Ocean?

19 A sporran would be worn with which item of traditional dress?

20 The company Birkenstock is famous for selling what type of clothing?

Answers to QUIZ 80 – Buildings

1	Hide	11	Florida
2	A church	12	Miss Marple
3	A greenhouse	13	17th century (1675-75)
4	Durham	14	Pavilion
5	Cloister	15	Maisonette
6	Warwickshire	16	Grade I
7	Scotland	17	Bricks
8	Daub	18	Garrison
9	School	19	A stable
10	A large impressive grave	20	A railway station

1   What is comfrey?

2   A liger is the offspring of a female tiger and a male of what species?

3   Which member of the royal family gave birth on May 6, 2019?

4   What word can mean both a small metal bolt and to fascinate?

5   Charlie Brooks played which character in *EastEnders*?

6   Who had a 1982 hit with *Fantastic Day*?

7   "Man Alive" is a traditional bingo call for which number?

8   What is the background colour of the Swedish flag?

9   In Greek mythology, what relation was Artemis to Apollo?

10   Who was the UK's Deputy Prime Minister from 1995 to 1997?

11   Which airport was previously known as Hurn Airport?

12   Which was the only Grand Slam tennis tournanment in which Tim Henman did not reach the semi-final?

13   What name is given to a dive into a swimming pool where the diver enters the water horizontally, making a large splash?

14   Which company bought the Rover group in 1994?

15   In which decade was the Angel of the North completed?

16   Christchurch lies on which island of New Zealand?

17   What was the name given to April 16, 1995, when an additional "1" was inserted into UK phone numbers?

18   What musical instruction is meant by the word *scherzo*?

19   In which county is the town of Brixham?

20   Who won the 2019 snooker World Championship?

Answers to QUIZ 81 – Pot Luck

1	*Dancing on Ice*	11	Lichfield
2	Nothing	12	Al Jolson
3	53	13	Gloucestershire
4	Guy Pearce	14	Suzanne Vega
5	Speed	15	Unanimous
6	Fairyhouse	16	The Mediterranean
7	Niacin	17	Ewe (sheep)
8	Phoebe Waller-Bridge	18	Cumbria
9	Coldplay	19	Cornrows
10	Dutch	20	Robyn (Miller)

Easy

1   Sulley is the nickname of the leading character in which 2001 film?

2   *Summer Vacation* was the subtitle of the 2018 release in which series?

3   The villainous Cruella De Vil features in which Disney film?

4   What animals are members of the "Rescue Aid Society" in the Disney film *The Rescuers*?

5   In which film did the Minions first appear?

6   What breed of dog is Lady in *Lady and The Tramp* (1955)?

7   Dug, voiced by Eddie Redmayne, was the hero of which 2018 film?

8   What is the name of Pongo's owner in *One Hundred and One Dalmatians*?

9   What is Cogsworth in the film *Beauty and the Beast*?

10 In which country was the 2018 film *Isle of Dogs* set?

Medium

11 What is the name of Woody's original owner in the *Toy Story* series of films?

12 *You Can Fly* and *A Pirate's Life* are songs from which 1953 film?

13 *When You Wish Upon a Star* is an Oscar-winning song from which film?

14 Which 1999 Disney film was based on a book by Edgar Rice Burroughs?

15 In the 2019 film *The Lego Movie 2: The Second Part*, of what are the aliens made?

16 What character was voiced by Eddie Murphy in the *Shrek* series?

17 Which Pixar film was released first, *Cars* or *Up*?

18 The 2019 film in the *How to Train Your Dragon* series had what subtitle?

19 What appliance completes the title of the 1987 film *The Brave Little ___*?

20 Who co-directed the 2005 film *Corpse Bride* with Mike Johnson?

Hard

Answers to QUIZ 82 – Fashion and Clothing

1	Florence, Italy	11	Fake
2	Poppy	12	ZZ Top
3	Donatella	13	Leg warmers
4	USA	14	Sir Hardy Amies
5	*Reward* (The Teardrop Explodes)	15	France
6	A sleeveless or short-sleeved jacket	16	Platform shoe
7	Biba	17	Mufti
8	Shoes	18	Bikini
9	Neil Diamond	19	A kilt
10	Feet	20	Shoes

ANSWERS ON PAGE 87

1   Who played Krystle Carrington in the 1980s TV series *Dynasty*?

2   In which county is Potters Bar?

3   Who presents *DIY SOS: The Big Build*?

4   The Pantiles is a Georgian colonnade in which Kent town?

5   What was the capital city of Nigeria until 1991?

6   Which pronoun can also mean a deep hole?

7   The question "Who was that masked man?" was associated with which fictional TV character?

8   A mufti is a jurist in which religion?

9   On which sport does former player Ken Brown (b.1957) commentate?

10 The song *Land of my Fathers* is associated with which part of the UK?

11 Morse Code was invented in which century?

12 Which article of the European Union must be triggered for a country to signal its withdrawal?

13 Which method of surveillance shares its name with the act of referencing individuals on Facebook™?

14 What do Americans call a handbag?

15 Around which part of the hand can you metaphorically wrap someone?

16 What is the term given to the isolation of a person or animal to prevent the spread of disease?

17 Which company manufactured the Camel fighter aircraft?

18 In which county was the TV series *Wycliffe* set?

19 Which confectionery company makes the Creme Egg?

20 Which volcano destroyed the Roman town of Herculanium?

Easy

Medium

Hard

Answers to QUIZ 83 – Pot Luck

1	A plant (of the borage family)	11	Bournemouth Airport
2	Lion	12	Australian Open
3	The Duchess of Sussex	13	Belly flop
4	Rivet	14	BMW
5	Janine Butcher	15	1990s (1998)
6	Haircut 100	16	South Island
7	Five	17	PhONEday
8	Blue	18	Lively
9	Brother and sister (twins)	19	Devon
10	Michael Heseltine (Baron Heseltine)	20	Judd Trump

Easy

1. What type of vessel was *Potemkin*, on which a mutiny occurred in 1905?
2. The saying "It'll be over by Christmas" was associated with which conflict?
3. Around the waters of which nation did the Battle of Jutland occur?
4. Which of Henry VIII's wives subsequently married Thomas Seymour?
5. Johannes Gutenburg invented the printing press during what century?
6. In which nation was the Solidarity trade union founded?
7. Christopher Columbus reached the new world in what century?
8. In 1930, who became the first female pilot to fly solo from England to Australia?
9. In which year was Tsar Nicholas II forced to abdicate?
10. Whom did Elizabeth I create Earl of Leicester in 1564?
11. In which decade did General Franco die?
12. The 1916 Easter Uprising occurred in which country?
13. Members of the Sealed Knot society recreate events from which conflict?
14. Which age preceded the Iron Age?
15. In what year did the Battle of Hastings take place?
16. Haile Selassie became Emperor of Abyssinia in which century?
17. The statue of which Greek God situated at Olympus was one of the Seven Wonders of the Ancient World?
18. Middleham Castle in North Yorkshire was the childhood home of which monarch, born in 1452?
19. Which happened first: the completion of the Eiffel Tower, or the presentation of the Statue of Liberty to America?
20. Whom did Brutus and Cassius, among others, assassinate?

Medium

Hard

Answers to QUIZ 84 – Animated Films

1	*Monsters, Inc.*	11	Andy
2	*Hotel Transylvania*	12	*Peter Pan*
3	*One Hundred and One Dalmatians*	13	*Pinocchio*
4	Mice	14	*Tarzan*
5	*Despicable Me*	15	Duplo®
6	Cocker spaniel	16	Donkey
7	*Early Man*	17	*Cars* (2006)
8	Roger	18	*The Hidden World*
9	A clock	19	Toaster
10	Japan	20	Tim Burton

1   Where are players sent when they are disciplined in ice hockey or rugby league?

2   What word describes a handwritten or typed document, particularly the original version of a book?

3   In which county is Watford?

4   Which verb meaning "to restart" is an anagram of "steer"?

5   What is the medical name for the gullet?

6   What shape is a chevron?

7   Which ship was the subject of the 1958 film *A Night to Remember*?

8   Who played the title role in the TV series *Thorne*?

9   On a standard keyboard, which letter is between T and U?

10 Who starred in the 1981 film *Whose Life Is It Anyway*?

11 Which 2011 French film, made in the style of a black and white silent film, won the Best Picture Oscar?

12 What is the name of the black cap worn at graduation ceremonies?

13 What name is given to the first day of Lent?

14 Whom did Alistair Darling succeed as Chancellor of the Exchequer?

15 The "Clean for the Queen" campaign was launched by which organisation in 2016?

16 What was the name of Noah Wyle's character in *ER*?

17 What word can mean both a cricket ground and a level of sound?

18 Who sang *It Had to Be You* in the 1989 film *When Harry Met Sally*?

19 How many nights are there in the full title of the collection of folk tales known as *The Arabian Nights*?

20 What type of dog is a cairn?

Easy

Medium

Hard

Answers to QUIZ 85 – Pot Luck

1	Linda Evans	11	19th century (1830s)
2	Hertfordshire	12	Article 50
3	Nick Knowles	13	Tagging
4	Tunbridge Wells	14	Purse
5	Lagos	15	Your little finger
6	Mine	16	Quarantine
7	The Lone Ranger	17	Sopwith
8	Islam	18	Cornwall
9	Golf	19	Cadbury
10	Wales	20	Mount Vesuvius

1 *Wild Wood* was an album released in 1993 by which singer?

2 Who starred as James West in the 1999 film *Wild Wild West*?

3 In which century was the novel *The Tenant of Wildfell Hall* first published?

4 Who starred as Johnny Strabler in the 1953 film *The Wild One*?

5 What is the more common name of the wild hyacinth?

6 Who wrote *Little House on the Prairie*?

7 How was gunfighter James Hickok more usually referred to?

8 Who had a 1981 hit with *Chequered Love*?

9 What nationality was novelist and playwright Thornton Wilder?

10 *Kings of the Wild Frontier* was the second studio album by which group?

11 The wildebeest belongs to which family of animals?

12 What term is given to unauthorised strike action?

13 Who played Joan Wilder in the 1984 film *Romancing the Stone*?

14 Which wildlife presenter shares his name with one of the Hairy Bikers?

15 The TV series *Wild at Heart* was set on which continent?

16 *Wild*, featuring Big Sean and Dizzee Rascal, was a top five hit for which female singer in 2013?

17 Who starred as Gail Hartman in the 1994 film *The River Wild*?

18 Proverbially, which wild animals are unable to make you do something you don't want to?

19 Who wrote *The Ballad of Reading Gaol* (1897)?

20 Who played the title role in the 1971 film *Willy Wonka and the Chocolate Factory*?

Answers to QUIZ 86 – History

1	Battleship	11	1970s (1975)
2	WWI	12	Ireland
3	Denmark	13	English Civil War
4	Catherine Parr	14	Bronze Age
5	15th century (c.1440)	15	1066
6	Poland	16	20th century (1930)
7	15th century (1492)	17	Zeus
8	Amy Johnson	18	Richard III
9	1917	19	The presentation of the Statue of Liberty (1886)
10	Robert Dudley	20	Julius Caesar

1   Which fictional presenter returned to television in 2019's *This Time*?

2   *Rockferry* was a Brit Award Best Album winner by which singer?

3   In 2017, who won a record eighth Wimbledon men's singles title?

4   What word can mean both an aisle between seats and a portable bridge for getting on or off a boat?

5   Who was the UK's Deputy Prime Minister from 2010 to 2015?

6   What substance and part of a room make up a two-word term describing a barrier to promotion?

7   The mountain of Skiddaw lies in which National Park?

8   What foodstuff completes the phrase "the land of milk and ___", meaning a fertile region?

9   What colour are the flowers on the wild garlic plant?

10 What nationality was the poet and novelist Robert Graves (d.1985)?

11 The 1971 film *The Boy Friend* starred which English model?

12 Which king ordered the dissolution of the monasteries in the 16th century?

13 Who recorded the song *Is She Really Going Out With Him?* in 1978?

14 Whitby is on the coast of which sea?

15 The name of which wasp is an anagram of a royal seat?

16 Which European capital city is situated at the confluence of the Danube and Sava rivers?

17 Which group had a hit with *Fernando* in 1976?

18 The binary number 11 has what decimal equivalent?

19 What word can mean both a psychiatric hospital and the permission for a refugee to stay in a foreign country?

20 What term is given to surgery carried out through small incisions?

Easy

Medium

Hard

Answers to QUIZ 87 – Pot Luck

1	The sin-bin	11	*The Artist*
2	Manuscript	12	Mortarboard
3	Hertfordshire	13	Ash Wednesday
4	Reset	14	Gordon Brown
5	Oesophagus	15	Keep Britain Tidy
6	V-shape	16	Dr John Carter
7	The *Titanic*	17	Pitch
8	David Morrissey	18	Harry Connick Jr
9	Y	19	*One Thousand and One*
10	Richard Dreyfuss	20	Terrier

1 In which part of the head does the cranial cavity lie?

2 The malleus, one of the ear bones, comes from the Latin for what?

3 To what does the prefix "haemo" refer?

4 What is inflamed with blepharitis?

5 On which part of the body would you find the bridge?

6 The brain is mostly composed of which substance?

7 What is the name of the body cavity that houses the heart and lungs?

8 Where is the fibula found?

9 The tendon at the top of the heel is named after which mythological Greek figure?

10 What is the more common name for the mandible?

11 "Hepatic" refers to which organ?

12 To which distance does the 20 in 20/20 vision refer?

13 Endocarditis affects which human organ?

14 What name is given to the 24-hour physiological cycles of living beings?

15 To which sense does the gustatory system refer?

16 What do the lachrymal glands produce?

17 Ophthalmology relates to which sense?

18 What is the most common blood type?

19 Vitiligo is a disease affecting which part of the body?

20 Which liquid in the body lends its name to anger towards someone or something?

Easy

Medium

Hard

Answers to QUIZ 88 – Wild

1	Paul Weller	11	Antelope
2	Will Smith	12	Wildcat strike
3	19th century (1848)	13	Kathleen Turner
4	Marlon Brando	14	Simon King
5	Bluebell	15	Africa
6	Laura Ingalls Wilder	16	Jessie J
7	Wild Bill Hickok	17	Meryl Streep
8	Kim Wilde	18	Wild horses
9	American	19	Oscar Wilde
10	Adam and the Ants	20	Gene Wilder

1 How many blackbirds were mentioned in *Sing a Song of Sixpence*?

2 What type of creature is a mudskipper?

3 Which fictional bear lived in a bear pit in Berne, Switzerland?

4 Golfer Colin Montgomerie is from which country?

5 Who had a 1996 hit with *Falling Into You*?

6 In which city is *One Hundred and One Dalmatians* set?

7 Who sang the 1981 song *I Go to Sleep*?

8 Glamorgan is the only first-class cricket club from which country of the UK?

9 In what century was the University of Oxford founded?

10 What type of substance was Linco-beer (originally Linc-O-Lin beer)?

11 *Cannonball* was a single from which *The X Factor* singers?

12 What is the meaning of the Latin phrase *tempus fugit*?

13 Chris Chittell plays which long-standing *Emmerdale* character?

14 Which city lies on the north bank of the Firth of Tay?

15 Which sign of the zodiac is represented by the Crab?

16 *Let's Hear it for the Boy* featured on the soundtrack of which 1984 film?

17 What is the term given to someone who studies codes and ciphers?

18 What word can mean both a small earring and a breeding stable?

19 The Cobham services on the M25 are in which county?

20 What sport does the LTA oversee?

Easy

Medium

Hard

Answers to QUIZ 89 – Pot Luck

1	Alan Partridge	11	Twiggy
2	Duffy	12	Henry VIII
3	Roger Federer	13	Joe Jackson
4	Gangway	14	North Sea
5	Sir Nick Clegg	15	Hornet (throne)
6	Glass ceiling	16	Belgrade
7	Lake District	17	ABBA
8	Honey	18	Three
9	White	19	Asylum
10	English	20	Keyhole surgery

Easy

1 "When your world is full of strange arrangements and gravity won't pull you through" is the opening line of which 1982 song?

2 *Celebration* and *Get Down on It* were 1980s hits for which band?

3 Released in 1985, what was the title of Marillion's only chart-topping album?

4 *Dancing with Tears in My Eyes* (1984) was a hit for which band?

5 With which band did Prince record *Purple Rain*?

6 *Hounds of Love* was a 1985 album by which singer?

7 Who released the 1984 song *The Riddle*?

8 Which group's debut album was entitled *Welcome to the Pleasuredome*?

9 "There's no time for us, there's no place for us" are the opening lyrics to which song by Queen?

10 Bernard Sumner and Peter Hook were co-founders of Joy Division and which other band?

11 *Invisible Touch* was a 1986 single and album by which group?

12 In which year did Madonna release the album *Like a Virgin*?

Medium

13 Which group's 1980s singles included *The King of Rock 'n' Roll* and *When Love Breaks Down*?

14 Which girl group released a cover of *Hazy Shade of Winter* in 1987?

15 The 1980 song *Show Me Heaven* featured on the soundtrack of which Tom Cruise film?

16 Which band released the 1980s albums *War* and *Rattle and Hum*?

17 "Guilty feet have got no rhythm" is a lyric from which 1984 song?

18 Released in 1987, *The Hit Factory* was a compilation of hits by which three music producers?

19 The band A-ha were formed in which country?

20 *Lessons in Love* was a 1986 single by which group?

Hard

Answers to QUIZ 90 – Biology

1	Skull	11	Liver
2	Hammer	12	20 feet
3	Blood	13	Heart
4	The eyelids	14	Circadian rhythms
5	The nose	15	Taste
6	Water (approximately 75%)	16	Tears
7	Thoracic cavity	17	Sight
8	In the lower leg	18	O
9	Achilles	19	Skin
10	Jaw (or jawbone)	20	Bile

1   Which term for a style of trousers can also refer to distress signals?

2   For which film did Paul Newman win his only Oscar?

3   The Piazza Navona lies in which European city?

4   Who had a 1978 hit with *Baker Street*?

5   What two letters can be added to "vanished" to make a term describing a complete defeat?

6   Minehead lies on the edge of which National Park?

7   Madonna had only two UK no.1 hits in the 1990s. *Vogue* was one, what was the other?

8   How many points is the letter D worth in Scrabble®?

9   In which county is the town of Looe?

10 Boss Hogg was a character in which US TV series made into a film in 2005?

11 What was the title of Shakespear's Sister's only no.1 hit?

12 What is an eddy?

13 On what vegetable crop does the Colorado beetle do particular damage?

14 By what name is the house plant *Monstera* usually known?

15 In 1970, which boxer became the first person to win the BBC Sports Personality of the Year for a second time?

16 What sporting measurement is equivalent to 220 yards?

17 Which punctuation mark is used to mark the omission of a letter, such as in the word shan't?

18 Which former player coached Sir Andy Murray from 2012 to 2014, rejoining his team in 2016?

19 The country of Cameroon is on which continent?

20 Cyril Fletcher and Pam Ayres both provided humorous poems on which long-running show first broadcast in 1973?

Answers to QUIZ 91 – Pot Luck

1	24	11	Little Mix
2	A fish	12	Time flies
3	Mary Plain	13	Eric Pollard
4	Scotland	14	Dundee
5	Celine Dion	15	Cancer
6	London	16	*Footloose*
7	The Pretenders	17	Cryptologist
8	Wales	18	Stud
9	11th century (1096)	19	Surrey
10	Shampoo	20	Tennis

1. Which girl group had a 1982 hit with *Shy Boy*?
2. Garam masala is a mixture of what type of foods?
3. The Yarra river flows through which Australian city?
4. Saab cars were manufactured in which country?
5. Taramasalata originates from which country?
6. In which country was comedian Dara Ó Briain born?
7. Maharajah is a title applied to princes in what country?
8. What term is given to a word formed of the rearranged letters of another word?
9. What was the first name of Humphrey Bogart's character in the film *Casablanca*?
10. In which continent is the Malay Peninsula?
11. What is the name of the focal table in a church?
12. In which city is the Maracanã football stadium?
13. What is the first name of the 44th president of the USA?
14. All species of lemurs are native to which island country?
15. Karnak in Egypt is the site of a complex of which type of buildings?
16. The war dance the haka originated in which country?
17. The alpaca is native to which continent?
18. From which country did the Armada set sail against England in 1588?
19. How is the fava bean usually known in the UK?
20. In which TV series did Amanda Abbington play Mary Morstan, later Mary Watson?

Easy

Medium

Hard

Answers to QUIZ 92 – 1980s Music

1. *The Look of Love* (ABC)
2. Kool and the Gang
3. *Misplaced Childhood*
4. Ultravox
5. The Revolution
6. Kate Bush
7. Nik Kershaw
8. Frankie Goes to Hollywood
9. *Who Wants to Live Forever*
10. New Order
11. Genesis
12. *1984*
13. Prefab Sprout
14. The Bangles
15. *Days of Thunder*
16. U2
17. *Careless Whisper* (George Michael)
18. Stock, Aitken and Waterman
19. Norway
20. Level 42

1   In which year did David Cameron first become UK prime minister?

2   Which city lies further north, Middlesbrough or Sunderland?

3   Nirvana is the ultimate goal of followers of which religion?

4   Which outer garment does Paddington Bear wear?

5   Irene Roberts, played by Lynn McGranger is a character in which long-running TV series?

6   *Love in an Elevator* was a 1989 hit for which US rock band?

7   What two words that sound the same but are spelt differently mean "a platform by water" and "an opening device"?

8   Who played the caretaker in the 1980 horror film *The Shining*?

9   Which ocean lies off the western coast of Australia?

10   Long on, silly mid-on and sledging are terms used in what sport?

11   Who played Arya Stark in the series *Game of Thrones*?

12   If someone is described as jaunty, are they feeling energetic or lethargic?

13   The US state of Alaska has a coast on two oceans, the Pacific and which other?

14   Which actress wrote the script for the 2005 film *Nanny McPhee*?

15   Who played James Bond in the 2012 film *Skyfall*?

16   Where were the 30th Olympic Games held?

17   In which month is the RHS Hampton Court Flower Show usually held?

18   Which singer had UK hits in the 1990s with *Breathe Again* and *Un-Break My Heart*?

19   What term for capital letters is derived from where they were stored by printers?

20   How is the word for "vaccination" spelt: innoculate, inocculate or inoculate?

Easy

Medium

Hard

Answers to QUIZ 93 – Pot Luck

1	Flares	11	*Stay* (1992)
2	*The Color of Money*	12	A gentle whirlpool
3	Rome	13	Potatoes
4	Gerry Rafferty	14	Swiss cheese plant
5	Qu (vanquished)	15	Sir Henry Cooper
6	Exmoor	16	Furlong
7	*Frozen* (1998)	17	Apostrophe
8	Two	18	Ivan Lendl
9	Cornwall	19	Africa
10	*The Dukes of Hazzard*	20	*That's Life!*

1   In investigating a criminal case, a detective may refer to the perpetrator's MO. For what do these letters stand?

2   Who was appointed Commissioner of the Metropolitan Police Service in 2017?

3   Which TV series was associated with the phrase "Don't have nightmares"?

4   What, in law, is a spoken defamation of character?

5   For what do the initials QC stand in the title of senior lawyers?

6   In which city was the TV series *New Street Law* set?

7   What two-word term is given to non-criminal legislation?

8   In 2007, who became the UK's first female Home Secretary?

9   What is the legal term for the information that is aimed at proving someone's guilt?

10 For what does the "B" stand in the term ASBO?

11 Which police force covers Berkshire, Buckinghamshire and Oxfordshire?

12 A Yardie is a member of a criminal gang based in which country?

13 What is the American term for a lawyer?

14 Who played the title role in the TV series *Murphy's Law*?

15 Which TV "judge" took part in the 2016 series of *Strictly Come Dancing*?

16 In which decade did the first private prison open in the UK?

17 Which TV series, first broadcast in 1997, was set in the fictional Boston law firm of Cage and Fish?

18 Which two-word French term is used to describe a notable law trial?

19 What term is given to rule of a country by the military?

20 In which decade was the Supreme Court of the United Kingdom established?

1 Which winter sport has a name that derives from a word meaning "small coasting sled"?

2 According to the proverb, you should cut your coat according to what?

3 Which member of a wedding day ceremony is traditionally tasked with keeping the wedding rings?

4 Which actor and martial arts expert plays Chon Wang in the films *Shanghai Noon* and *Shanghai Knights*?

5 Test cricket matches are typically played over how many days?

6 What is the name of Bruce Willis' character in the *Die Hard* films?

7 In which 2001 animated film does a tortured gingerbread man appear?

8 What word describes a shoe worn by ballet dancers?

9 What word can mean "spread", "glue" or "jewellery"?

10 Which of the *Friends* characters worked in a museum?

11 In which decade did Smokey Robinson and the Miracles originally release *Tears of a Clown*?

12 What nationality is tennis player Samantha Stosur?

13 The town of Chippenham is in which English county?

14 Which Nevada city is noted primarily for its gambling?

15 Eurydice was the wife of which Greek mythological character?

16 What is the name of the footbridge across the Thames that was originally referred to as "the wobbly bridge"?

17 Which 1977 hit includes the line "The pink champagne on ice"?

18 In which month is World Book Day held in the UK?

19 Baroness Marcia Falkender was the private secretary to which UK prime minister?

20 The name of which small snake is an anagram of a term for "tree juice"?

Easy

Medium

Hard

Answers to QUIZ 95 – Pot Luck

1	2010	11	Maisie Williams
2	Sunderland	12	Energetic
3	Buddhism	13	Arctic Ocean
4	Duffel coat	14	Dame Emma Thompson
5	*Home and Away*	15	Daniel Craig
6	Aerosmith	16	London (2012)
7	Quay and key	17	July
8	Jack Nicholson	18	Toni Braxton
9	Indian Ocean	19	Upper case
10	Cricket	20	Inoculate

1 What are you said to be full of, if you have lots of energy?

2 If you are absolutely certain about something, what food item are you sure about?

3 Which spice might be called to mind if you pay a small amount of money for your lodgings?

4 How much of which common condiment would a sceptic take?

5 If you make disparaging remarks about something you can't have, what fruit might you be eating?

6 What spilt liquid is it pointless shedding tears over?

7 Someone with an innocent look might be erroneously trusted to carry what dairy item in their mouth?

8 If something is not fit for its purpose, what salad plant would it fail to cut?

9 A person with many projects on might have what digit in what food items?

10 Which foodstuff might be said to be diametrically opposed to chalk?

11 What everyday packaged food might a fantastic new invention be considered to have surpassed?

12 If you thoroughly defeat an opponent, which seasonal item might you make of them?

13 A cherished person might be compared to which fruit in your eye?

14 Which food item might be contained in a pretty kettle, in a difficult situation?

15 Which fruit peel could be the cause of embarrassment if stepped on?

16 If you come to someone's rescue, what meat are you said to save?

17 Which part of the body is being referred to if you are told to "use your loaf"?

18 If you have more important things to do, what bigger food item would you be frying?

19 The colour of hair or cloth that is streaked black and white can be described as which two condiments?

20 Proverbially, what can you not have and eat it?

Answers to QUIZ 96 – Law and Order

1	*Modus operandi*	11	Thames Valley
2	Cressida Dick	12	Jamaica
3	*Crimewatch*	13	Attorney
4	Slander	14	James Nesbitt
5	Queen's Counsel	15	Robert Rinder
6	Manchester	16	1990s (1997 - HMP Altcourse)
7	Civil law	17	*Ally McBeal*
8	Jacqui Smith	18	*Cause célèbre*
9	Evidence	19	Martial law
10	Behaviour	20	2000s (2009)

1   *Clair de Lune* is a popular work by which French composer?

2   What is the final part of an ice dance competition?

3   What is the cube root of 27?

4   Which part of the eye is also another name for a student?

5   In cheesemaking, what is separated from the curds?

6   The San Andreas Fault runs through which US state?

7   From the 14th to the 17th century, which dynasty built the most extensive part of the Great Wall of China?

8   In which city is the 1970 animated film *The Aristocats* set?

9   Swiss Toni was a character on which sketch show of the 1990s?

10   What is the meaning of the word "clef"?

11   In which decade was the film *Moonstruck* released?

12   What word means both the time a single cricketer spends batting and the time batting for the whole side?

13   The city of Portsmouth lies in which county?

14   Which sailing move is an anagram of "way"?

15   What is the largest ballet company in the UK?

16   Who had a hit in 1989 with *All Around the World*?

17   The coastal region of Connemara lies in which Irish county?

18   Who co-starred with Zoë Wanamaker in the TV series *Love Hurts*?

19   Who composed the music to the 1975 film *Jaws*?

20   Arthur Negus and Hugh Scully were previous presenters of which long-running series?

Easy

Medium

Hard

Answers to QUIZ 97 – Pot Luck

1	Luge	11	1970s (1970)
2	Your cloth	12	Australian
3	Best man	13	Wiltshire
4	Jackie Chan	14	Las Vegas
5	Five	15	Orpheus
6	John McClane	16	Millennium Bridge
7	*Shrek*	17	*Hotel California* (Eagles)
8	Pointe	18	March
9	Paste	19	Harold Wilson (Baron Wilson of Rievaulx)
10	Ross	20	Asp (sap)

1   Proverbially, what animal is associated with a china shop?

2   Who writes the *Shopaholic* series of novels?

3   Which jewellery retailer takes its name from the first human woman in Greek mythology?

4   What colour were the "shield stamps" collected by shoppers from 1958 until 1991?

5   The Bait Shop is a business in which long-running Australian TV series?

6   Who played the jewellery salesman in the film *Love Actually*?

7   What is the main product sold in a French *boulangerie*?

8   In which decade did Cornershop have a hit with *Brimful of Asha*?

9   A shop steward is a representative of what type of organisation?

10 What was the first UK no.1 for the Pet Shop Boys?

11 What type of shop would you be visiting if you were in a turf accountant's?

12 The application Photoshop® was developed by which company?

13 Delphine Featherstone is a regular customer in which TV series?

14 What type of shop features in the musical *Little Shop of Horrors*?

15 A bucket shop is the term given to an establishment selling what, at a cheap price?

16 In which film does Tom Hanks play a duet with Robert Loggia on a foot-operated keyboard in a toy store?

17 What is the US term for a charity shop?

18 What formerly followed "Boots" in the name of the retail chain?

19 In what type of establishment did you often find a tuck shop?

20 What is the name of the convenience store in the TV series *The Simpsons*?

Answers to QUIZ 98 – Food Phrases

1	Beans	11	Sliced bread
2	Eggs (As sure as eggs is eggs)	12	Mincemeat
3	Peppercorn (rent)	13	Apple
4	A pinch of salt	14	Fish
5	Sour grapes	15	Banana skin
6	Milk	16	Bacon
7	Butter	17	The head (loaf of bread)
8	The mustard	18	Fish
9	Finger in many pies	19	Salt and pepper
10	Cheese	20	Your cake

ANSWERS ON PAGE 103

1 Emma Bunton was a judge on which TV show from 2010 to 2011?

2 In which country was Rudolf Nureyev born?

3 What is the title of the final part of *The Lord of the Rings* trilogy?

4 *Human Racing* was the 1984 debut album by which singer/songwriter?

5 In which county is the town of Corby?

6 Who starred in *Doctor Who* first, Sylvester McCoy or Peter Davison?

7 According to the proverb, what should sleeping dogs be left to do?

8 In which decade did London host the summer Olympic Games for the first time?

9 What information can you obtain from a chronograph?

10 Which shape is an anagram of "integral"?

11 Whom did Charles Kennedy succeed in 1999 as Leader of the Liberal Democrats?

12 What is a balalaika?

13 Who plays Ted Hastings in the TV series *Line of Duty*?

14 In which year of the 1990s did Robbie Williams leave Take That?

15 What is the name of the tiny holes on the surface of the skin?

16 The Kumbh Mela is a pilgrimage in which religion?

17 "Suits you sir!" was a phrase from which comedy sketch show?

18 The charleston dance first became popular in which decade?

19 What colour lies between green and indigo in a rainbow?

20 In which decade did Volkswagen launch the Golf GTI car?

Easy

Medium

Hard

Answers to QUIZ 99 – Pot Luck

1	Debussy	11	1980s (1987)
2	Free dance	12	Innings
3	Three	13	Hampshire
4	Pupil	14	Yaw
5	Whey	15	The Royal Ballet
6	California	16	Lisa Stansfield
7	Ming dynasty	17	County Galway
8	Paris	18	Adam Faith
9	*The Fast Show*	19	John Williams
10	Key	20	*Antiques Roadshow*

Easy

1   The owl was a symbol of which Greek goddess associated with wisdom?

2   The 1980s TV series *Falcon Crest* was set in the wine-making region of which US state?

3   Which bird featured in a series of iconic advertisements for Guinness beer from the 1930s to the 1980s?

4   Which south London football club is nicknamed "The Eagles"?

5   What was the name of the yellow bird used in marketing campaigns for the BT forerunner Post Office Telecommunications?

6   According to the proverb, what do birds of a feather do?

7   Which garden bird is most associated with Christmas card designs?

8   Which panel show featured "the Dove from Above"?

9   *The Dying Swan*, first presented in 1905, was a short ballet created for which Russian ballerina?

10   The thunderbird appears in the legends of several tribes of which people?

11   What type of bird was Professor Yaffle in *Bagpuss*?

12   The name of which bird of prey features in the name of a Bedfordshire town?

13   Native to North America, what type of bird is a bufflehead?

14   Who co-piloted the Millennium Falcon with Han Solo in the Star Wars film *A New Hope*?

15   Which bird is also known as the river hawk or fish hawk?

16   To which fictional character does the parrot Polynesia belong?

17   What name is given to a female peacock?

18   What two colours are the eyes of the owl on the TripAdvisor logo?

19   What was the official bird emblem of the Roman Empire?

20   Which species of bird has cirl, reed and snow varieties?

Medium

Hard

Answers to QUIZ 100 – Shops

1	Bull	11	Betting shop
2	Sophie Kinsella	12	Adobe®
3	Pandora	13	*Open All Hours* (and *Still Open All Hours*)
4	Green	14	Florist
5	*Home and Away*	15	Travel arrangements
6	Rowan Atkinson	16	*Big*
7	Bread	17	Thrift shop
8	1990s (1997)	18	The Chemist
9	Trade union	19	School
10	*West End Girls*	20	Kwik-E-Mart

1 What was the title of the first single by the Spice Girls that did not reach no.1 in the UK?

2 Which two countries hosted the 2019 Cricket World Cup?

3 Nikolaj Coster-Waldau played which character in the TV series *Game of Thrones*?

4 Who played the title role in the TV series *Wycliffe*?

5 In the rhyme, which building did Christopher Robin and Alice go to see in London?

6 What is the name of a building in which Quakers gather for worship?

7 What is the name of the small indentation in the skin from which a hair grows?

8 Chris Gascoyne plays which character in *Coronation Street*?

9 According to the proverb, what is someone who is penny wise?

10 *You're Gorgeous* was a 1996 hit for which band?

11 Which number is represented by five dashes in Morse Code?

12 In which English county is the town of Wilmslow?

13 Which comedy actor played Arthur Weasley in the Harry Potter films?

14 What is the main topping of a pizza described as "con funghi"?

15 *Penny Lane* was a double A-side release by the Beatles with which other song?

16 Which is the next prime number after 29?

17 Which group had a 1991 UK no.1 hit with *Goodnight Girl*?

18 In which country of the UK must a driver display an "R-plate" for the first year after passing their driving test?

19 Which word for the human mind or soul is taken from a figure in Greek mythology?

20 Who became the presenter of *Through the Keyhole* on its 2013 revival?

Answers to QUIZ 101 – Pot Luck

1	*Dancing on Ice*	11	Paddy Ashdown (Baron Ashdown of Norton-sub-Hamdon)
2	Russia		
3	*The Return of the King*	12	A (stringed) musical instrument
4	Nik Kershaw	13	Adrian Dunbar
5	Northamptonshire	14	1995
6	Peter Davison	15	Pores
7	Lie	16	Hinduism
8	1900s (1908)	17	*The Fast Show*
9	The time	18	1920s (1923)
10	Triangle	19	Blue
		20	1970s (1976)

Easy

Medium

Hard

Easy

1 What did the soldiers place on Jesus' head at his crucifixion?

2 Daniel is often depicted in the den of what animal?

3 Esau sold his birthright to whom?

4 How did Judas betray Jesus?

5 How many wives did Abraham have in the Old Testament?

6 The names of which two Old Testament figures are used to describe an unequal battle?

7 In which book of the New Testament is the story of Lazarus?

8 Mentioned in Revelations, how many Horsemen of the Apocalypse are there?

9 For whom did Jacob make a coat of many colours?

10 What is the second book of the New Testament?

11 Which creature tempted Eve in the Garden of Eden?

12 Which book covers Saul's conversion on the Road to Damascus?

13 In the New Testament, Elisabeth was whose mother?

14 How many gospels are there in the New Testament?

Medium

15 Which three-word saying, meaning to give every detail of a subject, is derived from the text of the Bible?

16 "The Lord is My Shepherd" comes from which psalm?

17 "Thou shalt not kill" and "Thou shalt not steal" are instructions in which Biblical set of principles?

18 Who was the father of Cain and Abel?

19 Which Old Testament figure was found in the bulrushes as a baby?

20 How many apostles did Jesus have?

Hard

Answers to QUIZ 102 – Birds

1	Athena	11	A woodpecker
2	California	12	Buzzard (Leighton Buzzard)
3	Toucan	13	Duck
4	Crystal Palace	14	Chewbacca
5	Buzby	15	Osprey
6	Flock together	16	Doctor Dolittle
7	Robin	17	Peahen
8	*Shooting Stars*	18	Red and green
9	Anna Pavlova	19	Eagle
10	Native Americans	20	Bunting

1   Which fashion designer had a son with Malcolm McLaren?

2   In which decade did New Zealand become a test cricket side?

3   Which lies further south, Northampton or Nottingham?

4   Who released the 1976 album *Oxygène*?

5   Unilever was formed by a merger of the British company Lever Brothers with a margarine company based in which European country?

6   Alex Reid won which reality show in 2010?

7   In which Scandinavian country did the band The Cardigans form?

8   Who plays the character of Julianne Potter in the 1997 film *My Best Friend's Wedding*?

9   The radio code word for which letter of the alphabet is also the name of a sport?

10   Which fish are said to be packed closely together?

11   Westphalia is a historical region in which modern-day country?

12   Which former leader of the Green Party became co-leader in 2016?

13   Theft by housebreaking is the equivalent of burglary in which country of the UK?

14   Mrs Bridges was the cook in which series first broadcast in 1971?

15   Does the borough of Bromley lie to the south-east or the south-west of London?

16   In which season is the Hindu festival of Diwali celebrated?

17   "I thought love was only true in fairytales" is the opening line to which 1966 song?

18   Who had a 2002 hit with *Sk8er Boi*?

19   Who was the original presenter of *Blankety Blank*?

20   What was the name of Dumbo's mother?

Answers to QUIZ 103 – Pot Luck

1	*Stop* (reached no.2)	11	Zero
2	England and Wales	12	Cheshire
3	Jaime Lannister	13	Mark Williams
4	Jack Shepherd	14	Mushrooms
5	Buckingham Palace	15	*Strawberry Fields*
6	Meeting house	16	31
7	Follicle	17	Wet Wet Wet
8	Peter Barlow	18	Northern Ireland
9	Pound foolish	19	Psyche
10	Babybird	20	Keith Lemon

QUIZ 106 – Medicine on Television

1. Which of the two original *The X Files* agents was a medical doctor?
2. Ellen Pompeo is the leading actress in which medical drama?
3. Which ward number featured in the title of a 1957-67 medical drama series?
4. What is Dr Nikki Alexander's profession in the series *Silent Witness*?
5. Which Channel 4 series was originally filmed in King's College Hospital, then moved to St George's Hospital in Tooting?
6. What nationality was Dr Finlay in the long-running series *Dr Finlay's Casebook*?
7. Which series, first aired in 1993, was set in the fictional town of Cardale?
8. What was the first name of the title character in the series *House*?
9. In which drama series did Dana Delany play medical examiner Megan Hunt?
10. What type of operation featured in the drama series *Nip/Tuck*?
11. George Clooney shot to fame in which medical drama?
12. Which fly-on-the-wall series has been broadcast from Southmead hospital in Bristol and Women's Hospital in Liverpool, amongst others?
13. Who plays Dr Patrick Turner in the TV series *Call the Midwife*?

14. Who was the original presenter of *Trust Me, I'm a Doctor* from 1996 to 1999?
15. Which actress played the title role in the 1990s series *Bramwell* and later appeared in *Holby City*?
16. The series *M*A*S*H* was set in which decade?
17. Helen Baxendale played Dr Claire Maitland in which 1990s series?
18. In which country was the drama series *The Flying Doctors* set?
19. Dr Pixie McKenna and Dr Dawn Harper are presenters on which medical series?
20. Who plays Henrik Hanssen in the TV series *Holby City*?

Answers to QUIZ 104 – The Bible

1. Crown of thorns
2. Lion
3. Jacob
4. With a kiss
5. Two (Sarah and Keturah)
6. David and Goliath
7. John
8. Four
9. Joseph
10. Mark
11. Serpent
12. Acts
13. John the Baptist
14. Four
15. Chapter and verse
16. Psalm 23
17. The Ten Commandments
18. Adam
19. Moses
20. Twelve

1 "Lonely water, won't you let us wander" is a lyric from which song?

2 What is the name of the seat behind the rider on a motorcycle?

3 What name is given to insurance protection taken out by an insurer to limit the potential exposure on losses?

4 What foodstuff might be in the form of radiatore?

5 What was the title of Kylie Minogue's first UK no.1 single, which topped the charts in 1987?

6 In which series of films does Liam Neeson play Bryan Mills?

7 A ninja is a practitioner of a martial art in which country?

8 Which river flows through the town of King's Lynn?

9 Which costumed character topped the UK charts at Christmas 1993 with a self-titled song?

10 What does IPA stand for in relation to alcohol?

11 A tunnel under and a bridge over the River Thames connect Thurrock in Essex with which Kent town?

12 Which cake is spelt the same as the name of a castle near Perth?

13 Faye Tozer was part of which group formed in the 1990s?

14 In which European city did the UEFA Cup final take place in 2019?

15 A monument to which ship was opened in Belfast in 2012?

16 Which fictional policeman was associated with the town of Kingsmarkham?

17 Which British owl is sometimes nicknamed "screech owl" because of its cry?

18 Who played the Genie in the 2019 film *Aladdin*?

19 An underground safe deposit facility in which area of London was famously burgled in 2015?

20 Who played the title role in the TV series *Boon*?

Easy

Medium

Hard

Answers to QUIZ 105 – Pot Luck

1	Dame Vivienne Westwood	11	Germany
2	1930s (1930)	12	Caroline Lucas
3	Northampton	13	Scotland
4	Jean-Michel Jarre	14	*Upstairs, Downstairs*
5	The Netherlands	15	South-east
6	*Celebrity Big Brother*	16	Autumn
7	Sweden	17	*I'm a Believer* (the Monkees)
8	Julia Roberts	18	Avril Lavigne
9	G (Golf)	19	Sir Terry Wogan
10	Sardines	20	Mrs Jumbo

1   What is a half-hitch an example of?

2   "The Magnolia State" is the nickname of which US state?

3   Who was the Hit Man in the title of the TV series *The Hit Man and Her*?

4   Who became the oldest recipient of the Best Actress Oscar for her role in the 1989 film *Driving Miss Daisy*?

5   In which country was Hitachi founded?

6   What nationality is rapper Missy Elliott?

7   Who played the title role in the 2005 film *Hitch*?

8   In what sport has Missy Franklin won Olympic gold medals?

9   What part of a building are you said to hit if you lose your temper?

10 Which Muppet has an on-off relationship with Kermit the Frog?

11 In which decade did Ray Charles record the song *Hit the Road Jack*?

12 What was the subtitle of the 2018 film in the *Mission: Impossible* franchise?

13 In the sitcom *Are You Being Served?*, who played Miss Brahms?

14 What item of clothing did Miss Havisham always wear in Dickens' *Great Expectations*?

15 Who directed the 1959 thriller *North by Northwest*?

16 What was the first name of the writer portrayed in the 2006 film *Miss Potter*?

17 "In the wilds of Borneo and the vineyards of Bordeaux" are lyrics from which 1978 single?

18 Which 1989 musical is based on Puccini's opera *Madama Butterfly*?

19 Who became Chancellor of Germany in 1933?

20 Miss Ellie was a character in which long-running TV series?

Answers to QUIZ 106 – Medicine on Television

1	Dana Scully	11	*ER*
2	*Grey's Anatomy*	12	*One Born Every Minute*
3	10 (*Emergency - Ward 10*)	13	Stephen McGann
4	Forensic pathologist	14	Dr Phil Hammond
5	*24 Hours in A&E*	15	Jemma Redgrave
6	Scottish	16	1950s
7	*Peak Practice*	17	*Cardiac Arrest*
8	Gregory	18	Australia
9	*Body of Proof*	19	*Embarrassing Bodies*
10	Plastic surgery	20	Guy Henry

Easy

Medium

Hard

ANSWERS ON PAGE 111

1 The troika is a vehicle from which country?

2 What type of fish is a dab?

3 What was the title of Take That's first UK no.1 single?

4 What two-word French term means a social blunder?

5 What completes the phrase: "Not in a month of ___" to indicate that something will not happen?

6 In which century was the Kingdom of Greece twice abolished before becoming a republic?

7 Who was appointed Secretary of State for International Trade in 2016?

8 What is the name of a long wooden bench on which people sit when attending church?

9 Foxton Locks and Watford Locks lie on which canal?

10 Which SI unit has the symbol Hz?

11 Who created the 2019 TV series *Years and Years*?

12 Which act had a 1957 hit with *Bye Bye Love*?

13 The town of Cheadle lies in which county?

14 What does a viticulturist grow?

15 On which channel is *Love Island* broadcast?

16 How long do the annual Burghley Horse Trials last?

17 What animals are featured in the 2000 film *Best in Show*?

18 In which English county was DH Lawrence born?

19 Which singer had a hit with *It's Raining Men* in 2001?

20 Who played the title role in the 2018 film *Colette*?

Easy

Medium

Hard

Easy

1   *Disco 2000* was a hit for which group?

2   The Happy Mondays came from which city in Greater Manchester?

3   *Jeepster* was an early hit for which band?

4   In which year did the Beatles release their first album *Please Please Me*?

5   *Best Song Ever* was a hit for which predominantly British boy band?

6   Which single won British Single of the Year at the 2019 Brit Awards?

7   The band Travis hails from which country?

8   Which Spice Girl featured with Lisa "Left Eye" Lopes on *Never Be The Same Again*?

9   Which reality TV winner had a UK no.1 with *Anything is Possible*?

10   What is Adele's surname?

Medium

11   *The Circus* and *Progress* were comeback albums by which band?

12   Charlie Watts is the drummer in which band?

13   *Dance Wiv Me*, *Holiday* and *Bonkers* have all been no.1 hits for which rapper?

14   Which Oasis album features the track *Wonderwall*?

15   Which female singer featured on the 1993 single *Relight My Fire*?

16   *See My Baby Jive* was a 1973 no.1 in the UK for which glam rock band?

17   *Our Version of Events* is a Brit Award Best Album winner by which act?

18   *Have a Nice Day* was a 2001 hit for which band?

19   Which band did Five team up with on the hit *We Will Rock You*?

20   *Frank* was the debut album by which singer?

Hard

Answers to QUIZ 108 – Hit and Miss

1	A knot	11	1960s (1961)
2	Mississippi	12	*Fallout*
3	Pete Waterman	13	Wendy Richard
4	Jessica Tandy	14	Her wedding dress
5	Japan	15	Sir Alfred Hitchcock
6	American	16	Beatrix
7	Will Smith	17	*Hit Me With Your Rhythm Stick* (Ian Dury and the Blockheads)
8	Swimming		
9	The roof	18	*Miss Saigon*
10	Miss Piggy	19	Adolf Hitler
		20	*Dallas*

1   What substance is measured in reams?

2   On *Countdown*, how many letters are there in the conundrum?

3   Rami Malek won the Best Actor Oscar for his portrayal of which singer in the 2018 film *Bohemian Rhapsody*?

4   Which Scottish city is known as "the Oil Capital of Europe"?

5   In the 1957 Disney film *Old Yeller*, what type of animal is the title character?

6   In what decade was the CIA founded?

7   What currency is used in the Republic of Ireland?

8   Prior to the reign of Elizabeth II, how many kings of England have been called Henry?

9   What does a tachometer measure?

10   The TV series *Big Brother* took its name from a character created by which author?

11   In which Shakespeare play do Portia and Bassanio fall in love?

12   How many points is the black ball worth in snooker?

13   Which Greek invented a famous screw that is still used today for raising water?

14   Canasta is a variety of which card game?

15   Dame Shirley Bassey was born in which Welsh city?

16   For which country did Ronaldo (b.1976) play international football?

17   How many players are there in a curling team?

18   Christian Louboutin is known for designing which item of clothing?

19   Which colour is an anagram of the name "Cilla"?

20   The philosopher Francis Bacon was born in which country?

Easy

Medium

Hard

Answers to QUIZ 109 – Pot Luck

1	Russia	11	Russell T Davies
2	A flatfish	12	The Everly Brothers
3	*Pray* (1993)	13	Staffordshire
4	*Faux pas*	14	Grape vines
5	Sundays	15	ITV2
6	20th century (1973)	16	Three days
7	Liam Fox	17	Dogs
8	Pew	18	Nottinghamshire
9	Grand Union Canal	19	Geri Horner (Halliwell)
10	Hertz	20	Keira Knightley

Easy

1   What time of day is it if you are wished *bon soir*?

2   Construction of the Notre Dame Cathedral began in which century?

3   What name is given to a native of Brittany?

4   What are *moules* known as in English?

5   Who became president of France in 2017?

6   In which century did the French Revolution take place?

7   The Grand Trianon and Petit Trianon are located in the grounds of which French palace?

8   At which Parisian station does the Eurostar stop?

9   Which is larger by area, France or Germany?

10 The port of La Rochelle lies on which body of water?

11 In which race is the *maillot jaune* awarded?

12 What is the internet country code for France?

13 Sancerre wine is what colour?

Medium

14 Which is the second-largest city in France?

15 What is the main ingredient in *pain perdu*?

16 In which century did the first line open on the Paris Métro?

17 According to a song from the musical *The Boyfriend*, in which city is it "nicer"?

18 What was the French currency unit before the euro?

19 Which French politician was the president of the European Commission from 1985 to 1995?

20 What is the English translation of the word *voiture*?

Hard

Answers to QUIZ 110 – British Music

1	Pulp	11	Take That
2	Salford	12	The Rolling Stones
3	T Rex	13	Dizzee Rascal
4	1963	14	*What's the Story (Morning Glory)?*
5	One Direction	15	Lulu
6	*One Kiss* (Calvin Harris and Dua Lipa)	16	Wizzard
7	Scotland (Glasgow)	17	Emeli Sandé
8	Mel C	18	Stereophonics
9	Will Young	19	Queen
10	Adkins	20	Amy Winehouse

1 In 2018, who became the second Paralympic athlete to take part in *Strictly Come Dancing*?

2 What was the name of the orphan girl adopted by Miss Havisham in *Great Expectations*?

3 Japan first hosted the Olympic Games in which season, summer or winter?

4 *Waiting for an Alibi* was a 1979 single by which band?

5 What word meaning to twist sounds like a piece of jewellery?

6 Who released the 1977 single *Solsbury Hill*?

7 Which Tom Hanks film was released first, *Splash* or *The Money Pit*?

8 The historic county of Roxburghshire is in which country of the UK?

9 What colour "Caps" are the New Zealand national cricket team known as?

10 What type of creature is a pale clouded yellow?

11 How many questions is a *University Challenge* team asked once a starter question has been correctly answered?

12 In which county is the town of Stow-on-the-Wold?

13 What sport completes the title of a 1986 novelty single by Chas and Dave, ___ *Loopy*?

14 Buffy Summers attended which fictional school in *Buffy the Vampire Slayer*?

15 With whom did Sir Elton John duet on his first UK no.1 single?

16 Northumbria University is located in which city?

17 Which political party was the successor of the Whigs?

18 Which European country has the international dialling code 0049?

19 In what capacity did Anna Raeburn give advice on Capital Radio in the 1970s and 1980s?

20 Which group had 1970s hits with *Angelo* and *Figaro*?

Answers to QUIZ 111 – Pot Luck

1	Paper	11	*The Merchant of Venice*
2	Nine	12	Seven
3	Freddie Mercury	13	Archimedes
4	Aberdeen	14	Rummy
5	A dog	15	Cardiff
6	1940s (1947)	16	Brazil
7	Euro	17	Four
8	Eight	18	Shoes
9	Engine speed	19	Lilac
10	George Orwell	20	England

Easy

1   Where was the midnight train going in the title of the 1973 hit for Gladys Knight and the Pips?

2   Who won the Booker Prize for the novel *Midnight's Children*?

3   What was the title of Dexys Midnight Runners' first UK no.1 single, released in 1980?

4   How is midnight represented on the 24-hour clock?

5   Who had a *Midnight Garden* in the title of a 1958 children's book?

6   "Send your camel to bed" is a line from which 1974 song by Maria Muldaur?

7   What midnight substance are you said to be burning if you stay up late?

8   Which British singer/songwriter released the 2002 album *A New Day at Midnight*?

9   What line follows "It came upon the midnight clear" in the Christmas carol?

10   What name is given to food eaten around midnight?

11   Which American patriot (d.1818) was famous for his "midnight ride" to warn of the approach of British forces?

12   In which decade was *In the Midnight Hour* a hit for Wilson Pickett?

13   "Midnight diamonds stud my heaven" is a line from which 1975 song?

14   Which band recorded the 1980 song *Living After Midnight*?

15   On which night is a midnight mass traditionally held?

16   Which fairy-tale character had to leave a ball abruptly when the clock struck midnight?

17   Which 1969 film starring Jon Voight and Dustin Hoffman won the Best Picture Oscar?

18   Which former Children's Laureate wrote the 2002 novel *Midnight*?

19   Midnight is a dark shade of which primary colour?

20   Where were Owen Wilson and Rachel McAdams at midnight in the title of a 2011 film?

Medium

Hard

Answers to QUIZ 112 – France

1	Evening	11	Tour de France (yellow jersey)
2	12th century	12	.fr
3	Breton	13	White
4	Mussels	14	Marseilles
5	Emmanuel Macron	15	Bread
6	18th century (1789)	16	20th century (1900)
7	Versailles	17	Nice
8	Gare du Nord	18	Franc
9	France	19	Jacques Delors
10	Bay of Biscay	20	Car

1 Cannock Chase lies in which English county?

2 *Love Me for A Reason* was a 1994 single for which group?

3 The RSPB reserve of Rathlin Island Cliffs is part of which country of the UK?

4 Which country is famous for its tea ceremony?

5 *Thank U* was a 1998 single by which singer/songwriter?

6 Which reality TV series took place on the island of Taransay?

7 What nationality is actress Rebel Wilson?

8 Which biscuit brand shares its name with a word meaning "to chat informally"?

9 The village of Loxley is associated with which legendary figure?

10 Which is the second-largest of the Channel Islands?

11 In the 2012 film *Les Misérables*, who played Cosette?

12 In 1785, which future US president was appointed the first American ambassador to Great Britain?

13 Which small Ford car was last produced in 1967 and replaced by the Escort?

14 Who recorded a version of *You Can Leave Your Hat On* for the soundtrack of the 1997 film *The Full Monty*?

15 In what month of 1914 did Britain declare war on Germany?

16 What is the singular form of the word "larvae"?

17 Who presented the series *Don't Forget Your Toothbrush*?

18 The name of which tree is also an eye colour?

19 How many batsmen are on the field at any one time in a game of cricket?

20 Which football team won the 2019 Premier League title?

Answers to QUIZ 113 – Pot Luck

1	Lauren Steadman	11	Three
2	Estella	12	Gloucestershire
3	Summer (1964)	13	*Snooker*
4	Thin Lizzy	14	Sunnydale High
5	Wring (ring)	15	Kiki Dee (*Don't Go Breaking My Heart*)
6	Peter Gabriel	16	Newcastle-upon-Tyne
7	*Splash* (1984)	17	Liberal Party
8	Scotland	18	Germany
9	Black	19	Agony aunt
10	A butterfly	20	Brotherhood of Man

1   Who wrote the play *A Streetcar Named Desire*?

2   Which play by Arthur Miller shares its title with the name of a pot used to heat substances in chemistry?

3   In which decade did *The Mousetrap* open in London?

4   The 1981 play *Way Upstream*, set on a cabin cruiser, was written by which dramatist?

5   Who wrote *War Horse*, which was subsequently adapted for the stage and film?

6   Tragedy is particularly associated with ancient plays from which European country?

7   Which play by Sir Noël Coward takes its name from two words in a poem by Shelley?

8   Sir Terence Rattigan's play *Separate Tables* was set in what type of building?

9   The 1973 play *Equus* was written by which dramatist?

10 What term is given to the genre of comedy written for the theatre between 1660 and 1710?

11 What nationality is playwright and director Stephen Poliakoff?

12 In the title of a 1977 play by Mike Leigh, which unseen character is having a party?

13 Which comedian and actor starred as Francis Henshall in the original 2011 London production of One Man, Two Guvnors?

14 The former name of which London theatre lent its name to farces staged in the 1950s and 1960s?

15 What nationality was the playwright Federico García Lorca?

16 Which US financial company that went bankrupt in 2008 is the subject of a play by Italian dramatist Stefano Massini?

17 In which decade did Harold Pinter write *Betrayal*?

18 *Small Island*, produced at the National Theatre in 2019, is based on a novel by which author?

19 Which play, adapted from a book by Susan Hill, has been running in the West End since 1987?

20 How are Olga, Maria and Irina known in the title of a play by Chekhov?

Easy

Medium

Hard

1 Which English football team won the 2019 Carabao Cup (League Cup)?

2 Which town lies further south, Blackpool, Middlesbrough or Scarborough?

3 Chan is the most popular form of Buddhist meditation in which country?

4 Which group had a 1986 hit with *Don't Dream It's Over*?

5 In the Old Testament, from whom did Jacob steal the "first-born" blessing?

6 Which character in *Friends* inspired a haircut based on her name?

7 *The Prince* (1979), a tribute to Prince Buster, was the first single by which band?

8 Charles Dickens and Florence Nightingale have both appeared on which bank note?

9 Cindy Beale famously arranged a hitman to shoot which character in *EastEnders*?

10 Myspace was founded in which country?

11 The 2019 Academy Awards ceremony went ahead without a main host after which comedian stepped down from the position?

12 Which hymn includes the line "Bring me my bow of burning gold"?

13 In which two events did Michael Johnson win gold in the 1996 Olympics?

14 Of what was Flora the Roman goddess?

15 Which medical advance occurred first, open-heart surgery or laser eye surgery?

16 In which decade was the film *Superman Returns* released?

17 The name of which US city preceded "Spinners" in the name of a Motown vocal group?

18 Which 1980s TV series was set in New York City High School for the Performing Arts?

19 Pete Shelley (d.2018) was the lead singer of which punk band?

20 What is the international car registration letter for Germany?

Answers to QUIZ 115 – Pot Luck

1	Staffordshire	11	Amanda Seyfried
2	Boyzone	12	John Adams (second US president)
3	Northern Ireland	13	Ford Anglia
4	Japan	14	Sir Tom Jones
5	Alanis Morissette	15	August
6	*Castaway 2000*	16	Larva
7	Australian	17	Chris Evans
8	Hobnob	18	Hazel
9	Robin Hood	19	Two
10	Guernsey	20	Manchester City

1 Gary Sparrow was the chief character in which TV series?

2 Gareth Keenan worked for which fictional company in a sitcom first broadcast in 2001?

3 Who played former senator Gary Hart in the 2018 film *The Front Runner*?

4 Gareth Hunt famously advertised which brand of coffee in the 1980s?

5 Who is Garth's mother in the sitcom *Birds of a Feather*?

6 What is the name of the Sunday morning Radio 5 programme presented by Garry Richardson?

7 The name Gareth originates from which country of the UK?

8 Which multiple golf Major winner was known for his trademark black clothes?

9 Whose debut solo album was entitled *The Pleasure Principle* (1979)?

10 Gareth Bale plays international football for which country?

11 Garth Brooks is famous for what genre of music?

12 For which 1952 film did Gary Cooper win his first Academy Award?

13 What is the name of Gary Lucy's *Hollyoaks* character?

14 As at June 2019, Gary Barlow has had how many UK solo no.1 albums?

15 Gareth Gates was the runner-up on which 2001-02 talent show?

16 In which city was Gary Lineker born?

17 Who played Gary in the sitcom *Miranda*?

18 What instrument does Gary Kemp play in Spandau Ballet?

19 Which position did Sir Gareth Edwards (b.1947) play in rugby union?

20 What was the name of Gary Oldman's character in the 2011 film *Tinker Tailor Soldier Spy*?

Answers to QUIZ 116 – Plays and Playwrights

1	Tennessee Williams	11	English
2	*The Crucible*	12	Abigail (*Abigail's Party*)
3	1950s (1952)	13	James Corden
4	Sir Alan Ayckbourn	14	Whitehall
5	Sir Michael Morpurgo	15	Spanish
6	Greece	16	Lehman Brothers (*The Lehman Trilogy*)
7	*Blithe Spirit*	17	1970s (1978)
8	A hotel	18	Andrea Levy
9	Sir Peter Shaffer	19	*The Woman in Black*
10	Restoration comedy	20	*Three Sisters*

1   Who had a hit in 1957 with *Great Balls of Fire*?

2   Cellist Dana Barrett was a character in which 1984 film?

3   What number is represented by the Roman numerals VIII?

4   Which company manufactures the X-Trail vehicle?

5   In which European country is the harbour town of Antibes?

6   The word *hacienda* means a home in which language?

7   At what age does a filly become a mare in the UK?

8   John Parrott is a former professional in which sport?

9   The rivalry between Vector and Gru is the plot of which 2010 animated film?

10 In which county is the main campus of Cranfield University?

11 What was the profession of the two main characters in the 1980s TV series *Don't Wait Up*?

12 What was the name of Ken Kercheval's character in the TV series *Dallas*?

13 How many points is the letter G worth in Scrabble®?

14 What name is given in horse-racing and motor-racing to the area where horses or cars are kept just before a race?

15 Which long-running BBC feedback programme has been presented by Barry Took and Sir Terry Wogan, amongst others?

16 Which is the next prime number after 37?

17 In which decade did David Bowie have his first UK no.1 album?

18 Where in the home would you find a counterpane?

19 Which character from Arthurian legend shares his name with a bird of prey?

20 Which nut is used to flavour frangipane?

Easy

Medium

Hard

Answers to QUIZ 117 – Pot Luck

1	Manchester City	11	Kevin Hart
2	Blackpool	12	*Jerusalem*
3	China	13	200m and 400m
4	Crowded House	14	Flowering of plants
5	Esau	15	Open heart surgery (1960s)
6	Rachel	16	2000s (2006)
7	Madness	17	Detroit
8	£10	18	*Fame*
9	Ian Beale	19	Buzzcocks
10	USA	20	D

QUIZ 120 – Literature

Easy

1. Ebenezer Scrooge features in which Dickens novel?
2. What word completes the title of a famous work by George Orwell, *The Road to ___ Pier*?
3. How many novels are there in The *Hunger Games* series?
4. *The Reckoning* was a 2018 legal thriller by which author?
5. *Robinson Crusoe* was published in which century?
6. Who wrote *For Whom The Bell Tolls* (1940)?
7. What flowers are the title of one of William Wordsworth's most famous poems?
8. Fitzwilliam Darcy is a main character in which 1813 novel?
9. *George's Marvellous Medicine* is a famous work by which children's author?
10. *Adam Bede* was the first novel by which Victorian writer?

Medium

11. Who wrote *The Last Chronicle of Barset* (1867)?
12. Michael Moorcock writes chiefly in which genre?
13. Who wrote *Three Sisters, Three Queens* (2016) and *The Last Tudor* (2017)?
14. *Dulce et Decorum est* is a famous work by which poet?
15. Who wrote *A Passage to India*?
16. *The Prime of Miss Jean Brodie* is set in a school in which city?
17. Nick and Amy Dunne are the main characters in which 2014 novel?
18. Who was "Obscure" in the title of a famous Thomas Hardy work?
19. During which century did Dylan Thomas live and die?
20. In which modern-day country was *Heart of Darkness* author Joseph Conrad born?

Hard

Answers to QUIZ 118 – Gary and Friends

1. *Goodnight Sweetheart*
2. Wernham Hogg *(The Office)*
3. Hugh Jackman
4. Nescafé
5. Tracey Stubbs
6. *Sportsweek*
7. Wales
8. Gary Player
9. Gary Numan
10. Wales
11. Country
12. *High Noon*
13. Luke Morgan
14. Two
15. *Pop Idol*
16. Leicester
17. Tom Ellis
18. Lead guitar
19. Scrum-half
20. George Smiley

120

1 The Manic Street Preachers hail from which part of the UK?

2 "Middle Way" is a term associated with which religion?

3 Which Hollywood actor starred in the 2019 TV series *MotherFatherSon*?

4 What word can mean both an impractical building and foolishness?

5 Which singer had no.1 UK singles in 2012 with *How We Do (Party)* and *R.I.P.*?

6 According to the proverb, when should hay be made?

7 Which famous mount in South Dakota, carved with the faces of American presidents, features in the film *North by Northwest*?

8 The 1977-79 TV series *Secret Army* was set in which country?

9 Which cartoon character was known as TC?

10 Which music legend did Taron Egerton play in the 2019 film *Rocketman*?

11 Which country has the internet code .dk?

12 The town of Broadstairs is located in which English county?

13 REM's *Everybody Hurts* was taken from which album?

14 Which animals are used to advertise the comparethemarket.com website?

15 What colour is sloe gin?

16 *The Daily Bugle* is a fictional newspaper in which series of comic books?

17 Is Galloway a region in the north-east or south-west of Scotland?

18 What is the last event in the men's heptathlon?

19 Who operated the roundabout in the 1960s TV series *The Magic Roundabout*?

20 The company Whitbread was originally founded to carry out what business?

Answers to QUIZ 119 – Pot Luck

1	Jerry Lee Lewis	11	Doctors
2	*Ghostbusters*	12	Cliff Barnes
3	Eight	13	Two
4	Nissan	14	Paddock
5	France	15	*Points of View*
6	Spanish	16	41
7	Four	17	1970s (*Aladdin Sane*, 1973)
8	Snooker	18	On a bed
9	*Despicable Me*	19	Merlin
10	Bedfordshire	20	Almond

1   What does a campanologist do?

2   How many hoops are used in a game of croquet?

3   Which popular board game was first published by Parker Brothers in 1935?

4   The Borrowdale valley, popular with walkers, lies in which English National Park?

5   In the UK, what is the lowest grade of music exam?

6   The *Maid of the Mist* is a tourist boat that takes sightseers to the foot of which famous North American water feature?

7   The phrase "Trick or treat" is associated with which night of the year?

8   In which country is the Muirfield golf course?

9   Tai chi originates from which country?

10   *Infinite Warfare* is the 2016 instalment of which video game series?

11   In which county is the Eden Project?

12   What French term is given to a restaurant's head waiter?

13   Zumba keep-fit sessions involve dance steps to what type of music?

14   In which decade did the first Center Parcs holiday village open in the UK?

15   Which piece is between a bishop and a castle at the start of a game of chess?

16   Which ship, open as a museum since 1971, is moored near Tower Bridge on the River Thames?

17   An asana is a pose in which form of exercise system?

18   What is shown on a brown road sign in the UK to indicate a beach?

19   England's National Exhibition Centre lies south-east of which city?

20   Which organisation manages the Suffolk nature reserve of Minsmere?

Easy

Medium

Hard

Answers to QUIZ 120 – Literature

1	*A Christmas Carol*	11	Anthony Trollope
2	*Wigan*	12	Sci-fi
3	Three	13	Philippa Gregory
4	John Grisham	14	Wilfred Owen
5	18th century (1719)	15	EM Forster
6	Ernest Hemingway	16	Edinburgh
7	*Daffodils*	17	*Gone Girl*
8	*Pride and Prejudice*	18	Jude
9	Roald Dahl	19	20th century (1914-53)
10	George Eliot	20	Poland

1   Which singer had his first solo hit in 1990 with *Blaze of Glory*?

2   Retired 400m runner Cathy Freeman was born in which country?

3   Which WWI battle occurred earlier, the Battle of Jutland or the Battle of the Somme?

4   What is the SI unit of luminous intensity, which takes its name from the Italian word for "candle"?

5   How many quavers are there in a crotchet?

6   What is verbena?

7   What five-letter word meaning "annoyed" is an anagram of a term for a lazy person?

8   Which group had 1970s hits with *Hersham Boys* and *Hurry Up Harry*?

9   The song *Under the Sea* features in which 1989 Disney film?

10 Wayne Bennett was appointed national rugby league coach of which team in 2016?

11 What is the name of Charlotte Bellamy's *Emmerdale* character?

12 Who played Elaine in the TV series *Seinfeld*?

13 In which London borough is the town of Orpington?

14 Which sporting event is an anagram of "a target"?

15 What word can describe both a place that is sheltered from sunlight and dishonest activities?

16 In the title of a 2019 film, what fictional creature is *King of the Monsters*?

17 What word for a light rug can also mean to fling?

18 Which band originally consisted of Kian, Markus, Shane, Brian and Nicky?

19 What general type of sporting equipment was a niblick?

20 2014 marked which anniversary of the first Band Aid record?

Answers to QUIZ 121 – Pot Luck

1	Wales	11	Denmark
2	Buddhism	12	Kent
3	Richard Gere	13	*Automatic for the People*
4	Folly	14	Meerkats
5	Rita Ora	15	Red
6	While the Sun shines	16	Marvel
7	Mount Rushmore	17	South-west
8	Belgium	18	1000m
9	Top Cat	19	Mr Rusty
10	Sir Elton John	20	Brewing

Easy

1 Who had a 1985 hit with *The Whole of the Moon*?

2 Who won the Best Supporting Actress Oscar for the 1973 film *Paper Moon*?

3 Who directed the 2009 film *Moon*?

4 "The moon has a face like the clock in the hall" is the first line of a verse by which author?

5 In which year did *Apollo 11* land on the moon?

6 Who plays *EastEnders'* Alfie Moon?

7 In which country is illegally-made whiskey called "moonshine"?

8 Which character in *Breakfast at Tiffany's* sings *Moon River*?

9 *New Moon* was the subtitle of which 2009 film, the second in a series?

10 Which band released the 1984 single *Killing Moon*?

11 Moon-Face, who inhabited the Magic Faraway Tree, was created by which children's author?

Medium

12 How are members of the Unification Church sometimes referred to?

13 *Walking on the Moon* was a 1979 hit for which band?

14 Which character in *Frasier* had the surname Moon?

15 Which musician famously named his daughter Moon Unit?

16 In which century was *The Moonstone* by Wilkie Collins first published?

17 What adjective means "of the moon"?

18 By what name is Beethoven's piano sonata No. 14 in C♯ minor better known?

19 Which James Bond character spoke his only words, "Well, here's to us", in the film *Moonraker*?

20 Who had a 1975 hit with *Moonlighting*?

Hard

Answers to QUIZ 122 – Leisure

1	Bell-ringing	11	Cornwall
2	Six	12	Maitre d' (hotel)
3	Monopoly™	13	Latin American
4	The Lake District	14	1980s (1987)
5	Grade I	15	Knight
6	Niagara Falls	16	*HMS Belfast*
7	Hallowe'en	17	Yoga
8	Scotland	18	Sandcastle
9	China	19	Birmingham
10	*Call of Duty*	20	RSPB

1 Which Devon city lends its name to a brand of gin?

2 The 2011 film *The Best Exotic Marigold Hotel*, starring Dame Judi Dench and Dame Maggie Smith amongst others, was set in which country?

3 Who won the Best Leading Actor BAFTA award in 2019 for his role in the series *Patrick Melrose*?

4 In which 2002 film did Tom Hanks' Carl Hanratty pursue Leonardo diCaprio's Frank Abagnale Jr?

5 What is the collective term for a group of vipers?

6 How many original members were there in the Spice Girls?

7 On a standard keyboard, which letter is between C and B?

8 Elected pope in 2005, what was the regnal number of Pope Benedict?

9 Which 1973 song by Stealers Wheel was famously used in Quentin Tarantino's *Reservoir Dogs*?

10 Which lies furthest north, Blackburn, Huddersfield or Leeds?

11 In which Greek city was Socrates born?

12 What two words that differ by one letter refer to a collection of subjects for study and a cold creamy dessert?

13 Which member of the Monty Python team has made several travel documentary series in places including Brazil and North Korea?

14 Which monarch reigned earlier, Henry IV or James I?

15 For how many years did David Dimbleby present *Question Time*?

16 In which county is the town of Evesham?

17 Who represented the UK in the Eurovision Song Contest in 2019?

18 Chesapeake Bay lies on the edge of Maryland and which other US state?

19 The Ranji Trophy is a first-class cricket competition played in which country?

20 Rocky Marciano was undisputed World Heavyweight Boxing Champion in which decade?

Easy

Medium

Hard

Answers to QUIZ 123 – Pot Luck

1	Jon Bon Jovi	11	Laurel Thomas
2	Australia	12	Julia Louis-Dreyfus
3	Battle of Jutland (June 1916)	13	Bromley
4	Candela	14	Regatta
5	Two	15	Shady
6	A flowering plant	16	Godzilla
7	Riled (idler)	17	Throw
8	Sham 69	18	Westlife
9	*The Little Mermaid*	19	Golf club (9 iron)
10	England	20	30th anniversary

Easy

1   Found in the North York Moors national park, what is Falling Foss?

2   Which walking trail runs from Winchester in Hampshire to Eastbourne in East Sussex?

3   Anfield is found in which English city?

4   What term is given to a small lake in an area of mountains, such as in the Lake District?

5   Spire FM is a radio station located in which UK city?

6   Which phrase from Shakespeare was used to describe the winter of 1978-79 in the UK?

7   The shortbread biscuit is associated with which country of the UK?

8   What is featured on the stamps issued on Lundy island?

9   Which city is most famously linked to Robin Hood?

10 In the British award, what does the "E" of CBE stand for?

11 What is the latest day on which British Summer Time can begin?

12 Which city has a ram as its emblem?

Medium

13 In which county is the town of Rugby?

14 Which is the closest city to the New Forest?

15 The NC500 is a scenic route in which country of the UK?

16 HR is the postcode for which UK city?

17 The Royal Albert Bridge connects the county of Cornwall with which city?

18 De Montfort University lies in which UK city?

19 What name is given to the commander of an army platoon in the UK?

20 What is the county town of Norfolk?

Hard

Answers to QUIZ 124 – The Moon

1	The Waterboys	11	Enid Blyton
2	Tatum O'Neal	12	Moonies
3	Duncan Jones	13	The Police
4	Robert Louis Stevenson	14	Daphne
5	1969	15	Frank Zappa
6	Shane Richie	16	19th century (1868)
7	USA	17	Lunar
8	Holly Golightly	18	*Moonlight Sonata*
9	*The Twilight Saga*	19	Jaws
10	Echo and the Bunnymen	20	Leo Sayer

1   Which 1980s TV series of monologues included *A Woman of No Importance* and *A Lady of Letters*?

2   In which country is the UNESCO World Heritage Site of Ravello?

3   Which Edward became King of England in 1901?

4   Which Harry Potter film was released first, *The Chamber of Secrets* or *The Goblet of Fire*?

5   What word can mean both fishing equipment and a manoeuvre in football?

6   In which English county is Herstmonceux Castle?

7   What is the largest organ of the human body?

8   Which famous singer won an Oscar for his role in the 1953 film *From Here to Eternity*?

9   The 19th-century *Hungarian Rhapsodies* were written by which composer?

10   Who starred in the 2019 TV series *The Widow*?

11   What nationality is football manager Jaap Stam?

12   Co is the chemical symbol for which element?

13   Mogadishu is the capital of which African country?

14   For what do the initials ERS stand in relation to voting?

15   Which is the correct spelling: acomodate, accomodate, or accommodate?

16   In which country is the TV series *Keeping Faith* set?

17   Jonah Barrington (b.1941) was a famous name in which indoor sport?

18   What is the name of the substance used to fill in the gaps between wall or mosaic tiles?

19   What event was the focus of the 1969 film *They Shoot Horses, Don't They*?

20   In which section of an orchestra would you find a glockenspiel?

Easy
Medium
Hard

Answers to QUIZ 125 – Pot Luck

1	Plymouth	11	Athens
2	India	12	Syllabus and syllabub
3	Benedict Cumberbatch	13	Sir Michael Palin
4	*Catch Me if You Can*	14	Henry IV (1399-1413)
5	Nest	15	25 (1994-2018)
6	Five	16	Worcestershire
7	V	17	Michael Rice
8	XVI	18	Virginia
9	*Stuck in the Middle With You*	19	India
10	Leeds	20	1950s (1952-56)

1   Ellie Taylor and Rachel Parris are regulars on which satirical news show?

2   The title of which current American newspaper is often abbreviated to *NYT*?

3   What term is given to a traditional larger format newspaper?

4   Who played journalist Cal McCaffrey in the 2009 film *State of Play*?

5   In which year did the *Independent* cease its printed format?

6   *The Last Leg* began as a show alongside which sporting event?

7   Who was the original host of *Have I Got News For You*?

8   What was the title of the UK newspaper, printed from 1986 to 1995, that was noted for its use of colour printing?

9   Haydn Gwynne, Stephen Tompkinson and Neil Pearson all found fame in which satirical TV series?

10 The 1976 film *All the President's Men* featured two journalists working on what newspaper?

11 Which *Good Morning Britain* presenter worked as a newspaper editor from the 1980s until 2004?

12 Which 2018 TV series featured the rivalry between fictional newspapers *The Herald* and *The Post*?

13 Amy Poehler, Chevy Chase and Dan Aykroyd all appeared on which US satirical show?

14 Which part of a newspaper takes its name from a high part of a ship?

15 What word is given to written material that is ready to be printed in a newspaper or posted on a website?

16 Which broadcasting company provided the UK's first 24-hour news television channel?

17 In which decade was the satirical programme *That Was the Week That Was* broadcast?

18 What subject does journalist Simon Calder cover?

19 Who chaired the 2011-12 inquiry into UK press standards?

20 In which 1987 film did Kevin Kline portray journalist Donald Woods?

Answers to QUIZ 126 – The UK

1	A waterfall	11	March 31
2	South Downs Way	12	Derby
3	Liverpool	13	Warwickshire
4	Tarn	14	Southampton
5	Salisbury	15	Scotland
6	Winter of Discontent (*Richard III*)	16	Hereford
7	Scotland	17	Plymouth
8	A puffin	18	Leicester
9	Nottingham	19	Lieutenant
10	Empire	20	Norwich

Easy

Medium

Hard

ANSWERS ON PAGE 131

1 Which new lifeline was introduced to *Who Wants to Be a Millionaire* in 2018?

2 Which city is furthest north, Birmingham, Sheffield or Bradford?

3 Cerebral is an adjective relating to which part of the body?

4 On which Italian island was Archimedes born?

5 For what do the letters HP stand in the name of the sauce?

6 What was the occupation of Caroline Quentin's character in the TV series *Men Behaving Badly*?

7 Does the Solway Firth lie off the east coast or the west coast of Great Britain?

8 What term is given to the account of someone's life when written by the person themself?

9 In which town is the Church of the Nativity located?

10 The Bond villain Le Chiffre appears in which novel and film?

11 Who had a 1991 hit with *Coming Out of the Dark*?

12 Johnnie Fingers was a member of which Irish band?

13 In which decade was a variable speed limit introduced on parts of the M25?

14 Which *Gardeners' World* presenter broadcast from his Barnsdale Gardens?

15 Which long-running series features Dictionary Corner?

16 For what do the letters LPA stand in the context of personal law?

17 What is the minimum number of games in which a tennis set can be won?

18 "Two households, both alike in dignity, in fair Verona" is the first line of which Shakespeare play?

19 Fyodor Dostoevsky lived and died during which century?

20 The town of Diss is situated in which English county?

Easy

Medium

Hard

Answers to QUIZ 127 – Pot Luck

1	*Talking Heads*	11	Dutch
2	Italy	12	Cobalt
3	Edward VII	13	Somalia
4	*The Chamber of Secrets* (2002)	14	Electoral Reform Society
5	Tackle	15	Accommodate
6	East Sussex	16	Wales
7	Skin	17	Squash
8	Frank Sinatra	18	Grout
9	Liszt	19	A dance marathon
10	Kate Beckinsale	20	Percussion

Easy

1   In the film *Carry On Cowboy*, who played The Rumpo Kid?

2   *C'era una volta il West* was the title of which 1968 film in the native language of its director?

3   The 1993 film *Tombstone* was set in which US state?

4   Who directed *Blazing Saddles*?

5   Which 1960 film was remade in 2016 with a cast that included Denzel Washington and Ethan Hawke?

6   Who played Rooster Cogburn in the 2010 remake of *True Grit*?

7   In which 1991 film, about a group of men visiting a cattle ranch, did Jake Gyllenhaal make his first screen appearance?

8   Where was the 3:10 train heading in the title of a 2007 film?

9   Which 1992 western won the Best Picture Oscar?

10   Who played the title role in the 1963 film *McLintock!*?

11   Which James Bond actor played the title role in the 2011 film *Cowboys & Aliens*?

12   In which decade was the Sam Peckinpah film *The Wild Bunch* released?

Medium

13   What word completes the titles of the classic films, *A Fistful of ___* and *A Few ___ More*?

14   Which 2005 Oscar-winning film was based on a short story by Annie Proulx?

15   Which fictional western hero's sidekick did Johnny Depp play in a 2013 film?

16   The town of Dirt was the setting for which 2011 animated western?

17   Who played "The Stranger" in the 1973 film *High Plains Drifter*?

18   In the 1994 film *Wyatt Earp*, who played the title role?

19   Who is the yodelling cowgirl that Woody meets in *Toy Story 2*?

20   What term describes western films made in Europe?

Hard

Answers to QUIZ 128 – In the News

1	*The Mash Report*	11	Piers Morgan
2	*New York Times*	12	*Press*
3	Broadsheet	13	*Saturday Night Live*
4	Russell Crowe	14	Masthead
5	2016	15	Copy
6	2012 Paralympic Games	16	Sky
7	Angus Deayton	17	1960s (1962-63)
8	*Today*	18	Travel
9	*Drop the Dead Donkey*	19	Lord Justice Leveson
10	*The Washington Post*	20	*Cry Freedom*

1   The musical *Viva Forever* was based on which group's singles?

2   Whose first single was *Move it/Schoolboy Crush*?

3   Who was prime minister first, Clement Attlee (First Earl Attlee) or Stanley Baldwin?

4   Who is the Greek equivalent of the Egyptian god Ra?

5   In which country was broadcaster Clive James born?

6   Which word meaning "pleasant" means "from birth" with the addition of one letter?

7   In the 2018 film *Skyscraper,* which actor starred as Will Sawyer?

8   What word refers both to the grip that something has on the ground and a medical treatment involving stretching?

9   What was the subtitle of the 2013 *Thor* film?

10   A sidewinder is what type of creature?

11   Which composer famously became deaf towards the end of his life but still produced music?

12   In the Star Wars films, what type of creature is Chewbacca?

13   What name is given to the tower over an oil well that is used to raise and lower the drill?

14   What condition is known in French as *mal de mer*?

15   Mn is the chemical symbol for which element?

16   The town of Louth is situated in which English county?

17   Who was the only person to speak in Mel Brooks' *Silent Movie*?

18   Which river flows through the town of Warwick?

19   In which country were the 2018 Commonwealth Games held?

20   Which disc jockey created the character of Captain Kremmen?

Answers to QUIZ 129 – Pot Luck

1	Ask the host	11	Gloria Estefan
2	Bradford	12	The Boomtown Rats
3	The brain	13	1990s (1995)
4	Sicily	14	Geoff Hamilton
5	Houses of Parliament	15	*Countdown*
6	Nurse	16	Lasting Power of Attorney
7	West coast	17	Six
8	Autobiography	18	*Romeo and Juliet*
9	Bethlehem	19	19th century (1821-81)
10	*Casino Royale*	20	Norfolk

Easy

1   Leona Lewis' hit *Run* was a cover of a song by which band?

2   Economist John Stuart Mill was born in which country?

3   In which sport would you hit a home run?

4   For what type of novels are Mills & Boon known?

5   What colour are runner beans?

6   How many years are there in a millennium?

7   The town of Runcorn lies in which county?

8   In which decade did Mill Reef win the Epsom Derby?

9   What word for a raised platform can also mean an area where an aircraft takes off?

10 Millefiori is an artistic technique used in what sort of material?

Medium

11 Runnymede lies on which river?

12 What nationality was playwright Arthur Miller?

13 Which commentator and former athlete created the Great North Run event?

14 Spike Milligan played the character of Eccles in which radio series?

15 In which decade did Bryan Adams have a hit with *Run to You*?

16 To whom was Heather Mills married from 2002 until their divorce in 2008?

17 Who starred in the 2007 film *Run, Fat Boy, Run*?

18 What type of "mill" is used to describe a routine, boring task?

19 Who played "K" in *Blade Runner 2049*?

20 Who is Ben Miller's comedy partner?

Hard

Answers to QUIZ 130 – Westerns

1	Sid James	11	Daniel Craig
2	*Once Upon a Time in the West*	12	1960s (1969)
3	Arizona	13	*Dollars*
4	Mel Brooks	14	*Brokeback Mountain*
5	*The Magnificent Seven*	15	Tonto (in *The Lone Ranger*)
6	Jeff Bridges	16	*Rango*
7	*City Slickers*	17	Clint Eastwood
8	Yuma	18	Kevin Costner
9	*Unforgiven*	19	Jessie
10	John Wayne	20	Spaghetti westerns

1. Who starred in the title role of the 2006 TV series *The Amazing Mrs Pritchard*?

2. What word can mean both a piece of leather for sharpening razors and a temper tantrum?

3. Who plays the title role in the TV series *Mum*?

4. Sufism is a mystical approach to which religion?

5. What nationality is actor Mads Mikkelsen (b.1965)?

6. What role does Millie Bright play in the England women's football team?

7. How is septicaemia more commonly known?

8. With which English county cricket team did Sir Ian Botham begin his domestic career?

9. In which county is the stately home of Audley End House?

10. The Kincardine Bridge spans which Scottish body of water?

11. In the TV series *Happy Days*, what was the Fonz's first name?

12. What nationality is tennis player Angelique Kerber?

13. New Orleans is in which US state?

14. Which character, created by Oscar Wilde, had a spooky picture in his attic?

15. Which part of the plant salsify is eaten as a vegetable?

16. In which Disney film would you hear the song *Be Our Guest*?

17. The 606 sports phone-in is broadcast on which national radio station?

18. "You walked into the party like you were walking onto a yacht" is the opening line of which song?

19. Is the European chub a freshwater fish or a sea fish?

20. Hobart is the capital of which Australian state?

Answers to QUIZ 131 – Pot Luck

1	The Spice Girls	11	Beethoven
2	Sir Cliff Richard	12	A wookiee
3	Stanley Baldwin (1923)	13	Derrick
4	Helios	14	Seasickness
5	Australia	15	Manganese
6	Congenial (congenital)	16	Lincolnshire
7	Dwayne Johnson	17	Marcel Marceau
8	Traction	18	Avon
9	*The Dark World*	19	Australia
10	Rattlesnake	20	Kenny Everett

1   What term is given to the individual parts of a World Rally Championship event, which can be up to 15 miles long?

2   At which circuit does the Belgian Grand Prix take place?

3   During which decade did Jim Clark win the British Grand Prix on four consecutive occasions?

4   Which TV chef (b.1972) made a documentary about his attempt to race in the Italian Mille Miglia?

5   In which country does the Le Mans 24-hour race take place?

6   In April 2019, which country hosted the 1000th Formula 1 Grand Prix?

7   What nationality is F1 driver Sergio Perez?

8   In which English county is Santa Pod Raceway?

9   Giuseppe "Nino" Farina, the first World Champion, came from which country?

10   What name is given to the volunteers at a race who are responsible for the safety of the competitors?

11   What is shown on a brown road sign in the UK to indicate a racing circuit?

12   Who was Lewis Hamilton's team-mate when he first joined Mercedes?

13   What name was the Formula 1 Racing Point team known as immediately prior to the 2019 season?

14   In which country does the last race of the World Rally Championship calendar take place?

15   For which team was Damon Hill driving when he won the Formula 1 World Championship in 1996?

16   Colin Turkington and Matt Neal compete in which form of motor racing?

17   As at 2019, in which decade did Brands Hatch last host the British Formula 1 Grand Prix?

18   The Catalunya racing circuit lies in which country?

19   Guy Martin took part in a car race against which former Formula 1 driver in a 2018 documentary?

20   Former racing driver Signor Trulli has what first name?

Easy

Medium

Hard

1   The town of Fareham is in which English county?

2   How was London known in Roman times?

3   Which English golfer topped the world rankings for the first time in November 2018?

4   Olly Murs was runner-up to which *The X Factor* winner?

5   How is 29 represented in Roman numerals?

6   By what nickname was the Roman emperor Constantine I known?

7   What was the name of the former telephone service provided by the Post Office that played pop music?

8   Which word meaning "attractive" was used to describe Bobby Shafto in the nursery rhyme?

9   In which decade was Kenneth Clarke Chancellor of the Exchequer?

10 What type of fish may be common, crucian or mirror?

11 Gavin Hastings played international rugby for which country?

12 How many members were there in the Boomtown Rats?

13 What country did former athlete Tom McKean (b.1963) represent at the Commonwealth Games?

14 In which decade did Goran Ivanišević win his only Grand Slam singles title?

15 With which long-running series was Phil Drabble associated?

16 Which is the correct spelling of the word meaning "to find not guilty": aquit, acquit or akquit?

17 What type of transport is a ketch?

18 Louisa Gradgrind is a character in which Charles Dickens novel?

19 What is the name of Tarzan's female companion in the Disney film?

20 What word can mean both a target and a description of information based on facts?

Easy

Medium

Hard

Answers to QUIZ 133 – Pot Luck

1	Jane Horrocks	11	Arthur
2	Strop	12	German
3	Lesley Manville	13	Louisiana
4	Islam	14	Dorian Gray
5	Danish	15	The root
6	Defender	16	*Beauty and The Beast*
7	Blood poisoning	17	Radio 5 Live
8	Somerset	18	*You're So Vain* (Carly Simon)
9	Essex (Saffron Walden)	19	Freshwater fish
10	Firth of Forth	20	Tasmania

Easy

1. "The Borogoves" were mentioned in which poem in *Through the Looking-Glass*?
2. Which Wonderland character uttered the words "Off with their heads!"?
3. In *Through the Looking-Glass*, who accompanied the Walrus in a poem?
4. What was the main colour of Alice's dress in the Disney film adaptation?
5. What relation is Tweedledum to Tweedledee?
6. The playing-cards painted what colour roses red?
7. Who was on trial for stealing tarts?
8. The Mad Hatter and the March Hare attempted to put which creature into a teapot?
9. Who directed the 2010 film *Alice in Wonderland*?
10. Which fantasy TV series had a 2011 spin-off set in Wonderland?

Medium

11. On what was the Caterpillar sitting when Alice first met him?
12. Which creatures were used as croquet mallets?
13. What did Alice become when she crossed the last brook in *Through the Looking-Glass*?
14. The Cook in Wonderland was prone to over-using which condiment?
15. What was the last thing visible on the Cheshire Cat when it disappeared?
16. In which decade was the Disney film *Alice in Wonderland* released?
17. Which nursery-rhyme creature was sitting on a wall when Alice met him?
18. What is the subtitle of *Through the Looking-Glass*?
19. Where were Alice and her sister sitting at the beginning of her adventures in Wonderland?
20. Over what did Tweedledum and Tweedledee fight?

Hard

Answers to QUIZ 134 – Motor Racing

1	Stages	11	Chequered flag
2	Spa	12	Nico Rosberg
3	1960's	13	Force India
4	James Martin	14	Australia
5	France	15	Williams-Renault
6	China	16	Touring cars
7	Mexican	17	1980s (1986)
8	Bedfordshire	18	Spain (Madrid)
9	Italy	19	Jenson Button
10	Marshals	20	Jarno

1   "All the Fives" is a traditional bingo call for which number?

2   *The Return to Jafar* was a follow up to which Disney film?

3   Stuart Milligan played Adam Klaus in which long-running TV series?

4   What does the French phrase *tout de suite* mean?

5   Where was Wallace and Gromit's destination on their *Grand Day Out*?

6   Why was cricket captain Eoin Morgan suspended for one match and fined following England's win against Pakistan in May 2019?

7   In which US TV series did Wentworth Miller play the character of Michael Scofield?

8   The island of Formentera belongs to which country?

9   Probate is the process of establishing the validity of what type of document?

10 From which country does the drink Campari® originate?

11 Natalie Dormer played which character in *The Hunger Games: Mockingjay Part 1*?

12 In which country was author JM Barrie born?

13 Mombasa is a coastal town and resort in which East African country?

14 What food is said to have been invented by an 18th-century earl of the same name, who wanted to continue gambling without having to stop to eat?

15 In Greek mythology, the siege of which city was ended by the "gift" of a wooden horse?

16 For which 2000 film did Julia Roberts win the Best Actress Oscar?

17 Who created the Muppets?

18 How many full notes are there in an octave?

19 What nationality was the artist Millais?

20 How many points is the letter B worth in Scrabble®?

Answers to QUIZ 135 – Pot Luck

1	Hampshire	11	Scotland
2	Londinium	12	Six
3	Justin Rose	13	Scotland
4	Joe McElderry	14	2000s (Wimbledon, 2001)
5	XXIX	15	*One Man and His Dog*
6	The Great	16	Acquit
7	Dial-a-Disc	17	(Sailing) ship
8	Bonny (or bonnie)	18	*Hard Times*
9	1990s (1993-97)	19	Jane
10	Carp	20	Objective

1   What was the name of Hyacinth's sister in *Keeping Up Appearances*?

2   *The Royle Family* was set in which city?

3   What are the names of Sally Webster's two daughters in *Coronation Street*?

4   Which 2019 series featured the Lyons family, headed by grandmother Muriel?

5   What was the first name of the oldest Crawley sister in *Downton Abbey*?

6   Jimmy McKenna plays Ashley Taylor Dawson's father in which long-running series?

7   What was the name of Tom's wife in *The Good Life*?

8   In *Doctor Who*, what relation is Graham to Ryan?

9   Who played Uncle Albert in *Only Fools and Horses*?

10   What is the name of Jay Pritchet's second wife in *Modern Family*?

11   Who was the head of the family in *The Sopranos*?

12   Uncle Fester is a relative of which fictional family?

13   What type of establishment did Beatrice and Evangeline Eliott run in the TV series *The House of Eliott*?

14   Stefan Dennis is the one of the original cast of *Neighbours*. To which family does his character belong?

15   What was the name of Victor Meldrew's wife?

16   How many children were there in the combined family *The Brady Bunch*?

17   Who is Ian Beale's mother in *EastEnders*?

18   Joanie and Richie were the siblings in which US series, first aired in 1974?

19   In which 1970s sitcom was Basil married to Sybil?

20   Who is Ellie's sister on *Gogglebox*?

Easy

Medium

Hard

Answers to QUIZ 136 – Alice's Adventures

1	*Jabberwocky*	11	A mushroom
2	The Queen of Hearts	12	Flamingos
3	The Carpenter	13	A queen
4	Blue	14	Pepper
5	Brother	15	Its grin
6	White roses	16	1950s (1951)
7	The Knave of Hearts	17	Humpty Dumpty
8	Dormouse	18	*and What Alice Found There*
9	Tim Burton	19	A riverbank
10	*Once Upon a Time*	20	A rattle

1 Who starred in the 1980s TV series *Chance in a Million*?

2 In which decade did Peter Schmeichel play for Aston Villa and Manchester City?

3 The NBA is the main North American League in what sport?

4 The Quantock Hills are located in which county?

5 What is the surname of the TV family who are *Lost in Space*?

6 Which *The Young Ones* actor recorded *Hole in My Shoe* in 1984?

7 Which annual trophy is contested between the winners of the Premier League and the holders of the FA Cup?

8 What condiment is served in a mill?

9 For what do the initials JK stand in the name of the Harry Potter author?

10 John Cleese provides the voice for King Harold in which animated series?

11 Which regional capital city of the UK is served by George Best Airport?

12 What word can denote "'an average", "being stingy" or "to intend"?

13 *It's Not Right, but It's Okay* was a hit for which female singer?

14 Which two old coins were used to describe an early form of bicycle?

15 Rosh Hashanah is the new year celebration in which religion?

16 What type of creature is a fieldfare?

17 On which sports surface would you find tramlines?

18 What is the international dialling code for the USA?

19 The four rocky planets in our solar system are Earth, Mars, Venus and which other?

20 Claire Sweeney played which character in *Brookside*?

Easy

Medium

Hard

Answers to QUIZ 137 – Pot Luck

1	55	11	Cressida
2	*Aladdin*	12	Scotland
3	*Jonathan Creek*	13	Kenya
4	Immediately	14	Sandwich
5	The Moon	15	Troy
6	Slow over-rate	16	*Erin Brockovich*
7	*Prison Break*	17	Jim Henson
8	Spain	18	Eight
9	A will	19	English
10	Italy	20	Three

Easy

1   Camilla is the first name of the Duchess of which county?

2   "Diction" indicates the clarity of what?

3   Chromecast is a digital media player manufactured by which company?

4   DKNY is a fashion house founded by whom?

5   Canaries are what colour?

6   Dawn was played by which actress in the TV series *The Office*?

7   Carnoustie golf course is in which country?

8   Dean Saunders (b.1964) played international football for which country?

9   Cabbage Patch dolls became popular in which decade?

10 Dill was the name of the dog in which children's TV series first shown in 1968?

11 Cava is a sparkling wine from which country?

12 Singer-dancer Dita Von Teese was born in which country?

13 Coll is part of which Scottish island group?

Medium

14 Drew Barrymore played the sister of which character in the 1982 film *E.T. the Extra-Terrestrial*?

15 Clive Owen played the legendary title character in which 2004 film?

16 *David*, by Michelangelo, can be seen in the Galleria dell'Accademia in which Italian city?

17 Calcutta is the former name of which Indian city?

18 Derby is the American term for what type of hat?

19 Casio is an electronics company based in which country?

20 Durum wheat is the basis for which foodstuff?

Hard

Answers to QUIZ 138 – TV Relatives

1	Daisy	11	Tony Soprano
2	Manchester	12	The Addams Family
3	Rosie and Sophie	13	Fashion house
4	*Years and Years*	14	The Robinsons (Paul Robinson)
5	Mary	15	Margaret
6	*Hollyoaks*	16	Six
7	Barbara	17	Kathy
8	Step-grandfather	18	*Happy Days*
9	Buster Merryfield	19	*Fawlty Towers*
10	Gloria Delgado	20	Izzi

1   Who is the Greek equivalent of the Roman god Cupid?

2   In which decade did Soviet leader Leonid Brezhnev die?

3   What is the dominant religion in Thailand?

4   The town of Alcúdia lies on which of the Balearic islands?

5   *What's Love Got to Do With It* was a 1984 hit for which singer?

6   How many different methods of dismissal are there in cricket?

7   What decade saw the publication of the *Chronicles of Narnia*?

8   What is the ninth sign of the zodiac?

9   Which size of paper measures 148mm by 210mm?

10 What word completes the title of the Everly Brothers hit *All I Have to Do is ___*?

11 John F Kennedy was assassinated in which year?

12 The logo of which Japanese car manufacturer features three red diamonds?

13 What is the name of Georgia Taylor's *Coronation Street* character?

14 What is the meaning of the word "coda"?

15 According to the nursery rhyme, what is Wednesday's child?

16 Which European nationality and a cleaning substance share the same spelling?

17 Which actor starred in *Doctor Who* first, Tom Baker or Colin Baker?

18 *Road Rage* was a 1998 hit by which band?

19 Lloyds Bank has its headquarters in which city?

20 Marty the Zebra is a leading character in which series of films?

Easy

Medium

Hard

Answers to QUIZ 139 – Pot Luck

1	Simon Callow	11	Belfast
2	2000s	12	Mean
3	Basketball	13	Whitney Houston
4	Somerset	14	Penny and farthing
5	Robinson	15	Judaism
6	Nigel Planer	16	A bird
7	FA Community Shield	17	Tennis court
8	Pepper	18	001
9	Joanne Kathleen	19	Mercury
10	*Shrek*	20	Lindsey Corkhill

1 Which football pundit famously advertises Walkers crisps?

2 Which TV series features a group known as "The Whisperers"?

3 Justin, Kevin, Kitty, Sarah and Tommy were the Walker siblings in which US series?

4 Who was appointed Speaker of the House of Commons in 2009?

5 The 1992 film *Fire Walk with Me* was a prequel to which TV series?

6 Which term for a raised platform on which to make a speech originated from the use of wooden shipping crates?

7 "Walking with my feet ten feet off of Beale" is a line from which song?

8 Proverbially, who have you been speaking about when someone arrives unexpectedly?

9 The long-distance walking route, the South West Coast Path, runs from Dorset through Devon and Cornwall to which other county?

10 Which writer invented the word "doublespeak"?

11 Who had a 1963 hit with *Walk on By*?

12 Coaches on which talent show, first broadcast in 2012, have included Boy George and Gavin Rossdale?

13 Polly Walker played legal adviser Gill Biggeloe in which TV series?

14 A chatterbox may be said to talk how many to the dozen?

15 Which comic group sang *I'm Walking Backwards for Christmas* in 1956?

16 "So baby talk to me, like lovers do" is a lyric from which 1983 song?

17 What was the title of the 1982 novel by Alice Walker, later made into a film starring Whoopi Goldberg?

18 Who co-starred with Rock Hudson in the 1959 film *Pillow Talk*?

19 *Walking in the Air* was a 1985 chart hit for which singer, now a TV presenter?

20 In what manner would a *sotto voce* remark be made?

Answers to QUIZ 140 – CD

1	Cornwall	11	Spain
2	Speech	12	USA
3	Google	13	Inner Hebrides
4	Donna Karan	14	Elliott
5	Yellow	15	*King Arthur*
6	Lucy Davis	16	Florence
7	Scotland	17	Kolkata
8	Wales	18	Bowler hat
9	1980s	19	Japan
10	*The Herbs*	20	Pasta

1 The island of Java is part of which country?

2 What would you use to play the gambling game *chemin de fer*?

3 Which of these major conflicts occurred earlier, WWI or the Spanish Civil War?

4 The Imperial March is the theme of which Star Wars villain?

5 Which 1950s prime minister used the phrase "You've never had it so good"?

6 The 2007 film *Hannibal Rising* was a prequel to which 1991 film?

7 Which herb has a name that means wise and learned?

8 Who plays Owen Grady in the *Jurassic World* films?

9 Fleet services are on which motorway?

10 The ballet term *rond de jambe* refers to which body part?

11 Who had a 2014 hit with *Shake It Off*?

12 Proverbially, what should you keep dry if you want to save resources for when they are most needed?

13 Whom did Flora MacDonald famously help to avoid capture by government troops in 1746?

14 The Bass Strait separates the Australian state of Victoria from which other state?

15 Which Scottish singer, nicknamed SuBo, found fame after appearing on *Britain's Got Talent*?

16 *Church of the Poison Mind* was a 1983 hit for which group?

17 In the *Godfather* films, who played the young Vito Corleone?

18 Where would you find sideburns?

19 What is the second event in a triathlon?

20 The radio code word for which two letters of the alphabet are characters in the title of a Shakespeare play?

Easy

Medium

Hard

1 Belgium has a border with how many countries?

2 In what year did Montenegro vote to split from Serbia?

3 Which Italian tourist attraction was the most popular in 2018, receiving 7.4 million visitors?

4 Lower Saxony is a state in the north-western part of which European country?

5 Which European country is closest to Tunisia?

6 In the Italian place name Isola Bella, what does *isola* mean?

7 Which language is known as *Deutsch* in its own language?

8 What animal is depicted on the city of Berlin's coat of arms?

9 St Peter's Basilica in the Vatican was completed in which century?

10 Which European country has the international car registration letter L?

11 Which European country is divided into 26 cantons?

12 In what year did the Maastricht Treaty create the European Union?

13 The Swiss town of Locarno lies at the foot of which range of mountains?

14 The Republic of San Marino is completely surrounded by which European country?

15 Which major river rises in Switzerland, flows into France and empties into the Mediterranean near Marseilles?

16 What is the name of the city of Naples in Italian?

17 Which is the highest mountain in Greece?

18 A Galwegian hails from which county of Ireland?

19 In which European city did the UEFA Europa Cup final take place in 2019?

20 How many countries does Andorra border?

Answers to QUIZ 142 – Walk the Talk

1 Gary Lineker
2 *The Walking Dead*
3 *Brothers and Sisters*
4 John Bercow
5 *Twin Peaks*
6 Soapbox
7 *Walking in Memphis* (Marc Cohn)
8 The devil
9 Somerset
10 George Orwell (in *Nineteen Eighty Four*)
11 Dionne Warwick
12 *The Voice UK*
13 *Line of Duty*
14 Nineteen
15 The Goons
16 *Here Comes the Rain Again* (Eurythmics)
17 *The Color Purple*
18 Doris Day
19 Aled Jones
20 In a soft voice

1. What colours are the two outside stripes on the German flag?

2. Who had a 1998 hit with the song *How Do I Live*?

3. In music what does *da capo* mean?

4. In the northern hemisphere, on what date are racehorses' birthdays celebrated?

5. How is 32 represented in Roman numerals?

6. What town links a Ricky Gervais sitcom with a poem by Sir John Betjeman?

7. In which book of the Bible is the story of Noah and the flood?

8. Which golfer and former Ryder Cup captain is nicknamed "Monty"?

9. In which key is a piece of music that has one sharp as its key signature?

10. E20 was a spin-off from which British soap?

11. Maggie Tulliver is the main character in which 1860 novel?

12. What was the surname of the Goods' neighbours in *The Good Life*?

13. Who won the Best Actor Oscar for his starring role in the 2006 film *The Last King of Scotland*?

14. In which county is the town of Malvern?

15. Which actress played Debbie Ocean in the film *Ocean's 8*?

16. Proverbially, what musical instrument are you said to play if you accept a subordinate role?

17. What is the name given to a bed that has vertical beams at each corner to hold up a canopy and enclosing curtains?

18. The supermarket Aldi was founded in which country?

19. Which actress played Nurse Sandra May in the 1967 comedy *Carry on Doctor*?

20. The name of which summer sport is also the name of a chirping, grasshopper-like insect?

Easy

Medium

Hard

Answers to QUIZ 143 – Pot Luck

1	Indonesia	11	Taylor Swift
2	Playing cards	12	Powder
3	WWI	13	Charles Edward Stuart (Bonnie Prince Charlie)
4	Darth Vader	14	Tasmania
5	Harold Macmillan (First Earl of Stockton)	15	Susan Boyle
6	*The Silence of the Lambs*	16	Culture Club
7	Sage	17	Robert De Niro
8	Chris Pratt	18	On the face
9	M3	19	Cycling
10	Leg	20	R and J (Romeo and Juliet)

Easy

1   Thomas wakes up in a metal elevator that brings him to a place called The Glade in which 2009 novel?

2   If *Insurgent* and *Allegiant* are book two and three respectively, what is book one?

3   The Peter Jackson film of which book by Philip Reeve was released in 2018?

4   Whose works include *Iggie's House*, *Tiger Eyes* and *Are you there God? It's Me, Margaret*?

5   Shailene Woodley and Ansel Elgort starred in a 2014 film based on which novel by John Green?

6   Who is the main protagonist in *The Catcher in the Rye*?

7   Max teaches Liesel to read whilst he is hiding from the Nazis in her foster parent's basement, in which novel?

8   What was the title of the fourth novel in the *Twilight* series?

9   Jean Louise Finch, nicknamed Scout, is the narrator in which novel?

10   Who wrote *The Hunger Games* series?

Medium

11   How many sisters are there in *Little Women* (1868)?

12   What is the name of the main female character in the *Twilight* series?

13   In which decade was a film released based on Lois Duncan's novel *I Know What You Did Last Summer*?

14   What is the name of the main character in Mark Haddon's *The Curious Incident of the Dog in the Night-Time*?

15   What word completes the tag line from the *Catching Fire* film poster "Remember who the _____ is"?

16   On what are the schoolboys stranded in *Lord of the Flies*?

17   Anne Frank wrote her diary while in hiding from the Nazis in which capital city?

18   Which series of novels charted the lives of Elizabeth and Jessica Wakefield?

19   Who played Sally Lockhart in the 2006 TV adaptation of Philp Pullman's *The Ruby in the Smoke*?

20   How often do the Hunger Games occur?

Hard

Answers to QUIZ 144 – Europe

1	Four (France, Germany, Luxembourg, The Netherlands)	11	Switzerland
2	2006	12	1992
3	Colosseum	13	Swiss Alps
4	Germany	14	Italy
5	Italy	15	The Rhône
6	Island	16	Napoli
7	German	17	Mount Olympus
8	Bear	18	Galway
9	17th century (1626)	19	Baku
10	Luxembourg	20	Two (France and Spain)

ANSWERS ON PAGE **149**

1   Natalie Cole with Nat King Cole won the 1991 Grammy for Record of the Year for which song?

2   What type of creature is a golden orfe?

3   In *The Good, the Bad and The Ugly*, Lee Van Cleef was The Bad and Eli Wallach was The Ugly. Who played The Good?

4   Who was appointed Shadow Chancellor of the Exchequer in September 2015?

5   What nationality is tennis player Petra Kvitova?

6   In which year was the Spotify service launched?

7   Who directed the 1976 film *Taxi Driver*?

8   In which decade were zebra crossings introduced in the UK?

9   What is the word for a person who predominately eats a vegetarian diet, but occasionally eats meat or fish?

10   Simone de Beauvoir was born in which country?

11   What type of alcoholic drink is Tanqueray?

12   Who is best known for playing Kim Fox-Hubbard in *EastEnders*?

13   Which big band leader recorded *In the Mood* (1939)?

14   What is made in a tannery?

15   Balsamic vinegar originated in which country?

16   In the title of the TV series *Quincy, ME*, for what do the letters *ME* stand?

17   Which actor delivered the famous line "You can't handle the truth" in the 1992 courtroom film *A Few Good Men*?

18   What is indicated in the UK by a brown road sign showing an elephant?

19   Which organisation launched in 1992 is associated with "yogic flying"?

20   Tag-teams contest matches in which sport?

Answers to QUIZ 145 – Pot Luck

1	Black and yellow	11	*The Mill on the Floss*
2	LeAnn Rimes	12	Leadbetter
3	Repeat from beginning	13	Forest Whitaker
4	January 1	14	Worcestershire
5	XXXII	15	Sandra Bullock
6	Slough	16	(Second) fiddle
7	Genesis	17	Four-poster
8	Colin Montgomerie	18	Germany
9	G	19	Dame Barbara Windsor
10	*EastEnders*	20	Cricket

Easy

1   What fabric are you said to be under when sleeping in a tent?

2   What material is said to be taken by a lawyer on becoming a QC?

3   *Spirits in the Material World* was a 1981 single by which group?

4   Jared Leto won an Oscar for playing the character of Rayon in which 2013 film?

5   Which pattern of curving shapes and colours shares its name with a Scottish town?

6   *Agadoo* was a 1984 hit for which group?

7   "Silk and satin, leather and lace" is a line from which song by the Steve Miller Band?

8   What is the translation of broderie anglaise?

9   Which rough fabric, used for making sacks, is known as "burlap" in the US?

10 "Moleskin" is a type of which fabric?

11 Which fabric shares its name with a Channel Island?

12 Worsted is what type of cloth?

13 Which actress starred as a 12-year-old in the 1944 film *National Velvet*?

14 What type of fabric is cheesecloth?

Medium

15 *Material Girl* was a 1985 single by which singer?

16 Which company ran an advertising campaign urging people to "Chuck out your chintz"?

17 What was the name of Dot Cotton's first husband on *EastEnders*?

18 Of what is Silk Cut a well-known brand?

19 For what is PVC an abbreviation?

20 Suede takes its name from the French for which country?

Hard

Answers to QUIZ 146 – Young Adult Fiction

1	*The Maze Runner*	11	Four
2	*Divergent*	12	Bella Swan
3	*Mortal Engines*	13	1990s (1997)
4	Judy Blume	14	Christopher
5	*The Fault in our Stars*	15	Enemy
6	Holden Caulfield	16	An island
7	*The Book Thief*	17	Amsterdam
8	*Breaking Dawn*	18	*Sweet Valley High*
9	*To Kill a Mockingbird*	19	Billie Piper
10	Suzanne Collins	20	Once a year

1   How many days of competition are there in each World Rally Championship event?

2   Which retail group, whose companies include Top Shop and Dorothy Perkins, shares its name with a play by Sir Tom Stoppard?

3   Who had a no.1 hit with *I'm Too Sexy*?

4   Who won his second Best Supporting Actor Oscar for his role in the 2018 film *Green Book*?

5   How many points is the letter P worth in Scrabble®?

6   What ten-letter word, meaning the official stopping of an activity for a period of time, is taken from the Latin for "delay"?

7   In cricket how many inches wide is each wicket (three stumps)?

8   What do the letters SME stand for in relation to commerce?

9   In which card game might you make a bid of "abundance"?

10 Which band released the 1990s albums *Achtung Baby* and *Zooropa*?

11 The TV series *Crossroads* was set near to which English city?

12 *Pure and Simple* was the song released by the winners of which talent show?

13 Which country has the internet code .es?

14 Who played the title role as an adult in the 2018 film *Christopher Robin*?

15 What colour is the "B" in the eBay logo?

16 In the English Civil War, what feature gave the Roundheads their nickname?

17 What planet precedes "flytrap" to make the name of a carnivorous plant?

18 In what position does footballer Ruben Loftus-Cheek play?

19 According to the lyrics of a 1973 song, Milly-Molly-Mandy was as sweet as what substance?

20 What is the ultimate goal for Buddhists?

Easy

Medium

Hard

Answers to QUIZ 147 – Pot Luck

1	*Unforgettable*	11	Gin
2	A fish	12	Tameka Empson
3	Clint Eastwood	13	Glenn Miller
4	John McDonnell	14	Leather
5	Czech	15	Italy
6	2008	16	Medical Examiner
7	Martin Scorsese	17	Jack Nicholson
8	1940s (1949)	18	Zoo
9	Flexitarian	19	Natural Law Party
10	France	20	Wrestling

1 What substance would someone be working with if they were using an adze?

2 The name of which artist's tool also means to improve someone's image?

3 Which tool used by a blacksmith shares its name with part of the ear?

4 The name of which cutting tool is also US slang for a guitar?

5 Which part of a knife is also an old-fashioned word for describing a dashing young man?

6 For what is a billhook used?

7 What can follow "band", "bow" and "buzz" to make the names of DIY tools?

8 The name of which DIY tool can also mean a routine exercise?

9 What word can refer both to a lifting tool and a sailor?

10 In which two sports would a mallet be used?

11 What word is a direction-finding device in the singular and a tool for drawing circles in the plural?

12 What cutting tool are you said to bury when you settle an argument?

13 Who would use a "last"?

14 Which DIY tool is an anagram of a word meaning "to practise boxing"?

15 The term for what peg is an anagram of "lowed"?

16 What is a mattock?

17 Which hand-held device is sometimes used in the kitchen to lightly brown the tops of dishes?

18 What word can mean both a smoothing hand tool and a computer storage document?

19 What DIY smoothing tool is also the name of a tree?

20 A set square is what shape?

Answers to QUIZ 148 – Material

1	Canvas	11	Jersey
2	Silk	12	Wool
3	The Police	13	Elizabeth Taylor
4	*Dallas Buyers Club*	14	Cotton
5	Paisley	15	Madonna
6	Black Lace	16	IKEA
7	*Abracadabra*	17	Charlie
8	English embroidery	18	Cigarettes
9	Hessian	19	Polyvinyl chloride
10	Cotton	20	Sweden

QUIZ 151 – Pot Luck

ANSWERS ON PAGE 153

1 How is Mildred Hubble referred to in the title of a book series by Jill Murphy?

2 The town of Esbjerg is in which European country?

3 Brian Potter is the owner of which fictional TV club?

4 Which European football club plays home games at the Mestalla?

5 Which wildlife film-maker wrote the 2015 biography *The Shark and the Albatross*?

6 Bryson DeChambeau (b.1993) plays which sport?

7 Who played Jenny Lind in the 2017 film *The Greatest Showman*?

8 What is the more common term for a soubriquet?

9 Which foremost Italian Renaissance architect engineered the dome for Florence Cathedral?

10 In which decade was *Children in Need* first broadcast?

11 How many "marks of existence" are there in Buddhist tradition?

12 How many times did Gordon Banks win the FIFA Goalkeeper of the Year award?

13 To the nearest million, how many drivers were there in the UK in 1939?

14 What is the nearest railway station to Epsom Downs racecourse?

15 Which group topped the charts in 2003 with *You Said No*?

16 Who played Gary Ewing in the *Dallas* spin-off *Knots Landing*?

17 Crocuses are members of which family?

18 To the nearest hundred miles, how far does the Andes mountain range stretch?

19 What was the two-word term used for the area of extremely low pressure that reached North America in early 2019?

20 The name of which historical location in Surrey translates to "meeting meadow"?

Answers to QUIZ 149 – Pot Luck

1	Three	11	Birmingham
2	Arcadia (Group)	12	*Popstars* (Hear'Say)
3	Right Said Fred	13	Spain
4	Mahershala Ali	14	Ewan McGregor
5	Three	15	Blue
6	Moratorium	16	Closely-cropped hair
7	Nine	17	Venus
8	Small and Medium-sized Enterprises	18	Midfield
9	Solo whist	19	Sugar candy
10	U2	20	Nirvana

1   Which group had the original hit with *The Great Pretender* (1955)?

2   *Auf Wiederseh'n Sweetheart* was a US no.1 for which singer?

3   Anthony Benedetto was the real name of which 1950s music star?

4   *Because You're Mine* was the name of a film and million-selling single by which star?

5   Ben E King sang lead vocals on *There Goes My Baby* (1959) with which group?

6   *Songs our Daddy Taught Us* was a 1950s album by whom?

7   Which group backed Gene Vincent?

8   *Cry! Cry! Cry!* was the first single released by which singer?

9   Eric Hilliard were the first real names of which US artist?

10   Which artist released the album *Gallopin' Guitars*?

11   Which Christmas song by Gene Autry was the first US no. 1 of the 1950s?

12   *Black Coffee* is the most acclaimed album release by which 1950s star?

13   Little Richard released *Tutti Frutti* in which year?

14   "The wind in the willow played love's sweet melody" is a line from which Fats Domino hit?

15   *Splish Splash* was the first single by which singer?

16   In which country was Winifred Atwell born?

17   What was the name of the group that had a 1957 hit with *At the Hop*?

18   What colour is the word "Elvis" on Presley's debut album cover?

19   What was Frank Sinatra's middle name?

20   In which year did the first Grammy Awards take place?

Answers to QUIZ 150 – Tools

1	Wood	11	Compass (compasses)
2	Airbrush	12	The hatchet
3	Anvil	13	A cobbler or shoemaker
4	Axe	14	Rasp (spar)
5	Blade	15	Dowel
6	Pruning and cutting	16	A large pick
7	Saw	17	Blowtorch or blowlamp
8	Drill	18	File
9	Jack	19	Plane
10	Croquet and polo	20	Triangle (right-angled)

1   In which US State is Pebble Beach Golf Course?

2   Doug Hopkins was the founder of which 1990s band who had a 1996 hit with *Follow You Down*?

3   What does the term "glissade" mean?

4   As at 2018, how many National Parks were there in Wales?

5   The song known as *Ye Banks and Braes* is about which Scottish river?

6   *The Fairy-Queen* is a 1692 semi-opera by which composer?

7   What type of creature is a whinchat?

8   What did the French company Panhard et Levassor manufacture?

9   In which county is the parliamentary constituency of Amber Valley?

10 With which flower was horticulturist David Austin (d.2018) particularly associated?

11 Sir David Jason played what role in *Porridge*?

12 What is temporarily stored in a bowser?

13 What is the name of the main town on Alderney?

14 CH is the postcode for which UK city?

15 Omar Ali is the leading character in which 1985 film?

16 In which year did Dick Fosbury win the high jump gold medal at the Olympic Games?

17 The village of Pennan, used as a location in the film *Local Hero*, is in which Scottish county?

18 What was the title of the second novel in Philip Pullman's *His Dark Materials* trilogy?

19 In which year did the Windsor Legoland site open?

20 The walled city of Urbino lies in which Italian region?

Easy

Medium

Hard

Answers to QUIZ 151 – Pot Luck

1	*The Worst Witch*	11	Three
2	Denmark	12	Six
3	The Phoenix Club	13	Three million
4	Valencia	14	Tattenham Corner
5	John Aitchison	15	Busted
6	Golf	16	Ted Shackelford
7	Rebecca Ferguson	17	Iris
8	Nickname	18	4300
9	Filippo Brunelleschi	19	Polar vortex
10	1980s (1980)	20	Runnymede

Easy

1. Which country is the setting for the series *No Activity*?
2. Who won the 2018 celebrity edition of the singing contest *All Together Now*?
3. What is Bob's surname in the animated sitcom *Bob's Burgers*?
4. Dr Spencer Reid is a leading character in which crime series?
5. In which year was the first series of *Coast* broadcast?
6. Who plays the title role in the series *The Marvelous Mrs Maisel*?
7. Which BBC sitcom was focused on events at the Department of Social Affairs and Citizenship?
8. The question "Are you local?" is associated with which series?
9. Constable Kevin Goody was a character in which sitcom?
10. The Princeton-Plainsboro Teaching Hospital was the setting for which medical drama?

Medium

11. Patrick Jane was the lead character in which series?
12. *King of The Hill* was set in which US state?
13. East Surrey provided the setting for which series starring Richard Briers?
14. Which famous US sitcom is based on the book of the same name by Candace Bushnell?
15. Jay Cartwright was a character in which sitcom?
16. The 1999 film *Guest House Paradiso* was based on which series?
17. The 2018 series of *Autumnwatch* was broadcast from which US state?
18. Philip Smith, played by Don Warrington, was a student and tenant in which series?
19. In what year did the last episode of *Friends* air?
20. How many series of *Keeping Up Appearances* were made?

Hard

Answers to QUIZ 152 – 1950s Music

1	The Platters	11	*Rudolph The Red Nosed Reindeer*
2	Dame Vera Lynn	12	Peggy Lee
3	Tony Bennett	13	1955
4	Mario Lanza	14	*Blueberry Hill*
5	The Drifters	15	Bobby Darin
6	The Everly Brothers	16	Trinidad and Tobago
7	The Blue Caps	17	Danny and the Juniors
8	Johnny Cash	18	Pink
9	Ricky Nelson	19	Albert
10	Les Paul	20	1959

1 In what decade was the Highway Code first printed in colour?

2 The town of Alberobello lies in which Italian region?

3 What was the name of the record label that was the original home of The Happy Mondays?

4 AirBaltic is based in which European country?

5 Which German football club plays home games at Signal Iduna Park?

6 For how many years was William IV king of Great Britain and Ireland?

7 What is henbane?

8 Who played Tom Jones in the 1963 film of the same name?

9 UK Prime Minister Spencer Perceval was assassinated in what year?

10 "Midnight creeps so slowly into hearts of men who need more than they get" is a lyric from which 1979 song?

11 What is the literal meaning of the French term *faux pas*?

12 If the Norse version is Freya, which goddess is the Greek version?

13 Which country's flag features a lion holding a sword?

14 Malvolio acts as a steward to which character in *Twelfth Night*?

15 In which decade was the Liberal Party formed in the UK?

16 Who was the first US president to be awarded the Nobel Peace Prize?

17 What is the national motto of Greece?

18 Dick Clement and Ian La Frenais created which 1960s sitcom set in Newcastle-upon-Tyne?

19 What word completes the title of the RM Ballantyne novel *The Coral ___*?

20 Which fruit used to be called a melonette?

Answers to QUIZ 153 – Pot Luck

1	California	11	Blanco (Webb)
2	Gin Blossoms	12	Water
3	Glide (in dancing)	13	St Anne
4	Three	14	Chester
5	River Doon	15	*My Beautiful Laundrette*
6	Henry Purcell	16	1968
7	(Small migratory) bird	17	Aberdeenshire
8	Cars	18	*The Subtle Knife*
9	Derbyshire	19	1996
10	Rose	20	Marche

1 The German inventor Siegfried Marcus (d.1898) built three experimental cars powered by what method?

2 Gary Numan's hit *Cars* was taken from which album?

3 Which car manufacturer acquired the Bugatti brand in 1998?

4 *From a Buick 8* (2002) is a novel by which American author?

5 In 1952, which nobleman founded the National Motor Museum at Beaulieu?

6 The Porsche logo includes the coat of arms of which German city?

7 *Cartrouble* was a 1981 Top 40 hit for which band?

8 In which year was the annual MOT test first required for cars over three years old?

9 In 2014 the London Film Museum opened an exhibition of cars from which film series?

10 What is the name of Nissan's electric car, which was rated World Car of the Year in 2011?

11 The BMW-owned Plant Oxford is in which area of greater Oxford?

12 What was the first name of automobile pioneer Renault?

13 The Riley motor company had its headquarters in which English city?

14 Which luxury car brand manufactures the Portofino?

15 What did the car manufacturer Toyo Kogyo Co change its name to in 1984?

16 Since 2001, NASCAR's Sprint Cup has consisted of how many stock car races over 10 months?

17 In *Driving in My Car* by Madness, where was the car bought?

18 What nationality was Juan Manuel Fangio, who dominated Formula 1's first decade?

19 In which decade was the first Haynes Manual published?

20 Who played Niki Lauda in the 2013 film *Rush*?

Answers to QUIZ 154 – Television

1	Australia	11	*The Mentalist*
2	Laurie Brett	12	Texas
3	Belcher	13	*Ever Decreasing Circles*
4	*Criminal Minds*	14	*Sex and the City*
5	2005	15	*The Inbetweeners*
6	Rachel Brosnahan	16	*Bottom*
7	*The Thick of It*	17	New Hampshire
8	*The League of Gentlemen*	18	*Rising Damp*
9	*The Thin Blue Line*	19	2004
10	*House*	20	Five

QUIZ 157 – Pot Luck

ANSWERS ON PAGE 159

1 Ceviche is a dish of raw fish eaten on which continent?

2 Who won the Best Supporting Actor Academy Award for his role in the 2007 film *No Country for Old Men*?

3 The Pinnawala Orphanage in Sri Lanka is set up for the care of which type of animal?

4 In which English county is the Blists Hill Victorian Town museum?

5 Carpo and Elara are moons of which planet?

6 In which four-person winter sport does the main piece of equipment have a maximum length of 3.8m?

7 Germany shares a border with how many other nations?

8 In 2009, Yang Yong-eun became the first Asian winner of a golfing major championship. In which country was he born?

9 How is the very small bird *Regulus Regulus* more commonly known?

10 What is the meaning of the plant name "saxifrage"?

11 From which US state does Bruce Springsteen hail?

12 In what decade was Rudyard Kipling born?

13 in which year of the 1990s did the "Russian Constitutional Crisis" occur?

14 How is Rose Louise Hovick better known?

15 Which British bird has the nickname "storm cock"?

16 What is a saraband?

17 The 2018 film *If Beale Street Could Talk* was based on a novel by which author?

18 What is the capital of Costa Rica?

19 In which year was Swansea given city status?

20 Which city is also *Doctor Who* star Jodie Whittaker's middle name?

Answers to QUIZ 155 – Pot Luck

1	1950s (1954)	11	False step
2	Apulia	12	Aphrodite
3	Factory	13	Sri Lanka
4	Latvia	14	Olivia
5	Borussia Dortmund	15	1850s (1859)
6	Seven (1830-37)	16	Theodore Roosevelt (1906)
7	(A poisonous) plant	17	Liberty or death
8	Albert Finney	18	*The Likely Lads*
9	1812	19	Island
10	*Boogie Wonderland* (Earth, Wind & Fire)	20	Kiwi fruit

Easy

1 The Gulf of Taranto is part of which sea within the Mediterranean?

2 The Borromean islands are situated in which Italian lake?

3 Horsetail Fall is a seasonal waterfall located in which US National Park?

4 In which country is Mardalsfossen, Northern Europe's highest waterfall?

5 Which of the Great Lakes is 193 miles in length and 53 miles wide?

6 In 1928, adventurer Richard Hallburton paid a toll of 36 cents to swim which waterway?

7 The waters around which island were designated England's first statutory Marine Conservation Zone?

8 The Kerch Strait separates the Sea of Azov from what other sea?

9 How is the African lake Nalubaale or Nyanza referred to in English?

10 The German city of Koblenz lies at the confluence of which two rivers?

Medium

11 What is the English name of the lake known in German as *Genfersee*?

12 In which European country does the coastal city of Makarska lie?

13 Lake Biwa is the largest freshwater lake in which Asian country?

14 What is the Scottish word for a small stream or brook?

15 Crummock Water lies in which National Park?

16 The river Darling is the third-longest river in which country?

17 In which strait does the Italian island of Pantelleria lie?

18 To the nearest ten, what percentage of Earth is covered by water?

19 In which decade was the water industry privatised in the UK?

20 The Wetlands centre of Caerlaverock is situated in which Scottish county?

Hard

Answers to QUIZ 156 – Cars

1	Petrol	11	Cowley
2	*The Pleasure Principle*	12	Louis
3	Volkswagen	13	Coventry
4	Stephen King	14	Ferrari
5	Lord Montagu (Third Baron Montagu of Beaulieu)	15	Mazda
6	Stuttgart	16	36
7	Adam and the Ants	17	Primrose Hill
8	1967	18	Argentinian
9	James Bond	19	1960s (1965)
10	Nissan Leaf	20	Daniel Brühl

QUIZ 159 – Pot Luck

ANSWERS ON PAGE 161

1 Which organisation bought Lucasfilm in 2014?

2 *Scandalous* was a 2003 hit for which girl group?

3 Which archipelago is home to the Soay and Boreray breeds of sheep, and a quarter of the world's northern gannets?

4 The Royal Oak Foundation is an American organisation that supports the work of which British charity?

5 How many books are there in the Tanakh (Hebrew Bible)?

6 Ferdinand was the name of how many Holy Roman Emperors?

7 In which European country is the town of Kranjska Gora?

8 In which popular novel and film do the title characters move from London to a Yorkshire house called *The Three Chimneys*?

9 Who released a cover of Soft Cell's *Say Hello, Wave Goodbye* in 2001?

10 Domhnall Gleeson plays which character in the *Star Wars* film *The Force Awakens*?

11 The man of the match trophy in the Rugby League Grand Final is named after which Australian?

12 In cuisine, what does "parmentier" mean?

13 What is the English meaning of *sous-chef*?

14 Henri Dunant was awarded the first Nobel Peace Prize for his part in founding which organisation?

15 In relation to communications, for what does the "I" stand in ISDN?

16 In which decade was nitrogen discovered and isolated?

17 Who plays the male lead in the 2012 film *Seeking a Friend for the End of the World*?

18 What does a hygrometer measure?

19 The Harz mountains are in which European country?

20 The world's first quartz wristwatch was invented by which company?

Easy

Medium

Hard

Answers to QUIZ 157 – Pot Luck

1	South America	11	New Jersey
2	Javier Bardem	12	1860s (1865)
3	Elephants	13	1993
4	Shropshire	14	Gypsy Rose Lee
5	Jupiter	15	Mistle thrush
6	Bobsleigh	16	(Spanish) dance
7	Nine	17	James Baldwin
8	South Korea	18	San José
9	Goldcrest	19	1969
10	Rock-breaker	20	Auckland

1   *Achilles and the Tortoise* is the best known of the famous paradoxes by which philosopher?

2   In which country was David Hume born in 1711?

3   *In Praise of Folly* (1509) is a work by which Dutch philosopher?

4   In what year did Jean-Paul Sartre refuse the Nobel Prize for Literature?

5   What word completes the title of Michel Foucault's first major work, *Madness and ___*?

6   *Justice as Fairness* (1985) was a work by which philosopher?

7   "Ecosophy" and "deep ecology" are terms associated with which Norwegian philosopher?

8   John Stuart Mill had a major influence on which philosopher (d.1970)?

9   What nationality is Noam Chomsky?

10 In what century did Søren Kierkegaard live and die?

11 What was the first name of the famous philosopher Machiavelli?

12 Which Austrian became a professor at Cambridge in 1929 after serving in WWI?

13 Who wrote the 13th-century work *Summa contra Gentiles*?

14 The principle of which philosophy was defined by its founder as "the greatest happiness of the greatest number that is the measure of right and wrong"?

15 *The Birth of Tragedy* (1872) is a work by which philosopher?

16 Which philosopher has a "razor" principle named after him?

17 Which Australian philosopher argued the case for veganism in his 1975 book *Animal Liberation*?

18 Which philosopher became a tutor to Queen Christina of Sweden in 1649?

19 Who wrote the 1798 work *An Essay on the Principle of Population*?

20 What term describes the belief that knowledge should be gained from practical experience rather than theories?

Answers to QUIZ 158 – Water

1	Ionian	11	Lake Geneva
2	Lake Maggiore	12	Croatia
3	Yosemite	13	Japan
4	Norway	14	Burn
5	Ontario	15	The Lake District
6	Panama Canal	16	Australia
7	Lundy	17	Strait of Sicily
8	Black Sea	18	70% (approximately 71%)
9	Lake Victoria	19	1980s (1989)
10	Rhine and Moselle	20	Dumfriesshire

1   Which Bob Hoskins gangster film was released in 1980?

2   Folic acid and folate are two forms of which vitamin?

3   Estoril is a motor-racing circuit in which country?

4   Which playwright wrote the screenplay for *The Go-Between* (1971)?

5   To the nearest year, for how many years was John Paul II pope?

6   For what would you use a muddler?

7   What was the middle name of the poet Emily Dickinson?

8   "Los Leones" (The Lions) is the nickname given to which Spanish La Liga team?

9   What is the real first name of Pixie Lott?

10 What was the name of the UK act who scored 0 points in the 2003 Eurovision Song Contest?

11 Which Irish city has a name meaning "marsh"?

12 Denton and Reddish is a parliamentary constituency in which metropolitan county?

13 *Boy in Da Corner* (2003) was a breakthrough album for which rapper?

14 Who played trapeze artist Anne Wheeler in the 2017 film *The Greatest Showman*?

15 Which writer said "Always forgive your enemies - nothing annoys them so much"?

16 What is the meaning of the Latin phrase *sui generis*?

17 Who was the frontman of the English rock band Kula Shaker?

18 The volcanic island of Jan Mayen belongs to which country?

19 Margaret Tudor, sister of Henry VIII, was married to which Scottish king?

20 In which decade did Barbra Streisand win the Best Actress Oscar in her debut musical?

Easy

Medium

Hard

Answers to QUIZ 159 – Pot Luck

1	Disney	11	Harry Sunderland
2	Mis-Teeq	12	With potatoes
3	St Kilda	13	Under-chef
4	National Trust	14	The Red Cross
5	24	15	Integrated
6	Three	16	1770s (1772)
7	Slovenia	17	Steve Carell
8	*The Railway Children*	18	Humidity
9	David Gray	19	Germany
10	General Hux	20	Seiko (Astron)

1   Who was the first person to voice Holly the computer in the TV series *Red Dwarf*?

2   In which decade was *Hollyoaks* first broadcast?

3   What was Buddy Holly's real first name?

4   How many universities make up the Ivy League?

5   What is the common name of the plant *Eryngium maritimum*?

6   Who preceded Holly Willoughby as the presenter of the dating show *Streetmate*?

7   Hollywood Burbank Airport is known by the name of which comedian?

8   Who played the character Poison Ivy in the 1997 film *Batman & Robin*?

9   Who played Ivy in the TV series *Last of the Summer Wine*?

10   Which group had a 1980 hit with a cover of *Poison Ivy*?

11   Who played the title role in the 1947 film *Ivy*?

12   For which 1987 film did Holly Hunter receive an Oscar nomination?

13   In the traditional carol *The Holly and the Ivy*, the holly's bark is described as being as bitter as what?

14   Who was the original lead singer of The Hollies?

15   Who played Ivy Tilsley in *Coronation Street*?

16   Whose novels included *Brothers and Sisters* (1929) and *Mother and Son* (1955)?

17   What did the famous Hollywood sign originally read?

18   What was the title of Holly Valance's 2002 debut album?

19   In which year of the 1960s was *Bake Off* judge Paul Hollywood born?

20   What was the title of Frankie Goes to Hollywood's second album?

Answers to QUIZ 160 – Philosophy

1	Zeno of Elea	11	Niccolo
2	Scotland	12	Ludwig Wittgenstein
3	Erasmus	13	Thomas Aquinas
4	1964	14	Utilitarianism (Jeremy Bentham)
5	*Civilization*	15	Friedrich Nietzsche
6	John Rawls	16	William of Ockham (Occam's Razor)
7	Arne Naess	17	Peter Singer
8	Bertrand Russell	18	René Descartes
9	American	19	Thomas Malthus
10	19th century	20	Empiricism

Easy

Medium

Hard

1   The title character of the TV series *Baptiste* originally appeared in which 2014 TV series?

2   The 1960s cartoon character Quick Draw McGraw was what type of animal?

3   Calamondin, kaffir and Persian are all types of what fruit?

4   From where does the Ragdoll breed of cat originate?

5   By what name was CS Lewis known to family and friends?

6   Which actress co-starred with Ginnifer Goodwin in the 2011 film *Something Borrowed*?

7   Who won the 1996 Grammy for Song of the Year with *Change the World*?

8   What is the name of the central prayer of the Jewish liturgy?

9   Eosophobia is the fear of what?

10   In which city was Archimedes born?

11   George Washington was elected first US President in what year?

12   The National Glass Centre lies in which UK city?

13   In golf, what term is given to the right to play first?

14   What is the only colour used in a grisaille painting?

15   What is the name of the monster in *Beowulf*?

16   Aneto is the highest mountain in which European range?

17   Which US state is nicknamed "The Cotton State"?

18   Which supermarket chain was founded by Karl and Theo Albrecht?

19   What is the nickname of Morgan Freeman's character in *The Shawshank Redemption*?

20   The Gothic villa Strawberry Hill House, located in Twickenham, was built for which author?

Easy
Medium
Hard

Answers to QUIZ 161 – Pot Luck

1	*The Long Good Friday*	11	Cork
2	B9	12	Greater Manchester
3	Portugal	13	Dizzee Rascal
4	Harold Pinter	14	Zendaya
5	(Just under) 27	15	Oscar Wilde
6	Mixing drinks	16	Unique
7	Elizabeth	17	Crispian Mills
8	Athletic Bilbao	18	Norway
9	Victoria	19	James IV
10	Jemini	20	1960s (1968, *Funny Girl*)

Easy

1 An atom of methane has a single carbon atom and four atoms of which gas?

2 What is measured by the SI unit the coulomb?

3 What nationality was physicist Paul Dirac (d.1984)?

4 Which metalloid chemical element has the atomic number 14?

5 Electron cooling was pioneered in Russia in which decade of the 20th century?

6 What is the term for the science of seemingly inexplicable happenings?

7 Jonas Salk developed the polio vaccination during what decade?

8 Aoede and Iocaste are moons of which planet?

9 Which scientist said "However difficult life may seem, there is always something you can do and succeed at"?

10 How is the bacillus Calmette-Guérin vaccine better known?

11 Whose law states "extension is proportional to load"?

12 Which branch of physics is concerned with the relationship of heat with other forms of energy?

13 In which decade was the London Science Museum founded?

14 Regarded as "the father of modern chemistry", what nationality was Antoine Lavoisier?

15 Which part of the human brain is the largest?

16 The South Downs Planetarium and Science Centre can be found in which UK city?

17 Which acid has the formula HNO_3?

18 Of what is petrology the study?

19 What is measured in siemens?

20 As at the end of 2018, how many elements were there in the periodic table?

Medium

Hard

Answers to QUIZ 162 – Holly and Ivy

1	Norman Lovett	11	Joan Fontaine
2	1990s (1995)	12	*Broadcast News*
3	Charles (Holley)	13	Any gall
4	Eight	14	Allan Clarke
5	Sea holly	15	Lynne Perrie
6	Davina McCall	16	Dame Ivy Compton-Burnett
7	Bob Hope	17	Hollywoodland
8	Uma Thurman	18	*Footprints*
9	Jane Freeman	19	1966
10	The Lambrettas	20	*Liverpool*

1   What other name is given to the caudal fin on a fish?

2   Gregor Mendel formed his laws of inheritance in what decade?

3   Symphony No.38 by Mozart is named after which European city?

4   Tiny Tim is a variety of which salad item?

5   Who played Alfred P Doolittle in the 1964 film *My Fair Lady*?

6   Which English motor manufacturer bought the Wolseley brand in 1927?

7   Where are the headquarters of the European Court of Justice?

8   What was the title of George Michael's third studio album, released in 1996?

9   For which team did Rubens Barrichello make his Formula 1 debut?

10 How many years did it take Michelangelo to paint the ceiling of the Sistine Chapel?

11 What is the meaning of the Latin word *passim*?

12 How are Charles Kelley, Hillary Scott and Dave Haywood collectively known?

13 Guadalcanal is part of which island group?

14 What is measured by a pluviometer?

15 Andy Abraham was runner up to which winner of *The X Factor*?

16 To which family of animals does the badger belong?

17 Which company declared "Living Coral" to be the 2019 "Color of the Year"?

18 "Old John of Gaunt, time honoured Lancaster" is the opening line of which Shakespeare play?

19 *Call for The Dead* (1961) was the first novel by which author?

20 The biggest selling album in America in the 1960s was the soundtrack to which film?

Easy
Medium
Hard

Answers to QUIZ 163 – Pot Luck

1	*The Missing*	11	1789
2	Horse	12	Sunderland
3	Lime	13	The honour
4	USA	14	Grey
5	Jack	15	Grendel
6	Kate Hudson	16	The Pyrenees
7	Eric Clapton	17	Alabama
8	Amidah	18	Aldi
9	Dawn	19	Red
10	Syracuse	20	Horace Walpole

1 Colin Smith, played by Sir Tom Courtenay, is the leading character in which film?

2 Who won the Directors' Guild Award for the feature film *Gravity* in January 2014?

3 Who wrote the screenplay for the 1997 film *The Full Monty*?

4 In which film does Hugh Grant play Will Thacker?

5 Who directed the 2014 thriller *Lucy*?

6 Which classic 1966 film was adapted from a 1963 play by Bill Naughton?

7 Who is the ordinary minifigure in *The Lego Movie* (2014), who is mistaken for the greatest Master Builder?

8 Who played Sidney Stratton in the 1951 film *The Man in the White Suit*?

9 In which year did George Lucas release the film *American Graffiti*?

10 Sir Noël Coward played Mr Bridger in which classic film?

11 Who directed the 1992 film *The Crying Game*?

12 How many Oscars did *Shakespeare in Love* (1998) win?

13 Roald Dahl helped write the script for which 1968 film?

14 Omar Sharif and Julie Christie played the lead roles in which classic 1965 film romance?

15 In which century is *The Hunchback of Notre-Dame* set?

16 Who directed the acclaimed 2000 film *Billy Elliot*?

17 Which playwright wrote the work on which *A Man For All Seasons* is based?

18 What do the main characters attempt to steal in *A Fish Called Wanda*?

19 *Portobello Road* is a song from which 1971 film musical?

20 Who wrote and directed the 2019 film *Fighting with My Family*?

Answers to QUIZ 164 – Science

1	Hydrogen	11	Hooke's Law
2	Electrical Charge	12	Thermodynamics
3	English	13	1850s (1857)
4	Silicon	14	French
5	1960s (1966)	15	Cerebrum
6	Phenomenology	16	Chichester
7	1950s (1955)	17	Nitric acid
8	Jupiter	18	Rocks
9	Stephen Hawking	19	Electrical conductance
10	BCG	20	118

ANSWERS ON PAGE 169

1   How many series of the sitcom *Goodnight Sweetheart* were made?

2   Which country won the 2011 Cricket World Cup, defeating Sri Lanka to earn victory?

3   What word can refer both to a red gemstone and a cluster of boils?

4   In which 2007 film does Simon Pegg play Nicholas Angel?

5   Cavendish is a variety of what fruit?

6   What is the meaning of the Latin word *antebellum*?

7   Esther Summerson is a main character in which Charles Dickens novel?

8   Which is the most northwesterly of the five Great Lakes?

9   Who was the Roman equivalent of the Greek goddess Demeter?

10   The villages of Frigiliana and Nerja can be found in which Spanish province?

11   The Golden Bear is the highest award given at which film festival?

12   Who won his first golfing major in 2011 after 20 years and 54 attempts?

13   The Bank of England was founded during the reign of which king?

14   Ralph and Piggy are central characters in which classic novel?

15   A "monkey" is slang for how many pounds?

16   Konstantin Stanislavski was foremost in developing what approach to acting?

17   In biology, of what is muscology the study?

18   Charles University is in which European capital city?

19   Who was Tom Mix, after whom the bingo call is named?

20   Which organisation was founded by Chad Varah in 1953?

Easy

Medium

Hard

Answers to QUIZ 165 – Pot Luck

1	Tail fin	11	Here and there or throughout
2	1860s (1863)	12	Lady Antebellum
3	Prague	13	The Solomon Islands
4	Tomato	14	Rainfall
5	Stanley Holloway	15	Shayne Ward
6	William Morris (First Viscount Nuffield)	16	Mustelidae
7	Luxembourg	17	Pantone®
8	*Older*	18	*Richard II*
9	Jordan	19	John le Carré
10	Four years	20	*West Side Story*

ANSWERS ON PAGE 170

1   Six men from Dorset who formed a Friendly Society of Agricultural Labourers in 1834 are also referred to by what two-word name?

2   Franklin D Roosevelt first became US President in which year?

3   Who was King of England from 1399 to 1413?

4   Who was emperor when the Romans first landed in Britain?

5   What year marked the end of the 20th-century Irish Civil War?

6   In which European city did William Caxton set up his first printing press?

7   Benito Mussolini came to power in Italy in what year?

8   In what decade was King Juan Carlos I of Spain born?

9   Lindum Colonia was the Roman name for which English city?

10   Why were UK driving tests suspended from November 1956 until April 1957?

11   Catherine de Medici married which French king?

12   In what century was India's Mughal Empire founded?

13   Known to history simply as "Cleopatra", what was her regnal number?

14   Who became king of Sweden in 1973?

15   The Battle of Prestonpans took place in 1745 in which country?

16   Who founded the school known as the Lyceum in Athens?

17   For how many months did Yuri Andropov reign as Communist party leader in the Soviet Union?

18   Who was married to Lord Guildford Dudley (d.1554)?

19   How many states were in the United States when Texas joined?

20   Which city housed the Court of Charles I during the English Civil War?

Answers to QUIZ 166 – Film

1	*The Loneliness of the Long Distance Runner*	11	Neil Jordan
2	Alfonso Cuarón	12	Seven
3	Simon Beaufoy	13	*Chitty Chitty Bang Bang*
4	*Notting Hill*	14	*Dr Zhivago*
5	Luc Besson	15	15th century (1482)
6	*Alfie*	16	Stephen Daldry
7	Emmet	17	Robert Bolt
8	Sir Alec Guinness	18	Diamonds
9	1973	19	*Bedknobs and Broomsticks*
10	*The Italian Job*	20	Stephen Merchant

1 The 2012 Ryder Cup was held in Medinah. In which US state is the course located?

2 Who was both the first prime minister and first president of Kenya?

3 Mark Morrison had a worldwide hit with *Return of the Mack* in which decade?

4 What is the name of Cisco Ramon's superhero alter-ego in the TV series *The Flash*?

5 Chinese lantern and Japanese lantern are alternative names for which shrub?

6 Who starred in the 1983 film *The Dead Zone*?

7 What type of drink is manzanilla?

8 What type of instrument is the Japanese samisen?

9 The 2011 novel *Snuff* was written by which author?

10 What competition did Planet Waves Forever Young Daydream Believers win in 2019?

11 What is Alain Ducasse's (b.1956) profession?

12 Henry VIII died in which year?

13 What is measured in phons?

14 Who wrote the 1807 poem *To William Wordsworth*?

15 What word can describe both waffle and a soft cloth?

16 How was Jeanne-Antoinette Poisson (d.1764) better known?

17 Of which country was Vicente Fox president from 2000-06?

18 The quagga, an extinct species that was native to South Africa, was what type of animal?

19 In what environment would you find a glasswort plant?

20 In what year was the novel *Catching Fire* published?

Answers to QUIZ 167 – Pot Luck

1	Six	11	Berlin
2	India	12	Darren Clarke
3	Carbuncle	13	William III (with Mary II)
4	*Hot Fuzz*	14	*Lord of the Flies*
5	Banana	15	500
6	Before the war	16	Method acting
7	*Bleak House*	17	Moss
8	Lake Superior	18	Prague
9	Ceres	19	Star of silent-film westerns
10	Malaga	20	The Samaritans

1   What was the first name of Bea Arthur's character in the TV series *The Golden Girls*?

2   The Arthur's Day music events held from 2009 to 2013 were held to promote which brand?

3   What did Andersen Consulting change its name to in 2001 after splitting from Arthur Anderson?

4   Who sang the theme song to the 1981 film *Arthur*?

5   In which TV series did Arthur Darvill play the Reverend Paul Coates?

6   What nationality was the tennis player Arthur Ashe (d.1993)?

7   Who provided the voice of Arthur in the 2011 film *Arthur Christmas*?

8   Which play by Arthur Miller centres on the character of Willy Loman?

9   Arthur Wellesley, 1st Duke of Wellington, was born in which capital city?

10 Which actor was the first person to record MacArthur Park?

11 Arthur's Seat is situated in which Edinburgh park?

12 In which decade did Chester Arthur serve as US President?

13 Who played the title role in the 2017 film *King Arthur: Legend of the Sword*?

14 What was the title of the first single released by James Arthur after winning *The X Factor*?

15 In the 2009 revival of Minder, what relation was Archie Daley to Arthur Daley?

16 Whom did Arthur Tudor marry in 1501?

17 Which political party did Arthur Scargill found in 1996?

18 Who played Arthur Fowler in *EastEnders*?

19 What does the "C" stand for in the name of the science-fiction writer Arthur C Clarke?

20 Who succeeded Arthur Balfour (1st Earl of Balfour) as UK Prime Minister?

Answers to QUIZ 168 – History

1	Tolpuddle Martyrs	11	Henry II
2	1933	12	16th century (1526)
3	Henry IV	13	VII
4	Claudius	14	Carl Gustav XVI
5	1923	15	Scotland
6	Bruges	16	Aristotle
7	1922	17	15
8	1930s (1938)	18	Lady Jane Grey
9	Lincoln	19	27
10	The Suez Crisis	20	Oxford

Easy

Medium

Hard

1   Who played King Arthur in *Monty Python and The Holy Grail*?

2   Shaktism is a denomination of which religion?

3   What is the airport code for the Da Vinci Airport in Rome?

4   Which European football club did Claudio Ranieri manage from 2012 to 2014?

5   The 1984 single *You Take Me Up* was the biggest hit for which new wave group?

6   Hernán Cortés led the Spanish conquest of Mexico in which century?

7   *Citrus sinensis* is the Latin name for what fruit?

8   In what year was the Bond film *The World is Not Enough* released?

9   Charon is a moon which orbits which body?

10 The Cavachon dog is a cross between a Bichon Frise and which other breed?

11 *Britain's Next Top Model* first aired on Sky in which year?

12 Which root vegetables were used as a sweetener in European countries before the arrival of cane sugar?

13 What is the decimal equivalent of the hexadecimal number 37?

14 How many countries were founder members of ASEAN?

15 *The Weirdstone of Brisingamen* (1960) was the debut work by which children's author?

16 Who wrote the 1936 play *French Without Tears*?

17 Of what is histology the study?

18 The Kamchatka Peninsula lies in which country?

19 In what organisation of Ancient Greece would you find the "phalanxes"?

20 In which century did Ivan the Terrible live?

Answers to QUIZ 169 – Pot Luck

1	Illinois	11	Chef
2	Jomo Kenyatta	12	1547
3	1990s (1996)	13	Loudness
4	Vibe	14	Samuel Taylor Coleridge
5	Physalis	15	Flannel
6	Christopher Walken	16	Madame de Pompadour
7	Sherry	17	Mexico
8	A guitar	18	A zebra
9	Sir Terry Pratchett	19	On a seashore or salt marsh
10	Best in Show at Crufts	20	2009

1 Who was the first Liberal to become UK Prime Minister?

2 What is the name of the only unitary authority in both West and East Sussex?

3 On which Scottish island can the standing stones at Callanish be seen?

4 Foinavon is the name of a fence on which English racecourse?

5 In which country of the UK was the Fosse Way Roman road?

6 Composer Frederick Delius was born in which city?

7 Hartland Point is on the coast of which county?

8 Which English town became the first to be twinned with Walt Disney World?

9 The Stephen Joseph Theatre is in which English seaside town?

10 Which British animal has the Latin name *Meles meles*?

11 In which building is Charles Darwin buried?

12 In which Bedfordshire village is there a group of trees planted in the shape of a cathedral?

13 What title is given to the second most senior judge in England and Wales?

14 The village of Glenridding lies on which body of water in the Lake District?

15 What is the UK's largest bird of prey?

16 In which county is the country estate of Wrest Park?

17 Old Sarum was an old settlement on the site of which English city?

18 The town of Ironbridge, famous for its part in the Industrial Revolution, lies on which river?

19 Which of the UK's lighthouses is situated the furthest north?

20 Which castle is the seat of the Duke of Northumberland?

Answers to QUIZ 170 – Arthur

1	Dorothy	11	Holyrood Park
2	Guinness	12	1880s (1881-1885)
3	Accenture	13	Charlie Hunnam
4	Christopher Cross	14	*Impossible*
5	*Broadchurch*	15	Nephew
6	American	16	Catherine of Aragon
7	James McAvoy	17	Socialist Labour Party
8	*Death of a Salesman*	18	Bill Treacher
9	Dublin	19	Charles
10	Richard Harris	20	Sir Henry Campbell-Bannerman

ANSWERS ON PAGE **175**

1 Who wrote the 1872 novel *Under the Greenwood Tree*?

2 The character of Apollo Creed appears in which series of films?

3 What type of atmosphere is described by the German word *gemütlich*?

4 What is the English title of the 2017 Danish series in which Lars Mikkelsen stars as a priest named Johannes?

5 Which country hosted the 2010 Commonwealth Games?

6 In which two consecutive years did Jedward represent Ireland in the Eurovision Song Contest?

7 Bechstein's is a species of which flying creature?

8 The stately home of Waddesdon Manor lies in which county?

9 What are the first names of the food writers Hemsley + Hemsley?

10 John Cleese and Jamie Lee Curtis starred in which 1988 comedy?

11 If someone was applying embouchure, what would they be doing?

12 What does an agrostologist study?

13 Which poem by John Keats includes the line "O for a beaker full of the warm South"?

14 The shrub bougainvillea is native to which continent?

15 What is a banderole?

16 The writers of the Hollies hit *The Air That I Breathe* were credited as co-writers on which Radiohead single following a copyright suit?

17 Who played Donatella Versace in the TV series *The Assassination of Gianni Versace*?

18 How many golden stars are there on the flag of the European Union?

19 In which decade was the Royal Society founded?

20 Boca Juniors is which country's most successful football club?

Easy

Medium

Hard

Answers to QUIZ 171 – Pot Luck

1 Graham Chapman

2 Hinduism

3 FCO (Fiumicino)

4 Monaco

5 The Thompson Twins

6 16th century (1519-21)

7 Orange

8 1999

9 Pluto

10 Cavalier King Charles Spaniel

11 2005

12 Parsnips

13 55

14 Five (Indonesia, Malaysia, Philippines, Singapore and Thailand)

15 Alan Garner

16 Sir Terence Rattigan

17 Tissue (animal and plant)

18 Russia

19 Army

20 16th century (1530-84)

1   What age of horse runs in the Triple Crown races?

2   Aside from red and white, which colour appears on the X Games logo?

3   Chris Evert won how many Grand Slam singles championships in her career?

4   Which US boxer (d.2014) was nicknamed "The Hurricane"?

5   Which two winter sports are governed by the IBSF?

6   Dame Kelly Holmes completed her famous 800m/1500m Olympic double in what year?

7   Who was appointed coach of the French national rugby union team in December 2017?

8   Which French football team plays home games at the Parc Du Princes?

9   Which university's cricket ground is called Fenners?

10 Which legendary Portuguese footballer was the top scorer at the 1966 World Cup?

11 Which team won the 2018 BBC Sports Personality Team of the Year award?

12 How long does the actual playing time last in total in an NHL game?

13 How many players are on each team in a game of Australian Rules football?

14 In what Olympic event did Jan Železný set records?

15 Which football club was managed by Rafael Benitez from 2013 to 2015?

16 The Wanamaker Trophy is awarded to the winner of which event?

17 In which sport would you encounter an oxer?

18 What is the name of Sussex's limited-overs team?

19 With which team did Jean Alesi end his racing career in 2001?

20 Sir Roger Bannister ran the first four-minute mile in which English city?

Answers to QUIZ 172 – The UK

1	Lord Palmerston (Third Viscount Palmerston)	11	Westminster Abbey
2	Brighton and Hove	12	Whipsnade
3	Isle of Lewis	13	Master of the Rolls
4	Aintree	14	Ullswater
5	England	15	White-tailed eagle
6	Bradford	16	Bedfordshire
7	Devon	17	Salisbury
8	Swindon	18	River Severn
9	Scarborough	19	Muckle Flugga
10	The badger	20	Alnwick Castle

1   In which province of Spain does the city of Astorga lie?

2   How is Helen Parr better known in *The Incredibles*?

3   Which of the US Great Lakes is only 210 feet deep and contains 116 cubic metres of water?

4   Pearl Jam were a 1990s band from which Pacific Coast city?

5   What term is given to the sheen produced by age on an item?

6   Chat Moss, the peat bog, is a feature of which North of England city?

7   Who played James Brown in the 2014 film *Get On Up*?

8   The Holburne Museum is located in which English city?

9   What legal term describes an action intended to annoy or embarrass the defendant?

10 Gwendolen Harleth is the main character in which 1876 work?

11 In what year did Hawaii become the USA's 50th state?

12 Which term for an outline drawing is taken from the name of a French politician?

13 In which year was the women's hammer throw first included in the Olympic Games?

14 In Greek mythology, who was the husband of Helen of Troy?

15 What name for a dungeon is taken from the French for "to forget"?

16 Mount Kosciuszko is the highest point in which mountain range?

17 Who composed the series of 20th-century short piano pieces entitled *Visions fugitives*?

18 Who created Clifford, the Big Red Dog?

19 In which American city was the TV series *ER* set?

20 Sir John Chester and Edward Chester feature in which Dickens work?

Answers to QUIZ 173 – Pot Luck

1	Thomas Hardy	11	Playing a wind or brass instrument
2	*Rocky*	12	Grasses
3	Warm and friendly	13	*Ode to a Nightingale*
4	*Ride Upon the Storm*	14	South America
5	India	15	A flag or pennant
6	2011 and 2012	16	*Creep*
7	Bat	17	Penélope Cruz
8	Buckinghamshire	18	12
9	Jasmine and Melissa	19	1660s (1660)
10	*A Fish Called Wanda*	20	Argentina

1   What internet company was founded and launched as Confinity?

2   In the term JPEG, for what does the "E" stand?

3   What general subject does the Ispot website cover, helping with identification and queries?

4   *Drake's Fortune* and *Among Thieves* are the first two instalments of which video game series?

5   Flash memory was invented by Toshiba in which decade?

6   What name was given to the first portable CD player manufactured by Sony?

7   The Nintendo® Famicom was released in what year?

8   In which country is the company Alibaba based?

9   For what does the "B" stand in the name of the programming language COBOL?

10 Larry Sanger was a co-founder of which Internet site?

11 What was the name of the Apple operating system released in late 2018?

12 In what form of communication does the company Mimecast specialise?

13 Which 1980 interactive computer game, the first of a trilogy, was subtitled *The Great Underground Empire*?

14 What is the name of the non-proprietary Unix-like operating system used by Android devices?

15 The video game *Pac-Man*™ was first released in which year?

16 In which country did Spotify originate?

17 What is the term given to software programmed into a read-only memory?

18 Which electronics company began life in 1938 as a grocery trading store in South Korea?

19 In what year was the first Blu-ray™ disc player launched in Japan?

20 Who manufactured the Dreamcast video games console?

Answers to QUIZ 174 – Sport

1	Three-year-old	11	England netball team
2	Black	12	60 minutes
3	18	13	18
4	Rubin Carter	14	Javelin
5	Bobsleigh and skeleton	15	Napoli
6	2004	16	US PGA tournament
7	Jacques Brunel	17	Showjumping
8	Paris Saint-Germain	18	The Sussex Sharks
9	Cambridge	19	Jordan
10	Eusebio	20	Oxford

ANSWERS ON PAGE 179

1   What year saw the release of Michael Anderson's film *The Dam Busters*?

2   In which winter sport do players "light the lamp"?

3   Who was the captain of the 2018 US Ryder Cup team?

4   How old was US President Abraham Lincoln at the time of his assassination?

5   For what does the "G" stand in the name of the author JG Ballard?

6   How many series of *My Family* were made?

7   Which two colours appear on the flag of Latvia?

8   What type of creature is a stone loach?

9   What is the real first name of singer Smokey Robinson?

10 Alina Zagitova and Yuzuru Hanyu were 2018 Olympic gold medallists in which sport?

11 What was the title of the 2018 sequel to the German TV series *Deutschland 83*?

12 Harold Shand and Victoria are the names of the main characters in which 1980 film?

13 Popular in the 17th and 18th centuries in France, what type of instrument was a musette?

14 What is the more common term for protanopia?

15 Which poet wrote *Ode to the West Wind* (1819)?

16 "In the government yard in Trenchtown" is a lyric from which song?

17 What is the common name of the tree *arbutus unedo*?

18 How many operas were written by Rimsky-Korsakov?

19 Ladywood is a parliamentary constituency in which English city?

20 What was the regnal number of the Scottish king known as Robert the Bruce?

Answers to QUIZ 175 – Pot Luck

1	León	11	1959
2	Elastigirl	12	Silhouette (Étienne de Silhouette)
3	Erie	13	2000
4	Seattle	14	Menelaus
5	Patina	15	Oubliette (from the verb *oublier*)
6	Salford	16	The Australian Alps
7	Chadwick Boseman	17	Sergei Prokofiev
8	Bath	18	Norman Bridwell
9	Vexatious	19	Chicago
10	*Daniel Deronda*	20	*Barnaby Rudge*

1. Moonlets can be found around which planet in the solar system?
2. Aphrodite Terra is the southern continent on which planet?
3. What was the name of the Chinese probe that landed on the far side of the moon in January 2019?
4. In what year was Pluto "demoted" to the status of a dwarf planet?
5. Lacus Mortis or the Lake of Death can be found on what body of the solar system?
6. Which organisation is reponsible for assigning names to celestial bodies?
7. Of which planet is the Adams Ring a feature?
8. Enceladus is a moon of which planet?
9. Named after the Dutch astronomer who proposed it, what is the name of the belt of icy debris beyond Neptune's orbit?
10. The Buran space programme was focused around visiting where?

11. What was the name of the first escape velocity spacecraft invented in Russia in the late 1950s?
12. Ananke orbits which planet?
13. Egyptian priests labelled which planet "Her Desher"?
14. The famous astronomer Edmond Halley hailed from which country?
15. How are the three bright stars Alnitak, Alnilam and Mintaka known collectively?
16. *Mariner 1* and *Mariner 2* were sent to visit which planet?
17. The Borealis Basin can be found on which planet?
18. In which decade is Halley's comet next predicted to be visible from Earth?
19. What was the name of the first space station, launched in 1971?
20. The ancient Tablet of Ammisaduqa shows an early awareness of which planet?

Answers to QUIZ 176 – Technology

1	PayPal™	11	Mojave
2	Experts (Joint Photographic Experts Group)	12	Email
3	Nature	13	Zork
4	*Uncharted*	14	Linux
5	1980s (c.1981)	15	1980
6	Discman	16	Sweden
7	1983	17	Firmware
8	China	18	Samsung
9	Business (COmmon Business - Oriented Language)	19	2003
10	Wikipedia	20	Sega

1 What is another name for the cor anglais?

2 In 2010 Nicaraguan troops accidentally invaded the neighbouring Costa Rica because of a mistake on what?

3 Richard Carstone and Ada Clare feature in which Dickens novel?

4 Frank Oz voiced which character in the Star Wars series of films?

5 The Variante Ascari sequence of bends is on which motor racing circuit?

6 *London Fields* is a 1989 novel by which author?

7 What was the destination of the *RMS Queen Elizabeth*'s maiden voyage in 1940?

8 Which big-band leader recorded *A String of Pearls* in 1941?

9 *Cynara scolymus* is the Latin name of which vegetable?

10 What type of substance is meerschaum, used in making pipes?

11 The TV series *Friends* first aired in what year?

12 *Quit Playing Games (With My Heart)* was a hit for which boy band?

13 How old was JFK when he was inaugurated as US President?

14 Who starred in the 2014 film *Tammy*?

15 Which Chancellor of the Exchequer introduced Premium Bonds?

16 *Idle Thoughts of an Idle Fellow* was an 1886 collection of essays by which writer?

17 Chetham's Library is found in which UK city?

18 Who was Oscar-nominated for her starring role in the 1950 film *Sunset Boulevard*?

19 In which year was the Kyoto Protocol on climate change signed?

20 Which snooker player topped the rankings in March 2019 for the first time since 2010?

Answers to QUIZ 177 – Pot Luck

1	1955	11	*Deutschland 86*
2	Ice hockey	12	*The Long Good Friday*
3	Jim Furyk	13	Bagpipes
4	56	14	(Red-green) colour-blindness
5	Graham	15	Shelley
6	11	16	*No Woman No Cry* (Bob Marley and the Wailers)
7	Red and white	17	Strawberry tree
8	A fish	18	15
9	William	19	Birmingham
10	Figure skating	20	I

Easy

1. In the term *homo sapiens*, what does "*sapiens*" mean?

2. What is a wynd?

3. Quantophrenia is the obsessive reliance on what?

4. What was the Ancient Greek legal term to describe a city and its surrounding area?

5. What animal used to be called a camelopard?

6. What is the name for a ballet enthusiast?

7. The word jentacular describes which meal of the day?

8. What is the translation of the word "Sikh"?

9. What is epigraphy the study of?

10. What is fear or dislike of strangers or foreigners known as?

11. A person lying flat on their back is said to be in what position?

Medium

12. Which first name comes from the ancient Celtic word meaning "ruler of the world"?

13. A group of which type of bird might be called a flamboyance?

14. What does the word "pulchritude" mean?

15. The plant columbine takes its name from the Latin for which bird?

16. What is the meaning of the Latin phrase *ceteris paribus*?

17. What six-letter word beginning with "m" describes a person's immediate environment?

18. What is a farrago?

19. The word "chelonian" describes which animal?

20. Of what is astraphobia the fear?

Hard

Answers to QUIZ 178 – Astronomy

1	Saturn	11	*Luna 1*
2	Venus	12	Jupiter
3	*Chang'e 4*	13	Mars
4	2006	14	England
5	The Moon	15	Orion's Belt
6	International Astronomical Union	16	Venus
7	Neptune	17	Mars
8	Saturn	18	2060s (2061)
9	Kuiper belt	19	*Salyut*
10	Mars	20	Venus

Easy

1   The USA invaded which country in 1983?

2   On a ship, what is an orlop?

3   What does a clinometer measure?

4   The Verso was produced by which car company from 2009 until 2018?

5   In which sitcom does the lead character stay in The Linton Travel Tavern for the first series?

6   Jade Ewen represented the UK in which year in the Eurovision Song Contest with *It's My Time*?

7   Who presents the TV series *The Moaning of Life*?

8   Despite being told, he may never walk again after a car crash in 1949, which golfer went on to win three of the four majors in 1953?

9   In what decade did the War of the Austrian Succession take place?

10 Which *Star Wars* character's most famous line was "It's a trap!"?

11 *Marguerita Time* was a 1983 single by which rock group?

12 Thomas Keneally won the 1982 Booker Prize for which novel?

13 In what year did the Panama Canal first open?

14 In which winter sport is "icing" considered a foul?

15 In which European city is the Borghese Gallery?

16 Which horse won the 2019 Epsom Derby?

17 Who won her second double indoor 1500m and 3000m championship in 2019?

18 How many storeys are there in the Empire State Building?

19 What type of creature is a moloch?

20 What is dulse?

Medium

Hard

Answers to QUIZ 179 – Pot Luck

1	English horn	11	1994
2	Google Maps	12	Backstreet Boys
3	*Bleak House*	13	43
4	Yoda	14	Melissa McCarthy
5	Monza	15	Harold Macmillan (First Earl of Stockton)
6	Martin Amis	16	Jerome K Jerome
7	New York	17	Manchester
8	Glenn Miller	18	Gloria Swanson
9	Globe artichoke	19	1997
10	Soft white clay	20	Ronnie O'Sullivan

Easy

1 Of what was Demeter the Greek goddess?

2 Which Roman goddess was the equivalent of Irene?

3 The selkie is said to take human form on land and what form in water?

4 In German literature, who is known as "The Knight of the Swan"?

5 Who was the Greek god of sleep?

6 The mythical country of Lyonesse was said to border which English county?

7 In Greek mythology, who was the mother of King Minos?

8 Surtr was a fire god in which branch of mythology?

9 Who was the Greek goddess of Spring?

10 Which small creature of British folklore is said to perform household chores at night while the owners are asleep?

11 In Greek mythology, which creature arose from the blood of Medusa?

12 In which month was the Roman festival of Saturn (Saturnalia) held?

13 Who was the Greek god of the Underworld?

14 Sir Terry Pratchett's *Discworld* is based on the myth of a world supported on which two different types of creatures?

Medium

15 Ptah, the god of architects, was a deity in which branch of mythology?

16 On which island was the Greek Labyrinth said to have been built?

17 Into what was the nymph Daphne turned to avoid the attentions of Apollo?

18 Who was the Roman equivalent of Dionysus?

19 According to legend, which giant built the Giant's Causeway in Northern Ireland?

20 The Æsir–Vanir War was a battle amongst deities in which branch of mythology?

Hard

Answers to QUIZ 180 – Words

1	Wise	11	Supine
2	A narrow urban lane or alley	12	Donald
3	Statistics	13	Flamingo
4	Polis	14	Beauty
5	Giraffe	15	Dove (or pigeon)
6	Balletomane	16	Other things being equal
7	Breakfast	17	Milieu
8	Student (or Disciple)	18	A mixture, usually a confused one
9	Ancient inscriptions	19	Turtle
10	Xenophobia	20	Thunder and lightning

ANSWERS ON PAGE **185**

1   Gwen Dickey was the lead singer with which 1970s group?

2   In what year was Napoleon exiled to Elba?

3   What is the first name of the lead character in the film *Kes*?

4   In which decade was the Ford Cortina first manufactured?

5   What does the second "A" stand for in the name of AA Milne?

6   Which financial organisation was formed at the 1944 Bretton Woods Conference?

7   What name is given to a chicken younger than one year?

8   "Buster" is the nickname of which retired US boxer (b.1960)?

9   Which emperor restored order to Rome in the years following the death of Nero?

10   What attraction opened in Tokyo on April 15, 1983?

11   In which century were Napier's Logarithms discovered?

12   What was the name of Robert Mitchum's character in the 1962 thriller *Cape Fear*?

13   London's Royal National Theatre is an example of what style of architecture?

14   Which famous singer starred in the 1988 comedy *Hairspray*?

15   Musician Lester William Polsfuss was better known by what name?

16   What is the main ingredient of the Irish dish "boxty"?

17   What is the dominant religion in Cambodia?

18   In which decade did Mikhail Baryshnikov defect to Canada?

19   Jeff Murdock and Susan Walker were the main characters in which 2000s sitcom?

20   Who was Oscar-nominated for his role in the 2017 film *Get Out*?

Easy

Medium

Hard

Answers to QUIZ 181 – Pot Luck

1	Grenada	11	Status Quo
2	The lowest deck	12	*Schindler's Ark*
3	Angle of elevation	13	1914
4	Toyota	14	Ice hockey
5	*I'm Alan Partridge*	15	Rome
6	2009	16	Anthony Van Dyck
7	Karl Pilkington	17	Laura Muir
8	Ben Hogan	18	102
9	1740s	19	A lizard
10	Admiral Ackbar	20	(Edible) seaweed

Easy

1   Which club sold Kaká to Real Madrid in 2009?

2   Which club's motto, "Power in Glory", was proposed by Maxim Gorky?

3   Jürgen Klopp managed which team from 2008 to 2015?

4   In 1993, which Serie A player won the Ballon D'Or?

5   "The Armymen" (or Army Men) is the nickname of which Bulgarian club?

6   Which French team famously plays in violet tops at home?

7   Which team was runner-up in the 2017 UEFA Champions League?

8   In which city is the BSC Young Boys based?

9   Which club plays home games at the Estádio José Alvalade?

10 What colour are the home shirts of Spartak Moscow?

11 Which club won the Copa Del Rey in both 2001 and 2004?

12 In which year was the European Cup renamed the UEFA Champions League?

13 Which European club plays at St Jakob-Park?

14 Which German striker scored 31 times in 65 matches for Bayern Munich between 1995 and 1997?

Medium

15 "Les Girondins" is the nickname of which French team?

16 Which English team won the UEFA Cup for the third time in 2001?

17 What nationality is centre-back Vedran Ćorluka (b.1986)

18 Which international manager spent most his playing career at Torsby between 1964 and 1971?

19 Lothar Matthäus played over 300 games for which club?

20 "Los Blancos" is a nickname of which Spanish club?

Hard

Answers to QUIZ 182 – Myth and Legend

1	Agriculture	11	Pegasus
2	Pax	12	December (17th)
3	Seal	13	Hades
4	Lohengrin	14	Elephants (four) and a turtle (Hindu)
5	Hypnos	15	Egyptian
6	Cornwall	16	Crete
7	Europa	17	A laurel bush
8	Norse	18	Bacchus
9	Persephone	19	Finn McCool (Fionn mac Cumhaill)
10	Brownie	20	Norse

1 Who starred as Terl in the 2000 film *Battlefield Earth*?

2 *The Woodlanders* was an 1887 novel by which author?

3 To the nearest hundred, for how many years did the Romanov Dynasty rule in Russia?

4 "This ain't love, it's clear to see" is a lyric from which 2014 song?

5 What was a farthingale?

6 Croatia finished in which position in their first ever World Cup in 1998?

7 Who was the first British pilot to fly Concorde?

8 Who won her third Best Actress Oscar for her portrayal of Eleanor of Aquitaine in the 1968 film *The Lion in Winter*?

9 In 1962, Sir Chris Bonington and Ian Clough became the first Britons to climb which mountain route?

10 In which decade was Mother Teresa awarded the Nobel Peace Prize?

11 How was the English city of Gloucester known in Roman times?

12 Which occurred first, the Spanish Civil War or the Korean War?

13 In which ballet does Franz become infatuated with a life-size dancing doll?

14 How many members in total were there when the UN Security Council was founded?

15 In which town is Hill House, designed by Charles Rennie Mackintosh?

16 What is the name of Australia's largest desert?

17 In what year was British Airways founded?

18 Peter Capaldi played Danny Oldsen in which 1983 British film?

19 In *The Carnival of the Animals* by Saint-Saëns, which instrument plays the sound of the cuckoo?

20 In which year did the Battle of Bosworth Field take place?

Easy

Medium

Hard

Answers to QUIZ 183 – Pot Luck

1	Rose Royce	11	17th century (1614)
2	1814	12	Max Cady
3	Billy	13	Brutalist
4	1960s (1962)	14	Deborah (Debbie) Harry
5	Alexander	15	Les Paul
6	The International Monetary Fund	16	Potato
7	Pullet	17	Buddhism
8	James Douglas	18	1970s (1974)
9	Vespasian	19	*Coupling*
10	Tokyo Disneyland	20	Daniel Kaluuya

1   Expressionism emerged in the early years of which century?

2   Also known as *Secret Hearts*, *Drowning Girl* was a famous 1963 painting by which pop artist?

3   Dadaism eventually developed into what other movement?

4   Hans van Meegeren was a famous forger of paintings by which artist?

5   In what century did Ford Madox Brown live?

6   The Pitti Palace museum is located in which European city?

7   In which US city was Andy Warhol born?

8   Which colour was most notably associated with the French artist Yves Klein?

9   Abbott NcNeill were the middle names of which famous artist?

10 What term is given to painting with the medium of egg yolk?

11 The Laing Art Gallery is located in which UK city?

12 Phillip IV of Spain had which famous artist as his court painter?

13 *A Dance to the Music of Time* is the most famous work by which artist? (d.1665)

14 Which painting was famously slashed by a suffragette in London's National Gallery?

15 The 1960 work *Ascending and Descending* is perhaps the most notable work by whom?

16 Which artist was born in Delft in 1632?

17 Several paintings of *The Judgement of Paris* in the 1630s are by which artist?

18 In which European city is the KattenKabinet, a small museum featuring works of art that include cats?

19 What is the term given to a wall decoration that has its design scratched through the plaster layer?

20 Olga Khokhlova was the first wife of which major 20th-century painter?

Answers to QUIZ 184 – European Football

1	AC Milan	11	Real Zaragoza
2	Dynamo Moscow	12	1992
3	Borussia Dortmund	13	FC Basel
4	Roberto Baggio	14	Jürgen Klinsmann
5	CSKA Sofia	15	Bordeaux
6	Toulouse	16	Liverpool
7	Juventus	17	Croatian
8	Berne	18	Sven-Göran Eriksson
9	Sporting Lisbon (Sporting Clube de Portugal)	19	Bayern Munich
10	Red	20	Real Madrid

1. What was the title of the 2014 film directed by Richard Linklater, which was filmed over the course of 12 years?

2. What is the currency of Egypt?

3. In which branch of the arts is Natalia Osipova famous?

4. For how many years did Joe Louis hold boxing's undisputed World Heavyweight title?

5. Elektra Abundance and Blanca Rodriguez are characters in which American TV series?

6. The Hindu demigod Hanuman led an army of which creatures?

7. What kind of creature was Jonathan Livingston in the title of the 1970 novel by Richard Bach?

8. The Cuban Missile Crisis took place in what year?

9. What name is given to a line that joins two parts of a circle?

10. What three colours feature on the flag of Iran?

11. The Taj Mahal was built in which century?

12. In which industry were the Boulting Brothers involved?

13. The bluebuck, an extinct species that was native to South Africa, was what type of animal?

14. What Australian city shares its name with an airport in Florida?

15. Which footballer appears on the global cover art for the FIFA 15 video game?

16. Who wrote the novels *The Book of Dave* (2006) and *Umbrella* (2012)?

17. What was the name of the orphaned human boy in the 2014 animated film *The Boxtrolls*?

18. John Whaite won which reality TV show in 2012?

19. The Blue Men of the Minch are mermaid-like creatures said to be found off the coast of which country?

20. Which horse won the Cheltenham Gold Cup in 2019?

Easy

Medium

Hard

Answers to QUIZ 185 – Pot Luck

1	John Travolta	11	Glevum
2	Thomas Hardy	12	The Spanish Civil War
3	300 (304)	13	*Coppélia*
4	*Stay With Me* by Sam Smith	14	11
5	A hooped petticoat	15	Helensburgh
6	Third	16	Great Victoria Desert
7	Brian Trubshaw	17	1974
8	Katharine Hepburn	18	*Local Hero*
9	The north face of the Eiger	19	Clarinet
10	1970s (1979)	20	1485

1   The political figure Che Guevara was killed in which South American country in 1967?

2   What was Lenin's middle name?

3   Cambodia gained independence from France during which decade?

4   Hubert Humphrey was vice president to which US president?

5   The EU was established in which year?

6   The Oireachtas is the national parliament of which country?

7   Who was the 33rd President of the USA?

8   Folketing, meaning "people's thing", is which Scandinavian country's national parliament?

9   How many "points" comprised Woodrow Wilson's famous plan?

10   Cristina Fernández de Kirchner became president of which country in 2007?

11   How old was Napoléon when he died?

12   Taiwan was ceded to Japan from which other nation in 1895?

13   The first election in the world with female candidates, held in Finland, occurred in what century?

14   In which year did Konstantin Chernenko become leader of the Soviet Union?

15   In which year did the dictatorship of Augusto Pinochet end in Chile?

16   To what did Greece lower the minimum voting age in 2016?

17   Lesotho and Barbados both gained independence during which decade?

18   In what decade was the African National Congress founded?

19   Zuzana Čaputová became the first female president of which European country in March 2019?

20   Who became Prime Minister of Italy in June 2018?

ANSWERS ON PAGE 191

1   Silas Wegg appears in which Dickens novel?

2   *Alive Till I'm Dead* is the title of the 2010 debut album by which singer?

3   Which dwarf planet was the first object to be discovered in the Kuiper Belt?

4   How many countries in the world are smaller than Monaco?

5   The TV series *Narcos* is centred around which real-life Colombian drug dealer?

6   What was the title of David Mitchell's 2014 award-winning novel?

7   Starting stalls were first used in horse-racing in the UK in which decade?

8   Sir Andrew Aguecheck appears in which Shakespeare play?

9   What was the name of Humphrey Bogart's character in the 1951 film *The African Queen*?

10   Holi is a major festival in which religion?

11   Be is the symbol for which element?

12   Who composed the 1827 set of eight piano pieces known as the *Impromptus*?

13   In which year was American actress Jennifer Lawrence born?

14   In which country is the town of Hallstatt, known for its production of salt?

15   Who was the winning candidate in 2019's *Comic Relief Does the Apprentice*?

16   Early Nantes is a variety of which vegetable?

17   Which Brazilian player's birth name was Ronaldo de Assis Moreira?

18   Which has the lower typical gestation period, a lion or a sheep?

19   Which part of the body may be protected by an article carrying the BS2724 British Standards label?

20   Frankfort is the capital of which US state?

Easy

Medium

Hard

Answers to QUIZ 187 – Pot Luck

1	Boyhood	11	17th century (1632-53)
2	Egyptian pound	12	The film industry
3	Ballet	13	An antelope
4	11	14	Melbourne
5	*Pose*	15	Lionel Messi
6	Monkeys	16	Will Self
7	A seagull	17	Eggs
8	1962	18	*The Great British Bake Off*
9	Chord	19	Scotland
10	Red, white and green	20	Al Boum Photo

1   Who featured on the 2014 hit single *Flawless* with Beyoncé?

2   Which band had a 1999 hit album with *Performance and Cocktails*?

3   How many keys does a modern piano have?

4   In which year was the Eurovision Song Contest held for the first time?

5   *Ave Maria* was composed by whom in 1825?

6   Which name for a chord literally means "a harp"?

7   *Un Ballo in Maschera* is an 1859 opera by which composer?

8   Darren Hayes was a member of which 1990s band?

9   To whom did Beethoven originally dedicate his 3rd Symphony (*Eroica*)?

10 Dan Reynolds is the lead singer with which American band?

11 In Prokofiev's *Peter and the Wolf*, the wolf itself is represented by three of which instrument ?

12 In the name of the 1990s group SWV, for what does the "S" stand?

13 What is the name usually given to most music composed between 1600 and 1750?

14 In the name of a band formed in 1995, what number followed Matchbox?

15 Who had a hit album in 2014 with *Caustic Love*?

16 Who composed *Tales from the Vienna Woods*?

17 Gustav Mahler was born in Bohemia, in which former Empire?

18 Which band performed the song for the James Bond film *The World is Not Enough*?

19 In which year did Alanis Morissette release *Ironic*?

20 The *Karelia Suite* was a 19th-century work by which composer?

Answers to QUIZ 188 – World Politics

1	Bolivia	11	51
2	Ilyich (Vladimir Illyich Ulyanor)	12	China
3	1950s (1953)	13	20th century (1907)
4	(Lyndon B) Johnson	14	1984
5	1993 (Treaty of Maastricht)	15	1990
6	Ireland	16	17
7	Harry S Truman	17	1960s (both in 1966)
8	Denmark	18	1910s (1912)
9	14	19	Slovakia
10	Argentina	20	Giuseppe Conte

QUIZ 191 – Pot Luck

1 For what does the "S" stand in the name of author CS Lewis?

2 In which year was the sequel to *My Big Fat Greek Wedding* released?

3 Maurice Greene won the 100m Olympic Gold Medal in what year?

4 In which country was the Roman emperor Trajan born?

5 The order of Hukam is associated with which religion?

6 What term is given to a baby bat?

7 What did Zara and Mike Tindall name their daughter who was born in 2014?

8 Which of these mountains is higher, Aconcagua or Mount Logan?

9 *Sycamore Row* was a 2013 best-seller written by which author?

10 The short-lived TV series *Eldorado* aired for the first time in which year?

11 What is the meaning of the Latin word *thesaurus*?

12 What colour are the flowers of an amaranth?

13 In what year was Yasser Arafat awarded the Nobel Peace Prize?

14 In which Italian city would you find the Bardini Museum?

15 Which system allows a neuron to pass an electrical impulse to another cell?

16 How many Oscars did the original *Mary Poppins* film win?

17 "The Valley of Sin" is found at which golf course?

18 Who played the title role in the 1948 film *Scott of the Antarctic*?

19 The Genesis is a luxury car made by which company?

20 In which year did Roald Amundsen become the first man to reach the South Pole?

Easy · **Medium** · **Hard**

Answers to QUIZ 189 – Pot Luck

1 *Our Mutual Friend*
2 Professor Green
3 Pluto
4 One (Vatican City)
5 Pablo Escobar
6 *The Bone Clocks*
7 1960s (1965 at Newmarket)
8 *Twelfth Night*
9 Charlie Allnut
10 Hinduism
11 Beryllium
12 Franz Schubert
13 1990
14 Austria
15 Kelly Hoppen
16 Carrot
17 Ronaldinho
18 A lion (110/152 days respectively)
19 The eyes
20 Kentucky

1 Which US singer had a 1980 hit with *It's My Turn*?

2 In which year did Tina Turner release the album *Private Dancer*?

3 What was it necessary to do to travel on a turnpike road?

4 In which decade was the first Turner Prize awarded?

5 "Turn down the lights, turn down the bed" are the opening lines to which Bonnie Raitt single?

6 In which 1990s TV series did Janine Turner play pilot Maggie O'Connell?

7 What type of creature is a turnstone?

8 *Turn the Music Up* was a 1979 hit for which US band?

9 Who might be referred to as a "turnkey"?

10 For which 1986 film did Kathleen Turner receive a Best Actress Oscar nomination?

11 What was the first year of the 21st century in which the Open golf championship was played at Turnberry?

12 What was the name of Aidan Turner's character in *The Hobbit* series of films?

13 In which decade did Cher have a hit with *If I Could Turn Back Time*?

14 For what does the "M" stand in the name of JMW Turner?

15 Which group released the 1965 album *Turn! Turn! Turn!*?

16 To what genus of plants do turnips belong?

17 Who played "Bootstrap Bill" Turner in the second and third Pirates of the Caribbean films?

18 What was the name of the dog that accompanied *Turner* in the title of a 1989 film starring Tom Hanks?

19 Viscount Charles Townshend, known as "Turnip Townshend" for his interest in agriculture, was born in which century?

20 *Turn it On Again* was a 1999 greatest hits album by which band?

Answers to QUIZ 190 – Music

1	Nicki Minaj	11	French horn
2	Stereophonics	12	Sisters (With Voices)
3	88	13	Baroque
4	1956	14	Twenty
5	Schubert	15	Paolo Nutini
6	Arpeggio	16	Johann Strauss II
7	Verdi	17	Austrian Empire
8	Savage Garden	18	Garbage
9	Napoléon	19	1996
10	Imagine Dragons	20	Sibelius

ANSWERS ON PAGE 195

1 In which year did Boris Yeltsin win his second election as Russian president?

2 The Mariana Islands are located in which ocean?

3 What form does an epistolary novel take?

4 Who played the Acid Queen in the 1975 film *Tommy*?

5 *The Battle of the Books* was a 1704 satire by whom?

6 What ten-letter word Latin word denotes approval to publish?

7 Who won the Best Supporting Actor Oscar for his role in the 1975 film *The Sunshine Boys* at the age of 80?

8 In which decade did the "Open Era" begin in tennis?

9 For which 1979 film did the title characters win the Best Actor and Best Actress Oscars?

10 In which country did the Rose Revolution take place in 2003?

11 What is the largest inland body of water in the world?

12 In which year did the Mark I Mini go on sale?

13 First made in 1972, what was the Sinclair Executive?

14 White Scar Cave is in which National Park?

15 In which decade did Sri Lanka become an official test playing cricket team?

16 *In the City* and *The Modern World* were 1977 singles by which band?

17 Who created the character of Fungus the Bogeyman?

18 From which country does the appaloosa horse originate?

19 Halakha are civil laws in which major religion?

20 Brick Lane is in which London borough?

Easy

Medium

Hard

Answers to QUIZ 191 – Pot Luck

1	Staples	11	Treasure
2	2016	12	Red
3	2000	13	1994
4	Spain	14	Florence
5	Sikhism	15	Synapse
6	A pup	16	Five
7	Mia	17	Old Course, St Andrews
8	Aconcagua	18	Sir John Mills
9	John Grisham	19	Hyundai
10	1992	20	1911

ANSWERS ON PAGE 196

1 *When We Were Kings* is an Oscar-winning documentary about which sport?

2 Which sporting team of 1919 featured in the film *Field of Dreams*?

3 In which decade was *Rocky II* released?

4 Who played jockey Red Pollard in the 2003 film *Seabiscuit*?

5 The 1986 film *The Color of Money* was a sequel to which 1961 film?

6 Who played Will Ferrell's ice skating partner in the 2007 film *Blades of Glory*?

7 Maggie Fitzgerald is the leading character in which boxing film?

8 Who directed the 1991 film *Point Break*?

9 What was the title of the 2005 film in the Herbie series of motor-racing films?

10 The 2014 film *Foxcatcher* focused on what sport?

11 Who played Harold Abrahams in the 1981 film *Chariots of Fire*?

12 Who directed the 1996 golf film *Tin Cup*?

13 *This Sporting Life* (1963) features which sport?

14 Who played Jess in the 2002 film *Bend it Like Beckham*?

15 Micky Ward was the leading character in which 2010 boxing film?

16 In which 1977 film did Paul Newman play ice hockey coach Reggie Dunlop?

17 Who played the title role in the 2000 golfing film *The Legend of Bagger Vance*?

18 Which British winter sports competitor did Taron Egerton portray in a 2015 film directed by Dexter Fletcher?

19 What was the title of the 1996 film that starred basketball player Michael Jordan?

20 Dorothy Boyd is the love interest of the title character in which 1996 film?

Answers to QUIZ 192 – About Turn

1	Diana Ross	11	2009
2	1984	12	Kili
3	Pay a toll	13	1980s (1989)
4	1980s (1984)	14	Mallord
5	*I Can't Make You Love Me*	15	The Byrds
6	*Northern Exposure*	16	Brassicas
7	A bird	17	Stellan Skarsgård
8	The Players Association	18	Hooch
9	A jailer or warder	19	17th century (1674)
10	*Peggy Sue Got Married*	20	Genesis

Easy
Medium
Hard

1   Which Scottish football club did actor Martin Compston sign for after leaving school?

2   In George Orwell's *Animal Farm*, what kind of animal is "Old Major"?

3   Which luxury car brand has its headquarters at Gaydon in Warwickshire?

4   Chantelle Houghton was the first "non-celebrity" to win which reality TV series?

5   Which female singer released the album *A Perfect Contradiction* (2014)?

6   Ivan the Terrible served as the Grand Prince of which city?

7   The film *Notes on a Scandal* was based on a novel by which author?

8   Who was man of the match in the 2002 FIFA World Cup final?

9   Pernicious anaemia is caused by the deficiency of which vitamin?

10 In what decade did Richard Branson found Virgin Atlantic?

11 The Great Basin Desert is on which continent?

12 In what year did Black Sabbath release the single and album *Paranoid*?

13 Tórshavn is the capital of which group of islands?

14 Which American actor starred in the 1989 film *The Tall Guy*?

15 What title is shared by a Rossini opera and a 1988 album by Marillion?

16 The division of North and South Korea occurred in which decade?

17 The original 1935 film *The Thirty-Nine Steps* starred whom as Richard Hannay?

18 In which French city is Merignac Airport located?

19 Deimos is a moon of which planet?

20 In which Indian city is Hawa Mahal, the Palace of the Winds?

Answers to QUIZ 193 – Pot Luck

1	1996	11	Caspian Sea
2	The Pacific	12	1959
3	A series of letters	13	Pocket calculator
4	Tina Turner	14	Yorkshire Dales
5	Jonathan Swift	15	1980s (1981)
6	*Imprimatur*	16	The Jam
7	George Burns	17	Raymond Briggs
8	1960s (1968)	18	USA
9	*Kramer vs. Kramer*	19	Judaism
10	Georgia	20	Tower Hamlets

Easy

1 To whom was Stevie Wonder's song *Happy Birthday* dedicated?

2 Who released the 2018 album *Staying at Tamara's*?

3 Who had a 1978 hit with *If I Can't Have You*?

4 Dave Hill and Don Powell were members of which group?

5 The single *Don't Stand So Close to Me* was taken from which album by the Police?

6 What was the title of Minnie Riperton's only UK chart hit?

7 *Wrecking Ball* appears on which Miley Cyrus album?

8 In which year did the Who release their eighth studio album *Who Are You*?

9 *Lovefool* was a 1996 single by which group?

10 *Bedshaped* and *Everybody's Changing* are tracks on which 2004 album by Keane?

11 Who composed the Monkees' hit *I'm a Believer*?

12 *Lost & Found* was the 2018 debut album of which singer?

13 On which island was the band Level 42 formed?

14 Which member of Queen wrote *Don't Stop Me Now*?

Medium

15 1997's *Everybody Knows (Except You)* was by which Northern Ireland group?

16 Which rapper featured on Katy Perry's 2010 single *California Gurls*?

17 In which year did Prince revert to using his name instead of a symbol?

18 Who won the British Breakthrough Act at the 2017 Brit Awards?

19 *Now Those Days Are Gone* (1982) was the second UK no.1 for which group?

20 What was the title of Olly Murs' sixth studio album, released in 2018?

Hard

Answers to QUIZ 194 – Sporting Films

1	Boxing	11	Ben Cross
2	Chicago White Sox	12	Ron Shelton
3	1970 (1979)	13	Rugby league
4	Tobey Maguire	14	Parminder Nagra
5	*The Hustler*	15	*The Fighter*
6	John Heder	16	*Slap Shot*
7	*Million Dollar Baby*	17	Will Smith
8	Kathryn Bigelow	18	Eddie "the Eagle" Edwards
9	*Herbie: Fully Loaded*	19	*Space Jam*
10	Wrestling	20	*Jerry Maguire*

1   What was the name of the 1991 novel by Martin Amis which runs backwards?

2   *Sigh No More* is a Brit Award Best Album winner by which band?

3   What nationality is author Anne Rice (b.1941)?

4   What is the literal meaning of the Latin term *in camera*?

5   *Hit That Perfect Beat* was a 1985 hit for which group?

6   Which German club plays home games at the BayArena?

7   What type of animal is a quoll?

8   Who starred as Charles van Doren in the 1994 film *Quiz Show*?

9   "The Five Thieves" is a central concept in which religion?

10   Esme Young and Patrick Grant are judges associated with which TV competition?

11   The Coral Sea lies to the west of which ocean?

12   What is the airport code for Beijing International?

13   *Couldn't Have Said it Better* was a 2003 album by which US singer?

14   Matt Dawson was runner-up to which other sportsman on *Strictly Come Dancing*?

15   Who directed the 1974 film *Chinatown*?

16   Which US state is nicknamed "The Land of the Midnight Sun"?

17   Who won the 2015 Australian Men's Open tennis championship?

18   In which decade was actor Toby Jones born?

19   Which celebrity's Oscar's selfie became one of the most re-tweeted photos of all time in 2014?

20   El Hierro and La Gomera are part of which archipelago?

Answers to QUIZ 195 – Pot Luck

1	Greenock Morton	11	North America
2	Pig (a boar)	12	1970
3	Aston Martin	13	The Faroe Islands
4	*Celebrity Big Brother*	14	Jeff Goldblum
5	Paloma Faith	15	*The Thieving Magpie*
6	Moscow	16	1940s (1948)
7	Zoë Heller	17	Robert Donat
8	Ronaldo	18	Bordeaux
9	B12	19	Mars
10	1980s (1984)	20	Jaipur

ANSWERS ON PAGE 200

Easy

1   The word "hundred" comes from the old Norse "hundrath" meaning how many?

2   Brazil is bordered by how many countries?

3   What position does theta occupy in the Greek alphabet?

4   An icosagon has how many sides?

5   A Goliath bet is the backing of eight horses, including how many doubles?

6   What letter is used to represent an imaginary number in mathematics?

7   Who had a 1979 hit with *Lucky Number*?

8   What is the subtitle of the Shakespeare play *Twelfth Night*?

9   How many seconds are there in six minutes?

10 Who played FBI agent Don Eppes in the TV series *NUMB3RS*?

11 What number is represented by the Roman numerals XLIX?

12 What is the fifth prime number?

Medium

13 The story of which missionary was told in the 1958 film *The Inn of the Sixth Happiness*?

14 What is four factorial, written as 4!?

15 What two numbers appear on a UK number plate for a car registered in September 2017?

16 The 1987 film *The Fourth Protocol* was based on a novel by which author?

17 In hexadecimal, what number does the letter B represent?

18 Which is the seventh book of the Old Testament?

19 Who recorded the song *Eighth Day*, included on the soundtrack of the 1980 film *Breaking Glass*?

20 How many books make up Euclid's *Elements*?

Hard

Answers to QUIZ 196 – Pop Music

1   Martin Luther King Jr
2   George Ezra
3   Yvonne Elliman
4   Slade
5   *Zenyatta Mondatta*
6   *Lovin' You* (1975)
7   *Bangerz*
8   1978
9   The Cardigans
10 *Hopes and Fears*
11 Neil Diamond
12 Jorja Smith
13 The Isle of Wight
14 Freddie Mercury
15 The Divine Comedy
16 Snoop Dogg
17 2000
18 Rag'n'Bone Man
19 Bucks Fizz
20 *You Know I Know*

1 Which of Dvorak's symphonies is known as the *New World Symphony*?

2 How many countries does Bolivia border?

3 Which of the Great Lakes is 307 miles in length and 118 miles at its widest?

4 What was the subtitle of the 2013 *Percy Jackson* film?

5 *Need You Now* was a 2009 hit for which group?

6 What would a quern-stone have been used for?

7 What is the name of the female panda who arrived at Edinburgh Zoo in 2011?

8 Smriti is a major text in which religion?

9 Who was the Roman equivalent of the Greek goddess Hestia?

10 In which European country is the Mateus Palace located?

11 The Welsh Grand National is run at which racecourse annually?

12 *Outlandos D'Amour* was the 1978 debut album by which group?

13 In which English county is the sitcom *White Gold* set?

14 Which actor returned to the boxing ring for a professional bout in 2014 aged 62?

15 The 1953 film *From Here to Eternity* was set in which US state?

16 Which occurred earlier, the second Boer War or the Boxer Rebellion?

17 Which car company uses the slogan "New Thinking, New Possibilities"?

18 The name of which condition comes from the Greek for "to breathe hard"?

19 What age was Edward VI when he became king of England?

20 What type of creature is a Swedish Blue?

Answers to QUIZ 197 – Pot Luck

1	*Time's Arrow*	11	Pacific Ocean
2	Mumford and Sons	12	PEK
3	American	13	Meat Loaf
4	In the room	14	Mark Ramprakash
5	Bronski Beat	15	Roman Polanski
6	Bayer Leverkusen	16	Alaska
7	Marsupial	17	Novak Djokovic
8	Ralph Fiennes	18	1960s (1966)
9	Sikhism	19	Ellen DeGeneres
10	*The Great British Sewing Bee*	20	The Canary Islands

Easy

1   According to the Schlieffen Plan, how many weeks was Russia expected to take to mobilise?

2   What was the first name of Commander Haig (d.1928)?

3   Ferdinand I was the tsar of which country during WWI?

4   German and Austrian forces defeated which nation in the Battle of Caporetto?

5   Which pandemic disease caused a massive loss of life at the end of the war?

6   What nickname was given to the Accrington battalion of the East Lancashire Regiment?

7   To which country did Kaiser Wilhelm II flee after abdicating in November 1918?

8   How was Margaretha Zelle better known during the war?

9   In 1918, Arthur Balfour held which Cabinet position in Britain?

10 In order to quell calls for his abdication, which Prince did the Kaiser appoint as chancellor of the German Empire from October 3 to November 9, 1918?

Medium

11 What was the first name of Lord Kitchener?

12 In what year was Ludendorff appointed German Chief of Staff?

13 In which country did the Battle of Passchendaele take place?

14 Messines Ridge was a battle site near which town?

15 Queen Wilhemina was the Queen of which country during WWI?

16 The Zimmerman Telegram was intended to urge which nation to attack the USA?

17 To the nearest month, how long did the Battle of Verdun, the longest battle of the war, last?

18 Vimy Ridge surrounded which Belgian city?

19 In what year did Russia and Germany sign the Treaty of Brest-Litovsk?

20 Who was the Prime Minister of France when Verdun was attacked in 1916?

Hard

---

1   Which former *Glee* actor won a Golden Globe award for his role in the TV series *The Assassination of Gianni Versace*?

2   Breguet, established in 1775, are world renowned manufacturers of what?

3   Brno is the second largest city of which European nation?

4   *The Admirable Crichton* was a work by which author?

5   The Napoleonic Wars lasted for how many years?

6   Who wrote the 2009 novel *One Day*?

7   Which 2010 film, set in the 1960s, dramatised a strike by sewing machinists?

8   The bittern is part of which family of birds?

9   Epistemology is the study of what?

10   "Superbad, Superdad" was the tag line of which 2010 animated film?

11   Framwellgate is an area in which North of England city?

12   Which well-known children's artist designed the *Blue Peter* logo?

13   In what decade did Iron Maiden release the album *The Number of the Beast*?

14   *Ursus maritimus* is the scientific name of which mammal?

15   Due to his habit of losing his temper on course, which golfer earned the nickname "The Towering Inferno"?

16   What was the name of the character played by Richard Ayoade in *The IT Crowd*?

17   Adrian Lewis (b.1985) is a leading player in which indoor game?

18   *Ascot Gavotte* is a song from which musical?

19   Bertha Mason was the first wife of which 19th-century literary character?

20   The Polden Hills lie in which English county?

Answers to QUIZ 199 – Pot Luck

1	Ninth	11	Chepstow
2	Five (Argentina, Chile, Brazil, Paraguay, Peru)	12	The Police
3	Michigan	13	Essex
4	*Sea of Monsters*	14	Mickey Rourke
5	Lady Antebellum	15	Hawaii
6	Grinding	16	Second Boer War
7	Tian Tian	17	Hyundai
8	Hinduism	18	Asthma
9	Vesta	19	Nine years old
10	Portugal	20	A duck

ANSWERS ON PAGE 204

Easy

1   Asakusa and Ginza are districts of which capital city?

2   Basutoland is the former name of which modern-day country?

3   Ticino is a region of which European country?

4   How is "the Savage Mountain" more widely known?

5   Dulles Airport serves which US city?

6   Which is the only South American country to have English as its official language?

7   Bellagio lies on the shore of which Italian lake?

8   If your geographical location was 0 degrees latitude and 0 degrees longitude, where in the world would you be?

9   The Ha'penny Bridge lies in which Irish city?

10   Monrovia is the capital of which African country?

11   The Iguazú Falls lie between which two South American countries?

12   Which city lies at the confluence of the River Itchen and the River Test?

13   Which American state has Topeka as its capital?

14   Kirstenbosch National Botanic Garden lies at the foot of which mountain?

Medium

15   How are the provinces of New Brunswick, Nova Scotia and Prince Edward Island collectively referred to?

16   In which country is St Hilarion castle, said to have inspired Walt Disney?

17   The Quechee Gorge is located in which US state?

18   Which Irish city lies on the River Corrib?

19   Which three colours are featured on the Hungarian flag?

20   In which country is the UNESCO-listed city of Valparaíso?

Hard

Answers to QUIZ 200 – World War I

1	Six weeks	11	Horatio (but known as Herbert)
2	Douglas	12	1916
3	Bulgaria	13	Belgium
4	Italy	14	Ypres
5	Spanish flu	15	The Netherlands
6	Accrington Pals	16	Mexico
7	The Netherlands	17	Ten months
8	Mata Hari	18	Arras
9	Foreign Secretary	19	1918
10	Maximillian (of Baden)	20	(Aristide) Briand

1 "Strawberry Thief" is a famous textile pattern by which designer?

2 Which 2003 novel features the characters of Henry DeTamble and Clare Abshire?

3 *Permission to Land* is a Brit Award Best Album winner by which band?

4 Is the Pays de la Loire region in the east of France or the west?

5 In what decade was John Grisham's novel *The Client* published?

6 The Giro d'Italia cycle race was first run in which decade?

7 What position does omicron occupy in the Greek alphabet?

8 What is the name of Alan Partridge's long suffering assistant in the TV series *I'm Alan Partridge*?

9 How many times is the water jump hurdled in a 3000m steeplechase event?

10 What is the capital of the US state of Florida?

11 What was the title of the 2017 release in the *Fast and Furious* franchise?

12 "Coming out of my cage and I've been doing just fine'" is a lyric from which song?

13 In heraldry, what word is used to describe an animal depicted standing on its hind legs?

14 *Dance Away* was a 1979 hit for which band?

15 What was the subtitle of the 1997 sequel to the film *Speed*?

16 Which English county shares its name with a horse-drawn carriage?

17 In what key is a piece of music that has four sharps as its key signature?

18 Ammonia is produced by mixing nitrogen with which other chemical element?

19 Which Hindu god is depicted with the head of an elephant?

20 GBG is the international car registration letter for which island?

Easy

Medium

Hard

Answers to QUIZ 201 – Pot Luck

1	Darren Criss	11	Durham
2	Watches	12	Tony Hart
3	Czechia/Czech Republic	13	1980s (1982)
4	JM Barrie	14	Polar bear
5	12	15	Tom Weiskopf
6	David Nicholls	16	Maurice Moss
7	*Made in Dagenham*	17	Darts
8	Heron	18	*My Fair Lady*
9	Knowledge	19	Mr Rochester (*Jane Eyre*)
10	*Despicable Me*	20	Somerset

Easy

1 Who wrote the novel *A Farewell to Arms* (1929)?

2 *O Captain! My Captain!* is a famous poem by which American poet?

3 For which book did Roddy Doyle win a Booker Prize?

4 *An Officer and a Spy* was a 2013 novel by which author?

5 The Prix Goncourt is the top literary prize given out in what nation?

6 What is Gulliver's first name in *Gulliver's Travels*?

7 What was the title of Ben Elton's 1989 debut novel?

8 In which modern-day country was the book and film *Out of Africa* set?

9 During which century was William Blake born?

10 Which Dickens novel is set during the Gordon Riots?

11 Which author created the character of Gaspode, a talking dog?

12 Who wrote the 1952 novel *Excellent Women*?

13 Luis Vaz De Camões is considered as the greatest poet to have been born in which country?

14 Who also published novels under the name Joseph Kell?

Medium

15 What does the "E" stand for in the name of EM Forster?

16 Which author's final work was *The Blue Flower*?

17 *The Love Song of J. Alfred Prufrock* was the first major work by which poet?

18 *The Turn of the Screw* was written by which literary figure?

19 What was the sequel to Jerome K Jerome's *Three Men in a Boat*?

20 What word completes the title of Martin Amis' 2014 award-winning novel, *The Zone of ___*?

Hard

1   What is the atomic number of beryllium?

2   In which decade did Adam Smith publish *The Wealth of Nations*?

3   Chelsee Healey was runner-up to which winner of 2011's *Strictly Come Dancing*?

4   Which 1987 horror comedy took its name from a group of characters in *Peter Pan*?

5   Which two British drivers made their Formula 1 debuts at the start of the 2019 season?

6   The Royal Rumble is an annual event in which sport?

7   The mini-series *Back To Earth* was part of which TV sitcom?

8   What is the name of Antarctica's largest lake?

9   Llandaff Cathedral lies in which Welsh city?

10   The code FLL indicates which US airport?

11   Who won the 2018 BBC Overseas Sports Personality of the Year award?

12   A lusophone is someone who speaks which language?

13   Whose law, published in 1678, concerns the force required to extend and compress springs?

14   In which year was the animated film *Tangled* released?

15   Which saint is considered to be the first Christian martyr?

16   Which horse won the 2014 Grand National?

17   Of what was Hebe the Greek goddess?

18   Novelist Ian Fleming was born in which decade?

19   How many series of *The IT Crowd* were made?

20   "Bunny" Manders is the sidekick of which fictional thief?

Answers to QUIZ 203 – Pot Luck

1	William Morris	11	*The Fate of the Furious*
2	*The Time Traveler's Wife* (Audrey Niffenegger)	12	*Mr Brightside* (The Killers)
3	The Darkness	13	Rampant
4	West	14	Roxy Music
5	1990s (1993)	15	*Cruise Control*
6	1900s (1909)	16	Surrey
7	15th	17	E (major)
8	Lynn	18	Hydrogen
9	Seven	19	Ganesha
10	Tallahassee	20	Guernsey

1. Who produced the original West End version of *Les Misérables*?

2. What is the name of the Wicked Witch of the West in *Wicked*?

3. In the musical *Cats*, which character sings the song *Memory*?

4. What is the title of the 2014 musical that features the music of The Kinks?

5. Nellie Forbush is a character in which musical?

6. Choreographer Jerome Robbins worked with Leonard Bernstein on which 1957 musical, made into a film in 1961?

7. Which *Mary Poppins Returns* actor created and originally starred in *Hamilton*?

8. How many Oscar nominations did the film *La La Land* receive?

9. Who was the subject of the 1998 musical *Spend Spend Spend*?

10. What is the title of the musical whose original cast was found via the BBC talent show *Let it Shine*?

11. In the 2001 film *Moulin Rouge!*, what was the name of Nicole Kidman's character?

12. Which stage and film musical is set on the fictional island of Kalokairi?

13. *Hello, Young Lovers* is a song from which 1951 musical?

14. Who wrote the music, lyrics and book for *Rent*?

15. Who presented the BBC Four series *Sound of Musicals* and *Sound of Film Musicals*?

16. The song *Who Wants to Be a Millionaire* first appeared in which 1956 film?

17. What was the name of Jeff Conaway's character in the 1978 film *Grease*?

18. In which decade did Fred Astaire and Ginger Rogers appear in *Follow the Fleet*?

19. *Class* and *Nowadays* are songs from which 1975 musical?

20. What is the name of Teyve's wife in *Fiddler on the Roof*?

Answers to QUIZ 204 – Literature

1	Ernest Hemingway	11	Sir Terry Pratchett
2	Walt Whitman	12	Barbara Pym
3	*Paddy Clarke Ha Ha Ha*	13	Portugal
4	Robert Harris	14	Anthony Burgess
5	France	15	Edward
6	Lemuel	16	Penelope Fitzgerald
7	*Stark*	17	TS Eliot
8	Kenya	18	Henry James
9	The 18th century (1757)	19	*Three Men on the Bummel*
10	*Barnaby Rudge*	20	*Interest*

1 What nationality were Roald Dahl's parents?

2 In which year was Brighton and Hove awarded city status?

3 Who directed the 2015 film *The Man from UNCLE*?

4 Who play the title characters in the TV series *Shakespeare & Hathaway: Private Investigators*?

5 The TV series *Crossroads* was set on the outskirts of which village?

6 What nationality is golfer Jon Rahm?

7 In which decade were hand signals dropped from the driving test?

8 What was David Essex's original surname?

9 Chris Froome was born in which African country?

10 What is the name of the school featured in *The Inbetweeners*?

11 In relation to railways, what is the English equivalent of a caboose?

12 In which month of 2019 was the Ultra Low Emission Zone introduced in London?

13 Associated with the tag line "Life's Good", what do the initials of the electronics company LG actually stand for?

14 What is the cube root of 216?

15 Which film won the Best Picture Oscar earlier: *Grand Hotel* or *Gone with the Wind*?

16 What is the first name of the escaped convict Magwitch in *Great Expectations*?

17 Which part of the body would be affected by myalgia?

18 The Korean war took place in what decade?

19 Why was Russia suspended from the G8 in 2014?

20 Who starred as Rob Gordon in the 2000 film *High Fidelity*?

Easy

Medium

Hard

Answers to QUIZ 205 – Pot Luck

1	4	11	Francesco Molinari
2	1770s (1776)	12	Portuguese
3	Harry Judd	13	Hooke's Law
4	*The Lost Boys*	14	2010
5	George Russell and Lando Norris	15	Saint Stephen
6	Wrestling (WWE)	16	Pineau de Re
7	*Red Dwarf*	17	Youth
8	Vostok	18	1900s (1908)
9	Cardiff	19	Four
10	Fort Lauderdale	20	Raffles

1   Arthur Stanley Jefferson was the real name of which comedian?

2   Which fictional character lives "under the name of Mr Sanders"?

3   How is *Soul Limbo,* by Booker T and the MGs better known on the radio?

4   What name is Vitamin B5 also known by?

5   Jacinth is another word for which mineral, which shares its name with a flower?

6   Which vegetable is also known as a kumara in New Zealand?

7   What is actress Emma Stone's real first name?

8   What is the alternative name for the UK's Western Isles?

9   New Holland was the historical European name given to which country?

10   Orville Burrell is the real name of which singer?

11   Windflower is an alternative name given to plants of which genus?

12   By what name is actor Mark Sinclair (b.1967) better known?

13   Which creature is also known as a cachalot?

14   What is the American name for candy floss?

15   By what name is Lev Bronstein (d.1940) better known?

16   Which US state is nicknamed "The Golden State"?

17   What stage name did singer-songwriter Steven Georgiou use before changing his name to Yusuf Islam in 1977?

18   In The *Lord of the Rings,* what alias did Frodo Baggins use when he began his travels?

19   What is the common name of the green and white houseplant *Chlorophytum comosum*?

20   How is comedian Cyril Mead (b.1942) better known?

Answers to QUIZ 206 – Musicals

1	Sir Cameron Mackintosh	11	Satine
2	Elphaba	12	*Mamma Mia!*
3	Grizabella	13	*The King and I*
4	*Sunny Afternoon*	14	Jonathan Larson
5	*South Pacific*	15	Neil Brand
6	*West Side Story*	16	*High Society*
7	Lin-Manuel Miranda	17	Kenickie (Murdoch)
8	14	18	1930s (1936)
9	Viv Nicholson	19	*Chicago*
10	*The Band*	20	Golde

1 What was the title of George Eliot's last novel?

2 The mountain K2 lies on the border between China and which other country?

3 Who won the British Breakthrough Act at the 2019 Brit Awards?

4 What nationality is cyclist Marianne Vos?

5 Richie and Eddie were the main characters in which London-based sitcom of the early 1990s?

6 The Treaty of Versailles was signed in what year?

7 Which conflict occurred first, the Battle of Blenheim or the Battle of Marston Moor?

8 What anniversary did the film *Snow White and the Seven Dwarfs* celebrate in 2017?

9 David Bryant (b.1931) won which World Championship three times between 1979 and 1981?

10 In which TV crime series did the character of Maria LaGuerta appear?

11 Which is the third-largest city in the Netherlands?

12 In which decade was TS Eliot born?

13 Who wrote the 1995 novel *The Horse Whisperer*?

14 Who directed and produced the 2008 film *Changeling*?

15 A Junkie XL remix of which Elvis single reached the top of the UK charts in 2002?

16 In contract bridge, what term is given to any trick taken above the number declared in the contract?

17 In what decade did *Open All Hours* first air on TV?

18 The German word *Kaiser* originates from which Latin word meaning "emperor"?

19 The French National Museum of Modern Art is located in which Parisian building?

20 What strait separates Sri Lanka from India?

Answers to QUIZ 207 – Pot Luck

1	Norwegian	11	Guard's van
2	2001	12	April
3	Guy Ritchie	13	Lucky GoldStar
4	Jo Joyner and Mark Benton	14	Six
5	King's Oak	15	*Grand Hotel* (1932)
6	Spanish	16	Abel
7	1970s (1975)	17	Muscles
8	Cook	18	1950s (1950-53)
9	Kenya	19	The Annexation of Crimea
10	Rudge Park	20	John Cusack

1 The liqueur chartreuse can be green or which other colour?

2 Denby Dale pie was created for which British king's recovery from an illness in 1788?

3 *Polpetta* is the Italian for which food?

4 What is the name of chef and TV presenter Tom Kerridge's two-Michelin-starred gastropub in Marlow, Buckinghamshire?

5 What is the meaning of the French cookery term *sous vide*?

6 What colour beans are known as *douchi* in Chinese cuisine?

7 Jack Daniel's bourbon comes from which US state?

8 Burpee's Golden is a variety of which vegetable?

9 Nasi goreng is a fried rice dish from which Asian country?

10 From what substance is a tandoor oven made?

11 Originating from Greece, what is manouri?

12 Gluten is classified as what type of substance?

13 In the UK, what is the maximum recommended adult daily intake of sugar, in grams?

14 A Negroni cocktail contains red vermouth, Campari® and what other alcoholic drink?

15 Which well-known whisky is distilled at the Glenturret Distillery?

16 In what decade was the Corona beer company founded in Mexico?

17 What item of food is a gigot?

18 Madeleines cakes are traditionally made in what shape?

19 To which family of plants do figs belong?

20 How many balls of marzipan traditionally appear on a Simnel cake?

Answers to QUIZ 208 – Also Known As

1 Stan Laurel
2 Winnie-the-Pooh
3 *Test Match Special* theme
4 Pantothenic acid
5 Hyacinth
6 Sweet potato
7 Emily
8 Outer Hebrides
9 Australia
10 Shaggy
11 Anemone
12 Vin Diesel
13 Sperm whale
14 Cotton candy
15 Leon Trotsky
16 California
17 Cat Stevens
18 Mr Underhill
19 Spider plant
20 Syd Little

QUIZ 211 – Pot Luck

ANSWERS ON PAGE 213

1 Which European country is called Hrvatska in its own language?

2 How many times did Seve Ballesteros win The Open?

3 Which US singer had a 2004 hit with *Breakaway*, co-written by Avril Lavigne?

4 Emma Reid is a main character in which daytime TV series?

5 What is meant by the Latin term *cave canem*?

6 *The Meltdown* is the title of a sequel to which 2002 animated film?

7 What type of animal is a Dorset Horn?

8 What does the "P" stand for in the name of jockey AP McCoy?

9 Daisy May Cooper and Charlie Cooper created and star in which mockumentary?

10 Leon Spinks was crowned Olympic boxing champion in what year?

11 Inspector Napoleon Bonaparte, created by Arthur Upfield, works in which country?

12 Which river flows through the town of Welshpool?

13 For which TV crime drama did Matthew McConaughey win a series of awards?

14 What colour is the background on the Isle of Man's flag?

15 Who succeeded Yitzak Rabin as the Prime Minister of Israel in 1977?

16 Who beat Shaun Ryder to win the tenth series of *I'm A Celebrity ...*?

17 Who starred as gardener Chance in the 1979 film *Being There*?

18 How many sides does a hendecagon have?

19 Lambeth Bridge joins Lambeth with which London borough?

20 In which country is the Franklin river?

Easy

Medium

Hard

Answers to QUIZ 209 – Pot Luck

1	*Daniel Deronda*	11	The Hague
2	Pakistan	12	1880s (1888)
3	Tom Walker	13	Nicholas Evans
4	Dutch	14	Clint Eastwood
5	*Bottom*	15	*A Little Less Conversation*
6	1919	16	Overtrick
7	Battle of Marston Moor (1644)	17	1970s (1976)
8	80th anniversary	18	Caesar
9	Indoor bowls	19	(Georges) Pompidou Centre
10	*Dexter*	20	Palk Strait

Easy

1 To the nearest ten, how many nations sent athletes to the 2014 Sochi Winter Olympics?

2 How many minutes is a penalty for a major rule infringement in ice hockey?

3 Whistler Creekside was the venue for which sport in the 2010 Winter Olympics?

4 In which sport do rings of eight feet and 12 feet play a central role?

5 Which country won the most medals in total at the 2018 Winter Olympics?

6 How many targets are there in each shooting round of a biathlon?

7 Which city was selected to host the 2022 Winter Olympics?

8 The National Ice Centre lies in which English city?

9 Which famous violinist represented Thailand at the Sochi 2014 Winter Olympics?

10 In which winter sport would a K-spot or K-point be used?

11 What colour is used to denote an intermediate ski trail in European resorts?

12 As at 2019, which country had won the most Olympic gold medals in speed skating?

13 Competitors in figure skating must be at least what age?

14 Who was the first athlete to win a snowboarding Olympic medal for Team GB?

15 In which four-person winter sport is the maximum weight of the equipment 630kg?

16 In the two years before *Bolero*, Torvill and Dean's free dance routines were set to the music of which two musicals?

17 Half-pipe and slopestyle are events in which category of skiing competition?

18 In which year did the first Paralympic Winter Games take place?

19 In which year did snowboarding make its debut at the Winter Olympic Games?

20 As at 2019, which is the only winter sport in which there is no women's competition in the Winter Olympics?

Medium

Hard

Answers to QUIZ 210 – Food and Drink

1	Yellow	11	Cheese
2	George III	12	Protein
3	Meatball	13	30g
4	The Hand and Flowers	14	Gin
5	Under a vacuum	15	Famous Grouse
6	Black	16	1920s (1925)
7	Tennessee	17	A leg of lamb
8	Beetroot	18	Shell-shaped
9	Indonesia	19	Mulberry
10	Clay (or metal)	20	11

ANSWERS ON PAGE 215

1   Colonel Castillo Armas served as the president of Guatemala during which decade?

2   Which Dickens novel features Madame Defarge?

3   Who directed the film *Black Swan*?

4   Sir Roysten Merchant was a much-referenced character in which satirical TV comedy?

5   Which of the Great Lakes is 160 miles at its widest point?

6   In March 2019, who became the first female jockey to ride a top-level Grade One Cheltenham Festival winner?

7   Who designed the cover for the Rolling Stones album *Sticky Fingers*?

8   Which character in *The Inbetweeners* was notorious for his constant lies?

9   Who directed the 1988 film *Beetlejuice*?

10 In which English resort did Abba win the Eurovision Song Contest in 1974?

11 In feet, how wide is a badminton court?

12 What letter precedes mu in the Greek alphabet?

13 In which room of a grand house would a scullion have been employed?

14 Doctor Calico is the villain in which 2008 Disney film?

15 What type of creature does a sericulturist breed?

16 What are male kangaroos called?

17 Which is larger by area, the Arabian Desert or the Gobi Desert?

18 Mary Tudor (Mary I) became Queen of England in what year?

19 Which car manufacturer makes the Sharan?

20 Who narrated *In The Night Garden*?

Answers to QUIZ 211 – Pot Luck

1	Croatia	11	Australia
2	Three times	12	Severn
3	Kelly Clarkson	13	*True Detective*
4	*Doctors*	14	Red
5	Beware of the dog	15	Menachem Begin
6	*Ice Age*	16	Stacey Solomon
7	A sheep	17	Peter Sellers
8	Peter	18	11
9	*This Country*	19	Westminster
10	1976	20	Australia

1   Which natural feature has a "shield" type, so called because of its resemblance to a warrior's shield lying on the ground?

2   To the nearest million, how many million square metres does the Sahara desert cover?

3   What is a zoolite?

4   The Krimml Waterfalls lie in which European country?

5   Within which of the Great Lakes is Georgian Bay?

6   What type of cloud is typically thin, consists of ice crystals, and is found at high altitude?

7   What type of natural feature is Dan-yr-Ogof in South Wales?

8   Lake Malawi, the sixth deepest lake in the world, lies across how many countries?

9   Sakura is the Japanese term for what plant?

10 To the nearest thousand, how many miles long is the Amazon River?

11 To be classed a desert an area must receive less than how many inches of rain annually?

12 The Blue Ridge Mountains are part of which US mountain range?

13 The Deccan Plateau lies in which country?

14 From what type of rock is Yosemite's El Capitan formed?

15 Which major river flows from the Plateau of Tibet to the South China Sea?

16 The Daintree Rainforest lies in which state of Australia?

17 What is the name of the frost that forms when water droplets in fog freeze onto the windward side of objects?

18 Which is the largest of Earth's tectonic plates?

19 What is the last period of the Paleozoic era?

20 In which Asian country is the UNESCO site of Ha Long Bay?

Answers to QUIZ 212 – Winter Sports

1	90 (88)	11	Red
2	Five minutes	12	The Netherlands
3	Alpine skiing	13	15 years old
4	Curling	14	Jenny Jones (2014)
5	Norway	15	Bobsleigh
6	Five	16	*Barnum* and *Mack and Mabel*
7	Beijing	17	Freestyle skiing
8	Nottingham	18	1976
9	Vanessa-Mae	19	1998
10	Ski jumping	20	Nordic Combined

1   In literature, what is the name of Don Quixote's horse?

2   Who wrote the sitcom *The IT Crowd*?

3   Syracuse is a province in which region of Italy?

4   *Head Music* and *A New Morning* were album releases by which band?

5   In which decade was the Care Quality Commission founded to inspect healthcare establishments?

6   Danny O'Donoghue was a judge on the first two series of which singing competition from 2012 to 2013?

7   What was the name of the Android operating system version released in 2018?

8   Which country hosted the inaugural Rugby League World Cup?

9   *Started Early, Took My Dog* is a 2010 novel by Kate Atkinson featuring which private detective?

10 In the 2008 film *Frost/Nixon*, who played Richard Nixon?

11 What is measured in ohms?

12 In what year were Andre Agassi and Lindsey Davenport crowned Olympic champions?

13 In which area of London was *My Family* set?

14 In *Little Women* (1868), what was the name of the youngest sister?

15 Which arts broadcaster was controller of BBC2 from 1987 to 1992 and BBC 1 from 1993 to 1996?

16 Les Dennis came runner-up to which other contestant on *Celebrity Big Brother 2*?

17 In what form are dahlias planted?

18 The moons Despina and Larissa orbit which planet?

19 Which film won the 2007 Best Animated Feature Oscar, *Cars* or *Happy Feet*?

20 The jay belongs to which family of birds?

Easy

Medium

Hard

Answers to QUIZ 213 – Pot Luck

1	1950s (1954-57)	11	20ft
2	*A Tale of Two Cities*	12	Lambda
3	Darren Aronofsky	13	The kitchen
4	*Drop the Dead Donkey*	14	*Bolt*
5	Lake Superior	15	Silkworm
6	Bryony Frost	16	Bucks (or jacks)
7	Andy Warhol	17	Arabian Desert
8	Jay	18	1553
9	Tim Burton	19	Volkswagen
10	Brighton	20	Sir Derek Jacobi

QUIZ 216 – Duos

1   With whom did Tina Turner duet on the 1990 single *It Takes Two*?

2   What name accompanies Farrow in the name of a paint and wallpaper manufacturer?

3   Which duo released the 1979 singles *Beat the Clock* and *The Number One Song in Heaven*?

4   Tracey Thorn and Ben Watt formed which 1990s duo?

5   Which comedy duo's theme song was entitled *Dance of the Cuckoos*?

6   "Who's on first?" was a routine by which comedy duo?

7   *Wednesday Morning, 3 A.M.* (1964) was the first album released by which duo?

8   In which decade did Bonnie and Clyde go on a crime spree?

9   Which group released the 1998 song *Mulder and Scully*?

10 Who is the ruling Prince of Verona in Shakespeare's *Romeo and Juliet*?

11 In *The Ren and Stimpy Show*, what type of cat is Stimpy?

12 Who composed the music for the 1877 ballet *Samson and Delilah*?

13 *The Blues Brothers* film was developed from a musical sketch on which US TV show?

14 *Change* and *Shout* were hits for which duo in the 1980s?

15 What were the real surnames of Eric and Ernie?

16 1981's *Don't Stop the Music* was the biggest hit for which US duo?

17 Who was Herc's partner in the early series of *The Wire*?

18 What are the surnames of TV presenters Sam and Mark?

19 Elizabeth and Philip Jennings were the main characters in which TV series first aired in 2013?

20 The Duke of Plaza-Toro appears in which work by Gilbert and Sullivan?

Answers to QUIZ 214 – Planet Earth

1	Volcano	11	Ten inches
2	Nine million	12	Appalachian Mountains
3	A fossilised animal	13	India
4	Austria	14	Granite
5	Huron	15	The Mekong
6	Cirrostratus	16	Queensland
7	Cave	17	Rime
8	Three (Malawi, Tanzania, Mozambique)	18	The Pacific Plate
9	Cherry blossom	19	Permian
10	4000 (c.4010)	20	Vietnam

ANSWERS ON PAGE 219

1   In what field is the Frenchman Thomas Piketty (b.1971) a well-known name?

2   Which part of the brain regulates body temperature?

3   In which country was crime writer Ngaio Marsh born?

4   Which US actress was presented with an honorary damehood by Queen Elizabeth II in 2014 for her anti-war campaigns?

5   British player Nigel Short famously challenged and failed to win which World Championship in 1993?

6   In which county is the parliamentary constituency of Mole Valley?

7   Who played Merry in Peter Jackson's *The Lord of the Rings* trilogy?

8   The second race of the annual Cheltenham festival is named after which legendary horse?

9   What is the name of Captain Ahab's ship in the novel *Moby-Dick*?

10 "Welcome to a new kind of tension all across the alien nation" is a lyric from which song?

11 Who created the TV series *Are You Being Served?*?

12 *Viking* 1 landed on which planet in 1976?

13 What was the first name of the composer Mussorgsky?

14 In which year did Fidel Castro oust Fulgencio Batista from power in Cuba?

15 How many masts were there on a xebec sailing ship?

16 James Dean Bradfield is the frontman with which band?

17 What type of creature is a lilac-breasted roller?

18 Which occurred first, the Battle of the Nile or the Battle of Trafalgar?

19 Diane Murray, played by Bernie Nolan, was a character in which long-running series?

20 In which sport was Yokozuna a world champion in the 1990s?

Easy

Medium

Hard

Answers to QUIZ 215 – Pot Luck

1	Rosinante	11	Electrical resistance
2	Graham Linehan	12	1996
3	Sicily	13	Chiswick
4	Suede	14	Amy
5	2000s (2009)	15	Alan Yentob
6	*The Voice UK*	16	Mark Owen
7	Pie	17	Tubers
8	France (1954)	18	Neptune
9	Jackson Brodie	19	*Happy Feet*
10	Frank Langella	20	Corvidae (crows)

Easy

1 Andri Ólafsson is a policeman in which foreign-language crime drama?

2 Who played Mark Latimer in *Broadchurch*?

3 The series *A Touch of Frost* was set in which fictional town?

4 What was the name of Graham Cole's character in *The Bill*?

5 Blythe Duff played Jackie Reid in which long-running TV crime drama series?

6 In which decade was the TV series *Prime Suspect* first aired?

7 Who played Huggy Bear in the original TV series of *Starsky and Hutch*?

8 What was the name of Sonny Crockett's partner in the TV series *Miami Vice*?

9 Pathologist Max DeBryn appears in which police series?

10 *The Abominable Bride* and *The Lying Detective* were episodes in which series?

11 DS Justin Ripley, played by Warren Brown, was a character in which series?

12 Who played Bert Lynch in the series *Z-Cars*?

13 Which series featured the text message "Urgent exit required"?

14 Pauline Moran played which character in *Agatha Christie's Poirot*?

Medium

15 In which series has the lead character owned dogs called Sykes and Paddy?

16 How is the series *Forbrydelsen* better known in the UK?

17 What is the name of Catherine's sister in *Happy Valley*?

18 Who plays Rhona Kelly in the TV series *Shetland*?

19 Danny Williams is a detective in which series, first shown in the 1960s and remade in 2010?

20 In which country was the second series of *Top of the Lake* set?

Hard

Answers to QUIZ 216 – Duos

1	Sir Rod Stewart	11	Manx
2	Ball	12	Saint-Saëns
3	Sparks	13	*Saturday Night Live*
4	Everything But the Girl	14	Tears for Fears
5	Laurel and Hardy	15	Bartholomew and Wiseman
6	Abbott and Costello	16	Yarbrough and Peoples
7	Simon and Garfunkel	17	(Ellis) Carver
8	1930s	18	Nixon and Rhodes
9	Catatonia	19	*The Americans*
10	Prince Escalus	20	*The Gondoliers*

1 Who was pope earlier, Clement XIV or Pius X?

2 Which model made her film debut playing Polly in the 2007 film *St Trinian's*?

3 Bobby Darin won a Golden Globe for his role in which 1961 film?

4 The 2018 novel *Forever and a Day* by Anthony Horowitz is about the early life of which fictional character?

5 The highest mountain in the Alps, Mont Blanc, is how high to the nearest thousand metres?

6 County Wicklow is located in which province of Ireland?

7 Which European football club plays its home games at the Philips Stadion?

8 In which Swiss lakeside town is there a bronze statue of Freddie Mercury?

9 What is the first name of Inspector Maigret?

10 Which country is the largest by area, Mali, Mexico or Mozambique?

11 How many times did Miguel Induráin win the Tour de France?

12 *In Utero* was a 1993 album by which band?

13 What is the translation of the Latin motto *Nemo me impune lacessit*?

14 Which 1841 ballet tells the story of a peasant girl whose ghost protects her lover after her premature death?

15 The 1892 play *The Master Builder* was written by which dramatist?

16 What was the title of Whitney Houston's first UK no.1?

17 Which US state has Olympia as its capital?

18 *Take Me Bak 'Ome* was a 1972 no.1 in the UK for which rock band?

19 In which year did *Only Fools and Horses* first air?

20 The KCOM Stadium, shared by a football club and a rugby league club, is in which city?

Answers to QUIZ 217 – Pot Luck

1	Economics	11	Jeremy Lloyd and David Croft
2	Hypothalamus	12	Mars
3	New Zealand	13	Modest
4	Angelina Jolie	14	1959
5	Chess	15	Three
6	Surrey	16	Manic Street Preachers
7	Dominic Monaghan	17	A bird
8	Arkle	18	Battle of the Nile
9	*Pequod*	19	*Brookside*
10	*American Idiot* (Green Day)	20	WWF (wrestling)

1   What was the title of Orange Juice's only hit, released in 1983?

2   What colour is viridian?

3   Blue vitriol was an old name for which chemical compound?

4   What is the heraldic word for purple?

5   What colour T-shirt does Shaggy wear in the *Scooby-Doo* TV series?

6   I RAM RENAULT is an anagram of what colour?

7   What colour is Delftware?

8   What colour is the Air Berlin Logo?

9   Who wrote the 2018 TV series *Black Earth Rising*?

10 Sir Steve Redgrave won his first Olympic gold medal in which year?

11 What was the occupation of Sidney Stratton in the film *The Man in The White Suit*?

12 In a game of pool, what colour is the eight-ball?

13 Which Indian city is known as "the Pink City"?

14 Who rode the winning horse in the 2019 Cheltenham Gold Cup?

15 Hooker's and Hunter are shades of which colour?

16 What colour are the crescent and star on the flag of Algeria?

17 Which actor starred in the title role of the 1999 film *Grey Owl*?

18 What colour are the home shirts of Colombia's national football team?

19 A blue hydrangea would typically be growing in which type of soil, acid or alkaline?

20 What does the red horse represent in the Four Horsemen of the Apocalypse?

Answers to QUIZ 218 – Crime Drama

1	*Trapped*	11	*Luther*
2	Andrew Buchan	12	James Ellis
3	Denton	13	*Line of Duty*
4	Tony Stamp	14	Miss Lemon
5	*Taggart*	15	*Midsomer Murders*
6	1990s (1991)	16	*The Killing*
7	Antonio Fargas	17	Clare Cartwright
8	Ricardo (Rico) Tubbs	18	Julie Graham
9	*Endeavour*	19	*Hawaii Five-O*
10	*Sherlock*	20	Australia

1   Who wrote the 1915 novel *Of Human Bondage?*

2   The Colossus of Rhodes was a statue of which Greek god?

3   "I would say I'm sorry if I thought that it would change your mind" is a lyric from which 1979 song?

4   What nationality is footballer Zlatan Ibrahimović (b.1981)?

5   What is the meaning of the Latin phrase *tabula rasa*?

6   In which decade was *One Foot in the Grave* first broadcast?

7   In which European country is the city of Coimbra?

8   Ernie Banks (d.2015) was a famous name in what sport?

9   Mediacity UK is located in which English city?

10 The Delian League was founded in Athens as protection against which people?

11 In which county is the parliamentary constituency of Bosworth?

12 The group 10cc were formed in which city?

13 In what decade was author Graham Greene born?

14 On which planet was Luke Skywalker raised in the *Star Wars* films?

15 The Rocky Mountains stretch from British Colombia in Canada to which US state?

16 What type of creature is a glasswing?

17 In which year did Zimbabwe (formerly known as Southern Rhodesia) become an independent country?

18 Who played Marion Cunningham in the sitcom *Happy Days?*

19 Hans Hass (d.2013) was known for making documentaries filmed in which environment?

20 How old was Emperor Hirohito when he died in 1989?

Answers to QUIZ 219 – Pot Luck

1	Clement XIV	11	Five
2	Lily Cole	12	Nirvana
3	*Come September*	13	No-one provokes me with impunity
4	James Bond	14	Giselle
5	5000m (4810m)	15	Henrik Ibsen
6	Leinster	16	*Saving All My Love For You*
7	PSV Eindhoven	17	Washington
8	Montreux	18	Slade
9	Jules	19	1981
10	Mexico	20	Hull

1   Saaremaa is the largest island belonging to which country?

2   The T-Bana is the name given to the underground rail system in which capital?

3   In which region of Italy is La Sila plateau located?

4   Which mountain in Catalonia shares its name with a Caribbean island?

5   Which three cities in Germany are states in their own right?

6   In which capital city is there a museum dedicated to inventor Nikola Tesla?

7   Who became King of Spain in 2014?

8   Lake Bled lies in which small country?

9   Wawel Castle is situated in which city?

10 What is the internet code for Hungary?

11 The Little Yellow Train runs through which mountain range?

12 Barajas Airport can be found in which capital city?

13 In which two countries does the Bernina Express train operate?

14 The Mauritshuis art musem is located in which city in the Netherlands?

15 In which decade did Finland host the Olympic Games?

16 The Medici family rose to prominence in Florence in what century?

17 Off which European country is the Bay of Kotor?

18 At which racecourse is the French Derby run?

19 The Sporades islands lie off the east coast of which country?

20 In which country is Turku Airport?

Easy · **Medium** · **Hard**

Answers to QUIZ 220 – Colours

1	*Rip It Up*	11	Chemist
2	Green	12	Black
3	Copper sulphate	13	Jaipur
4	Purpure	14	Paul Townend
5	Green	15	Green
6	Ultramarine	16	Red
7	Blue	17	Pierce Brosnan
8	Red	18	Yellow
9	Hugo Blick	19	Acid soil
10	1984	20	War

1   Which Danish footballer played for Rangers between 1994 and 1998?

2   In which year did Toyota launch its revolutionary Prius model?

3   "Take a bow for the new revolution" is a lyric from which 1971 song?

4   What type of vehicle was a Sunderland?

5   What was the first name of Madame Bovary in the 1856 novel?

6   In 2019, who became the oldest winner of *Britain's Got Talent*?

7   The Megacorporation Buy N Large is a central organisation in which animated film?

8   In which country was Sir Bradley Wiggins born?

9   The town of Arundel is in which county?

10 Simon Baker is the leading actor in which TV series?

11 Mount Erebus is on which Antarctic island?

12 Which city became England's 50th city in the 50th year of Elizabeth II's reign?

13 Where was the children's series *Pingu* set?

14 Who hosted *Countdown* from 2007 to 2008?

15 In which European city is the Charlottenburg Palace?

16 What is the term for a marriage between two people of unequal rank that does not raise the lower ranked partner?

17 What type of creature is a minivet?

18 Lake Rotorua lies in which country?

19 In what key is a piece of music that has two flats as its key signature?

20 Field Marshal von Hindenburg (d.1934) had what first name?

Answers to QUIZ 221 – Pot Luck

1	W Somerset Maugham	11	Leicestershire
2	Helios	12	Manchester
3	*Boys Don't Cry* (The Cure)	13	1900s (1904)
4	Swedish	14	Tatooine
5	A blank tablet (or clean slate)	15	New Mexico
6	1990s (1990)	16	Butterfly
7	Portugal	17	1980
8	Baseball	18	Marion Ross
9	Salford	19	Underwater
10	Persians	20	87

Easy

Medium

Hard

1 Which 1960s band was fronted by Eric Burdon?

2 *The Defamation of Strickland Banks* was a 2010 album by which rapper?

3 What is the first name of singer Ms Goldfrapp?

4 Who won British Album of the Year at the Brit Awards in 2014 for *AM*?

5 The single *A Different Beat* (1996) was a hit for which group?

6 What was the title of Billie Piper's first no.1 of the 2000s?

7 *Babel* (2012) was the second studio album by which group?

8 Which country provided the title of a 2006 Razorlight hit?

9 Which band was fronted by Graham Gouldman?

10 *Spirit* (2007) was the debut album of which talent show winner?

11 *Valerie*, a hit for Amy Winehouse, was written by which band?

12 What was the title of Duffy's follow-up single to *Mercy*?

13 Who was the lead singer of the Happy Mondays?

14 Which female singer featured on Professor Green's single *Just Be Good to Green*?

15 *Everything Must Go* (1996) was a Brit Award Best Album winner by which band?

16 Graham Coxon played lead guitar in which band?

17 How many consecutive top 20 hits did Slade have?

18 *Every Teardrop is a Waterfall* was a 2011 single by which band?

19 Who replaced Siobhán Donaghy in the Sugababes?

20 Mike Skinner (b.1978) found fame under what name?

Answers to QUIZ 222 – Europe

1	Estonia	11	Pyrenees
2	Stockholm	12	Madrid
3	Calabria	13	Italy and Switzerland
4	Montserrat	14	The Hague
5	Berlin, Bremen and Hamburg	15	1950s (1952)
6	Belgrade	16	15th century
7	Felipe VI	17	Montenegro
8	Slovenia	18	Chantilly
9	Kraków	19	Greece
10	.hu	20	Finland

ANSWERS ON PAGE 227

1   Which was the first film to feature fictional spy Harry Palmer?

2   Botanically, what is alstroemeria?

3   For what does the "C" of ACAS stand?

4   Sir John Mills played Ordinary Seaman Shorty Blake in which 1942 film?

5   Fetlar belongs to which island group?

6   The Indus River flows through which three countries?

7   How is the rugby league position five-eighth also known?

8   Who played Guinevere (Gwen) in the 2008-12 TV series *Merlin*?

9   The King George VI Chase is traditionally run on which day of the year?

10 John Stapleton, Hugh Scully and Lynn Faulds Wood have all been presenters on which consumer affairs programme?

11 Mowbray Park is in which North of England city?

12 Which London financial institution is based at 1 Lime Street?

13 Which actress won the Best Actress Oscar first, Bette Davis or Joan Fontaine?

14 In which decade was the band The Boomtown Rats founded?

15 What birthday is Tom Good celebrating in the first episode of *The Good Life*?

16 Which Charles Dickens novel features the character of Mr Fezziwig?

17 Which group released the 2018 album *LM5*?

18 Bimini is an area of which group of islands?

19 First presented in 1949, who is given a silver medal at The Open golf championship?

20 What name is given to carvings made from shells or other materials by sailors?

Easy

Medium

Hard

Answers to QUIZ 223 – Pot Luck

1	Brian Laudrup	11	Ross Island
2	1997 (in Japan)	12	Preston
3	*Won't Get Fooled Again* (The Who)	13	Antarctica
4	Flying boat	14	Des O'Connor
5	Emma	15	Berlin
6	Colin Thackeray (89)	16	Morganatic
7	*WALL-E*	17	A bird
8	Belgium	18	New Zealand
9	West Sussex	19	B-flat major
10	*The Mentalist*	20	Paul

1 The famous Inca site of Machu Picchu is believed to have been built as an estate for which emperor?

2 In 2000, Colombia won its first ever Olympic gold medal in which sport?

3 With whom did Gabriela Sabatini win the Wimbledon ladies' doubles Championship in 1988?

4 The Interoceanic Highway, opened in 2011, connects Brazil with which other nation?

5 How many terms did Porfirio Diaz serve as Mexican leader?

6 From the Quechua for "inn", what was the name of the Inca structure often used for military purposes?

7 Protests occurred in which nation in 2002 aimed at the removal of President Macchi?

8 What is the eight-letter acronym of the South American sports governing body Confederação Sul-Americana de Futebol?

9 What is the name of the small, flat griddle used in Mexico to cook tortillas and meat?

10 The Caranqui civilisation once thrived in which nation?

11 Where did Juan Peron head to exile in 1955?

12 What is the name of the 21st-century South American trading bloc?

13 General Romero was ousted from power in El Salvador in which decade?

14 The Broad Front Coalition won the 2009 and 2014 elections in what country?

15 What is the official language of Suriname?

16 Geographer Francisco Velasco published the first maps of which nation in 1901?

17 In which year was Gabriel García Márquez awarded the Nobel Prize in Literature?

18 The 1983 film *Under Fire* was set in which country?

19 In 2006, who became Chile's first female president?

20 In Mexican cuisine, what is pozole?

Answers to QUIZ 224 – British Music

1	The Animals	11	The Zutons
2	Plan B	12	*Warwick Avenue*
3	Alison	13	Shaun Ryder
4	Arctic Monkeys	14	Lily Allen
5	Boyzone	15	Manic Street Preachers
6	*Day and Night*	16	Blur
7	Mumford and Sons	17	17
8	America	18	Coldplay
9	10cc	19	Heidi Range
10	Leona Lewis	20	The Streets

ANSWERS ON PAGE 229

1 Limnology is the study of what geographical feature?

2 What is the name of the founder of Alibaba, now one of the world's largest companies?

3 *A Boor Asleep* and *Interior of an Alehouse* are works by which Flemish-born painter?

4 Which retired golfer has the nickname "Supermex"?

5 Which English band released their debut album *Rocka Rolla* in 1974?

6 In 1975, what did Junko Tabei become the first woman to do?

7 What is the capital city of Dominica?

8 A red circle and a green triangle make up the logo of which Russian political party?

9 Who played Tom Denning in the 1951 mystery film *Mr Denning Drives North*?

10 In 1899, which racing driver became the first person to officially exceed 60 mph?

11 What is the national animal of Afghanistan?

12 St Isidore of Seville is often depicted surrounded by which insects?

13 Which author wrote "Wine is the most civilised thing in the world"?

14 Subject of the BBC drama *Our Zoo*, who founded Chester Zoo?

15 Which German football team is known as "The Red Devils"?

16 What does a quidnunc like to hear?

17 In the TV series *The Hour*, who played Freddie Lyon?

18 What is the decimal equivalent of the hexadecimal number AD?

19 A wall is what type of tiny creature?

20 Which element has the chemical symbol Sb?

Answers to QUIZ 225 – Pot Luck

1	*The Ipcress File*	11	Sunderland
2	Lily	12	Lloyd's of London
3	Conciliation	13	Bette Davis
4	*In Which We Serve*	14	1970s (1975)
5	Shetland Islands	15	His 40th birthday
6	China, India and Pakistan	16	*A Christmas Carol*
7	Stand-off	17	Little Mix
8	Angel Coulby	18	The Bahamas
9	Boxing Day	19	The leading amateur golfer
10	*Watchdog*	20	Scrimshaw

1   Who was the commander of the Roman forces when they lost the Battle of the Teutoburg Forest?

2   Robert Bloet was the second pre-reformation bishop of which English city?

3   Alexander the Great defeated which leader at the Battle of Gaugamela in 331 BC?

4   In which decade were driving licences first introduced in the UK?

5   Noviomagus Reginorum was the Roman name for which UK city?

6   At its greatest extent in 1935, how many members did the League of Nations have?

7   How long did it take Charles Lindbergh to cross the Atlantic for the first time in 1927?

8   Whose army famously sheltered under a banyan tree?

9   What decade saw the publication of the Communist Manifesto?

10 How many "Great Realms" existed in ancient India?

11 Joan of Arc lifted the siege of Orléans in which year?

12 Frederick the Great rose to power in Prussia in what decade?

13 In 79 AD who succeeded Vespasian as emperor of Rome?

14 Which Greek mathematician died in 212 BC?

15 What was the birth name of Pope Innocent X?

16 Which UK Prime Minister served only 119 days in office?

17 Along with France, which other nation signed the Sykes-Picot Agreement concerning the partition of the Middle East?

18 What was the name of Archduke Franz Ferdinand's wife who was assassinated alongside him in 1914?

19 Which city became the first twinned city in the world when it formed a relationship with formerly named Stalingrad during WWII?

20 The Battle of the Nile took place in what year?

Answers to QUIZ 226 – Central and South America

1	Pachacuti	11	Paraguay
2	Weightlifting	12	Mercosur (Southern Common Market)
3	Steffi Graf	13	1970s (1979)
4	Peru	14	Uruguay
5	Seven	15	Dutch
6	Tambo	16	Colombia
7	Paraguay	17	1982
8	CONMEBOL	18	Nicaragua
9	Comal	19	Michelle Bachelet
10	Ecuador	20	A soup

Easy

Medium

Hard

1   "Always Faithful" is the motto of which UK city?

2   Bryan Abrams and Sam Watters were original members of which American band, originally formed in the 1990s?

3   Norman and Ethel Thayer are main characters in which 1981 film?

4   The kouprey is a south-east Asian species of which type of animal?

5   Which artist painted the 1953 picture *Fun Fair at Daisy Nook*?

6   Anne Michaels won the Orange Prize for Fiction for which work?

7   What type of food is the Japanese dish *tamagoyaki*?

8   Which mythological bird appears on the crest of Sussex County Cricket Club?

9   On what date is International Women's Day celebrated?

10 Which TV competition did Brian Chesney win in 2018?

11 In 1981, who became the first British winner of the Pritzker Architecture Prize?

12 Camogie is the women's variant of what sport?

13 How was artist Emmanuel Radnitzky (d.1976) better known?

14 What does a pedologist study?

15 In which country is the Svir river?

16 The film *A Diamond in the Mind* featured which pop group in concert in 2011?

17 Who wrote the 1996 play *Stones in His Pockets*?

18 "How my achievements mock me" is a quote from which Shakespeare play?

19 Who became the first female mayor in England when she was elected in Aldeburgh in 1908?

20 Which is the largest city on the central European River Mur?

Answers to QUIZ 227 – Pot Luck

1	Lakes	11	Snow leopard
2	Jack Ma	12	Bees
3	(Adriaen) Brouwer	13	Ernest Hemingway
4	Lee Trevino	14	George Mottershead
5	Judas Priest	15	FC Kaiserslautern
6	Climb Mount Everest	16	Gossip
7	Roseau	17	Ben Whishaw
8	Yabloko	18	173
9	Sir John Mills	19	A butterfly
10	Camille Jenatzy	20	Antimony

Easy

1   Where does a lithophyte plant grow?

2   Which type of natural formation accumulates to form a moraine?

3   Lake Onega lies in which country?

4   Glass, jewel and rhomboid are types of which animal?

5   Which bird is the largest living ratite?

6   What type of creature is a blue morpho?

7   Helminthology is the study of which creature?

8   Birds of the order *Strigiformes* are more commonly known by what name?

9   What process is known as ecdysis?

10 In which country is the Wadi Rum desert?

11 The Waitomo caves in New Zealand are noted for their population of which insect?

12 The group of animals known as "monotremes" are the only mammals who do what?

13 What name is given to the temporary nest structures that army ants construct from their own bodies to protect their queen?

Medium

14 What type of animal is a cavicorn?

15 The sheatfish is a member of which family?

16 What is the name of the third-highest mountain in the world?

17 The solenodon, a burrowing mammal, is found only on Cuba and which other island?

18 Often called the Arctic Oasis, what is a polynya?

19 With a top speed of 16 metres per hour, what is the world's slowest fish?

20 Also known as the kri-kri, what type of creature is an agrimi?

Hard

Answers to QUIZ 228 – History

1	Varus	11	1429
2	Lincoln	12	1740s
3	King Darius III	13	Titus
4	1900s (1903)	14	Archimedes
5	Chichester	15	(Giovanni Battista) Pamphilli
6	58 (from 1934 to 1935)	16	George Canning
7	33 hours 30 mins	17	United Kingdom
8	Alexander the Great	18	Sophie
9	1840s (1848)	19	Coventry
10	16	20	1798

1   What is the English translation of the Latin name Cicero?

2   Which band released the albums *Look into the Future* (1976) and *Trial by Fire* (1996)?

3   André Masson (d.1987) was associated with what two types of art?

4   *Either/Or* (1843) is a major work by which philosopher?

5   Of what is palaeography the study?

6   At which Formula 1 Grand Prix in 1982 did Michele Alboreto win his first race?

7   Which empire lasted for c. 623 years until the early 20th century?

8   Maseru is the capital of which country?

9   Which is the largest living member of the cormorant family?

10   John Part is a famous name in which indoor sport?

11   Of what is ochlophobia a fear?

12   What can be categorised as "loessic"?

13   Bernard Leach (d.1979) was a noted figure in which branch of the arts?

14   What is a kukri?

15   In which city was Sir Frank Whittle, the inventor of the jet engine, born?

16   Which actors played Marlene and Jacob in the 2011 film *Water for Elephants*?

17   Porto-Novo is the capital of which small African country?

18   Who wrote the 1933 novel *Love on the Dole*?

19   What was the name of Taraji P Henson's character in the TV series *Person of Interest*?

20   *Back to Methuselah* is a 1922 play by which author?

Answers to QUIZ 229 – Pot Luck

1	Exeter	11	Sir James Stirling
2	Color Me Badd	12	Hurling
3	*On Golden Pond*	13	Man Ray
4	An ox	14	Soil
5	LS Lowry	15	Russia
6	*Fugitive Pieces*	16	Duran Duran
7	Omelette	17	Marie Jones
8	Martlet	18	*Troilus and Cressida*
9	March 8	19	Elizabeth Garrett Anderson
10	*Mastermind*	20	Graz (in Austria)

1   Simone Signoret won the Best Actress Oscar for her role in which 1959 British film?

2   Which film, originally made in 1938, is based on *The Wheel Spins* by Ethel Lina White?

3   What was the name of Walter Pidgeon's character in the 1956 film *Forbidden Planet*?

4   Which character did Harold Ramis play in the 1984 film *Ghostbusters*?

5   Who composed the soundtrack to the 1969 version of *The Italian Job*?

6   For which film did Amy Adams receive her first Oscar nomination?

7   Who directed *The Shawshank Redemption*?

8   Which 1987 film was written and directed by Bruce Robinson?

9   Ilene Woods provided the voice for which leading character in a 1950 Disney film?

10 In what decade did Orson Welles direct *The Magnificent Ambersons*?

11 The Oscar-winning 2018 documentary film *Free Solo* featured which climber?

12 Which film was released in the USA under the name *Young Scarface*?

13 What was the surname of Gregory in *Gregory's Girl* (1981)?

14 Amandla Stenberg plays which character in the first *Hunger Games* film?

15 Who played Dr Kananga/Mr Big in the 1973 film *Live and Let Die*?

16 What type of animal is Ziggy in the 1967 animated version of *The Jungle Book*?

17 In the 2010 film *The Way*, which pilgrimage route was Martin Sheen's character following?

18 What was the name of Nicole Kidman's character in the 2018 film *Aquaman*?

19 Which 1992 film had the working title *The Soldier's Wife*?

20 Who played the title role in the 1994 film *Il Postino*?

Answers to QUIZ 230 – Natural World

1	On a rock	11	Glow-worm
2	A glacier	12	Lay eggs
3	Russia	13	Bivouac
4	Squid	14	Any one with hollow horns
5	Ostrich	15	Catfish
6	Butterfly	16	Kanchenjunga (India/Nepal)
7	Parasitic worm	17	Hispaniola
8	Owls	18	Sea lake surrounded by ice
9	Shedding of an arthropod or snake's skin	19	Seahorse
10	Jordan	20	A goat

1   In which Asian country does the Kalka-Shimla railway run?

2   What, on the human body, is the calcaneus?

3   The engineer Augustus Siebe (d.1872) developed a helmet used in which pursuit?

4   Eddie Vedder was the lead singer with which 1990s band?

5   Confucius was born in what century?

6   Aleksandr Loran invented what safety device in 1904?

7   The takahe is a flightless bird native to which country?

8   Onychophagia is the technical term for what habit?

9   "Progress, Industry, Humanity" is the motto of which North of England city?

10 In 1932 Colombia declared war on which other nation?

11 Which American novelist and screenwriter created the TV series *ER*?

12 In which US state was TS Eliot born?

13 Which is the only country to have rugby league as its national sport?

14 Who played Ayesha in *Guardians of the Galaxy: Vol 2 (2017)*?

15 *Kuay teow* is a Thai soup usually containing what main ingredient?

16 By area, what was the largest UK parliamentary constituency in 2019?

17 Which body of water is also known as Lake Tiberius, amongst other names?

18 What is the full Latin phrase often abbreviated to *infra dig*?

19 Bernice Rubens won the Booker Prize for which 1969 novel?

20 What type of animal was "Fuleco", the mascot for the 2014 FIFA World Cup in Brazil?

Answers to QUIZ 231 – Pot Luck

1	Chickpea	11	Crowds
2	Journey	12	Wind-blown sediment
3	Surrealism and automatic drawing	13	Pottery
4	Søren Kierkegaard	14	A knife (with a curved blade)
5	Handwritings of the past	15	Coventry
6	US (Caesars Palace)	16	Reese Witherspoon and Robert Pattinson
7	Ottoman Empire	17	Benin
8	Lesotho	18	Walter Greenwood
9	Flightless or Galapagos cormorant	19	Joss Carter
10	Darts	20	George Bernard Shaw

1. Who composed the 1801 ballet *The Creatures of Prometheus*?

2. "The object of nature is man. The object of man is style" is a quote by which Dutch artist?

3. Constructivism, an artistic and architectural philosophy, originated in which country?

4. Which famous artist designed the costumes and sets for the 1920 ballet *Pulcinella*?

5. In what year did Manet paint *Olympia*?

6. In 2013, a painting entitled *Self-portrait Wearing a White Feathered Bonnet* was attributed to which old master?

7. What was the title of the most performed play in US high schools in 2017-18?

8. In what country was Ford Madox Brown born?

9. In the ballet *La Bayadère*, how does Nikiya die?

10. *Cire-perdue* is a technique used in which branch of the arts?

11. *Emilie Flöge* (1902) is a famous work by which artist?

12. In what century was the first known ballet performed?

13. The painter Marc Chagall was born in 1887 in which present-day country?

14. *Widowers' Houses* (1892) was the first play to be staged by which playwright?

15. What word completes this title of a work by Georgia O'Keeffe, *Red Hill and White ___*?

16. Which French ballet dancer's birthday is now observed as International Dance Day?

17. Who was the sculptor of the Colossus of Rhodes?

18. Who wrote the 18th-century play *Don Carlos*?

19. El Greco belonged to which artistic school?

20. Which Irish-born dancer is regarded as the "godmother" of English ballet?

Answers to QUIZ 232 – Film

1	*Room at the Top*	11	Alex Honnold
2	*The Lady Vanishes*	12	*Brighton Rock*
3	Doctor Morbius	13	Underwood
4	Egon Spengler	14	Rue
5	Quincy Jones	15	Yaphet Kotto
6	*Junebug* (2005)	16	Vulture
7	Frank Darabont	17	*El Camino de Santiago*
8	*Withnail and I*	18	Atlanna
9	Cinderella	19	*The Crying Game*
10	1940s (1942)	20	Massimo Troisi

ANSWERS ON PAGE 237

1   The 1949 US no.1 *I Can Dream, Can't I* was recorded by which singers?

2   Which Roman emperor succeeded Nerva in AD 98?

3   In Cuba, the rum and coke cocktail known elsewhere as Cuba libre is called mentirita. What does this mean?

4   In 1952, which toy was the first to be advertised on American television?

5   The Battle of Little Big Horn took place in what year?

6   What is the capital city of Mauritius?

7   What is the sum of all the numbers on a roulette wheel?

8   What type of bird is a cahow?

9   212 is a perfume range from which fashion house?

10   Both Luke and Acts of the Apostles in the New Testament are addressed to whom?

11   Prussic acid is the poison contained in what nut?

12   Who played Prince Charles in the 2006 film *The Queen*?

13   *Daughters of the Vicar* was a short story by which writer (b.1885)?

14   Which card game has variants of Chinese and Rubicon?

15   The Battle of Iwo Jima took place in what year?

16   Who created the sci-fi TV series *Babylon 5*?

17   Which iconic American pop music band was originally called The Pendletones?

18   In 1766, who discovered hydrogen?

19   Kat Ashley was a governess to which future monarch?

20   Whose 94th symphony, written in 1791, is known as *The Surprise Symphony*?

Easy

Medium

Hard

Answers to QUIZ 233 – Pot Luck

1	India	11	Michael Crichton
2	Heel bone	12	Missouri (St Louis)
3	Diving	13	Papua New Guinea
4	Pearl Jam	14	Elizabeth Debicki
5	6th century BC (551)	15	Noodles
6	Foam fire extinguisher	16	Ross, Skye and Lochaber (12,000 square km)
7	New Zealand	17	The Sea of Galilee
8	Nail biting	18	*Infra dignitatem*
9	Bradford	19	*The Elected Member*
10	Peru	20	Armadillo

1 The Swedish dish *ärtsoppa* is a soup primarily containing which vegetable?

2 *Laulau* is a dish of steamed pork and fish served in which island group?

3 Which seafood is known as *huitres* in French?

4 *Curcuma longa* is the technical term for which spice?

5 Famous for the 1963-73 TV series *The French Chef*, who is regarded as the USA's equivalent of Elizabeth David in popularising French cuisine?

6 In the Lebanon, what type of food is *sfouf*?

7 What are *jau gok* in Chinese cuisine?

8 What is the name of the stock used to form the basis of miso soup?

9 The traditional Lebanese dessert, *meghli*, is typically eaten to mark what event?

10 What type of food is *menudo* in Mexico?

11 *Yoshoku* is the Japanese culinary term for what?

12 Ben Lear and Early Black are varieties of what fruit?

13 *Diospyros kaki* is the Latin name for what?

14 How would something be cooked if it was described as *brouillé*?

15 Made in Switzerland, what type of food is *schabziger*?

16 From which island country does the ugli fruit originate?

17 With what is the Mediterranean alcoholic drink *arak* flavoured?

18 Blackstrap is what sugar processing by-product?

19 Literally meaning "witch", *strega* is a liqueur from which European country?

20 What are the two main traditional ingredients of the Irish soup brotchan foltchep?

Answers to QUIZ 234 – The Arts

1	Beethoven	11	Gustav Klimt
2	Theo van Doesburg	12	16th century (1581-*Ballet des Polonais*)
3	Russia	13	Belarus
4	Picasso	14	George Bernard Shaw
5	1863	15	*Shell*
6	Rembrandt	16	Jean-Georges Noverre
7	*Almost Maine*	17	Chares (of Lindos)
8	France	18	Friedrich Schiller
9	She is bitten by a snake	19	Mannerism
10	Sculpture (making a duplicate cast)	20	Dame Ninette de Valois

1   The former UN Secretary General Kofi Annan was born in which country?

2   Joey Kramer is the drummer for which American band?

3   Who was the captain of the US team in the first six Ryder Cups?

4   What was the former name of Lake Turkana in Kenya?

5   Which country used the cruzado as its currency unit until 1994?

6   How old was Tchaikovsky when he died?

7   "In the room women come and go/Talking of Michelangelo" is a line from which 1915 poem?

8   Which European football club plays its home games at the Stadion Maksimir?

9   Who is the Baron Administrator of Cloud City in the *Star Wars* films?

10 In which US state was the TV series *House* set?

11 *Dei donum* appears on the coat of arms of which Scottish city?

12 Donald Watson (d.2005) coined what term to describe an individual's diet?

13 What breed of bird was first released in Central Park in 1890 and is said to be responsible for the bulk of its US population?

14 King Filimer ruled which people in Oium, south-east Europe?

15 Which Austrian football club is known as "The Green-Whites"?

16 Johann Sebastian Bach's mini opera *Schweigt stille, plaudert nicht* (be still, stop chattering) is about a woman who is addicted to what drink?

17 Who was the England cricket captain during the 1932/33 Bodyline series?

18 Which city did Samuel Johnson describe as "a city of philosophers"?

19 The drink *cha yen* is the Thai equivalent of which popular beverage?

20 What was the name of Guy Pearce's character in the TV series *Neighbours*?

Answers to QUIZ 235 – Pot Luck

1	The Andrews Sisters	11	Almond
2	Trajan	12	Alex Jennings
3	Little lie	13	DH Lawrence
4	Mr Potato Head	14	Bezique
5	1876	15	1945
6	Port Louis	16	J Michael Straczynski
7	666	17	The Beach Boys
8	A petrel (Bermudan petrel)	18	Henry Cavendish
9	Carolina Herrera	19	Elizabeth I
10	Theophilus	20	Haydn

1   El Djem of Thysdrus, the Roman amphitheatre, is in which North African country?

2   How many stars appear on the flag of Comoros?

3   What is the longest freshwater lake in the world?

4   What is the capital of the Italian region of Abruzzo?

5   In which Adriatic country is the Krka National Park?

6   To the nearest ten square miles, how big is Malta?

7   How many countries border Afghanistan?

8   In which European country are the cities of Budva and Cetinje?

9   The Kinabatangan River is the second longest river in which country?

10   The UNESCO-listed Ellora Caves, a site of worship, lie in which Asian country?

11   What is the name of the highest (dormant) volcano in Antarctica?

12   The Amargosa River runs through which desert?

13   Which archipelagic country has c. 700 islands?

14   Mount Triglav is the highest point in which European country?

15   In which capital city is Sheremetyevo Airport?

16   Belmopan is the capital of which country?

17   A summer ferry runs from Kylerhea on Skye to which village on the Scottish mainland?

18   In which century did Mount Fuji last erupt?

19   In which African country can the Cango Caves be found?

20   To the nearest metre, how high is the Great Pyramid of Giza?

Answers to QUIZ 236 – Food and Drink

1	Peas	11	Western food
2	Hawaii	12	Cranberry
3	Oysters	13	Persimmon
4	Turmeric	14	Scrambled
5	Julia Child	15	Cheese
6	(Almond-semolina) Cake	16	Jamaica
7	Dumplings	17	Anise
8	Dashi	18	Molasses
9	Birth of a baby	19	Italy
10	Soup	20	Leek and oatmeal

1   *Shadow Dance* (1966) was the debut novel by which female author?

2   From what does a clootie dumpling take its name?

3   Which German football club plays at the Volksparkstadion?

4   Claude Monet was born in which decade?

5   Who plays Jim Strange in the TV series *Endeavour*?

6   Genghis Khan died in what year?

7   Venta Belgarum was the Roman name for which English city?

8   In which country did the poet Byron die?

9   Which English singer had a 1960 UK no.1 hit with a cover of *Why*?

10   A tyrosemiophile is someone who collects labels from boxes containing what?

11   Which philosopher said "Thinking: the talking of the soul with itself"?

12   The post-punk band the Futureheads are from which UK city?

13   *Denis Duval* was an unfinished final novel by whom?

14   The city of Seville lies on which river?

15   How is the British singer Dylan Mills better known?

16   Which two Norwegians shared the Nobel Peace Prize in 1921?

17   On what day in September did the Gregorian Calendar begin in Britain?

18   Tejo was declared the national sport of which nation in 2001?

19   In which country are the Fox Glacier and the Franz Josef Glacier?

20   Which company created the 1978 game *Space Invaders*?

Easy

Medium

Hard

Answers to QUIZ 237 – Pot Luck

1	Ghana (originally Gold Coast)	11	Dundee
2	Aerosmith	12	Vegan
3	Walter Hagen	13	Starling
4	Lake Rudolf	14	The Goths
5	Brazil	15	(Rapid) Vienna
6	53	16	Coffee
7	*The Love Song of J Alfred Prufrock*	17	Douglas Jardine
8	Dinamo Zagreb	18	Lichfield
9	Lando Calrissian	19	Iced tea
10	New Jersey	20	Mike Young

1   Which Indian religion traces its succession through 24 teachers?

2   Ah Mun was the god of agriculture in which civilisation?

3   The Dalit movement (Buddhism) emerged in which century?

4   What name is given to a place of public worship for followers of Shintoism?

5   In which Asian country was the Tenrikyo religion formed?

6   "Silent illumination" is a form of meditation in which religion?

7   The Vedic god Agni represents which element?

8   Kagura is a dance in which Asian religion?

9   The Samaritans of the Levant are based around which mount?

10 Joseph Albo (d.1444) is a key figure in the history of which religion?

11 Lakshmi is the wife of which Hindu god?

12 In the Shinto religion, from which part of Izanagi is Susanoo born?

13 Trinity Sunday is celebrated one week after which other holy day in the Christian calendar?

14 In which Asian country was Hoahoism founded in 1939?

15 What is the name given to bad deeds in Buddhism?

16 What is the meaning of "Vulgate" as in the Vulgate Bible?

17 Shogi Effendi is a key figure in which religion?

18 Followers of which religion believe in the Chinvat Bridge of Judgement?

19 A stupa is a burial ground for followers of which religion?

20 Who was the son of Cush in the Bible, known as a mighty hunter?

Answers to QUIZ 238 – Geography

1	Tunisia	11	Mount Sidley
2	Four	12	The Mojave Desert (Death Valley)
3	Lake Tanganyika	13	The Bahamas
4	L'Aquila	14	Slovenia
5	Croatia	15	Moscow
6	120 (122)	16	Belize
7	Six (Iran, Turkmenistan, Tajikistan, China, Uzbekistan, Pakistan)	17	Glenelg
8	Montenegro	18	18th century (1707)
9	Malaysia	19	South Africa
10	India	20	147m

1   Which European country's parliament is called the Eduskunta?

2   *Smoke + Mirrors* (2015) was the second album released by which band?

3   In which century did composer Thomas Tallis live?

4   *Kyoyasai* is a term for vegetables originating from where in Japan?

5   Lordosis affects which part of the human body?

6   "With God's Help, Our Labour is Successful" is the motto of which UK city?

7   The Scythians originated from which modern-day country?

8   A variation of cricket called kilikiti is the national sport of which island nation?

9   Which chemist, better known as an inventor, discovered potassium and sodium?

10 What was the name of the *Last of the Mohicans* in the famous novel and film?

11 The underwater city of Rapture and the Big Daddy character appear in which video game?

12 What type of creature is a bleak?

13 In which capital city is Zvartnots airport?

14 Which philosopher said "The journey of a thousand miles begins with a single step"?

15 Who led the Romans at the Battle of Aquae Sextiae?

16 John Cade was involved in developing the use of which chemical element?

17 What was the name of the "winning" horse in the 1993 Grand National which was famous for being declared void?

18 In what year is the animated sci-fi film *WALL-E* set?

19 Etosha National Park is in which African country?

20 Which legendary character did Sean Maguire play in the TV series *Once Upon a Time*?

Answers to QUIZ 239 – Pot Luck

1	Angela Carter	11	Plato
2	The strip of cloth in which it is boiled	12	Sunderland
3	Hamburger SV	13	William Makepeace Thackeray
4	1840s (1840)	14	The Guadalquivir
5	Sean Rigby	15	Dizzee Rascal
6	1227	16	Christian Lange and Hjalmar Branting
7	Winchester	17	September 14
8	Greece	18	Colombia
9	Anthony Newley	19	New Zealand
10	Cheese	20	Taito

Easy

1 The band Focus were formed in which European country?

2 *Never Say Die* (1978), *Turn up the Night* (1982) and *TV Crimes* (1992) were UK Top 40 hits for which band?

3 The North Wales International Music Festival is held annually in which city?

4 What was the only no.1 hit for The Troggs?

5 What is the real name of the rapper Childish Gambino?

6 *Belshazzar's Feast* was a 1931 cantata by which British composer?

7 Who won the 2012 Mercury Music Prize with the album *An Awesome Wave*?

8 First performed in St Petersburg in 1824, *Missa Solemnis* is a work by which composer?

9 Composer Isaac Albéniz was born in 1860 in which country?

10 From which country does the band Babymetal originate?

Medium

11 Which band started their career as The New Yardbirds?

12 To which composer did Elizabeth I grant a monopoly of sheet music?

13 *Chattanoogie Shoe Shine Boy* was a 1950 US no.1 for which singer?

14 In what year did the first Proms take place?

15 *Clutching at Straws* was a 1987 album by which band?

16 What was the name Stevie Ray Vaughan gave to his second Stratocaster guitar?

17 A Gamelan is a traditional orchestra in which country?

18 Who composed the late 16th-century choral work *Stabat Mater*?

19 Jasper Cini was the real name of which 1950s American singer?

20 What was the first name of the Austrian composer Webern (d.1945)?

Hard

Answers to QUIZ 240 – Religion

1	Janism	11	Vishnu
2	Mayan	12	Nose
3	20th century (1935)	13	Pentecost
4	Haiden	14	Vietnam
5	Japan	15	Akusala
6	Zen Buddhism	16	Common version
7	Fire	17	Baha'i
8	Shinto	18	Zoroastrianism
9	Gerizim	19	Buddhism
10	Judaism	20	Nimrod

ANSWERS ON PAGE 245

1 Not open to the general public, an adytum was an inner room found in what type of old building?

2 Pendeford Airfield was the original site of an airport in which UK city?

3 Charlemagne was crowned Holy Roman Emperor in what year?

4 Kate Grenville won the Orange Prize for Fiction for which 1999 novel?

5 Drivers from which Formula 1 team won the first two World Championships?

6 *The Hollow Men* (1925) and *Ash-Wednesday* (1927) are works by which poet?

7 Fyodor Pirotsky was a key figure in the invention of what mode of transport?

8 Stolichno and Shumensko beers are from which European country?

9 Emily Osment played which character in the 2009 *Hannah Montana* film?

10 "In time we hate that which we often fear" is a quote from which Shakespeare play?

11 In the Bible, Hagar was the handmaiden to whom?

12 What is the motto of the British Order of the Garter?

13 What is the national sport of Turkey?

14 *Shochu* is what type of drink in Japan?

15 *Emma Brown* is an unfinished final novel by which author?

16 The Riigikogu is which European country's parliamentary assembly?

17 Which computing company announced Satya Nadella as its new CEO in February 2014?

18 In the 1987 film *The Princess Bride*, who played Inigo Montoya?

19 Port Moresby is the capital city of which country?

20 Which item of medical equipment was invented by René Laennec?

Easy

Medium

Hard

Answers to QUIZ 241 – Pot Luck

1   Finland
2   Imagine Dragons
3   16th century
4   Kyoto
5   The spine
6   Sheffield
7   Iran
8   Samoa
9   Sir Humphry Davy (First Baronet)
10 Uncas
11 *BioShock*
12 A (small freshwater) fish
13 Yerevan (Armenia)
14 Lao Tzu
15 Gaius Marius
16 Lithium
17 Esha Ness
18 2085
19 Namibia
20 Robin Hood

1. What is the term for the branch of chemistry related to fermentation in brewing?
2. What is the SI unit of catalytic activity?
3. Antonie van Leeuwenhoek is known as the "father" of which branch of science?
4. The Latin name for Copenhagen gives which chemical element its name?
5. What is the medical term for fainting?
6. How many elements comprise the lanthanides series in the periodic table?
7. With whom did Pierre and Marie Curie share the Nobel Prize in Physics in 1903?
8. Named after a Russian inventor, what do the Korotkov sounds listen for?
9. In which year did *Sputnik* 1 fall out of orbit and burn up in the Earth's atmosphere?
10. Cholecystitis affects what part of the human body?
11. What does a tribologist study?
12. The Pauli exclusion principle is part of which branch of physics?
13. What is measured by a henry?
14. How many zeros follow the "1" in a British quadrillion?
15. What term is given to the study of the motion of bodies without reference to mass or force?
16. Crural refers to which body part?
17. In Earth days what is the orbital period of Mercury?
18. How many thoracic vertebrae are there in the human body?
19. What does a galvanometer measure?
20. Which mineral derives its name from the Persian for "golden"?

Answers to QUIZ 242 – Music

1	The Netherlands	11	Led Zeppelin
2	Black Sabbath	12	Thomas Tallis
3	St Asaph	13	Red Foley
4	*With a Girl Like You*	14	1895
5	Donald Glover Jr	15	Marillion
6	Sir William Walton	16	Lenny
7	alt-J	17	Indonesia (Java and Bali)
8	Beethoven	18	Palestrina
9	Spain	19	Al Martino
10	Japan	20	Anton

Easy

Medium

Hard

1   Frenchman Jean Courbet belonged to which artistic school?

2   Attraction were crowned champions of which reality show?

3   *Low Budget* (1979), *Sleepwalker* (1977), and *Word of Mouth* (1984) were albums by which British band?

4   Which US president said "Happiness lies in the joy of achievement and the thrill of creative effort"?

5   Where in the body is the Organ of Corti?

6   "The Wall" and "Mr Dependable" were nicknames of which Indian cricketer?

7   In the Bible, the Book of Lamentations is attributed to whom?

8   Which club won the 2000 UEFA Cup Final on penalties?

9   The official motto of which capital city is "She is tossed to the waves but doesn't sink"?

10 How is the number "a chiliad" more commonly known?

11 The flag of Cape Verde contains how many stars?

12 For what did the Incas use a quipu?

13 The Wills Memorial Building can be found in which UK city?

14 "Los Che" is the name given to which Spanish football club?

15 The Thai dessert *kanom khrok* consists of what flavour pancakes?

16 George Orwell was born in which decade?

17 What is the name given to the German city where Martin Luther was a prominent visitor?

18 Marien was an ancient territory in which Caribbean country?

19 What does the Arabic word *kitab* mean?

20 What was the subtitle of the 2014 film *Birdman*?

Easy

Medium

Hard

Answers to QUIZ 243 – Pot Luck

1	A temple	11	Sarah
2	Wolverhampton	12	*Honi soit qui mal y pense*
3	800	13	Oil wrestling
4	*The Idea of Perfection*	14	Distilled spirit
5	Alfa Romeo	15	Charlotte Brontë
6	TS Eliot	16	Estonia
7	The electric tram	17	Microsoft®
8	Bulgaria	18	Mandy Patinkin
9	Lilly (Truscott)	19	Papua New Guinea
10	*Antony and Cleopatra*	20	The stethoscope

1 What does the "L" stand for in the name of writer Dorothy L Sayers?

2 In which decade did Franz Kafka publish *Metamorphosis*?

3 In which building was Jane Austen buried?

4 "Had We but World Enough and Time" is the opening line of which poem?

5 Who won the 2018 Booker Prize for her novel *Milkman*?

6 *Amelia*, published in 1751, was the last novel by which author?

7 Who wrote the 1946 novel *All The King's Men*?

8 What was the middle name of Elizabeth Gaskell?

9 *Barrack-Room Ballads and Other Verses* was the title of a collection of poems by which writer?

10 Which sport is featured in PG Wodehouse's 1909 novel *Mike*?

11 Which city was designated as England's first UNESCO City of Literature in 2012?

12 British author William Boyd was born in which country?

13 Ali Smith won the 2012 Hawthornden Prize for which novel?

14 *Elric at the End of Time* and *The Chronicles of Corum* are works by which author?

15 Which poet, who died in 1824, had the first names George Gordon?

16 In what decade did Lewis Carroll publish *Alice's Adventures in Wonderland*?

17 *Buddenbrooks* is a 1901 novel by which literary figure?

18 Boccaccio's *Decameron* was the main source of which Shakespeare play?

19 Camberg was the maiden name of which Scottish author?

20 The early poet Valmiki wrote in which language?

Answers to QUIZ 244 – Science

1	Zymurgy	11	Friction
2	Katal	12	Quantum mechanics
3	Microbiology	13	Electrical inductance
4	Hafnium	14	24
5	Syncope	15	Kinematics
6	15	16	Leg
7	Antoine Henri Becquerel	17	88
8	Blood pressure	18	12
9	1958	19	Small electric currents
10	Gall bladder	20	Zircon

1   Joe Venuti is famous for playing which instrument?

2   The Battle of Balaclava took place in which year?

3   In 2007, Italy replaced which country in the Women's Six Nations rugby tournament?

4   How many of Emily Dickinson's poems were published during her lifetime?

5   What was the name of Gina McKee's character in the first series of *Line of Duty*?

6   Walter Gropius founded which architecture school in 1919?

7   What was the stage name of entertainer Matilda Wood (d.1922)

8   What kind of "tree" featured in the title of a Pulitzer Prize winning collection of poetry by Robert Frost?

9   The National Diet is which country's parliament?

10 Helen Dunmore won the 1996 Orange Prize for Fiction for which novel?

11 Which Scottish architect was knighted for his design of Coventry Cathedral?

12 Which band entitled their 1981 debut album *Too Fast for Love*?

13 Who directed the 2016 remake of *Ghostbusters*?

14 Three species of which seabird are known in the USA as "jaegers"?

15 What is the capital city of St Kitts and Nevis?

16 Cuboid bones are found in which part of the human body?

17 For what kind of plays was Aristophanes noted?

18 Which bird is the state bird of seven US states?

19 What is the modern name of the capital city referred to by the Romans as Olisipo?

20 Of what is phengophobia a fear?

Answers to QUIZ 245 – Pot Luck

1	Realism	11	Ten
2	*Britain's Got Talent* (2013)	12	Counting
3	The Kinks	13	Bristol
4	Franklin D Roosevelt	14	Valencia
5	In the ear	15	Coconut-rice
6	Rahul Dravid	16	1900s (1903)
7	Jeremiah	17	Lutherstadt
8	Galatasary (defeated Arsenal)	18	Haiti
9	Paris	19	Book
10	1000	20	*The Unexpected Virtue of Ignorance*

Easy

1   Bob Beamon caused a sensation in 1968 when he smashed the world record in what event?

2   At which golf course did the first 12 Open championships take place?

3   1981 Formula 1 World Championship runner-up Carlos Reutemann was from which country?

4   Which French football club has retired the no.17 shirt to honour Marc-Vivien Foé?

5   In what year did the first official Ryder Cup take place?

6   A famous cross-country horse steeplechase race has been run in Pardubice in which country since 1874?

7   Named after its inventor, what is the Australian name for a googly?

8   Which event saw a change in technique in the 1950s to the Däscher Technique?

9   Air & Style and X-Trail Jam are contests in which extreme sport?

10 Barry Bonds (b.1964) is a retired player of what sport?

11 In which US state do the Pacers basketball team play?

12 Which Dutch football club is nicknamed "The Light Bulbs"?

13 The Wimbledon tennis championships were first held in which decade?

Medium

14 What do the initials WFDF stand for in the organisation that oversees the sport known as Ultimate?

15 Erwin Baker was NASCAR's first commissioner. What was his nickname?

16 In 1897, the first ever Rugby League Challenge Cup final was held between St Helens and which other team?

17 How many people are there in a war canoe team?

18 James J Jeffries was an undisputed boxing champion in what decade?

19 Bisque, pioneer ball and pivot ball are terms used in which sport?

20 What did the company that first sponsored the Tour de France green jersey produce?

Hard

Answers to QUIZ 246 – Literature

1	Leigh	11	Norwich
2	1910s (1915)	12	Ghana
3	Winchester Cathedral	13	*There But For The*
4	*To His Coy Mistress* (Andrew Marvell)	14	Michael Moorcock
5	Anna Burns	15	Lord Byron
6	Henry Fielding	16	1860s (1865)
7	Robert Penn Warren	17	Thomas Mann
8	Cleghorn	18	*All's Well That Ends Well*
9	Rudyard Kipling	19	Dame Muriel Spark
10	Cricket	20	Sanskrit

1. The Morning Runners' song *Gone Up in Flames* was the theme tune to which sitcom?

2. The 19th-century operetta *White Horse Inn* is set near which Austrian town?

3. Germany has which flower as a national symbol?

4. What type of creature is a *Scaptia beyonceae*?

5. Who is the frontman of the Lemonheads rock band?

6. What nationality was the choreographer August Bournonville?

7. What is an epistaxis?

8. What age was Juan Manuel Fangio when he became the oldest man to win a Formula 1 world title?

9. Honiara is the capital of which Pacific country?

10. Kenai is the leading character in which 2003 Disney film?

11. Which football club won its first French league title in 2012?

12. Fernand Leger belonged to which school of art?

13. The historical region of Numidia lies mostly in which modern-day country?

14. In what year was Napoleon Bonaparte born?

15. In what year BC did the famous Battle of Marathon occur?

16. How was the 10th-century Russian ruler Oleg styled?

17. Which fruit flavours the Finnish liqueur *lakka*?

18. Which golfer is represented on the top of the Ryder Cup?

19. *The Bookshop* (1978) and *Offshore* (1979) are works by which author?

20. In 1905, who became the first woman to be awarded the Nobel Peace Prize?

Answers to QUIZ 247 – Pot Luck

1	Violin	11	Sir Basil Spence
2	1854	12	Mötley Crüe
3	Spain	13	Paul Feig
4	Seven	14	Skua
5	Jackie Laverty	15	Basseterre
6	Bauhaus	16	The foot
7	Marie Lloyd	17	Comedies
8	*A Witness Tree*	18	The Northern cardinal
9	Japan	19	Lisbon
10	*A Spell of Winter*	20	Natural light

Easy

1   *Open All Hours* and *Porridge* were a result of which show of one-off comedy episodes starring Ronnie Barker?

2   What was the name of Susan Tully's character in *Grange Hill*?

3   Who composed the theme tune for *The Vicar of Dibley*?

4   The first three series of *Police Interceptors* followed officers from which county?

5   Natalee Harris appeared on which reality series broadcast from 2012 to 2014?

6   Birch Avenue was the fictional setting of which 1970s sitcom?

7   What was the name of Tom Hiddleston's character in the English version of *Wallander*?

8   Jonathon Morris and Victor McGuire played brothers in which 1980s sitcom?

9   Who played barrister Jo Mills in the series *Judge John Deed*?

10 In what year in the UK was Freeview launched?

11 Manny Bianco was a character in which sitcom?

12 In which year did the Open University first broadcast on TV?

13 Who narrates on the reality show *First Dates*?

Medium

14 Which two actresses were the focus of the first series of *Feud*?

15 In what capacity does Darren Bett appear on television?

16 Kadiff Kirwan and Samson Kayo are lead actors in which comedy series?

17 Michael Rice was the first winner of which talent show?

18 *Bouncing Back* was the autobiography of which fictional character?

19 Sir Antony Jay and Jonathan Lynn created which series, first aired in 1980?

20 Barnaby Walker and Nina Morales are the main characters in which comedy drama?

Hard

Answers to QUIZ 248 – Sport

1	Long jump (he broke the record by 21²/₃ in (55cm))	11	Indiana
2	Prestwick	12	PSV Eindhoven
3	Argentina	13	1870s (1877)
4	Lyon	14	World Flying Disc Federation
5	1927	15	Cannon Ball
6	Czechia/Czech Republic	16	Batley
7	Bosie (after Bernard Bosanquet)	17	15
8	Ski jumping	18	1900s
9	Snowboarding	19	Croquet
10	Baseball	20	Lawnmowers

1   In what month of 1918 did WWI end?

2   *EastEnders* produced its first live broadcast for which anniversary?

3   Full backs in rugby union wear which number on their shirt?

4   Which African country is bordered by Algeria to the west and Libya to the east?

5   Who was the original host of *Question Time*?

6   What colour is Chianti wine?

7   Jools Holland played what instrument when he was a member of Squeeze?

8   Which part of the body does glaucoma affect?

9   What is the radio code word for the last letter of the alphabet?

10   Who directed the 1945 classic *Brief Encounter*?

11   For how many series was Ricky Wilson a judge on *The Voice UK*?

12   In which decade was the fashion label Biba founded?

13   What is the name of the Spanish Mediterranean region that includes the resorts of Malaga and Torremolinos?

14   Which team did England beat to win the SheBelieves football trophy in 2019?

15   Which actor was awarded the Golden Raspberry for Worst Actor for his performance in the 2017 film *The Mummy*?

16   Expedia and Trivago specialise in what business?

17   What term is given to someone who always thinks that bad things will happen?

18   Who starred in the 1997 film *Liar Liar*?

19   *My Camera Never Lies* was a 1982 no.1 for which group?

20   Commemorated with a statue in Edinburgh, what type of animal was Greyfriars Bobby?

Easy

Medium

Hard

Answers to QUIZ 499 – Pot Luck

1	Malabo	11	Garlic
2	Lloyd Price	12	Kidney
3	Maserati	13	Henri Rousseau
4	*True Detective*	14	Dame Beryl Bainbridge
5	Samoa	15	Austria
6	EM Forster	16	Lady Helen Colquhoun
7	Russia (near St Petersburg)	17	*All's Well That Ends Well*
8	Argentina	18	Lech Poznań
9	*The Ferryman* (Jez Butterworth)	19	Demi Moore
10	*Obsession*	20	Alfalfa

1 What caused the cancellation of the Cheltenham Gold Cup in 2001?

2 A privileged person is said to be born with what silver item in their mouth?

3 Which singer had a hit in 1993 with *Fields of Gold*?

4 Which US state is nicknamed "the Silver State"?

5 A Golden Delicious is what type of fruit?

6 Which two items of cutlery are used in silver service?

7 A silver bullet is said to be the only way to kill which mythical creature?

8 What part of the head might be described as "silver" in a persuasive person?

9 What nationality was Franz Lehár, composer of the *Gold and Silver Waltz*?

10 What role did Jay Silverheels famously play in a TV western series?

11 The 1985 film *Silverado* is in what genre?

12 The Golden Fleece features in which Greek myth?

13 For how many pieces of silver did Judas betray Jesus?

14 Who played James Bond in the 1964 film *Goldfinger*?

15 Which 1960s song begins with the words "You're everywhere and nowhere baby"?

16 In which decade was Goldie Hawn born?

17 Which Australian state has a Gold Coast?

18 What colour medal is awarded at Chelsea Flower Show for a garden between silver and gold standard?

19 Which fairy-tale character is also known as Mr Gold in the TV series *Once Upon a Time*?

20 Who played James Bond for the second time in the 1974 film *The Man With the Golden Gun*?

Answers to QUIZ 500 – Musicals

1	Richard Beymer	11	*Cinderella* (1950)
2	*Oklahoma!*	12	*Avenue Q*
3	*Rent*	13	1999
4	Herbert Kretzmer	14	Damien Chazelle
5	*Paint Your Wagon*	15	*The Broadway Melody* (1929)
6	*Fiddler on the Roof*	16	Katharine McPhee
7	Dame Gillian Lynne	17	*Xanadu*
8	*Stop the World - I Want to Get Off*	18	F Scott Fitzgerald
9	Brian Roberts	19	Jule Styne
10	Fred Casely	20	*Me and My Girl*

1   How many members are there in an athletics relay team?

2   *It Must Have Been Love* by Roxette featured on the soundtrack to which 1990 film?

3   Which American river flows from Minnesota to a delta in Louisiana and into the Gulf of Mexico?

4   What type of creature is a twite?

5   How many points is the letter F worth in Scrabble®?

6   What is indicated in the UK by a brown road sign showing a duck?

7   According to the proverb, what is worth two in the bush?

8   In which south-western US state is the city of Albuquerque?

9   What nationality is the singer José Carreras?

10 The proposed merger of Sainsbury's with which other supermarket was vetoed in April 2019?

11 In cycling, what did the name of Team Sky change to in 2019?

12 Which city forms the main setting for the film *Trainspotting*?

13 Which fort was the location of a game show presented by Melinda Messenger?

14 In which country is the 1977 novel *The Thorn Birds* set?

15 Which book of the Old Testament is a word for a mass departure?

16 Who played the title role in the 2018 film *Robin Hood*?

17 In which year did Croatia join the European Union?

18 In the British civil honours such as MBE and OBE, for what does the E stand?

19 What genre is the Lonesome Dove series of novels, written by Larry McMurtry?

20 Which sporting tournament did Gary Woodland win for the first time in June 2019?

Answers to QUIZ 251 – Pot Luck

1	November	11	Three
2	25th anniversary	12	1960s (1964)
3	15	13	Costa del Sol
4	Tunisia	14	Japan
5	Sir Robin Day	15	Tom Cruise
6	Red	16	Travel
7	Piano	17	Pessimist
8	The eyes	18	Jim Carrey
9	Zulu	19	Bucks Fizz
10	Sir David Lean	20	A dog

1 In 2011, who became a permanent co-presenter on *The One Show* alongside Alex Jones?

2 The characters of Alison McIntosh and Sandy Wilson appear in which crime drama series?

3 Chris Barrie starred in which sitcom set in a leisure centre?

4 Who was the original host of *Bargain Hunt*?

5 *Killing Eve* was adapted from novels by Luke Jennings by which actress and writer?

6 "Who shot Phil Mitchell?" was a famous 2001 storyline in which long-running drama series?

7 Which decade was the setting for the 2019 series *Traitors*?

8 In what type of institution is *Grey's Anatomy* set?

9 *The Third* and *Goes Forth* were series titles of which sitcom?

10 Who hosts the singing competition *All Together Now*?

11 Lauren Pope is associated with which reality show?

12 Who presents the TV series *This Time Next Year*?

13 The *Fawlty Towers* waiter Manuel was from which country?

14 What relation was Cersei Lannister to Tyrion Lannister in *Game of Thrones*?

15 The murder of Danny Latimer formed the basis of which crime drama series?

16 Ria's cooking was the source of amusement in what sitcom first broadcast in 1978?

17 Jimmi Harkishin plays which character in *Coronation Street*?

18 Which 2018 series featured John Goodman as an international prosecution barrister?

19 Compo was a famous character from which series?

20 Which 2019 talent competition was won by 14-year-old Ellie Fergusson?

Answers to QUIZ 252 – Gold and Silver

1	Foot-and-mouth disease	11	Western
2	Spoon	12	Jason and the Argonauts
3	Sting	13	30
4	Nevada	14	Sir Sean Connery
5	Apple	15	*Hi Ho Silver Lining*
6	Spoon and fork	16	1940s (1945)
7	Werewolf	17	Queensland
8	The tongue	18	Silver-gilt
9	Austro-Hungarian	19	Rumplestiltskin
10	Tonto (*The Lone Ranger*)	20	Sir Roger Moore

ANSWERS ON PAGE 257

1   Rhinology is associated with which part of the body?

2   Which band had a hit in 1998 with *My Favourite Game*?

3   Billy Bunter was the most famous pupil of which fictional school?

4   National Hunt racing in the UK is divided into two branches – steeplechasing and which other?

5   The Gordano services in Somerset are on which motorway?

6   Which European country has the international dialling code 0034?

7   What is a besom?

8   What nationality is golfer Tommy Fleetwood?

9   *First Contact* and *Into Darkness* are film titles in which series?

10 Ligue 1 is the top footballing league in which country?

11 Which large rodent is a national emblem of Canada?

12 The video to which Peter Gabriel single included stop-motion animation and claymation?

13 What role does Portia play at Antonio's trial in *The Merchant of Venice*?

14 What type of creature is a chub?

15 With which children's programme is the phrase "Here's one I made earlier" associated?

16 What is the occupation of Ben Stiller's character in the *Zoolander* films?

17 *Lungs* was a Brit Award Best Album winner by which group?

18 What sport is played by the Atlanta Braves?

19 Which French city is the official seat of the European parliament?

20 Which member of Hear'Say left the group several months before they disbanded?

Easy

Medium

Hard

Answers to QUIZ 253 – Pot Luck

1	Four	11	Team Ineos
2	*Pretty Woman*	12	Edinburgh
3	Mississippi	13	Fort Boyard
4	A bird (of the finch family)	14	Australia
5	Four	15	Exodus
6	Nature reserve	16	Taron Egerton
7	A bird in the hand	17	2013
8	New Mexico	18	Empire
9	Spanish	19	Western
10	Asda	20	US Open Golf

Easy

1 For which international team did George Best play?

2 Phil Taylor is a multiple world title winner in which sport?

3 Former England Test cricket captain Graham Gooch captained which county side?

4 In which city does the end of season ATP Masters Tennis event take place?

5 In which year did Steve Cram win his only Olympic medal?

6 Former Rally driver and WRC team principal Tommi Mäkinen is from which country?

7 Which ex-footballer and former World Player of the Year became president of his country in 2018?

8 "Kiwis" is the nickname of which nation's rugby league team?

9 Which colour ball is worth one point in snooker?

10 Which football club won Serie A every year from 2012 to 2019?

Medium

11 In which city do the Redskins play their NFL games?

12 Golfer Charl Schwartzel is from which country?

13 Lindsay Vonn retired from competing in which sport in 2019?

14 In which UK city did the 2014 Tour de France start?

15 Which football club won the Dutch league in 2019 for the 34th time?

16 Yorkshire's limited-overs county side have what name?

17 Long Track is a variation of which winter sport?

18 Mike Ashley bought which football club in 2007?

19 The MLB is the name of the main North American league in what sport?

20 What is the maximum number of people in a game of Olympic badminton?

Hard

Answers to QUIZ 254 – Television

1	Matt Baker	11	The Only Way is Essex
2	Shetland	12	Davina McCall
3	The Brittas Empire	13	Spain (Barcelona)
4	David Dickinson	14	Sister
5	Phoebe Waller-Bridge	15	Broadchurch
6	EastEnders	16	Butterflies
7	1940s	17	Dev Alahan
8	Hospital	18	Black Earth Rising
9	Blackadder	19	Last of the Summer Wine
10	Rob Beckett	20	The Greatest Dancer

1 For which 2011 film did Jean Dujardin win the Best Actor Oscar?

2 What verb can mean both "to cool" and "to frighten"?

3 What is the length of an Olympic swimming pool in metres?

4 *Rebel Rouser* and *Peter Gunn* were 1950s hits for whom?

5 Which Olympic rower became the oldest member of a winning Boat Race crew in 2019 at the age of 46?

6 What traditional instrument does Alastair Campbell play?

7 How is 53 represented in Roman numerals?

8 In which month are two of the UK's patron saints celebrated?

9 What type of creature is a gopher?

10 Commissioner James Gordon is most closely associated with which superhero?

11 The capital of which US state shares its name with a port in Kent?

12 Which actor (d.2015) wrote the autobiography *The World Was My Lobster*?

13 *Europe's Most Wanted* is the title of the third film in which animated series?

14 Which company manufactures the NEXO car model?

15 In which county is Hemel Hempstead?

16 Miss Hannigan is a character in which musical?

17 How many points must a snooker player score within one visit at the table to make a century break?

18 Lord Farquaad is the villain in which series of films?

19 What type of illumination also means to take a second job on the side?

20 Which actress presented the TV series *Watercolour Challenge*?

Answers to QUIZ 255 – Pot Luck

1	Nose	11	Beaver
2	The Cardigans	12	*Sledgehammer*
3	Greyfriars	13	Lawyer
4	Hurdles	14	A fish
5	M5	15	*Blue Peter*
6	Spain	16	Fashion model
7	A broom (made of twigs and a pole)	17	Florence and the Machine
8	English	18	Baseball
9	*Star Trek*	19	Strasbourg
10	France	20	Kym Marsh

Easy

1 *The Brothers Karamazov* is a famous Russian novel by whom?

2 *Tess of the D'urbevilles* was written by whom?

3 *The Canterbury Tales* was started in which century?

4 What nationality was poet and playwright Seamus Heaney (d.2013)?

5 *The Silmarillion* is a novel by which writer?

6 Who wrote a trilogy of 1970s novels about the fictional Mallen family?

7 Who wrote the 2018 novel *Transcription*?

8 Published in 1996, what is the title of Alex Garland's most famous work?

9 What was the middle name of writer Richard Sheridan?

10 Which Brontë sister was the oldest?

11 What word completes the 14th-century work by Dante, *The Divine ___*?

Medium

12 What nationality was the writer and preacher John Bunyan (d.1688)?

13 *The Hound of the Baskervilles* was written by which author?

14 Who wrote the classic work *The Water Babies*?

15 Who was announced as the new Poet Laureate in May 2019?

16 Room 101 features in which 1949 novel?

17 What nationality was Miguel de Cervantes?

18 For what does the "T" stand in the name of TS Eliot?

19 Wackford Squeers is a key character in which Dickens work?

20 Who wrote the 1989 spy novel *The Russia House*?

Hard

Answers to QUIZ 256 – Sport

1	Northern Ireland	11	Washington
2	Darts	12	South Africa
3	Essex	13	Alpine skiing
4	London	14	Leeds
5	1984 (1500m silver)	15	Ajax
6	Finland	16	Vikings
7	George Weah (Liberia)	17	Speed skating
8	New Zealand	18	Newcastle United FC
9	Red	19	Baseball
10	Juventus	20	Four

1   *That'll Be The Day* was a 1958 album by which singer?

2   Mongolia is bordered by Russia and which other major Asian country?

3   Gaz and Horse are leading characters in which 1997 film?

4   What was the name of the US president for whom New York's Idlewild Airport was renamed in 1963?

5   Which piece of cricket equipment when new must weigh between 156g and 163g?

6   The zodiac sign Aquarius covers which two calendar months?

7   On which show did One Direction find fame?

8   Which 1972 film included the line "I'm gonna make him an offer he can't refuse"?

9   The Eucharist is a key part of which religion?

10   Who won the Best Leading Actress BAFTA award in 2019 for her role in the series *Killing Eve*?

11   What nationality is golfer Francesco Molinari?

12   John Boyega plays which *Star Wars* character in *The Force Awakens*?

13   Which is the shortest race in the decathlon?

14   What does a trainee lawyer and courtroom advocate become when he or she is "called to the bar"?

15   Proverbially, what do you work to the bone if you are working very hard?

16   Which UK prime minister introduced the "Cones hotline" for reporting apparently unnecessary traffic cones?

17   Bamm-Bamm Rubble is a character in which animated TV series?

18   Which US state includes the major cities of Philadelphia, Pittsburgh and Allentown?

19   What is the radio code word for the second letter of the alphabet?

20   Which is the second longest river in China?

Easy
Medium
Hard

Answers to QUIZ 257 – Pot Luck

1	*The Artist*	11	Delaware (Dover)
2	Chill	12	George Cole
3	50m	13	*Madagascar*
4	Duane Eddy	14	Hyundai
5	James Cracknell	15	Hertfordshire
6	Bagpipes	16	*Annie*
7	LIII	17	100
8	March (St David and St Patrick)	18	*Shrek*
9	A rodent	19	Moonlight
10	Batman	20	Hannah Gordon

1 What does a phlebotomist specialise in?

2 Ronnie Barker played a shopkeeper in which sitcom?

3 Which 2007 Simon Pegg film revolves around police officers?

4 What is the term given to someone who writes work that is officially credited to someone else?

5 In what environment does an aquanaut work?

6 What is the term given to the person responsible for recording proceedings in a courtroom?

7 Someone in which profession is also known as a coiffeur?

8 What was the profession of the title character in the 2019 TV series *Warren*?

9 Where does a barista work?

10 The 1966 film *Blow-Up* is about what kind of artist?

11 Which occupation is sometimes referred to as "the rag trade"?

12 What is the name given to someone who plays the flute?

13 In the traditional song, what was Old MacDonald?

14 What kind of shop is owned by Hugh Grant's character in *Notting Hill*?

15 What is the English term for an American janitor?

16 For what is Marie Kondo famous?

17 What was Ben Harper's occupation in the TV series *My Family*?

18 In the New Testament, what was the profession of Mary's husband Joseph?

19 What is the profession of the leading characters in *Withnail and I*?

20 In the Kirsty MacColl song, where did the guy work who swore he was Elvis?

Answers to QUIZ 258 – Literature

1	Fyodor Dostoevsky	11	*Comedy*
2	Thomas Hardy	12	English
3	14th century (c.1387)	13	Sir Arthur Conan Doyle
4	Irish	14	Charles Kingsley
5	JRR Tolkein	15	Simon Armitage
6	Dame Catherine Cookson	16	*Nineteen Eighty-Four*
7	Kate Atkinson	17	Spanish
8	*The Beach*	18	Thomas
9	Brinsley	19	*Nicholas Nickleby*
10	Charlotte	20	John le Carré

1   In which fictional city is *Monsters, Inc.* set?

2   *Club Tropicana* was a 1983 hit for which duo?

3   How many golf holes have been played when someone "is at the turn"?

4   Which two words that sound the same but are spelt differently mean "a clerical dignitary" and "a large gun"?

5   What name did Manuel give to his pet hamster in a famous episode of *Fawlty Towers*?

6   *I'll Be There for You* was the theme tune to which US series?

7   Which is the most southerly city, Canterbury, Cardiff or Colchester?

8   For which country did Kapil Dev (b.1959) play cricket?

9   On a standard keyboard, which is the left-most letter on the middle row?

10 What nationality is retired sprinter Usain Bolt?

11 Who wrote, co-directed and starred in the 1977 film *High Anxiety*, a parody of Sir Alfred Hitchcock films?

12 Which sports commentator (d.2013) was the original commentator on *Dancing on Ice*?

13 The mysterious Nazca Lines, ancient patterns that can only be clearly seen from the air, are in which South American country?

14 The town of Fakenham is situated in which English county?

15 Who plays the title role in the TV series *Keeping Faith*?

16 The abbreviation "re" is short for which word?

17 What is the name given to the landing gear of large passenger aeroplanes?

18 Which Steven Spielberg film was released first, *Catch Me if You Can* or *Jurassic Park*?

19 The name of which Canadian province includes the names of two dog breeds?

20 What was Fred Dibnah's (d.2004) occupation?

Easy

Medium

Hard

Answers to QUIZ 259 – Pot Luck

1	Buddy Holly	11	Italian
2	China	12	Finn
3	*The Full Monty*	13	100m
4	John F Kennedy	14	Barrister
5	Ball	15	Your fingers
6	January and February	16	Sir John Major
7	*The X Factor*	17	*The Flintstones*
8	*The Godfather*	18	Pennsylvania
9	Christianity	19	Bravo
10	Jodie Comer	20	The Yellow River

1   Rievaulx Abbey lies in which National Park?

2   In which Dorset town was the novel *The French Lieutenant's Woman* set?

3   Which Hampshire town is famous for its international air show?

4   What is the lowest grade given to a listed building?

5   How many counties are there in Northern Ireland?

6   From what substance are the White Cliffs of Dover mostly formed?

7   Mull is part of which group of islands?

8   In the UK, what name is given to the subdivision of an army company?

9   Ledecestre is the name given to which UK city in the Doomsday Book?

10 The Scottish Parliament is based in which city?

11 The castles of Bamburgh and Dunstanburgh lie on the coast of which county?

12 Sotonians are from which UK city?

13 Opened in 2016, in which English town is the National Horseracing Museum?

14 Who became the UK's first female Defence Secretary in May 2019?

15 Which Midlands police force takes its name from an ancient kingdom?

16 The Cornish village of Tintagel lies on which body of water?

17 Birdoswald was a Roman fort alongside which historical structure?

18 DH is the postcode for which UK city?

19 The area known as "Silicon Fen" can be found in which UK city?

20 An Arthurian Round Table hangs in the Great Hall of the castle in which Hampshire city?

Answers to QUIZ 260 – Occupations

1	Drawing blood	11	Fashion (or clothing)
2	*Open All Hours*	12	Flautist
3	*Hot Fuzz*	13	A farmer
4	Ghost writer	14	Bookshop
5	Underwater	15	Caretaker
6	Stenographer	16	Decluttering or organising
7	Hairdressing	17	Dentist
8	Driving instructor	18	Carpenter
9	In a coffee shop or café	19	Acting
10	Photographer	20	Chip shop

1   Which plotter is remembered on November 5?

2   How tall in inches must cricket stumps be?

3   Who directed *Four Weddings and a Funeral?*

4   Corinthians is a text in which religion?

5   Which country has the international car registration letters EIR?

6   What was the title of the 2018 film in the Spider-Man franchise?

7   How many leaves are there on a shamrock?

8   What type of creatures are Chip 'n' Dale in the cartoon series?

9   Who won the Best Supporting Actress Oscar for her role in the 2018 film *If Beale Street Could Talk?*

10 Gary Kemp was a member of which group formed in 1979?

11 The South Hams is a local government area in which English county?

12 What is the name of Gillian Taylforth's character in *EastEnders?*

13 Victoria Beckham was known as which "Spice"?

14 Which cartoon hero has been voiced by both Sir David Jason and Alexander Armstrong?

15 Who was the lead guitarist with the Beatles?

16 Which old coin precedes the words "a pocket full of rye" in the children's song?

17 Which Caribbean island is linked with Tobago?

18 In the saying meaning that everything is all right, who is your uncle?

19 What is the result of multiplying the number of players in a football team by the number of players in a netball team?

20 Which UK prime minister said of the Battle of Britain pilots in 1940, "Never was so much owed by so many to so few'"?

Easy

Medium

Hard

Answers to QUIZ 261 – Pot Luck

1	Monstropolis	11	Mel Brooks
2	Wham!	12	Tony Gubba
3	Nine	13	Peru
4	Canon and cannon	14	Norfolk
5	Basil	15	Eve Myles
6	*Friends*	16	Regarding
7	Canterbury	17	Undercarriage
8	India	18	*Jurassic Park* (1993)
9	A	19	Newfoundland and Labrador
10	Jamaican	20	Steeplejack

1   The song *Hold On* was a 1990 no.1 for which group?

2   Who is Phil Tufnell's opposite number on *A Question of Sport*?

3   What was the name of the puppet who accompanied Phillip Schofield on Children's BBC in the 1980s?

4   Who played Phyllis in the 1970 film *The Railway Children*?

5   *EastEnders'* Phil Mitchell is played by which actor?

6   The Philippines lie in which ocean?

7   Who married Captain Mark Phillips in 1973?

8   Dame Emma and Sophie Thompson are the daughters of which actress?

9   What is the name of the TV series presented by Phil Spencer and Kirstie Allsopp in which homeowners have their house altered before deciding whether or not to sell?

10 What relation are sporting coaches Phil Neville and Tracey Neville?

11 What does a cinephile love?

12 In which building is the London Philharmonic Orchestra based?

13 What does a philatelist collect?

14 Who played the title role in the 2013 film *Philomena*?

15 What term of Biblical origin is used to describe a person who is not interested in culture?

16 Philadelphia is a brand of what type of foodstuff?

17 Who played Philippa in the TV series *dinnerladies*?

18 What was the first name of the spy Mr Philby?

19 What term is given to a person who donates money and help to those in need?

20 Leslie Ash played Steph in which 1979 film that starred Phil Daniels as a mod?

Answers to QUIZ 262 – The UK

1	North York Moors	11	Northumberland
2	Lyme Regis	12	Southampton
3	Farnborough	13	Newmarket
4	Grade III	14	Penny Mordaunt
5	Six	15	West Mercia Police
6	Chalk	16	Atlantic Ocean
7	Inner Hebrides	17	Hadrian's Wall
8	Platoon	18	Durham
9	Leicester	19	Cambridge
10	Edinburgh	20	Winchester

1. What word can describe both a chemical substance and a cutting remark?

2. Which county in the north-east of England includes Newcastle-upon-Tyne, Gateshead and Sunderland?

3. The 1998 film *The Truman Show* starred which actor in the title role?

4. What is the name of Donald Duck's girlfriend?

5. What shape is the indentation in a Jammie Dodger biscuit?

6. In which 1955 film did Sir Alec Guinness play Professor Marcus?

7. What was Whitney Houston's first UK no.1 hit of the 1990s?

8. According to the proverb, what does a watched pot never do?

9. What is the most westerly major town in Cornwall?

10. In which decade did the shell suit become popular?

11. What part of the body precedes "wave" to make a word meaning a sudden flash of inspiration?

12. Who wrote the 1986 novel *A Matter of Honour*?

13. How many US states have only four letters in their names?

14. Which former player was appointed coach of the Spanish national football team in 2018?

15. The Met Office symbol for sunny intervals shows the sun on which side of the cloud?

16. What bread product of Jewish origin is made by shaping and boiling the dough before baking?

17. *Sweet Georgia Brown* is the theme tune of which basketball team?

18. What is Madonna's surname?

19. In which English county is the town of Pickering?

20. What colour are the doubles on a standard dartboard?

Easy

Medium

Hard

Answers to QUIZ 263 – Pot Luck

1	Guy Fawkes	11	Devon
2	28 inches	12	Kathy Beale
3	Mike Newell	13	Posh Spice
4	Christianity	14	Danger Mouse
5	Republic of Ireland	15	George Harrison
6	*Spider-Man: Into the Spider-verse*	16	Sixpence
7	Three	17	Trinidad
8	Chipmunks	18	Bob
9	Regina King	19	77 (11 x 7)
10	Spandau Ballet	20	Sir Winston Churchill

Easy

1   In what form are alliums planted?

2   "Rosebud" is the final word in which 1941 film?

3   *Edelweiss* is a song from which musical film?

4   Which TV series featured Daisy Haggard as Miri, a recently-released prisoner?

5   Which playwright wrote "What's in a name? That which we call a rose. By any other name would smell as sweet"?

6   Inspector Raymond Flower was a character in which TV series?

7   What line follows "Ring a ring o' roses" in the nursery rhyme?

8   In George Orwell's *Animal Farm*, what type of creature is Clover?

9   Rose Leslie appeared as housemaid Gwen Dawson in which ITV historical drama series?

10 Which variety of daffodil takes its name from the French term for a private conversation?

Medium

11 *Love Don't Live Here Any More* was a 1978 single by which group?

12 The word for which part of a flower also means something to be ashamed of?

13 In which Gilbert and Sullivan opera does the character of Little Buttercup appear?

14 What were the names of Daisy Duke's cousins in the TV series *The Dukes of Hazzard*?

15 Which company makes Roses chocolates?

16 Who played Miss Eglantine Price in the 1971 film *Bedknobs and Broomsticks*?

17 Who did Heather Morris play in the TV series *Glee*?

18 What common garden flower lends its name to a make of rubber gloves, usually yellow?

19 Adding unnecessary adornment is referred to as gilding which flower?

20 What type of animal is Flower in the animated film *Bambi*?

Hard

---

1   Which former Dutch striker (b.1969) famously has a fear of flying?

2   In which year was *EastEnders* first broadcast?

3   What is the name given to the small cycle-powered boat found on boating lakes?

4   What nationality is former tennis player Pete Sampras?

5   In what item of crockery is a storm said to take place over a small matter?

6   Which 1952 classic musical starring Gene Kelly, Donald O'Connor and Debbie Reynolds is set as the silent films are taken over by talkies ?

7   What type of ship acts as a runway for military jets?

8   For what does *ER* stand in the title of the US drama series?

9   What is the Internet domain code for the Republic of Ireland?

10 In April 2019, who won the 1000th Formula 1 Grand Prix?

11 What nationality was the composer Rimsky-Korsakov?

12 In what year did Japan enter WWII?

13 Which UK prime minister introduced the idea of "the Big Society"?

14 Craig Charles and Chris Barrie are stars of which sci-fi series, first broadcast in 1988?

15 What type of dog lends its name to a long-winded story?

16 What two-word term is given to the theory of the rapid expansion of the universe?

17 "Well, it's one for the money, two for the show" are the opening lines of which 1955 song?

18 The song *You've Got a Friend in Me* features in which series of animated films?

19 Which is the second largest and second most populous continent?

20 Which officer in the army is responsible for the supply of all equipment?

Answers to QUIZ 265 – Pot Luck

1	Caustic	11	Brain
2	Tyne and Wear	12	Jeffrey Archer
3	Jim Carrey	13	Three (Iowa, Ohio and Utah)
4	Daisy Duck	14	Luis Enrique
5	A heart	15	On the right
6	*The Ladykillers*	16	Bagel
7	*I Will Always Love You* (1992)	17	Harlem Globetrotters
8	Boil	18	Ciccone
9	Penzance	19	North Yorkshire
10	1980s	20	Green

1   Which room in Arles formed the title of three paintings by Vincent van Gogh?

2   Degas belonged to which artistic school?

3   Who was Henry VIII's court painter?

4   How many panels does a diptych altarpiece have?

5   Complete the title of a famous Manet work of 1863: *Luncheon on the___*?

6   *Impression, Sunrise* (1872) is a famous work of art by which painter?

7   Is gouache paint opaque or transparent?

8   In which century did abstract art originate?

9   In which English city was Damien Hirst born?

10 Ceramic items are made from what substance?

11 Who painted *Four Marilyns*?

12 The village of Dedham and its surroundings were associated with which English painter?

13 Which famous artwork had both its painted versions stolen and subsequently recovered from galleries in Oslo in 1994 and 2004?

14 The Biennale art exhibition takes place in which Italian city?

15 Which 17th-century Dutch artist was particularly noted for his self-portraits?

16 In which gallery can Botticelli's *Birth of Venus* be seen?

17 What colour paint is obtained by mixing blue and yellow?

18 In which American city is the Guggenheim Museum?

19 Which modelling material takes its name from the French for "chewed paper"?

20 The 1536-41 fresco *The Last Judgement* was painted by which artist?

Answers to QUIZ 266 – Flowers

1	Bulbs	11	Rose Royce
2	*Citizen Kane*	12	Stigma
3	*The Sound of Music*	13	*HMS Pinafore*
4	*Back to Life*	14	Bo and Luke
5	William Shakespeare	15	Cadbury
6	*The Thin Blue Line*	16	Dame Angela Lansbury
7	A pocket full of posies	17	Brittany S Pierce
8	A horse	18	Marigold
9	*Downton Abbey*	19	The lily
10	Tête-à-tête	20	Skunk

1 The character of Colonel Pickering appears in which musical?

2 *It's All Coming Back to Me Now* was a hit for which female singer in 1996?

3 In which film did Tom Hanks first play Professor Robert Langdon?

4 Which city in the north-east of the USA is famous for its "tea party" political protest in 1773?

5 The positions of "short leg" and "short third man" are used in which sport?

6 In which Middle Eastern city is The Dome of the Rock situated?

7 Which day of the week is named after the ancient Norse god of thunder and lightning?

8 In which 1960 film did Kirk Douglas play the leader of a slave revolt in ancient Rome?

9 The promontory of Portland Bill, on the coast of Dorset, stretches into which body of water?

10 What is the name of the walkway that runs along the side of a canal?

11 Which part of the body would a reflexologist be concerned with?

12 Shabbat candlesticks are used in which religion?

13 "Tumble out of bed and stumble to the kitchen" is a lyric from which song?

14 The headquarters of Bloomingdale's is located in which US city?

15 Which player in a football team traditionally wears the number nine shirt?

16 The Ganges flows through India and which other country?

17 What will there be over the white cliffs of Dover, according to the wartime song?

18 Who played Raquel Watts in *Coronation Street*?

19 Ailsa Craig is a variety of which salad ingredient?

20 How long is the run in an Olympic triathlon?

Easy

Medium

Hard

Answers to QUIZ 267 – Pot Luck

1	Dennis Bergkamp	11	Russian
2	1985	12	1941
3	Pedalo	13	David Cameron
4	American	14	*Red Dwarf*
5	Teacup	15	Shaggy dog
6	*Singin' in the Rain*	16	Big Bang (Theory)
7	Aircraft carrier	17	*Blue Suede Shoes*
8	Emergency Room	18	Toy Story
9	.ie	19	Africa
10	Lewis Hamilton	20	Quartermaster

Easy

1   In the USA, what type of food is chowder?

2   The Greek spirit ouzo has what flavour?

3   What cookery term describes a sauce or other mixture that has split into different parts?

4   What are traditionally eaten on Shrove Tuesday?

5   Gravadlax is what type of fish?

6   What is folded into a half-moon shape to make a calzone?

7   Which fruit has the Latin name *Citrus limon*?

8   In Italian cuisine, what is pollo?

9   Which English city is famous for its Brown Ale?

10 What Japanese term refers to a soy sauce marinade, often applied to meat dishes?

11 Navel is a popular variety of what type of fruit?

12 Garlic is a member of which family of plants?

13 Tortillas and nachos are dishes from which country?

Medium

14 What sweet foodstuff was taken in the boat in Edward Lear's *The Owl and the Pussycat*?

15 Which order of monks lends its name to an Italian coffee?

16 What part of the plant horseradish is used to make sauce?

17 Does a fresh egg sink or float if dropped into a bowl of water?

18 Trocken is a drier style of which country's wine?

19 What does "on the rocks" mean in relation to a drink?

20 In what is bread dipped to make French toast?

Hard

Answers to QUIZ 268 – Art

1	Bedroom	11	Andy Warhol
2	Impressionism	12	John Constable
3	Hans Holbein (the Younger)	13	*The Scream* (Edvard Munch)
4	Two	14	Venice
5	*Grass*	15	Rembrandt
6	Monet	16	The Uffizi (Florence)
7	Opaque	17	Green
8	20th century	18	New York
9	Bristol	19	*Papier-mâché*
10	Clay	20	Michelangelo

ANSWERS ON PAGE 273

Easy

1   Which part of a car benefits from ABS?

2   Which leading Shakespeare character has a sword fight with Laertes?

3   King Triton is a character in which 1989 Disney film?

4   Which lies furthest north: Derby, Nottingham or Stoke-on-Trent?

5   In relation to metal, for what does the "N" stand in EPNS?

6   Of what is seismology the study?

7   What did an apothecary sell?

8   *Consider Yourself* was a hit song from which musical film?

9   How many points is the letter H worth in Scrabble®?

10 Who created and played the Sheriff of Nottingham in the series *Maid Marian and Her Merry Men*?

11 Nikita Khrushchev died during which decade?

12 Ti is the chemical symbol for which element?

13 Shelley Kerr was appointed captain of which UK country's women's football team in 2017?

14 What fruit are you said to have two bites at, if you get a second attempt at something?

15 Who wrote the 1993 novel *The Man Who Made Husbands Jealous*?

16 Which Canadian province, capital Edmonton, was named after one of Queen Victoria's daughters?

17 Jade, Perrie, Leigh-Anne and Jesy form which group?

18 What type of creature is a green-veined white?

19 What is the name given to the aeroplane used to transport the US president and his entourage?

20 If you want to diversify, which items should you avoid putting in one basket?

Easy

Medium

Hard

Answers to QUIZ 269 – Pot Luck

1	*My Fair Lady*	11	Feet
2	Celine Dion	12	Judaism
3	*The Da Vinci Code*	13	9 to 5
4	Boston	14	New York
5	Cricket	15	Centre-forward
6	Jerusalem	16	Bangladesh
7	Thursday (Thor)	17	Bluebirds
8	*Spartacus*	18	Sarah Lancashire
9	English Channel	19	Tomato
10	Towpath	20	10km

1   In Prokofiev's *Peter and the Wolf*, which instrument represents the duck?

2   The painted wolf is a member of which family of animals?

3   Lake Wolfgang lies in which European country?

4   The novel *Wolf Hall* was set in which century?

5   As whom did the Big Bad Wolf disguise himself in the tale of *Little Red Riding Hood*?

6   "Wolves" is the nickname of which West Midlands football club?

7   Which journalist and broadcaster co-wrote the sitcom *Raised by Wolves* with her sister Caroline?

8   Who starred as Scott Howard in the 1985 film *Teen Wolf*?

9   Where was the American Werewolf in the title of the 1981 film directed by John Landis?

10 What adjective is used to describe a wolf?

11 Which TV series, first broadcast in 1977, featured the character of Wolfie Smith?

12 A 2007 memoir by former stockbroker Jordan Belfort was the basis for which 2013 film?

13 What has someone done if they are accusing of "crying wolf"?

14 What name is given to the young of a wolf?

15 Wolfram is the old name for which chemical element?

16 In which 2000 film did Hugh Jackman first play the character of Wolverine?

17 Who released the 2009 album *She Wolf*?

18 How many Oscars did the 1990 film *Dances with Wolves* win from its 12 nominations?

19 What nationality is Mercedes F1 team principal Toto Wolff?

20 What type of transport featured in the 1980s TV series *Airwolf*?

Answers to QUIZ 270 – Food and Drink

1	Soup	11	Orange
2	Aniseed	12	Alliums
3	Curdled	13	Mexico
4	Pancakes	14	Honey
5	Salmon	15	Capuchin (cappuccino)
6	A pizza	16	The root
7	Lemon	17	Sink
8	Chicken	18	Germany
9	Newcastle-upon-Tyne	19	With ice
10	Teriyaki	20	Egg

1   Mia Dolan and Sebastian Wilder were the main characters in which 2016 film?

2   What was the title of the 2018 sequel to *Wreck-it Ralph*?

3   Brookfield Farm is the main location of which radio series?

4   Which word for a sore is an anagram of "cruel"?

5   Peach, Bloat, Gurgle and Bubbles are all characters in which animated film?

6   What two-word Latin term means "way of working"?

7   What colour flag does a starter use to organise the horses ahead of a race?

8   A short time can be compared to two shakes of what young animal's tail?

9   In which county is the seaside town of Aldeburgh?

10 The M6 Toll road bypasses which city?

11 In which sitcom did James Beck play Private Joe Walker?

12 *Walk Like an Egyptian* was a 1986 hit for which group?

13 What type of "wave" do sports spectators sometimes perform in an arena?

14 A wolf is said to disguise itself in what other animal's clothing to appear innocent?

15 Who composed *An American in Paris*?

16 Which singer had a 1972 hit with *Starman*?

17 Which gymnastic move involves a sideways somersault onto the hands and back onto the feet?

18 The radio code word for which letter of the alphabet is the name of a month?

19 What is a Roman candle?

20 Sweden is connected by the Øresund Bridge and the Drogden tunnel to which other country?

Answers to QUIZ 271 – Pot Luck

1	Brakes (Anti-lock braking system)	11	1970s (1971)
2	Hamlet	12	Titanium
3	*The Little Mermaid*	13	Scotland
4	Stoke-on-Trent	14	Cherry
5	Nickel	15	Jilly Cooper
6	Earthquakes	16	Alberta
7	Medicine	17	Little Mix
8	*Oliver!*	18	A butterfly
9	Four	19	Air Force One
10	Sir Tony Robinson	20	Eggs

1   How many countries share a land border with Cape Verde?

2   Bohemia is a historical region in which modern-day country?

3   Of which Australian state is Adelaide the capital city?

4   In which European country is Zeeland a province?

5   What colour is the central stripe on the German flag?

6   The Hokkaido Shrine is devoted to which religion?

7   On what continent is the 3900-mile Yangtze River?

8   Llandrindod Wells lies in which Welsh county?

9   What is Spain's largest city, by population?

10 The Sahara Desert is found on what continent?

11 Winnipeg is the capital of which Canadian province?

12 What is the largest city in South Africa, with 3.7 million residents?

13 The Indian city of Chennai lies off which bay?

14 What is the name given to any flag that has a design of three vertical or horizontal stripes?

15 Helmand Province is part of which Asian country?

16 The escarpment of Wenlock Edge lies in which English county?

17 Which country contains the mouth of the river Amazon as it flows into the South Atlantic Ocean?

18 In which US state is the city of Fresno?

19 Which two countries border Sweden?

20 What continent covers the South Pole?

Answers to QUIZ 272 – Wolves

1	Oboe	11	*Citizen Smith*
2	Dogs	12	*The Wolf of Wall Street*
3	Austria	13	Raised a false alarm
4	16th century (1500–1535)	14	Cub
5	Little Red Riding Hood's grandmother	15	Tungsten
6	Wolverhampton Wanderers	16	*X-Men*
7	Caitlin Moran	17	Shakira
8	Michael J Fox	18	Seven
9	London	19	Austrian
10	Lupine	20	A helicopter

Easy

Medium

Hard

1   The Cullinan, the Hope and the Koh-i-Noor are famous examples of which gemstone?

2   Which queen is associated with the phrase "We are not amused"?

3   Which Southern Californian city is the second largest US city in terms of population?

4   In *The Great Escape*, which actor's character attempted a motorcycle jump to freedom?

5   Harry Styles was a member of which group?

6   What relative to you is your mother's mother's sister?

7   What nationality is tennis player Naomi Osaka?

8   The Murray is one of the longest rivers in which Commonwealth country?

9   Proverbially, if nothing is ventured, what is gained?

10 Pak choi is a type of which vegetable?

11 What accompanied *Green Eggs* in the title of a Dr Seuss book?

12 In which 2000 film was a FedEx executive stranded on a desert island?

13 Where would you find a lychgate?

14 "Once a jolly swagman camped by a billabong" are the opening lyrics to which song?

15 Which children's character has colleagues Elvis Cridlington, Penny Morris and Station Officer Norris Steele?

16 Who was the UK Leader of the Opposition from 1975 to 1979?

17 What name is given to a package of uneaten food taken home from a restaurant, said to be for a household pet?

18 The town of Billericay is in which county?

19 *Don't Stop Moving* was a 2001 UK no.1 hit for which group?

20 Which country on the Asian side of the Pacific Rim has Hanoi as its capital city?

Answers to QUIZ 273 – Pot Luck

1	*La La Land*	11	*Dad's Army*
2	*Ralph Breaks the Internet*	12	The Bangles
3	*The Archers*	13	Mexican wave
4	Ulcer	14	A sheep's clothing
5	*Finding Nemo*	15	George Gershwin
6	*Modus operandi*	16	David Bowie
7	White	17	Cartwheel
8	Lamb	18	N (November)
9	Suffolk	19	A firework
10	Birmingham	20	Denmark

1   What sweet thing lends its name to a driver's trick of spinning a car in a circle on one spot to leave a circular mark on the road?

2   Which English football team shares its name with a type of toffee?

3   Nougat and Honeycomb are versions of which operating system?

4   What dessert food, which may also be made as a savoury dish, is proverbially flat?

5   Liquorice sweets are usually what colour?

6   What sweet things complete the phrase "selling like ___" when applied to something that is much in demand?

7   Which part of a dartboard shares its name with a boiled sweet?

8   In *Doctor Who*, which actor introduced jelly babies as the Doctor's favourite snack?

9   Which Dickens character used the phrase "Bah humbug"?

10   Which chocolates were advertised by the slogan "All because the lady loves…"?

11   What old silver coin is traditionally put into a Christmas pudding?

12   In Italy, which frozen dessert is similar to sorbet?

13   Which Scottish dessert is usually made from cream, raspberries, oats and whisky?

14   In Haiti, what is méringue?

15   In which children's book were Everlasting Gobstoppers first introduced?

16   Which American dessert takes its name from its resemblance to the banks of a major river?

17   What form of medicinal sweet shares its name with a diamond shape?

18   In which decade did the Sweet have all their top twenty hits?

19   What flavour was the Pink Panther chocolate bar?

20   In the fairy tale involving a gingerbread house, who is Hansel's sister?

Answers to QUIZ 274 – Geography

1	None (it is an island country off Senegal)	11	Manitoba
2	Czechia/Czech Republic	12	Johannesburg
3	South Australia	13	Bay of Bengal
4	The Netherlands	14	Tricolour
5	Red	15	Afghanistan
6	Shinto	16	Shropshire
7	Asia	17	Brazil
8	Powys	18	California
9	Madrid	19	Finland and Norway
10	Africa	20	Antarctica

1   What was the title of the 2018 *Johnny English* film?

2   What nationality is 1964 Ballon d'Or winner Denis Law?

3   Brahmins are the teachers of which religion?

4   What is an NHL puck made of?

5   Robert Browning was born and died in which century?

6   How many eyes does the *Monsters Inc* character Mike Wazowski have?

7   UK driving tests were suspended in 1939 because of WWII. In what year did they resume?

8   The Gorbals is an area in which Scottish city?

9   Amelle Berrabah is a former member of which girl group?

10 What does *tostada* mean in English?

11 In which year did the Battle of Mons take place?

12 *All the Young Dudes* was a 1972 hit for which group?

13 Who, from ancient Greece, is known as the "father of medicine"?

14 What is the name of the city of Milan in Italian?

15 In which decade was Baron Dennis Healey Chancellor of the Exchequer?

16 On which Scottish motorway are the Hamilton services?

17 The town of Ludlow lies in which county?

18 Which former head of Royal Bank of Scotland had his knighthood annulled in 2012?

19 What is the name of the Indian's chief's daughter in *Peter Pan*?

20 Which team won the 2018 FA Community Shield?

Answers to QUIZ 275 – Pot Luck

1	Diamond	11	Ham
2	Queen Victoria	12	*Cast Away*
3	Los Angeles	13	In a churchyard (roofed gateway)
4	Steve McQueen's character	14	*Waltzing Matilda*
5	One Direction	15	Fireman Sam
6	Great aunt	16	Baroness Margaret Thatcher
7	Japanese	17	Doggy bag
8	Australia	18	Essex
9	Nothing	19	S Club 7
10	Cabbage	20	Vietnam

Easy

1 Which annual garden event was originally known as the RHS's "Great Spring Show"?

2 What is Liam Gallagher's full first name?

3 What is another name for the spines on a porcupine's back?

4 The young of which creature are nicknamed "humbugs" due to their striped appearance?

5 What is almond paste more usually called?

6 Which bird is also known as a "hedge-sparrow"?

7 "The Big O" was the nickname given to which singer (d.1988)?

8 What was the country now called Belize previously called?

9 Which US state is nicknamed "The Last Frontier"?

10 Prince Harry has what actual first name?

Medium

11 What nine-letter word beginning with "e" means another name for a thing that people do not want to directly speak about?

12 Which number has the nickname "Coming of Age" in bingo?

13 "The Forces Sweetheart" is a nickname for which singer?

14 Which English monarch was known as "Good Queen Bess"?

15 Someone nicknamed a Canuck is from which country?

16 Which Shakespearean character speaks the words: "What's in a name?"

17 Which 1980 comedy disaster film was known as *Flying High!* in several countries?

18 "Maccy D's" refers to which fast-food chain?

19 What is the American dish mac and cheese called in the UK?

20 What is actor Kit Harington's full first name?

Hard

1. What type of creature is a chequered skipper?

2. In which decade was the TV series *Mad Men* set?

3. What name for the head straps of a horse precedes the word "way" to make the name of a trail for horse riders?

4. Which UK prime minister, first elected in the 20th century, was famous for his "Third Way" policies?

5. According to the proverb, to which city do all roads lead?

6. "Garden Gate" is a traditional bingo call for which number?

7. If you overpack you are said to be taking everything except for which item found in the home?

8. Which Mediterranean country lies in both Asia and Europe and borders Bulgaria and Greece on its European side?

9. What type of act was *Britain's Got Talent* winner Spellbound?

10. In which 1983 film did Eddie Murphy play street hustler Billy Ray Valentine?

11. Which flower has the Latin name *Digitalis*?

12. In which country was Sir Garfield Sobers born?

13. Which Teletubby is green?

14. In golf, what is the name of the mown stretch of grass that connects the tee to the green?

15. What word follows English, Irish and Red to make the names of breeds of dog?

16. Who is the lead singer of Travis?

17. A dish described as "Wellington" has what on the outside?

18. In August 2018, which retail store chain was bought by businessman Mike Ashley?

19. Who presented the 2019 quiz show *The Family Brain Games*?

20. In the film *Life of Pi*, what four-legged creature accompanies Pi in the lifeboat on the film posters?

Answers to QUIZ 277 – Pot Luck

1	*Johnny English Strikes Again*	11	1914
2	Scottish	12	Mott the Hoople
3	Hinduism	13	Hippocrates
4	(Vulcanised) rubber	14	Milano
5	19th century (1812-1889)	15	1970s (1974-79)
6	One	16	M74
7	1946	17	Shropshire
8	Glasgow	18	Fred Goodwin
9	Sugababes	19	Tiger Lily
10	Toasted	20	Manchester City

Easy

1   As at 2019, who was the youngest person to be elected US president?

2   In what century did Benjamin Disraeli serve as UK prime minister?

3   Who succeeded Charles Kennedy in 2006 as Leader of the Liberal Democrats?

4   Who was the UK home secretary from 1997 to 2001?

5   How many years did Boris Yeltsin serve as president of Russia?

6   Sirimavo Bandaranaike served three terms as the head of state in which country?

7   Which UK prime minister said "Success is not final, failure is not fatal: it is the courage to continue that counts"?

8   Emperor Akihito abdicated as emperor of which country in April 2019?

9   Which former deputy prime minister is nicknamed "Prezza"?

10 In what year was Bill Clinton elected President of the USA?

11 Mao Zedong established the People's Republic of China in what decade?

12 Which former prime minister published his memoir *A Journey* in 2010?

13 Which vegetable did former US president George HW Bush famously dislike?

14 In which decade did François Mitterrand become president of France?

15 What is the name of the lower chamber of the US Congress?

Medium

16 Who was the acting leader of the Labour party between Gordon Brown's resignation and Ed Miliband's appointment?

17 In which century did Warren Harding become US president?

18 Who held the post of UK foreign secretary from 2010 to 2014?

19 Which Cabinet position did Theresa May hold immediately before becoming prime minister?

20 What was the original date scheduled in 2019 for Britain's exit from the European Union?

Hard

Answers to QUIZ 278 – Also Known As

1	Chelsea Flower Show	11	Euphemism
2	William	12	18
3	Quills	13	Dame Vera Lynn
4	Wild boar	14	Elizabeth I
5	Marzipan	15	Canada
6	Dunnock	16	Juliet
7	Roy Orbison	17	*Airplane!*
8	British Honduras	18	McDonalds
9	Alaska	19	Macaroni cheese
10	Henry	20	Christopher

ANSWERS ON PAGE **283**

1   What was the first name of the German composer Wagner?

2   "In sooth, I know not why I am so sad" is the opening line of which Shakespeare play?

3   *Toot Sweets* is a song from which musical film?

4   In a medley swimming race, which stroke do most swimmers use on the last freestyle leg?

5   Which word meaning a dazzling light is an anagram of "regal"?

6   In Irish folklore, what colour are leprechauns usually dressed in?

7   Which pigment is responsible for a sunbather's brown colour?

8   In which country was Walmart founded?

9   *Gonna Make You a Star* was a 1974 hit for which singer?

10 Who was given the award for Worst Actor of the Century at the 2000 Razzie awards?

11 Which actress won the Best Actress Oscar first, Audrey Hepburn or Sophia Loren?

12 In what key is a piece of music that has one flat as its key signature?

13 Merlene Ottey is a former competitor in which sport?

14 What is the name of the block of flats which is home to Del Trotter in *Only Fools and Horses*?

15 Where would you find a sleeping policeman?

16 From which London station does the Gatwick Express depart?

17 What name is given to the early part of the evening when drinks in a pub are sold at a lower price?

18 How is 18 represented in Roman numerals?

19 Which river rises in the Cambrian mountains and flows through Shropshire, Worcestershire and Gloucestershire and into the Bristol Channel?

20 Lumbar disc herniation occurs in which part of the human body?

Answers to QUIZ 279 – Pot Luck

1	A butterfly	11	Foxglove
2	1960s	12	Barbados
3	Bridle (way)	13	Dipsy
4	Tony Blair	14	Fairway
5	Rome	15	Setter
6	Eight	16	Fran Healy
7	Kitchen sink	17	Pastry
8	Turkey	18	House of Fraser
9	Gymnastics act	19	Dara Ó Briain
10	*Trading Places*	20	Tiger

Easy

1 What feelings would a person have towards their *bête noire*?

2 What term is given to occasions when day and night are of equal length?

3 If someone is described as lugubrious, are they cheerful or sad?

4 Which part of a shoe has the same name as part of the mouth?

5 What word meaning "to do again" is an anagram of "tea tier"?

6 In Cockney rhyming slang, what is a "butcher's"?

7 What is the correct spelling for a pirate: bucaneer, buccaneer, or buccanneer?

8 What does someone described as a charlatan pretend to have?

9 How many vowels are there in the alphabet?

10 In what container would something be cooked if it was braised?

Medium

11 What is a buffoon?

12 Which language shares its name with a citrus fruit?

13 What word is the antonym of the noun "exit"?

14 Kayak, deed and rotor are examples of what type of word?

15 The cochlea bone takes its name from the Greek for the shell of what creature?

16 What does "hirsute" mean?

17 On what island was the Manx language spoken?

18 What word can mean idle talk or the sound of a brook?

19 Which word meaning "twisted" is an anagram of "wary"?

20 Which chord shares its name with an old secret Chinese society?

Hard

Answers to QUIZ 280 – Politics

1	John F Kennedy (43)	11	1940s (1949)
2	19th century	12	Tony Blair
3	Menzies (Ming) Campbell (Baron Campbell of Pittenweem)	13	Broccoli
		14	1980s (1981)
4	Jack Straw	15	House of Representatives
5	Eight	16	Harriet Harman
6	Sri Lanka	17	20th century (1921)
7	Sir Winston Churchill	18	William Hague (Baron Hague of Richmond)
8	Japan	19	Home Secretary
9	John Prescott (Baron Prescott)	20	March 29
10	1992		

1 What is an auricula?

2 *X and Y* is a Brit Award Best Album winner by which band?

3 What number shirt does the lock in rugby league traditionally wear?

4 Who provided the voice of Duke Caboom in *Toy Story 4*?

5 What is the meaning of the Latin phrase *nil desperandum*?

6 Which word can mean both a pool of money and a carnival vehicle?

7 "We'll be lookin' flashy in my Mercedes Benz" is a lyric to which song?

8 Which country hosted the 2019 Eurovision Song Contest?

9 Which Leonardo DiCaprio film was released first, *The Aviator* or *The Departed*?

10 In the New Testament, what was the trade of Andrew, one of the twelve apostles?

11 Which TV drama series, broadcast in both English and its native language, is known in its homeland as *Un Bore Mercher*?

12 Louie Spence became famous on a documentary about which London dance studio?

13 What is the county town of Shropshire?

14 What term for delaying acceptance of an invitation originates from the ticket stub given to baseball fans when a game is cancelled because of bad weather?

15 In which sport do competitors keep their missiles in a quiver?

16 Which children's TV series is set in Bikini Bottom?

17 From which French wine region does claret come?

18 Which three zodiac star signs are traditionally depicted by horned animals?

19 The 2014 film *Selma* is set in which country?

20 What imperial weight is equal to 28.35 grams?

Easy

Medium

Hard

Answers to QUIZ 281 – Pot Luck

1	Richard	11	Audrey Hepburn (1954)
2	*The Merchant of Venice*	12	F major
3	*Chitty Chitty Bang Bang*	13	Athletics (sprinter)
4	Front crawl	14	Nelson Mandela House
5	Glare	15	On a road (speed hump)
6	Green	16	Victoria
7	Melanin	17	Happy hour
8	USA	18	XVIII
9	David Essex	19	River Severn
10	Sylvester Stallone	20	The back

1 What type of zoo animal is Alex, the character voiced by Ben Stiller in the *Madagascar* films?

2 Sasha Fierce is the alter-ego of which singer?

3 In which year was *The Angry Birds Movie* released?

4 Who was the fourth president of the United States?

5 Is the George Cross a civilian or military medal?

6 What accompanies crossbones on a pirate flag?

7 The tale of the *Three Billy Goats Gruff* originated in which country?

8 What is a madrigal?

9 Sierra Madre is a town in which US state?

10 Bathsheba Everdene is a central character in which 1874 novel?

11 *Suddenly* by Angry Anderson was used in which series during the wedding of Charlene and Scott?

12 Charing Cross station lies between Hungerford Bridge and which London street?

13 The group of writers known as the Angry Young Men were so named in which decade?

14 What type of creature is a crossbill?

15 Madrid is the capital of which country?

16 What type of animal was the grumpy internet celebrity Tardar Sauce?

17 If you dot the "i's", which letters do you cross?

18 Who played Don Draper in the TV series *Mad Men*?

19 Oscar the Grouch appears on which TV programme?

20 Who starred in the 1957 film *12 Angry Men*?

Answers to QUIZ 282 – Words

1	Dislike	11	A foolish person
2	Equinox	12	Mandarin
3	Sad	13	Entrance
4	Tongue	14	Palindrome
5	Iterate	15	Snail
6	Look (butcher's hook)	16	Hairy
7	Buccaneer	17	Isle of Man
8	Specialist skills or knowledge	18	Babble
9	Five	19	Awry
10	A pan	20	Triad

1   *Rat Rapping* was a single by which TV puppet?

2   Which Biblical couple are used as rhyming slang for "believe"?

3   In which winter sport do competitors steer a sled with their calf and shoulder muscles?

4   Which young bird sounds like a type of ring?

5   Who captained Australia during the 2013 Ashes series?

6   In 1965, which prime minister officially opened London's Post Office Tower?

7   Which city follows the names of Princess Beatrice and Princess Eugenie?

8   What type of house can precede the words cheese, loaf and pie to make items of food?

9   Which sports company's logo is a tick shape known as "the swoosh"?

10 Is Nottingham in the East Midlands or the West Midlands?

11 Which major cathedral in London has an area called Poets' Corner?

12 Which police force covers the National Rail network?

13 Ellis Hollins plays which character in *Hollyoaks*?

14 Which biscuit is named after a large French city on the Mediterranean coast?

15 What is the title of the 1976 comedy gangster movie where all the actors are children?

16 Which Spanish area's name translates into English as "white coast"?

17 In the 1963 film *Cleopatra*, who played the title role?

18 What type of racing takes place at the Belle Vue stadium in Manchester?

19 Where is Parkhurst prison located?

20 Who played the Master of Lake-town in *The Hobbit* films?

Easy

Medium

Hard

Answers to QUIZ 283 – Pot Luck

1	A flower (also called bear's ear)	11	*Keeping Faith*
2	Coldplay	12	Pineapple
3	13	13	Shrewsbury
4	Keanu Reeves	14	Rain check
5	Never despair	15	Archery
6	Float	16	*SpongeBob SquarePants*
7	*Get the Party Started* (Pink)	17	Burgundy
8	Israel	18	Aries (ram), Capricorn (goat) and Taurus (bull)
9	*The Aviator* (2004)	19	USA
10	Fisherman	20	Ounce

1   *I Surrender* and *All Night Long* were chart hits for which rock band?

2   What is the name of Bruce Springsteen's backing band?

3   Adam Clayton is a long-serving member of which band?

4   In which trio was Frank Beard the only member who did not sport a long beard?

5   Taken from the soundtrack to *Armageddon*, which band recorded the song *I Don't Want to Miss a Thing*?

6   Keith Moon played drums in which band?

7   Which band reached no.1 in the USA with the song *Jump* in 1984?

8   Chris Difford and Glenn Tilbrook founded which band in 1974?

9   What was Queen's first UK no.1 single?

10   From what country are the band Simple Minds?

11   Jerry Garcia was a member of which band?

12   *Keep the Faith* was a 1992 album release by which band?

13   Which band featured in the 1976 film *The Song Remains the Same*?

14   Thin Lizzy were formed in which country?

15   Which band released the 1973 single *The Ballroom Blitz*?

16   What was Status Quo's only UK no.1?

17   Jim Morrison (d.1971) was the lead singer with which band?

18   Who released the 2019 album *Shine a Light*?

19   Gene Simmons and Paul Stanley founded which band in 1973?

20   *Use Somebody* was a 2008 single by which band?

Answers to QUIZ 284 – Angry

1	Lion	11	*Neighbours*
2	Beyoncé	12	The Strand
3	2016	13	1950s
4	James Madison	14	A bird
5	Civilian	15	Spain
6	Skull	16	A cat
7	Norway	17	The "t's"
8	A song	18	Jon Hamm
9	California	19	*Sesame Street*
10	*Far from the Madding Crowd*	20	Henry Fonda

1   Which country won the Women's Six Nations trophy in 2019?

2   What type of creature is a redwing?

3   In 2019, who won the Masters golf tournament for the first time since 2005?

4   Which band had a hit album with *A Day at the Races*?

5   Jutland is a northern European peninsula shared by Germany and which other country?

6   What courageous nickname was given to Richard I, the 12th-century king of England?

7   Which company created the perfume known as No.5?

8   What two words precede Iced Tea in the name of a cocktail?

9   Dr Teeth and the Electric Mayhem was the house band on which TV comedy series?

10 What is the name of the picture format that is taller than it is wide?

11 Derbyshire, Lincolnshire, South Yorkshire and which other county border Nottinghamshire?

12 According to the well-known phrase, what is the spice of life?

13 Which UK prime minster has been played by Albert Finney in *The Gathering Storm* and Timothy Spall in *The King's Speech*?

14 What was the ancient Egyptian paper made from a grassy plant called?

15 In which country was Nando's restaurant chain first established?

16 What is the common name of the teeth that grow right at the back of the jaw in adults?

17 What is the name of the pack of cards used by fortune tellers and which includes The High Priestess and Wheel of Fortune?

18 Russell Crowe played boxer James Braddock in which 2005 film?

19 What nautical measure of depth of six feet can also mean "understand"?

20 Which country lies across the Tasman Sea from Australia?

Answers to QUIZ 285 – Pot Luck

1	Roland Rat	11	Westminster Abbey
2	Adam and Eve	12	British Transport Police
3	Luge	13	Tom Cunningham
4	Cygnet (signet)	14	Nice biscuit
5	Michael Clarke	15	*Bugsy Malone*
6	Harold Wilson (Baron Wilson of Rievaulx)	16	Costa Blanca
7	York	17	Elizabeth Taylor
8	Cottage	18	Greyhound racing
9	Nike	19	Isle of Wight
10	East Midlands	20	Stephen Fry

1   Who duetted with Peter Gabriel on *Don't Give Up*?

2   *Especially for You* was a 1988 no.1 duet by which two singers?

3   Who is Jenny's viewing companion in the TV series *Gogglebox*?

4   Which two singers duetted on *Dancing in the Street* in 1985?

5   Which woman's name accompanies "Darby" in a traditional term for an elderly couple?

6   How were Bodie and Doyle known in the title of a TV series first aired in 1977?

7   Which comedy duo starred in the TV series *Peep Show*?

8   Which two actors, who later sang together, portrayed Dave Tucker and Paddy Garvey in the TV series *Soldier, Soldier*?

9   Bob Carolgees is accompanied by what puppet dog?

10 Which duo had a hit in 1974 with a cover of *Jambalaya (On the Bayou)*?

11 Which female impressionist teamed up with Alistair McGowan in the TV series *The Big Impression*?

12 Famous in the fashion world for their surnames, how are Italians Domenico and Stefano better known?

13 Which comedian often said of his partner "You can't see the join"?

14 What were the first names of the title characters of the TV series *Hart to Hart*?

15 Who replaced Ant McPartlin as presenter of *I'm a Celebrity* for the 2018 series?

16 In the cartoon series, what creatures were Tom and Jerry?

17 Which duo released the 1966 song *Hazy Shade of Winter*?

18 In which two Grand Slam tennis tournaments did Jamie Murray and Bruno Soares win the men's doubles in 2016?

19 How were Jim Carrey and Jeff Daniels described in the title of a 1994 comedy film?

20 Which duo had a 1977 hit with *Sorry, I'm a Lady*?

Answers to QUIZ 286 – Rock Music

1	Rainbow	11	The Grateful Dead
2	The E Street Band	12	Bon Jovi
3	U2	13	Led Zeppelin
4	ZZ Top	14	The Republic of Ireland
5	Aerosmith	15	Sweet
6	The Who	16	*Down Down*
7	Van Halen	17	The Doors
8	Squeeze	18	Bryan Adams
9	*Bohemian Rhapsody*	19	Kiss
10	Scotland	20	Kings of Leon

1   The zodiac sign Capricorn covers which two calendar months?

2   What are you said to paper over if you make temporary repairs to something without solving the underlying problems?

3   Who was US president first, Abraham Lincoln or Andrew Jackson?

4   Before decimalisation, how many shillings were there in a pound?

5   Which George became king of the United Kingdom in 1910?

6   In which year did Red Rum win his final Grand National?

7   When did *Britain's Got Talent* first air on TV?

8   What word can mean both a type of deer and an unused field in farming?

9   What type of companies are Equifax and Experian?

10 *How to Dismantle an Atomic Bomb* and *No Line on the Horizon* are albums by which group?

11 Which is the next prime number after 67?

12 *Waldorf Salad* was an episode of which sitcom?

13 Which US city completes the film title *Fear and Loathing In ___*?

14 Which Premier League football team has a mascot named Fred the Red?

15 The ferry from Holyhead to Dublin crosses which body of water?

16 What was the title of the 1944 Cary Grant film about a newly-married man who visits his two elderly and murderous aunts?

17 How were Cameron Diaz, Drew Barrymore and Lucy Liu known collectively in the title of a 2000 film?

18 What are jump leads used for?

19 Jon Voight is the father of which Hollywood actress?

20 Ne is the chemical symbol for which element?

Answers to QUIZ 287 – Pot Luck

1	England	11	Leicestershire
2	A bird	12	Variety
3	Tiger Woods	13	Sir Winston Churchill
4	Queen	14	Papyrus
5	Denmark	15	South Africa
6	The Lionheart	16	Wisdom teeth
7	Chanel	17	Tarot cards
8	Long Island	18	*Cinderella Man*
9	*The Muppet Show*	19	Fathom
10	Portrait	20	New Zealand

1   Callisto and Io are moons that orbit which planet?

2   In medical terms, what is hypotension?

3   What is meant by the term "heliocentric"?

4   In renal failure, which organ is not working correctly?

5   What is measured in joules?

6   Does a cation have a positive or negative charge?

7   Sn is the chemical symbol for which element?

8   Brass consists of zinc and which other material?

9   Chinese astronomers called which planet the "fire star"?

10 What is the characteristic smell of hydrogen sulphide?

11 Neuropathology is the branch of medicine dealing with diseases in which system of the body?

12 In chemistry, what is an alloy?

13 What is the name for the scientific study of sound?

14 Which chemical compound has the formula CO?

15 Geology and geography are part of which group of sciences?

16 What is the SI unit of time?

17 In which part of the body is the carotid artery located?

18 Riboflavin is part of which group of vitamins?

19 In what century did William Herschel discover Uranus?

20 What is the chemical formula for water?

Answers to QUIZ 288 – Duos

1	Kate Bush	11	Ronni Ancona
2	Kylie Minogue and Jason Donovan	12	Dolce and Gabbana
3	Lee	13	Eric Morecambe (about Ernie Wise)
4	Sir Mick Jagger and David Bowie	14	Jennifer and Jonathan
5	Joan	15	Holly Willoughby
6	*The Professionals*	16	Cat and mouse
7	Mitchell and Webb	17	Simon and Garfunkel
8	Robson Green and Jerome Flynn	18	Australian Open and US Open
9	Spit	19	*Dumb and Dumber*
10	The Carpenters	20	Baccara

1   Which Quentin Tarantino film was released first, *Jackie Brown* or *Pulp Fiction*?

2   The album of which band's 1994 reunion tour was entitled *Hell Freezes Over*?

3   What was the occupation of Edith Cavell during WWI?

4   What was the title of the Netflix series about Earth, narrated by Sir David Attenborough and first broadcast in April 2019?

5   In which country was the religion Jainism founded?

6   Which group had a 1988 UK no.1 hit with a cover of *With a Little Help from My Friends*?

7   Which sport has the nickname "Chess on Ice"?

8   *What Makes You Beautiful* was a worldwide hit for which group?

9   Is the Firth of Forth on the east coast or the west coast of Scotland?

10 What colour lies between red and yellow in a rainbow?

11 Which country has the internet code .mx?

12 The Zafira car model was made by which company?

13 Who had a hit in 1990 with *Justify My Love*?

14 What is the score in a game of tennis after the server has won the first point of the game?

15 In the Bible, for how many days was Lazarus dead before being restored to life?

16 On a standard keyboard, which letter is between J and L?

17 The retail chain Next has its headquarters in which county?

18 In *Coronation Street*, what type of building is Underworld?

19 On which continent is the republic of Guinea?

20 What nationality is former tennis player Jimmy Connors?

Answers to QUIZ 289 – Pot Luck

1	December and January	11	71
2	The cracks	12	*Fawlty Towers*
3	Andrew Jackson (1829)	13	Las Vegas
4	20	14	Manchester United FC
5	George V	15	Irish Sea
6	1977	16	*Arsenic and Old Lace*
7	2007	17	*Charlie's Angels*
8	Fallow	18	Starting a car from a battery
9	Credit reference agencies	19	Angelina Jolie
10	U2	20	Neon

Easy

1 In *This is The House that Jack Built*, what animal ate the malt?

2 Who starred in the *Ace Ventura* films?

3 How many playing cards are used to play a game of contract bridge?

4 Queen Latifah played Matron Mama Morton in which 2002 film musical?

5 What "jack" is the name given to the card game pontoon, or twenty-one, when played in a casino?

6 Who starred in the 1958 film *King Creole*?

7 How many court cards are there in a pack of playing cards?

8 The ace of which suit is traditionally decorated more elaborately than the others?

9 *She Loved Like Diamond* was a 1982 single by which New Romantic group?

10 What word can mean both "a series of cards" and "to redden"?

Medium

11 Which of the seven deadly sins involves a love of food?

12 According to the advertising jingle, "If you want a lot of chocolate on your biscuit", what should you join?

13 In mythology, the Three Graces were the daughters of which god?

14 An adult female of which household pet is called a queen?

15 Proverbially, what does absence make the heart do?

16 The Joker is the enemy of which superhero?

17 Hank, Peggy and Bobby were the main characters in which animated US sitcom first broadcast in 1997?

18 Which part of a garment might you have an ace up, if you have a secret weapon?

19 How many green bottles were originally hanging on a wall in the children's song?

20 At the start of a game of chess, the queen is between the king and which other piece?

Hard

Answers to QUIZ 290 – Science

1	Jupiter	11	Nervous system
2	Low blood pressure	12	A mixture of metals
3	Having the sun at the centre	13	Acoustics
4	Kidney	14	Carbon monoxide
5	Energy or work	15	Earth sciences
6	Positive	16	Second
7	Tin	17	Neck
8	Copper	18	Vitamin B (B2)
9	Mars	19	18th century (1781)
10	Rotten eggs	20	H_2O

1   Which Hollywood actor appeared in both *An Officer and a Gentleman* and *The Second Best Exotic Marigold Hotel*?

2   Ben Nevis is located in which range of mountains?

3   Which fish lends its name to an item of winter sports kit?

4   What is the name of the court convened to hear cases subject to military law?

5   What type of animal is the North American prairie dog?

6   In 1997, the TCCB became which cricket governing body?

7   In which century did the Manchester Ship Canal open?

8   Who played tenor horn player Andy Barrow in the 1996 comedy *Brassed Off*?

9   What word follows five o'clock to make a phrase meaning stubble?

10 Troy and Gabriella are the main characters in which series of films?

11 Which river flows into the Dead Sea?

12 Who was *Getting' Jiggy Wit It* in 1999?

13 Is St David's in north or south Wales?

14 What is the term given to the right-hand side of a boat or ship when facing forwards?

15 What is the first name of the title character of the 1971 and 2000 films *Get Carter*?

16 In which parade ground does the Trooping of the Colour ceremony take place?

17 What metric measure of length is equal to 3,280 feet 10 inches?

18 The slogan "Because I'm worth it" is associated with which personal care company?

19 Which South American country is more than ten times longer than it is wide?

20 The Feathers was the local pub in which Granada sitcom?

Easy

Medium

Hard

Answers to QUIZ 291 – Pot Luck

1	*Pulp Fiction* (1994)	11	Mexico
2	The Eagles	12	Vauxhall
3	Nurse	13	Madonna
4	*Our Planet*	14	Fifteen-love
5	India	15	Four
6	Wet Wet Wet	16	K
7	Curling	17	Leicestershire
8	One Direction	18	Factory (making textiles)
9	East coast	19	Africa
10	Orange	20	American

1   Who won the Best Actress Oscar for her role in the 2018 film *The Favourite*?

2   What is the full name of the awards given for the worst films in any given year?

3   *Gregory's Girl* (1981) is set in which country?

4   Dame Emma Thompson played Elinor Dashwood in which Jane Austen adaptation?

5   Who played James Bond in *Dr No*?

6   On which continent is *The Lion King* set?

7   Who played Albert Perks in the 1970 version of *The Railway Children*?

8   *Continental Drift* is the fourth sequel to which animated film?

9   During which century is *A Man for All Seasons* (1966) set?

10   What is Lara Croft's profession in the video game on which the Tomb Raider films are based?

11   Who directed the 1987 film *Hope and Glory*?

12   Which 1965 British film is based on a novel by Boris Pasternak?

13   *The Edge of Reason* was a sequel to which romcom?

14   Which 2018 film became the first superhero film to be nominated for the Best Picture Oscar?

15   Who directed the 1979 film *Apocalypse Now*?

16   The *Pet Sematary* films are based on a novel by which author?

17   What was the first name of the character played by Macaulay Culkin in the *Home Alone* series?

18   In which *Star Wars* film did Chewbacca first appear?

19   *Withnail and I* is set in which city?

20   What was the first film in which Elvis Presley made an appearance?

Answers to QUIZ 292 – Playing Cards

1	The rat	11	Gluttony
2	Jim Carrey	12	Our club
3	52	13	Zeus
4	*Chicago*	14	Cat
5	Blackjack	15	Grow fonder
6	Elvis Presley	16	Batman
7	12	17	*King of the Hill*
8	Ace of spades	18	Your sleeve
9	Spandau Ballet	19	Ten
10	Flush	20	Bishop

1   Flutes, oboes, clarinets and bassoons are included in which section of a classical orchestra?

2   How many points is the letter W worth in Scrabble®?

3   According to the comic song by Sir Noël Coward, mad dogs and who go out in the midday sun?

4   What beetle is known as a lightning bug in America?

5   Who had a 1965 hit with the title song to the film *What's New Pussycat*?

6   Which castle near the River Thames was originally built by William the Conqueror in the 11th century?

7   What unit of currency completes the phrase: "You can bet your bottom ___ "?

8   The radio code word for which letter of the alphabet is also the name of a drink?

9   How many metres is one lap of an athletics track?

10   What device in a car indicates how fast the vehicle is going?

11   How is 83 represented in Roman numerals?

12   Birmingham is the largest city of which US state?

13   Proverbially, what is thicker than water?

14   *The Man Who* was a Brit Award Best Album winner by which band?

15   What colour were the coats worn by staff in the TV series *Hi-de-Hi!*?

16   What word meaning of limited duration can also refer to crumbly pastry?

17   Which South Yorkshire city has the football teams, Wednesday and United?

18   The line "He's not the Messiah, he's a very naughty boy" is from which Monty Python film?

19   The town of Bishop Auckland lies in which English county?

20   Which two-word French term means "in a body"?

Easy
Medium
Hard

Answers to QUIZ 293 – Pot Luck

1	Richard Gere	11	River Jordan
2	Grampian Mountains	12	Will Smith
3	Skate	13	South Wales
4	Court martial	14	Starboard
5	A rodent	15	Jack
6	ECB	16	Horse Guards Parade
7	19th century (1894)	17	Kilometre
8	Ewan McGregor	18	L'Oréal
9	Shadow	19	Chile
10	*High School Musical*	20	*The Royle Family*

1 Laverne Cox plays Sophia Burset in which Netflix series?

2 Pinto is what type of food?

3 Lena Headey played which character in the TV series *Game of Thrones*?

4 Pesos are used as a unit of currency in the Philippines and several countries on which continent?

5 Leah Clearwater is a character in which series of novels and films?

6 Paul McKenna became famous for what form of entertainment?

7 Lactose is a sugar that occurs in what substance?

8 Puck appears in which Shakespeare play?

9 La Scala is a famous opera house in which European city?

10 *Parks and Recreation* featured which Hollywood star as the upbeat Chris Traeger?

11 Leon Brittan (Baron Brittan of Spennithorne) held the position of Home Secretary to which UK prime minister?

12 Pedro is the Spanish form of which English name?

13 *Lock, Stock and Two Smoking Barrels* (1998) was written and directed by whom?

14 Pyrex™ is a brand of cookware made from a tough version of what?

15 Lava lamps originally became popular in which decade?

16 Pastrami is a spiced version of what type of meat?

17 Lady Gaga co-starred with which actor in the 2018 film *A Star is Born*?

18 Patience as a card game is known by what name in the US?

19 Leek is a town in which English county?

20 Patricia Cornwell writes novels in which genre?

Answers to QUIZ 294 – Film

1	Olivia Colman	11	John Boorman
2	The Golden Raspberries	12	*Doctor Zhivago*
3	Scotland	13	*Bridget Jones's Diary*
4	*Sense and Sensibility*	14	*Black Panther*
5	Sir Sean Connery	15	Francis Ford Coppola
6	Africa	16	Stephen King
7	Bernard Cribbins	17	Kevin
8	*Ice Age*	18	*A New Hope*
9	16th century	19	London
10	Archaeologist	20	*Love Me Tender*

1. What does the "C" stand for in the name of the author CS Lewis?

2. What colour properties are The Angel Islington and Euston Road on a Monopoly™ board?

3. Who is the Greek equivalent of the Roman god Jupiter?

4. Who had a no.1 hit single in 1979 with *Hot Stuff*?

5. Druids and Hawthorn Hill are points on which motor-racing circuit?

6. In the phrase meaning "vehemently", what implement accompanies tongs?

7. What type of creature is a rudd?

8. Which British actor starred in the 2002 film *The Transporter*?

9. Followers of which religion would adhere to the Puranas?

10. What colour card is shown as a caution to a footballer?

11. Who directed the Oscar-winning 2013 film *12 Years a Slave*?

12. Which instrument can be acoustic, classical or Spanish?

13. "Never knowingly undersold" is the motto of which department store?

14. What is the name of Fred Flintstone's daughter?

15. At which major London church are coronation ceremonies held?

16. In which month is the official start of spring in the UK?

17. The island of Spitsbergen belongs to which country?

18. What colour flag is traditionally waved to signify surrender?

19. Mandarin is the most-spoken version of the language used by people in which country?

20. What was the name given to an illicit drinking bar in America during the period of Prohibition?

Easy

Medium

Hard

Answers to QUIZ 295 – Pot Luck

1	Woodwind	11	LXXXIII
2	Four	12	Alabama
3	Englishmen	13	Blood
4	Firefly	14	Travis
5	Sir Tom Jones	15	Yellow
6	Tower of London	16	Short
7	Dollar	17	Sheffield
8	W (Whiskey)	18	*Monty Python's Life of Brian*
9	400m	19	County Durham
10	Speedometer	20	*En masse*

1   A person who feigns sadness is said to cry the tears of what animal?

2   If you are obsessed about something, what are you said to have in your headwear?

3   A determination to confront an issue can be compared to taking what animal by the horns?

4   What marine creature might the sky's cloud formation be described as?

5   Someone who can't keep a secret might let what animal out of the bag?

6   The hair of what animal is jokingly said to cure a hangover?

7   Someone who is out of their comfort zone might be compared to which creature out of its environment?

8   Which creature might be mentioned in relation to a scheme that has not been properly thought through?

9   Giving a gift that might not be fully appreciated could be compared to throwing pearls before what animals?

10 Pursuing a fruitless errand could be said to be like chasing what type of bird?

11 Earning enough to live on is said to keep which creature from the door?

12 If you are making your final appearance in something it could be compared to the song of which bird?

13 A lovesick person might cast the eyes of what animal in the direction of the admired person?

14 If you do things in the wrong order, what vehicle are you putting before what animal?

15 Which marine creature might lead you astray in the plot of a murder mystery?

16 Which creature always gets the main share of something?

17 If you look down your nose at people you are said to be on what high animal?

18 A useless object might be described as what colour creature?

19 If you are prone to exaggeration, you could be accused of making mountains out of what creature's endeavours?

20 Mentioning a contentious issue could be compared to stirring up the home of what type of insect?

Answers to QUIZ 296 – LP

1	*Orange is the New Black*	11	Baroness Margaret Thatcher
2	Bean	12	Peter
3	Cersei (Lannister)	13	Guy Ritchie
4	South America	14	Glass
5	*Twilight*	15	1960s (invented in 1963)
6	Hypnotism	16	Beef
7	Milk	17	Bradley Cooper
8	*A Midsummer Night's Dream*	18	Solitaire
9	Milan	19	Staffordshire
10	Rob Lowe	20	Crime fiction

1   What is the decimal equivalent of the binary number 10?

2   What is the international car registration letter for Italy?

3   BSL is the abbreviation for what language?

4   Who is the last person mentioned in the rhyme *Tinker Tailor*?

5   What nationality is tennis player Simona Halep?

6   *Jumpin' Jack Flash* was a 1968 hit for which band?

7   Which character from Charles Dickens *A Christmas Carol* has been played on screen by Alastair Sim and Sir Michael Caine, amongst others?

8   Which New England US state has a name that is based on the French words for "green" and "mountain"?

9   In what year was the *Lusitania* sunk by German U-boats?

10 What two letters from the phonetic alphabet appear in the title of a 2013 Steve Coogan film?

11 What type of bird is Harry Potter's Hedwig?

12 In which South American country is the majority of the Orinoco river?

13 What word follows "short" in the name of an electrical fault?

14 Which TV series for young children involved square, round and arched windows?

15 What symbol features in the centre square of a Scrabble® board?

16 In which Hertfordshire town was Lewis Hamilton born?

17 Which martial arts expert starred in the films *Fist of Fury* and *Enter the Dragon*?

18 Which Scottish comedian and actor married Pamela Stephenson in 1989?

19 What type of writers featured in the title of a 1989 film starring Robin Williams and Ethan Hawke?

20 Which cartoon series is set in the fictional US town of Springfield?

Easy

Medium

Hard

Answers to QUIZ 297 – Pot Luck

1	Clive	11	Steve McQueen
2	Light blue	12	Guitar
3	Zeus	13	John Lewis
4	Donna Summer	14	Pebbles
5	Brands Hatch	15	Westminster Abbey
6	Hammer	16	March
7	A fish	17	Norway
8	Jason Statham	18	White flag
9	Hinduism	19	China
10	Yellow	20	Speakeasy

Easy

1   What is the name of the telephone service, reached by dialling 123 on a BT line, that provides an accurate time?

2   The instant noodle was developed in Japan during which decade?

3   What is the writing system used by people who are visually impaired?

4   Which was invented first: the cathode-ray tube or the telephone?

5   Which early car was nicknamed "Tin Lizzie"?

6   The first example of what form of road control was set up outside the Houses of Parliament in 1868?

7   In which decade was the FIFA World Cup first televised?

8   The Millennium Dome, now named the O2 Arena, lies on which London peninsula?

9   Which brand of drink, originally intended as a medicine, had the main original ingredients of coca leaves and kola nuts?

10 Which On the Buses actor made the first ever withdrawal from an automatic cash machine, in 1967?

11 Which was the first motorway service station open to all types of traffic?

12 In which century was the UK Patent Office established?

Medium

13 Which prime minister reintroduced the post of First Minister of Scotland in 1999?

14 The world's first artificial satellite was launched by which country?

15 What is the name of the environmental group that held two weeks of protests in Central London in April 2019?

16 What name is given to the thin piece of wire inside a light bulb?

17 The PlayStation® was developed during which decade?

18 What is the name of Amazon's subscription service?

19 Which piece of ship's equipment can calculate the depth of the sea by using sound waves?

20 In which decade was the Windows® operating system first released?

Hard

Answers to QUIZ 298 – Animal Idioms

1	Crocodile	11	The wolf
2	A bee (in your bonnet)	12	Swan
3	The bull	13	Sheep
4	Mackerel	14	(The cart before) the horse
5	The cat	15	Red herring
6	The dog	16	Lion
7	A fish out of water	17	Horse
8	Hare (hare-brained)	18	White elephant
9	Swine	19	Mole (molehills)
10	Wild goose	20	Hornet (hornets' nest)

1   Les Gray was the long-time lead vocalist for which group?

2   Which philosopher was brought up in the Chinese province of Lu?

3   In the Bible, who was Esau's twin?

4   "Brexit" is a combination of which two words?

5   Which metal lends its name to a species of beech?

6   In what decade was Checkpoint Charlie set up in Berlin?

7   What was the name of Dawn's original boyfriend in *The Office*?

8   In the TV series *The Young Ones*, who portrayed Vyvyan?

9   Which European country has the international dialling code 0033?

10   Into what do long jump competitors land?

11   Oldham and Stockport are boroughs in which metropolitan county?

12   George Stephenson and the Duke of Wellington have appeared on which bank note?

13   What word for a part of a boat can also mean "authoritarian"?

14   Gemma Andrews was accidentally killed in *Emmerdale* by which member of the Dingle family?

15   Which football team won the 2019 Scottish Premiership, their eighth victory in a row?

16   What colour is the inside of a kiwi fruit?

17   In which film would you find "The Self Preservation Society"?

18   The stately home of Harewood House is located near which West Yorkshire city?

19   The fictional Winchester club, run by barman Dave, featured in which TV series?

20   In the abbreviated title HE, given to governors and ambassadors, for what does the "E" stand?

Easy

Medium

Hard

Answers to QUIZ 299 – Pot Luck

1	2	11	Owl
2	I	12	Venezuela
3	British Sign Language	13	Circuit
4	Thief	14	*Play School*
5	Romanian	15	Star
6	The Rolling Stones	16	Stevenage
7	Ebenezer Scrooge	17	Bruce Lee
8	Vermont	18	Sir Billy Connolly
9	1915	19	Poets (*Dead Poets Society*)
10	Alpha Papa (*Alan Partridge: Alpha Papa*)	20	*The Simpsons*

1. How many celebrities take part in an edition of Richard Osman's *House of Games*?

2. On *Countdown*, how many numbers are selected in each round?

3. Who hosts *The Chase*?

4. Charles Ingram, the "Coughing Major", was found to have cheated on which TV quiz show?

5. In which decade did Jeremy Paxman first ask the questions on *University Challenge*?

6. Which song by the Eurythmics lends its name to a panel show hosted by Rob Brydon?

7. Who presented *A Question of Sport* from 1979 to 1997?

8. "Possibly the Greatest Quiz Team in Britain" is the tag line of which quiz show?

9. Which radio station broadcasts the *Round Britain Quiz*?

10. Who presented *Telly Addicts*?

11. In which decade was *Mastermind* first broadcast?

12. What is the penultimate round in *Pointless*?

13. *In It to Win it* and *Winning Lines* were broadcast as part of which weekly event?

14. Who hosts *Insert Name Here*?

15. Which show featured "the walk of shame"?

16. The 2019 revival of *Blockbusters* was hosted by which comedian?

17. On which quiz show, broadcast in 2015-16, did contestants have to both answer a question and find the answer in a hexagonal grid?

18. *Only Connect* takes its name from a phrase in which EM Forster novel?

19. Who was the original host of *Ask the Family*?

20. How many contestants start each game of a quiz that has been hosted by both William G Stewart and Sandi Toksvig?

Answers to QUIZ 300 – Inventions and Initiatives

1	Speaking clock	11	Newport Pagnell (1959)
2	1950s	12	19th century (1852)
3	Braille	13	Tony Blair
4	The telephone	14	Soviet Union (*Sputnik 1*)
5	Model T Ford	15	Extinction Rebellion
6	Traffic lights	16	Filament
7	1950s (1954)	17	1990s (1994)
8	Greenwich Peninsula	18	Amazon Prime
9	Coca-Cola	19	Sonar
10	Reg Varney	20	1980s (1985)

1 Dim sum feature in the cuisine of which country?

2 Which Canadian singer had a hit with the 2002 song *Complicated*?

3 What clothing measure that is 6 in London, would be 8 in New York or 39 in Paris?

4 Patty Simcox is a character in which musical film?

5 Which film set a new record on its release in April 2019 as the quickest film to take $1 billion at the box office?

6 What does Shylock require a pound of, in *The Merchant of Venice*?

7 *Save Tonight* was a 1998 hit for which Swedish singer?

8 Sid Waddell famously commentated on which sport?

9 The Hood is the main villain in which children's TV series?

10 Which US horse race did Country House win in 2019 after the winner on the day was disqualified?

11 What colour is indicated by the word "sanguine"?

12 The Italian southern region of Campania has what city as its capital?

13 Which punctuation mark is used to indicate possession?

14 What are the two official languages of Canada?

15 Who topped the UK singles charts in 2019 with *Vossi Bop*?

16 The Netherlands has land borders with Germany and which other country?

17 What word completes the phrase "horses for ___", meaning that different tactics are appropriate for different situations?

18 Which fictional detective has a surname that is a word for a picture puzzle?

19 The name of which food plant is traditionally muttered by crowd-scene actors?

20 What "milk" is used to settle an upset stomach?

Answers to QUIZ 301 – Pot Luck

1	Mud	11	Greater Manchester
2	Confucius	12	£5
3	Jacob	13	Stern
4	British exit	14	Belle
5	Copper	15	Celtic FC
6	1940s (1947)	16	Green
7	Lee	17	*The Italian Job*
8	Adrian Edmondson	18	Leeds
9	France	19	*Minder*
10	Sandpit	20	Excellency

Easy

Medium

Hard

Easy

1   Which month is most associated with showers?

2   *It Might As Well Rain Until September* was a 1962 hit for which singer/songwriter?

3   Which two signs of the zodiac cover December?

4   Who starred as the Russian submarine Captain Marko Ramius in the 1990 thriller *The Hunt for Red October*?

5   "When I look into your eyes, I can see a love restrained" is the opening line to which 1992 song?

6   How many weeks are there in a lunar month?

7   What month is named *marzo* in Italian?

8   How many months does a typical human pregnancy last?

9   Whom did Theresa May succeed as UK prime minister?

10   Pearl and moonstone are the birthstones associated with which month?

11   How many days are there in August?

12   Which stone, usually blue, is associated with September?

13   "It's late September and I really should be back at school" is a lyric from which song?

Medium

14   Brian May and which other original member of Queen continue to tour under that name?

15   Which month lends its name to a word meaning "dignified"?

16   Valentine's day is celebrated in which month?

17   How many times a year does a bi-monthly event take place?

18   Which actress played June in the 1979-87 TV series *Terry and June*?

19   Proverbially, what animal may look at a king?

20   What nationality is actress January Jones?

Hard

Answers to QUIZ 302 – Quiz Shows

1	Four	11	1970s (1972)
2	Six	12	Head to Head
3	Bradley Walsh	13	National Lottery Draw
4	*Who Wants to Be a Millionaire?*	14	Sue Perkins
5	1990s (1994)	15	*The Weakest Link*
6	*Would I Lie to You?*	16	Dara Ó Briain
7	David Coleman	17	*Hive Minds*
8	*Eggheads*	18	*Howards End*
9	Radio 4	19	Robert Robinson
10	Noel Edmonds	20	Fifteen (*Fifteen-to-One*)

1   In which county is the town of Droitwich?

2   Wednesday and Pugsley are children in which fictional family?

3   In which English county is the administrative region of Torbay?

4   Who starred in *Doctor Who* first, Patrick Troughton or Jon Pertwee?

5   The name of what painting gave Nat King Cole his first US no.1 of 1950?

6   Which children's character has a red van with the number plate PAT 1?

7   Which European country includes the cities of Kraków and Łódź?

8   Presenters of which morning TV show, last aired in 2002, included Chris Evans and Johnny Vaughan?

9   How is 13 represented in Roman numerals?

10 What colour is the logo of Keep Britain Tidy?

11 *A Whole New World* featured in which Disney film?

12 Ronald Reagan was elected US president in which year?

13 *The Phantom Menace* has what episode number in the Star Wars series of films?

14 Who was king of the United Kingdom first, George IV or William IV?

15 Which water bird's name also means to submerge under water or the failure to score in cricket?

16 Carl Fredricksen is the main character in which 2009 animated film?

17 What colour is the background of the official Emirates airline logo?

18 In what century was Royal Ascot racecourse founded?

19 Which part of a theatre is someone said to be playing to, if they are courting popularity?

20 Central Park is in which borough of New York?

Easy

Medium

Hard

Answers to QUIZ 303 – Pot Luck

1	China	11	Red
2	Avril Lavigne	12	Naples
3	Shoe size	13	Apostrophe
4	*Grease*	14	English and French
5	*Avengers: Endgame*	15	Stormzy
6	Flesh	16	Belgium
7	Eagle-Eye Cherry	17	Courses
8	Darts	18	Inspector Rebus
9	*Thunderbirds*	19	Rhubarb
10	Kentucky Derby	20	Milk of magnesia

1   A drop goal in rugby union is worth how many points?

2   Beach volleyball is contested between teams of how many players?

3   When a snooker game commences, what colour ball is at the middle of the table?

4   In which sport are the goal shooter and goal attack the only players allowed to attempt to score?

5   Which country hosted the Copa America football tournament in 2016?

6   How many balls are used in the game of billiards?

7   The song *I'm Forever Blowing Bubbles* is associated with which London football club?

8   What sport has a Crown Green variety?

9   Diamond and battery are terms used in which US sport?

10 In feet, how high is the centre of the net on a tennis court?

11 In which season of the year is the Super Bowl played?

12 On what surface is shinty usually played?

13 How many players, maximum, would you find in a standard rugby union scrum?

14 How is ping-pong also known?

15 The modern game of golf originated in which country?

16 What nationality is tennis player Juan Martin del Potro?

17 What sport is played by the Boston Red Sox?

18 How many players are on each team in a game of polo?

19 In which decade was the women's FA cup first played?

20 What is the call in tennis to indicate that a serve needs to be replayed?

Easy

Medium

Hard

Answers to QUIZ 304 – Months

1	April	11	31
2	Carole King	12	Sapphire
3	Sagittarius and Capricorn	13	*Maggie May* (Sir Rod Stewart)
4	Sir Sean Connery	14	Roger Taylor
5	*November Rain* (Guns N' Roses)	15	August
6	Four	16	February (14th)
7	March	17	Six
8	Nine	18	Dame June Whitfield
9	David Cameron	19	A cat
10	June	20	American

1   Pistachio is a shade of what colour?

2   What is the last event in the women's heptathlon?

3   The Corrs were formed in which country?

4   Where was the king in *Sing a Song of Sixpence*?

5   During which conflict is *The English Patient* set?

6   Which TV presenter joined *Strictly Come Dancing* in 2014?

7   What was the first name of Ashley Tisdale's character in the High School Musical films?

8   Who won the men's London Marathon for the fourth time in 2019?

9   Which country is made up of 31 states including Chihuahua and Tabasco?

10 In which book of the Bible is the story of Jacob told?

11 *Goodnight Girl* was a 1992 chart-topper for which group?

12 What are you said to be fishing for, if you are trying to obtain praise for yourself?

13 The Red Sea is connected via the Gulf of Aden to which ocean?

14 Proverbially, what is truth stranger than?

15 In which decade was *Never Say Never Again* released?

16 A Cavalier King Charles is a small breed of which type of dog?

17 The name of which Scandinavian country's capital is derived from "Merchant's Harbour" in its own language?

18 Brookes University can be found in which UK city?

19 The resorts of Paphos and Ayia Napa lie on which Mediterranean island?

20 Which of the following spellings is correct: perffume, perfume or perrfume?

Answers to QUIZ 305 – Pot Luck

1	Worcestershire	11	*Aladdin*
2	The Addams Family	12	1980
3	Devon	13	One
4	Patrick Troughton	14	George IV (1820)
5	*Mona Lisa*	15	Duck
6	Postman Pat	16	*Up*
7	Poland	17	Red
8	*The Big Breakfast*	18	18th century (1711)
9	XIII	19	The gallery
10	Green	20	Manhattan

Easy

1. In TS Eliot's *Old Possum's Book of Practical Cats*, who is the Railway Cat?

2. Which series of books were the most-loaned books from public libraries between 2000 and 2010?

3. What number does Thomas the Tank Engine have painted on his side?

4. How are Peter, Janet, Jack, Barbara, George, Pam and Colin better known?

5. *The Amazing Maurice and His Educated Rodents* was written by which author of fantasy books?

6. Which book series features Jared and Simon Grace and their older sister Mallory?

7. Which award for children's literature was first won by Arthur Ransome for *Pigeon Post* in 1936?

8. *The Voyage of the Dawn Treader* is a sequel to which novel?

9. Lyra and her daemon Pantalaimon first appeared in which series of books?

10. What colour cat is Orlando, in the series of books by Kathleen Hale?

Medium

11. Aunt Spiker and Aunt Sponge are characters from which Roald Dahl novel?

12. Who wrote *Jabberwocky* and *The Hunting of the Snark*?

13. Which children's writer created Whoville and its tiny residents?

14. Mr Badger and the Chief Weasel feature in which novel?

15. Which 12-year-old, in a 2005 novel by Rick Riordan, discovers he is the son of a mortal woman and the Greek god Poseidon?

16. What did the Ugly Duckling turn into?

17. In which book, set during WWII, is William evacuated to live with Tom Oakley?

18. What type of creature is Hazel, one of the leading characters in the Richard Adams novel *Watership Down*?

19. Arrietty and Pod are characters in which 1952 children's novel by Mary Norton?

20. Which range of children's books, first printed in 1914, takes its name from a colourful insect?

Hard

Answers to QUIZ 306 – Ball Sports

1	Three	11	Winter
2	Two	12	Grass
3	Blue	13	16
4	Netball	14	Table tennis
5	USA	15	Scotland
6	Three	16	Argentinian
7	West Ham United FC	17	Baseball
8	Bowls	18	Four
9	Baseball	19	1970s (1970-71)
10	Three feet	20	Let

QUIZ 309 – Pot Luck

ANSWERS ON PAGE 311

1   Which US state's name can follow the word "West" to make another state, whose capital is Charleston?

2   What kind of animal is Sergeant Tibbs in One Hundred and One Dalmatians?

3   In which long-running TV series did Noele Gordon play a character called Meg?

4   The Heston services in Greater London are on which motorway?

5   Which fruit also means an unwanted third person?

6   According to the nursery rhyme, what was the colour of the pear on My Little Nut Tree?

7   What word completes the phrase: "by hook or by ___", meaning by any means possible?

8   Who was the beaten finalist in the 2019 snooker World Championships?

9   Who was the US president in 2006?

10 Which actress was recreated by CGI in a television advert for Galaxy chocolate?

11 What do you jump to, if you make a hasty decision based on incomplete received information?

12 Senegal is the westernmost country on the mainland of which continent?

13 The Talmud is a key text in which religion?

14 Alesha Dixon has been a judge on which talent show since 2012?

15 Who was the host of the improvisation show Whose Line is it Anyway?

16 What is the name given to the party thrown for the bride of an upcoming wedding?

17 In which English county is the town of Okehampton?

18 How were Plácido Domingo , José Carreras and Luciano Pavarotti collectively known?

19 What is the term for the rows of upturned spikes used by some meditators and illusionists?

20 For what do the letters UAE stand in the name of the Middle Eastern federation?

Easy

Medium

Hard

Answers to QUIZ 307 – Pot Luck

1	Green	11	Wet Wet Wet
2	800m	12	Compliments
3	The Republic of Ireland	13	Indian Ocean
4	In his counting house	14	Fiction
5	WWII	15	1980s (1983)
6	Claudia Winkleman	16	Spaniel
7	Sharpay	17	Denmark (Copenhagen)
8	Eliud Kipchoge	18	Oxford
9	Mexico	19	Cyprus
10	Genesis	20	Perfume

1   *Black Sails* is a TV series that is a prequel to which Robert Louis Stevenson novel?

2   Berkeley Square was a setting to hear which bird, in the classic 1939 song?

3   *Baum* is the German word for what?

4   Barm cake, originating in the north-west of England, is what type of foodstuff?

5   Baz Luhrmann directed a 2013 film adaptation of which F Scott Fitzgerald novel?

6   Biffo the Bear originally appeared in which comic?

7   Boho, describing hippy-influenced fashion, is short for what word?

8   Brad Pitt played Tyler Durden in which 1999 film?

9   Barra is an island off the coast of which country?

10 Becky Sharp is the central character in which 1848 novel?

11 Bros were the subject of which 2018 documentary?

12 Brussels is the capital city of which European country?

13 Belle Dingle, played by Eden Taylor-Draper, is a character in which long-running TV series?

14 Bilbo Baggins is what relation to Frodo in Tolkien's novels?

15 "Bluff" can mean both an act of deception and what geographical feature?

16 Boise is the capital of which US state?

17 Boris Becker won his three Wimbledon championships in which decade?

18 Bravo represents which letter in the phonetic alphabet?

19 "Blotto" is a word meaning what?

20 Bruce Springsteen was born in which decade?

Answers to QUIZ 308 – Children's Literature

1   Skimbleshanks
2   *Tracy Beaker*
3   1
4   The Secret Seven
5   Sir Terry Pratchett
6   *The Spiderwick Chronicles*
7   Carnegie Medal
8   *The Lion, the Witch and the Wardrobe*
9   *His Dark Materials* (Philip Pullman)
10 Marmalade
11 *James and the Giant Peach*
12 Lewis Carroll
13 Dr Seuss
14 *The Wind In the Willows*
15 Percy Jackson
16 A swan
17 *Goodnight Mr Tom*
18 Rabbit
19 *The Borrowers*
20 Ladybird

1 Who captained Australia during the 2005 Ashes series?

2 In which county is the city of Salisbury?

3 What type of vegetable are petit pois?

4 Which 1981 film opens with athletes running along a beach to a soundtrack by Vangelis?

5 What name is given to an individual day of competition in a World Rally Championship event?

6 Which imperial paper size, larger than the metric A4, was named after its traditional jester's hat watermark?

7 How long did Peter Mayle spend in Provence, according to the title of his 1989 memoir and subsequent TV adaptation?

8 What name is given to a look-out post high up on an ship's mast?

9 Sir Elton John featured in the 2018 Christmas advert for which retail chain?

10 What was Krakatoa, in the title of the disaster film *Krakatoa, East of Java*?

11 Proverbially, what bird's back is unbothered by water?

12 For what does the acronym SWALK stand?

13 Who won the Best Supporting Actor BAFTA award in 2019 for his portrayal of Norman Scott in *A Very British Scandal*?

14 Which religion recites five Salahs per day?

15 In March 2019, who was confirmed as the new main presenter of *Newsnight*?

16 What name is given to the musical director of an orchestra who directs the musicians during performances?

17 What nationality is retired jockey Steve Cauthen?

18 In which county is the village of Helford?

19 What was the name of Hyacinth Bucket's long-suffering husband in *Keeping Up Appearances*?

20 Who recorded the 1985 festive no.1 *Merry Christmas Everyone*?

Answers to QUIZ 309 – Pot Luck

1	Virginia (West Virginia)	11	Conclusions
2	A cat	12	Africa
3	*Crossroads*	13	Judaism
4	M4	14	*Britain's Got Talent*
5	Gooseberry	15	Clive Anderson
6	Golden	16	Hen night
7	Crook	17	Devon
8	John Higgins	18	The Three Tenors
9	George W Bush	19	Bed of nails
10	Audrey Hepburn	20	United Arab Emirates

1   The city of Brescia lies at the foot of which range of mountains?

2   The forint is the currency of which European country?

3   What is the name of the city at the mouth of the Rhine which has the largest cargo port in Europe?

4   Which country has the international car registration letters CH?

5   The famous Sorbonne university is in which European capital city?

6   What is the Spanish word for "tomorrow"?

7   Which European country is shaped like a boot?

8   The Wiener schnitzel dish is a speciality of which country?

9   Fjords are particularly associated with which Scandinavian country?

10   The Riviera is a coastal region on which sea?

11   Which sea lies off the north-west coast of the Netherlands?

12   *Liberté, égalité, fraternité* is the national motto of which country?

13   Which colour is the cross on the Danish flag?

14   *Buon giorno* is the greeting for "good day" in which language?

15   What is the main ingredient of the sauce for cod Portuguese?

16   In which European city does the Marriage of the Sea ceremony take place every year?

17   What is the English equivalent of an *Hôtel de Ville* in France?

18   What is the capital of Iceland?

19   Proverbially, which ancient city was not built in a day?

20   What nationality can precede the word "courage" to meaning alcohol-induced bravery?

Answers to QUIZ 310 – Plan B

1	*Treasure Island*	11	*After the Screaming Stops*
2	Nightingale	12	Belgium
3	Tree	13	*Emmerdale*
4	A bread roll	14	Cousin
5	*The Great Gatsby*	15	A steep bank or cliff
6	*The Beano*	16	Idaho
7	Bohemian	17	1980s (1985, 1986, 1989)
8	*Fight Club*	18	B
9	Scotland	19	Very drunk
10	*Vanity Fair*	20	1940s (1949)

1 In which decade was actor Liam Hemsworth born?

2 What condiment might be said to be rubbed into a wound to make a situation worse?

3 What tree follows "witch" to make the name of an astringent lotion?

4 In which year was *Dancing on Ice* first shown on TV?

5 What item of refereeing equipment is proverbially very clean?

6 How many kings of England prior to Queen Elizabeth II were called Charles?

7 What adjective preceded Stevie Wonder's name on his early recordings?

8 What is the radio code word for the third letter of the alphabet?

9 Which series, designed for hearing-impaired children, featured "The Gallery" of viewer's paintings?

10 What kind of animal is Hamm in the Toy Story films?

11 What are roasting on an open fire, in the first line of a festive song?

12 The England football team exited the Euro 2016 tournament after losing to which island country?

13 Who played the title role in the 2015 film *Mr Holmes*?

14 Hong Kong is on the south-east coast of which country?

15 What name is given to the act of scoring three goals in a football match or the taking of three wickets in three balls in cricket?

16 Author Peter James writes in which genre?

17 What sort of tree would be created by a genealogist?

18 What word precedes "gap" to make a phrase indicating the difference in outlook between parents and their children?

19 What colour is a Samoyed dog?

20 A pasha is the name for a former governor in which country?

Easy

Medium

Hard

Answers to QUIZ 311 – Pot Luck

1	Ricky Ponting	11	A duck
2	Wiltshire	12	Sealed with a loving kiss
3	Peas	13	Ben Whishaw
4	*Chariots of Fire*	14	Islam
5	Leg	15	Emily Maitlis
6	Foolscap	16	Conductor (or maestro)
7	A year	17	American
8	Crow's nest	18	Cornwall
9	John Lewis	19	Richard
10	Volcano	20	Shakin' Stevens

Easy

1   Which actor was the star of *Doctor Who* when Billie Piper first played Rose Tyler?

2   Which *Star Trek* villains famously use cloaking devices on their starships?

3   *Life, the Universe and Everything* (1982) was the third novel in which series?

4   Which husband and wife team produced the children's 1960s sci-fi series *Fireball XL5*?

5   In what year was the Star Wars film *The Force Awakens* released?

6   Originally played by DeForest Kelley in the TV series and films, what is the nickname of the *Star Trek* character Dr McCoy?

7   Optimus Prime is a character in which sci-fi franchise?

8   Which TV presenter created the TV series *Black Mirror*?

9   Which actor reprised his role as Rick Deckard in the 2017 film *Blade Runner 2049*?

10   What was the subtitle of the 2016 *Independence Day* sequel?

Medium

11   Who wrote the 1951 novel *The Day of the Triffids*?

12   The sinister "cigarette-smoking man" appeared in which sci-fi series?

13   Killer Frost is the alter-ego of which character in *The Flash*?

14   In which decade was the film *Westworld* released?

15   Which *Doctor Who* spin-off is an anagram of that title?

16   The Adama family appeared in which sci-fi series?

17   Who wrote the 1932 novel *Brave New World*?

18   Released in 1927, which was the first full-length sci-fi film?

19   Who plays Offred in the TV series *The Handmaid's Tale*?

20   The 2017 TV series *Electric Dreams* was based on short stories by which author?

Hard

Answers to QUIZ 312 – Europe

1	The Alps	11	The North Sea
2	Hungary	12	France
3	Rotterdam	13	White
4	Switzerland	13	Italian
5	Paris	15	Tomato
6	*Mañana*	16	Venice
7	Italy	17	Town hall
8	Austria	18	Reykjavík
9	Norway	19	Rome
10	Mediterranean	20	Dutch

1 "Take a look at her hair, it's real" is a lyric from which song?

2 Which is the largest and longest spinal nerve in the body?

3 Richard DeVere was a main character in which sitcom?

4 David Beckham played for which major Spanish club from 2003 to 2007?

5 What was the theme of the 2019 series of *Great British Menu*?

6 What rodent-related phrase means the general rush of working life?

7 The musical *Rent* is set in which US city?

8 Who directed the 2019 film *Yesterday*?

9 Is the historical region of Aquitaine in the south-east or south-west of France?

10 Proverbially, what should you not throw the baby out with?

11 Whom did Henry VIII marry first, Anne Boleyn or Jane Seymour?

12 Which is the correct spelling: accquire, acquire or aquire?

13 Who wrote the 1993 TV series *Lipstick on Your Collar*?

14 What is the lowest council tax band?

15 Grimsby is a port in which English county?

16 Which musical term for a type of a note can also mean "unintentional"?

17 Which UK prime minister introduced the ASBO, which was superseded in 2014?

18 Epsom Downs racecourse is in which English county?

19 What is indicated in the UK by a brown road sign showing a sheep?

20 By area, which country is larger: Australia, India or Russia?

Easy

Medium

Hard

Answers to QUIZ 313 – Pot Luck

1	1990s (1990)	11	Chestnuts
2	Salt	12	Iceland
3	Hazel	13	Sir Ian McKellen
4	2006	14	China
5	A whistle	15	Hat trick
6	Two	16	Crime fiction
7	Little	17	Family tree
8	Charlie	18	Generation
9	*Vision On*	19	White
10	Pig	20	Turkey

Easy

1   In which year did the future Queen Elizabeth II marry Philip Mountbatten?

2   Francis Drake circled the world in what century?

3   Which Kingdom became part of the United Kingdom in 1800?

4   In what year did the "February Revolution" take place in Russia?

5   The Moguls were rulers of which modern-day country?

6   In which century was Charles Edward Stuart, known as Bonnie Prince Charlie, born?

7   Who was the first king to rule England from the House of Lancaster?

8   Ellis Island, the former immigration processing point for the USA, lies in the harbour of which city?

9   In 1880, education became compulsory in the UK for children until they were how old?

10 Which public school did Sir Winston Churchill attend?

11 George I was born in which German city?

12 Brazil was colonised by which empire in 1500?

Medium

13 In 1800, who became the first US president to take up residence in the White House?

14 How many years were there between the end of WWI and the start of WWII?

15 In which century did the Gunpowder Plot occur?

16 What nationality was explorer Abel Tasman?

17 In which decade was the voting age for women in the UK reduced to 21?

18 Which European war took place from 1936 to 1939?

19 Which two superpowers were the main parties involved in the Cold War?

20 In which century was the first census taken in the UK?

Hard

ANSWERS ON PAGE 319

1   Leonardo da Vinci completed the *Mona Lisa* in which century?

2   *Never Had a Dream Come True* was a 2000 no.1 hit for which group?

3   The novel *Charlotte Gray* (1999) was written by which author?

4   How many umpires are on the field during a cricket match?

5   Silverside is a cut of which meat?

6   In which century was Marks and Spencer founded?

7   In which year did *Smooth* by Santana win the Grammy for Record of The Year?

8   What is the meaning of the word "amen"?

9   Who preceded Nicolas Sarkozy as president of France?

10 Who died first, Mary II or her husband William III?

11 Proverbially, who does fortune favour?

12 What type of device was a "reel to reel"?

13 Nick Ross and Sue Cook were presenters of which police-related programme?

14 Which team won the 2014 FIFA World Cup, beating Argentina in the final?

15 In the UK, what is the highest grade of a standard music exam?

16 Which of the senses would detect something that was noisome?

17 In which 1992 animated film do the characters go on a magic carpet ride?

18 Which of Roger Hargreaves' Mr Men is a perfectionist?

19 What star sign is someone whose birthday is on October 1?

20 A flounder is what type of fish?

Easy

Medium

Hard

Answers to QUIZ 315 – Pot Luck

1	*Living Doll* (Sir Cliff Richard)	11	Anne Boleyn
2	Sciatic nerve	12	Acquire
3	*To The Manor Born*	13	Dennis Potter
4	Real Madrid	14	Band A
5	British pop muic	15	Lincolnshire
6	Rat race	16	Accidental
7	New York	17	Tony Blair
8	Danny Boyle	18	Surrey
9	South-west	19	Farm park
10	The bathwater	20	Russia

Easy

1 Which single won Song of the Year at the 2018 Brit awards?

2 Justin Bieber was born in which country?

3 What was Elvis Presley's middle name?

4 Which "year" provided Taylor Swift with a record-breaking album?

5 Who had a 2014 hit with *Thinking Out Loud*?

6 The band Coldplay formed in which country?

7 Which actress covered the Kirsty MacColl hit *They Don't Know* in 1983?

8 Who duetted with Donna Summer on the no.1 hit *No More Tears (Enough is Enough)*?

9 What word completes the title of the Rolling Stones' hit: *Gimme ___*?

10 Britney Spears released *Baby One More Time* in which year?

Medium

11 What followed *I Would Do Anything For Love* in the title of the Meat Loaf hit?

12 Which US band had hits with *Radioactive* and *Demons*?

13 *thank u, next* was a 2019 chart-topping album for which singer?

14 Sir Elton John performed five songs on the soundtrack to which Disney film?

15 In 1991, which female vocalist had a US no.1 with the song *Someday*?

16 What was Mel C's Spice Girls nickname?

17 For which song did Eric Clapton win the 1992 Grammy Song of the Year?

18 Who wanted to *Fly Away* in 1999?

19 The band Pulp were from which British city?

20 Shane Filan was the lead singer with which group?

Hard

Answers to QUIZ 316 – History

1	1947	11	Hanover
2	16th century (1577-80)	12	Portuguese Empire
3	Kingdom of Ireland	13	John Adams
4	1917	14	21
5	India	15	17th century (1605)
6	18th century (1720)	16	Dutch
7	Henry IV	17	1920s (1928)
8	New York	18	Spanish Civil War
9	Ten years old	19	Soviet Union and USA
10	Harrow	20	19th century (1801)

1. Which town lies furthest north: Basingstoke, Folkestone or Slough?

2. Tennis player Rafael Nadal was born on Manacor in which group of islands?

3. Lisa Faulkner won which TV competition in 2010?

4. In which Star Wars film did Yoda first appear?

5. In the US, what vegetables follow the word "small" to indicate that something is of little importance?

6. In which century was the first Cambridge University college founded?

7. What nationality is Formula 1 driver Kimi Räikkönen?

8. Located in South America, what is the world's fifth-largest country by area?

9. What has "got groove, it's got meaning" in the title track to a 1978 film?

10. In 2004, who became the youngest player to score a goal for the England national football team?

11. What colour was the famous three-wheeled van in *Only Fools and Horses*?

12. In which county is the RSPB reserve of Snettisham?

13. *Bad Boys* was a single from which *The X Factor* winner?

14. What was the name of the UK telephone communications market regulator prior to 2004?

15. In 2009 what became the second animated film in history to be nominated for a Best Picture Oscar?

16. What are men encouraged to grow to support the men's health Movember campaign?

17. What is the most southerly capital city in the world?

18. The 1996 film *Twister* featured what weather phenomena?

19. Which age followed the Stone Age?

20. The 1997 song by Puff Daddy, *I'll Be Missing You*, sampled which Police song?

Answers to QUIZ 317 – Pot Luck

1	16th century (c.1517)	11	The brave
2	S Club 7	12	Tape recorder
3	Sebastian Faulks	13	*Crimewatch (UK)*
4	Two	14	Germany
5	Beef	15	Grade eight
6	19th century (1884)	16	Smell
7	1999	17	*Aladdin*
8	So be it	18	Mr Fussy
9	Jacques Chirac	19	Libra
10	Mary II (1694)	20	Flatfish

Easy

1 Which comedian hosted the 2019 TV series *The Ranganation*?

2 Who played Twinkle in the sitcom *dinnerladies*?

3 Leslie Nielsen played Frank Drebin in which film series?

4 Who are the two team captains on *Would I Lie to You*?

5 Which 1984 spoof spy film marked Val Kilmer's acting debut?

6 Who directed the 1982 film *The King of Comedy*?

7 In which English city is the stand-up venue The Comedy Store?

8 Which two members of the Countdown team appear in *8 Out of 10 Cats Does Countdown*?

9 In which decade was the first Carry On film, *Carry on Sergeant*, released?

10 The TV series *Upstart Crow* is written by which comedian?

11 What would make a noise on a jester's cap?

12 Who created and starred in the 2019 black comedy series *After Life*?

Medium

13 Which major Scottish city hosts a fringe comedy festival?

14 In which European country did *commedia dell'arte* originate?

15 Who issues the challenges in the series *Taskmaster*?

16 What term is given to someone who interrupts a stand-up comedian?

17 What nationality is comedian Adam Hills?

18 Gladioli are associated with which comedy character created by Barry Humphries?

19 Who presented the TV series *The Last Resort*?

20 "Mockumentary" is a combination of which two words?

Hard

Answers to QUIZ 318 – Pop Music

1	*Human* (Rag'n'Bone Man)	11	*(But I Won't Do That)*
2	Canada	12	Imagine Dragons
3	Aaron	13	Ariana Grande
4	1989	14	*The Lion King*
5	Ed Sheeran	15	Mariah Carey
6	England	16	Sporty
7	Tracey Ullman	17	*Tears in Heaven*
8	Barbra Streisand	18	Lenny Kravitz
9	*Shelter*	19	Sheffield
10	1999	20	Westlife

1   UB40 topped the US chart in which decade with (*I Can't Help*) *Falling in Love With You*?

2   Mr Toad is a key character in which novel?

3   Which three colours feature on the flag of the Netherlands?

4   Nigel Starmer-Smith commentates on which sport?

5   The town of Tewkesbury lies in which county?

6   Which Yorkshire and England cricketer (d.2006) was known as "Fiery Fred"?

7   C is the chemical symbol for which element?

8   How was Torchy described in the title of a 1960s children's TV series?

9   What name is given to a sudden narrowing of a road system that often causes hold-ups?

10 Antony Costa is a member of which pop group?

11 What is measured in bauds?

12 In which country is the Great Ocean Road?

13 Which English football club took the second part of their name from their original home of Alexandra recreation ground?

14 In which capital city did the post-war peace conference begin in 1919?

15 Nick Bottom appears in which Shakespeare play?

16 What sort of animal was Rikki-Tikki-Tavi in the Rudyard Kipling short story?

17 Singer-songwriter Amy Macdonald (b.1987) was born in which country?

18 Which 1989 stage musical famously gives the illusion of a helicopter taking off?

19 In relation to computers, what is UNIX?

20 Which US actress starred in the 2014 film *Lucy*?

Answers to QUIZ 319 – Pot Luck

1	Slough	11	Yellow
2	Balearic Islands	12	Norfolk
3	*Celebrity Masterchef*	13	Alexandra Burke
4	*The Empire Strikes Back*	14	Oftel
5	Potatoes	15	*Up*
6	13th century (1284)	16	A moustache
7	Finnish	17	Wellington (New Zealand)
8	Brazil	18	Tornadoes
9	Grease	19	Bronze Age
10	Wayne Rooney	20	*Every Breath You Take*

Easy

1 Which hair-tidying tool is proverbially daft?

2 Who had a 2003 hit with *Crazy in Love*?

3 *Fool Again* was a 2000 hit for which group?

4 What rhyming name traditionally follows "Silly"?

5 Which Roman god was called "stupid" in the title of a 1958 song by Connie Francis?

6 Who wrote the play *Absurd Person Singular*?

7 *Silly Love Songs* was a 1976 hit for which band?

8 What word completes the title of the 2011 film, *Crazy, Stupid, ___*?

9 What are the first names of the two main characters in the Dumb and Dumber films?

10 *Land of Confusion* was a 1986 single by which band?

11 What is the name of a lift used in a restaurant to deliver food?

12 The first day of which month is known as "Fool's Day"?

13 Where was the fool in the title of the Beatles song?

14 What is added to fruit to make a fool?

Medium

15 Daft Punk is an electronic music duo from which country?

16 What word precedes "crazy" in the term for restlessness from being confined in one place?

17 The town of Dumbarton lies north-west of which Scottish city?

18 Which profession is said to have a silly season in the summer?

19 What word follows "horses" in the theme song to *Only Fools and Horses*?

20 What, proverbially, is there no fool like?

Hard

Answers to QUIZ 320 – Comedy

1	Romesh Ranganathan	11	Bells
2	Maxine Peake	12	Ricky Gervais
3	*Naked Gun*	13	Edinburgh
4	David Mitchell and Lee Mack	14	Italy
5	*Top Secret!*	15	Greg Davies
6	Martin Scorsese	16	Heckler
7	London	17	Australian
8	Rachel Riley and Susie Dent	18	Dame Edna Everage
9	1950s (1958)	19	Jonathan Ross
10	Ben Elton	20	Mock and documentary

1   How many points is the letter X worth in Scrabble®?

2   What legal character is proverbially sober?

3   The sultanate of Oman lies on which continent?

4   Which gas does a plant take in during the process of photosynthesis?

5   Buttons appears in which pantomime?

6   What word describes a surface that curves inwards at the centre?

7   Which household pet was sacred to the Egyptians?

8   Which two English football teams contested the 2019 Europa Cup?

9   What is written on a stave?

10   In the Harry Potter films, what colour is the Hogwarts Express?

11   What unit of currency was used in the Netherlands prior to the euro?

12   The unsweetened cake known as a bannock originated in which country?

13   Who released the 2000 single *I'm Like a Bird*?

14   Moving anti-clockwise on a dartboard, what number is next to 10?

15   Of what is somniphobia a fear?

16   The Strait of Dover is the narrowest part of which body of water?

17   Which country's national cricket team is nicknamed the Proteas?

18   What style of hat did the fancy-dress shopkeeper wear in the TV cartoon series *Mr Benn*?

19   Brisket is a cut of what type of meat?

20   Who provides the voice of Rocket in the *Guardians of the Galaxy* films?

Easy

Medium

Hard

Answers to QUIZ 321 – Pot Luck

1	1990s (1993)	11	Phone line speed
2	*The Wind In The Willows*	12	Australia
3	Red, white and blue	13	Crewe Alexandra FC
4	Rugby	14	Paris
5	Gloucestershire	15	*A Midsummer Night's Dream*
6	Fred Trueman	16	A mongoose
7	Carbon	17	Scotland
8	The Battery Boy	18	*Miss Saigon*
9	Bottleneck	19	An operating system
10	Blue	20	Scarlett Johansson

Easy

1. Which US state includes Walt Disney World and Palm Beach?

2. The character of Professor Plum appears in which board game?

3. How many pawns are there on the board at the start of a game of chess?

4. What name is given to the part of a theatre in which the audience sit?

5. At what event would you find a big top?

6. How many houses is a hotel worth in Monopoly™?

7. What was the location of the first Center Parcs village to open in the UK?

8. In which leisure pursuit would you "hang ten"?

9. What would you be doing if you were using bias binding?

10. What is the English equivalent of a *bibliothèque*?

11. A third of which city lies in the Peak District National Park?

12. What is the name of the playground game where players throw small stones and jump across a numbered grid of squares on the ground?

Medium

13. Who "says" in a game where players have to exactly follow the lead of the organiser?

14. What four colours are used in the game of Twister®?

15. At which studio tour, based in Watford, can you visit an exhibition about the making of the Harry Potter films?

16. What is indicated in the UK by a brown road sign showing a lion?

17. What is used to play a game of craps?

18. A greenkeeper may be employed to maintain a bowling green or which other sporting surface?

19. In which country is the ski resort of Méribel?

20. What would you be doing if you were creating petit point?

Hard

Answers to QUIZ 322 – Silly

1	A brush	11	Dumb waiter
2	Beyoncé	12	April
3	Westlife	13	On the hill
4	Billy	14	Cream
5	Cupid	15	France
6	Sir Alan Ayckbourn	16	Stir
7	Wings	17	Glasgow
8	*Love*	18	Journalism
9	Harry and Lloyd	19	Work
10	Genesis	20	An old fool

ANSWERS ON PAGE 327

1   The Footlights dramatic club belongs to which university?

2   Which former footballer and England captain (b.1957) has the nickname "Captain Marvel"?

3   What organ of the body is treated by the process of dermabrasion?

4   "Have you come here to play Jesus To the lepers in your head" is a lyric from which 1992 song?

5   What is the chemical symbol for chlorine?

6   What is a col?

7   Which band headlined the last night of the 2019 Glastonbury festival?

8   London official taxi cabs are usually what colour?

9   What nationality was the philosopher Karl Marx?

10   What grammatical term modifies a "doing word"?

11   What does the saying "gone dark" mean when applied to a theatre?

12   How high in inches is the net in table tennis?

13   In what decade did Miguel Induráin win the Tour de France several times?

14   What is the full name of the animal known as a hippo?

15   Which animal has traditionally been used to locate truffles?

16   A beaver and a polar bear appear on coins from which Commonwealth country?

17   Frank Butcher was a famous character in which long-running series?

18   Which two general food groups are not mixed under kosher laws?

19   Which brand of razor, advertised by Roger Federer and Thierry Henry, has the slogan "the best a man can get"?

20   What are the occupations of the title characters in the 2005 film *Mr & Mrs Smith*?

Easy

Medium

Hard

Answers to QUIZ 323 – Pot Luck

1	Eight	11	Guilder
2	A judge	12	Scotland
3	Asia	13	Nelly Furtado
4	Carbon dioxide	14	6
5	*Cinderella*	15	Sleep
6	Concave	16	English Channel
7	A cat	17	South Africa
8	Arsenal and Chelsea	18	A fez
9	Music	19	Beef
10	Red	20	Bradley Cooper

ANSWERS ON PAGE 328

Easy

1 Gravesend in Kent lies across the Thames from which historic port?

2 Which form of entertainment is most associated with London's West End?

3 Which actress co-starred with Steve Carell in the 2012 film *Seeking a Friend for the End of the World*?

4 *Endeavour* was the Royal Navy ship used by which English explorer?

5 Southend-on-Sea lies in which English county?

6 How is endive more usually known in the UK?

7 The word "endgame" is applied to the final stages of which board game?

8 Is an endomorph skinny or plump?

9 Land's End is the beginning of a popular journey that ends at which Scottish village on the north coast?

10 Endocrinology is the study of glands and which substances?

11 Where would you find an endpaper?

12 What is the French term for a dead end?

Medium

13 *End of the Road* was a hit for Boyz II Men in which decade?

14 In which country of the United Kingdom does Bridgend lie?

15 In what "end" are you said to be, if you face a difficult situation without experience?

16 Who wrote the 1818 poem *Endymion*?

17 An endowment mortgage is intended to be linked to which other financial product?

18 Which black comedy film of 1989 starred Andrew McCarthy and Jonathan Silverman?

19 Wallsend lies on which river?

20 *The End of the Affair* was a 1951 novel by which English author?

Hard

Answers to QUIZ 324 – Leisure

1	Florida	11	Sheffield
2	Cluedo®	12	Hopscotch
3	16	13	Simon
4	Auditorium	14	Blue, green, red and yellow
5	Circus	15	Warner Bros
6	Five	16	Safari park
7	Sherwood Forest	17	Two dice
8	Surfing	18	Golf course
9	Sewing	19	France
10	Library	20	Needlework or embroidery

1   On which motorway are the Newport Pagnell services?

2   Which animal lends its name to a nickname for police cars?

3   What are you lacking if you are dehydrated?

4   On which album cover are the Beatles using a zebra crossing?

5   What word can mean both a financial product and "to stick"?

6   Which city is also an inner London borough?

7   How long does a period last in a game of ice hockey?

8   Which athletics event is known as the "metric mile"?

9   What was the profession of someone who wrote and copied documents before printing was invented?

10   On what festive occasion is the French phrase *joyeux Noël* appropriate?

11   What is the name of Matthew Wolfenden's *Emmerdale* character?

12   What appears in the centre of the flag of Argentina?

13   Does hot air fall or rise?

14   Who created the TV series *The West Wing*?

15   What does a pedometer measure?

16   What nationality is actor Hugh Jackman?

17   In which decade was the first *The Hangover* film released?

18   Which purplish-red colour is used in printing ink?

19   Windsor Castle is close to which river?

20   Who is the patron saint of children?

Answers to QUIZ 325 – Pot Luck

1	Cambridge	11	There is no show
2	Bryan Robson	12	Six inches
3	Skin	13	1990s
4	*One* (U2)	14	Hippopotamus
5	Cl	15	Pig
6	A mountain pass	16	Canada
7	The Cure	17	*EastEnders*
8	Black	18	Meat and milk
9	German	19	Gillette
10	Adverb	20	Assassins

Easy

1. Which position is found in rugby union but not in rugby league?

2. Which four letters denote the international governing body of the sport?

3. As of 2018, who are the current World Cup holders?

4. How many points is a try worth?

5. Gained from a conversion or a penalty, how many points is a goal worth?

6. The annual All Stars match is played in which country?

7. In which country is the Catalans Dragons team based?

8. "Kangaroos" is the nickname for which country's rugby league team?

9. How many teams does the Super League have, as at 2019?

10. As at the beginning of 2019, who was the most capped player in the history of the England rugby league team?

11. What shirt number does a fullback typically wear?

12. The Challenge Cup final is traditionally held at which stadium?

Medium

13. As at 2019, which is the only team, other than Great Britain and Australia, to win the World Cup?

14. Winning it 19 times, which is the most successful club in Challenge Cup history, as at 2018?

15. From which governing body did rugby league originally split?

16. As at the end of the 2018 season, which club held the most Super League titles?

17. The Rugby League Varsity Match is played by which two universities?

18. Who was appointed chairman of the Rugby Football League in 2013?

19. What colour card is shown by a referee to indicate a sin-bin offence?

20. The 2019 Super League season is denoted by which Roman numerals?

Hard

Answers to QUIZ 326 – In the End

1	Tilbury	11	In a book
2	Theatre	12	*Cul-de-sac*
3	Keira Knightley	13	1990s (1992)
4	Captain James Cook	14	Wales
5	Essex	15	The deep end
6	Chicory	16	John Keats
7	Chess	17	Insurance
8	Plump	18	*Weekend at Bernie's*
9	John O'Groats	19	Tyne
10	Hormones	20	Graham Greene

ANSWERS ON PAGE 331

1 "Cry God for Harry, England and Saint George!" is a famous quote from which Shakespeare play?

2 In which book of the New Testament does the shortest verse in the Bible appear?

3 The zodiac sign Sagittarius covers which two calendar months?

4 The Grolsch brewery was founded in which country?

5 Which Kevin Costner film was released first, *The Postman* or *Tin Cup*?

6 In which year was *Strictly Come Dancing* first broadcast?

7 Which automobile company manufactures the Supra?

8 What is verbascum?

9 Chiang Kai-shek was the leader of which country from 1928 to 1975?

10 What word describes an illness that lasts for a long time?

11 What name is given to the young of a domestic fowl?

12 The Italian *per favore* and Spanish *por favor* mean what in English?

13 What is the name given to a list at the back of a book that explains technical or unusual terms?

14 In cycling, which classification is used to award the white jersey?

15 In what decade did driver Mike Hawthorn become Formula 1 World Champion?

16 Which group had a hit in 1999 with *I Want it That Way*?

17 What branch of physics studies the behaviour and properties of atoms and molecules?

18 What is kept in a hangar?

19 Longmeadow garden belongs to which TV presenter?

20 Who played the title role in the 1968 film *Bullitt*?

Easy

Medium

Hard

Answers to QUIZ 327 – Pot Luck

1	M1	11	David Metcalfe
2	Panda	12	Sun
3	Water	13	Rise
4	*Abbey Road*	14	Aaron Sorkin
5	Bond	15	A person's steps
6	City of Westminster	16	Australian
7	20 minutes	17	2000s (2009)
8	1500m	18	Magenta
9	Scribe	19	River Thames
10	Christmas	20	St Nicholas

ANSWERS ON PAGE 332

Easy

1 Which social media site was originally designed and launched as "Picaboo"?

2 The world's first portable CD player was invented by which company?

3 What two colours are used on the Pinterest logo?

4 Which 2014 app had 50 million downloads shortly after launch but was withdrawn days later?

5 What is the name for the symbol in music notation that is the same as the hashtag symbol?

6 *Advanced Warfare* is the 2014 instalment of which video game series?

7 Which app, launched in 2012, has resulted in the phrase "swipe right"?

8 What do the letters "DP" stand for in GDPR?

9 The text messaging application WhatsApp was bought in February 2014 for $19 billion by which company?

10 In which country was the Tamagotchi™ toy invented?

Medium

11 What term beginning with "p" is given to the practice of attempting to obtain money by sending fake emails?

12 On a standard keyboard, which letter is between F and H?

13 Which country has the internet code .gr?

14 The Galaxy S Series of mobile phones is made by which manufacturer?

15 What term is given to someone who reads comments on websites and social media without contributing themselves?

16 Which operating system displays a blue screen after a system crash?

17 What item of equipment connects a computer to the Internet?

18 In which decade did cameras first become available on mobile phones?

19 What is the name for a program that prevents an unauthorised user gaining access to a computer on a network?

20 The adverts for which TV service featured comedian Johnny Vegas and a knitted monkey?

Hard

Answers to QUIZ 328 – Rugby League

1	Flank	11	One
2	RLIF	12	Wembley
3	Australia	13	New Zealand
4	Four	14	Wigan Warriors
5	Two	15	RFU
6	Australia	16	Leeds Rhinos (eight)
7	France	17	Oxford and Cambridge
8	Australia	18	Brian Barwick
9	12	19	Yellow
10	James Graham	20	XXIV

1   According to the nursery rhyme, on which day of the week did Solomon Grundy die?

2   The 2016 documentary film *Supersonic* told the story of which Manchester group?

3   Proverbially, which pearl-making shellfish is the world, if all options are open?

4   Which football club was founded as a result of Wimbledon's relocation in 2004?

5   The jewellery and watch company Cartier was founded in which country?

6   What name is given to the rounded end of a church?

7   The rocky headland of Strumble Head is on the coast of which Welsh county?

8   Who played Tinker Bell in the 1991 film *Hook*?

9   Which boxing weight has a maximum of eight stone?

10 *Because You Loved Me* was a 1996 single by which singer?

11 Which group had a hit in 1975 with *Three Steps to Heaven*?

12 Which actress played the title role in the 2019 TV series *Gentleman Jack*?

13 From what do golfers drive the ball?

14 Which city was the setting for the TV series *Rab C Nesbitt*?

15 "A cup of joe" is American slang for a cup of which hot drink?

16 In what does cellulose naturally occur?

17 Cheddar Gorge lies in which English county?

18 What term is given to a baby whale?

19 Who duetted with Ed Sheeran on the 2019 single *I Don't Care*?

20 Which pair of organs filter waste products from blood in humans?

Easy

Medium

Hard

Answers to QUIZ 329 – Pot Luck

1	*Henry V*	11	Poult (or chick)
2	John (Jesus wept)	12	Please
3	November and December	13	Glossary
4	The Netherlands	14	Best rider under 26
5	*Tin Cup* (1996)	15	1950s (1958)
6	2004	16	Backstreet Boys
7	Toyota	17	Particle physics
8	A flowering plant, also called mullein	18	Aircraft
9	China	19	Monty Don
10	Chronic	20	Steve McQueen

ANSWERS ON PAGE 334

1   Which duo sang about *Rainy Days and Mondays* in 1971?

2   How many raindrops are there on the Met Office symbol for heavy rain?

3   Which Scottish band asked *Why Does it Always Rain on Me?*

4   "Rain keeps falling, rain keeps falling Down, down, down" is a line from which 1985 song?

5   What name is given to rain that has been polluted by industrial processes?

6   Who starred as the title character in the 1990s TV series *Maisie Raine?*

7   In which year was Prince's single *Purple Rain* originally released?

8   Audrey Raines, played by Kim Raver, was a character in which TV series?

9   What was the name of Jessica Raine's character in *Call the Midwife?*

10   Which group's cover of *I Can't Stand the Rain* reached the top ten in 1978?

11   A heavy downpour is proverbially referred to as raining which two animals?

12   Who played Charlie Babbitt in the 1988 film *Rain Man?*

13   What follows the words "Raindrops on roses" in the song *My Favourite Things?*

14   *Raining in My Heart* was a 1959 no.1 for which singer?

15   Who wrote the 1995 novel *The Rainmaker?*

16   *The Rain in Spain* is a song from which musical?

17   What is the French phrase for "It's raining"?

18   What name is given to the practice of storing rainwater on site for reuse?

19   Which US state completes the title of the 1960s song *Rainy Night in ___?*

20   Which group released the 1983 single *Walking in the Rain?*

Answers to QUIZ 330 – Technology

1	Snapchat	11	Phishing
2	Sony	12	G
3	Red and white	13	Greece
4	*Flappy Bird*	14	Samsung
5	Sharp	15	Lurker
6	*Call of Duty*	16	Windows®
7	Tinder	17	Router
8	Data Protection	18	2000s (2000)
9	Facebook™	19	Firewall
10	Japan	20	ITV Digital

1 In 1991 Madonna released which *Collection*?

2 Cadbury uses what main colour for its chocolate wrappers?

3 The character of Marilyn Chambers, played by Emily Symons, appears in which long-running TV series?

4 Which US family group had a 1972 hit with *Crazy Horses*?

5 In relation to computing, for what do the initials MSN® stand?

6 Steve Waugh and Allan Border played what sport at international level?

7 Which is the correct spelling: calandar, calander or calendar?

8 "It's a sad, sad situation and it's getting more and more absurd" are lyrics from which Sir Elton John song?

9 In a theatre, what name is given to the areas at the side of the stage?

10 What, proverbially, is the sky if there are no restrictions?

11 What grilled item was one of the Teletubbies' favourite foods?

12 How many lords are a-leaping in *The Twelve Days of Christmas*?

13 In what decade was Bill Gates born?

14 What do Americans call trousers?

15 Which actor played Bruce Nolan in the film *Bruce Almighty*?

16 How old was Tiger Woods when he won the Masters tournament for the first time?

17 Cindy Cunningham is a long-serving character in which soap?

18 Which two teams played in the FA Cup final in May 2019?

19 What word is the opposite of "symmetrical"?

20 According to the nursery rhyme, which child is "loving and giving"?

Easy

Medium

Hard

Answers to QUIZ 331 – Pot Luck

1	Saturday	11	Showaddywaddy
2	Oasis	12	Suranne Jones
3	Oyster	13	The tee
4	MK (Milton Keynes) Dons	14	Glasgow
5	France	15	Coffee
6	Apse	16	Plants
7	Pembrokeshire	17	Somerset
8	Julia Roberts	18	Calf
9	Flyweight	19	Justin Bieber
10	Celine Dion	20	Kidneys

Easy

1   What two colours are used on the circle quarters in the BMW logo?

2   What colour are Dorothy's slippers in *The Wizard of Oz*?

3   Which of these is the correct spelling for a red colour: crimmson, crimson or crimsson?

4   Which part of the human eye provides the colour?

5   Shades of which colour include "Oxford" and "powder"?

6   Traditionally, what colour is the cover of Wisden?

7   What colour follows "Parma" to make the name of a sweet?

8   The Orange Free State is a former region in which country?

9   When a new Pope has been elected, what colour smoke is seen at the Vatican?

10 What is the English translation of *Moulin Rouge*?

11 What colour is the background of the Linkedin logo?

12 *Blue is the Colour* is associated with which football club?

Medium

13 Which two colours are used to play a game of chess?

14 What colour is touchpaper usually described as in a common phrase?

15 Blu-ray™ discs were designed to enhance the storage capacity of which format?

16 What is the first colour of the rainbow?

17 Amethysts are what colour?

18 What colour was the racehorse Desert Orchid?

19 What colour is the engine James in the stories by Reverend W Awdry?

20 In which book of the Bible is the story of Joseph's coat of many colours?

Hard

Answers to QUIZ 332 – Rain

1	The Carpenters	11	Cats and dogs
2	Two	12	Tom Cruise
3	Travis	13	And whiskers on kittens
4	*Don't You (Forget About Me)* (Simple Minds)	14	Buddy Holly
5	Acid rain	15	John Grisham
6	Pauline Quirke	16	*My Fair Lady*
7	1984	17	*Il pleut*
8	24	18	Rainwater harvesting
9	Jenny Lee	19	*Georgia*
10	Eruption	20	Modern Romance

1 What substance does an hourglass contain?

2 Irene Adler is associated with which fictional detective?

3 In the phrase "con-trick", for what is "con" an abbreviation?

4 Which Formula 1 driver formed his own airline in 1979?

5 In the Old Testament, how many stone tablets were the Ten Commandments written on?

6 What name is given to the amount of money owed by the government of a country?

7 Proverbially, when is the sky red to delight a shepherd?

8 Which London underground line serves Amersham and Chesham?

9 In cookery, what do you remove if you are paring a fruit or vegetable?

10 On what type of transport is the 2013 film *Captain Phillips* mostly set?

11 Broccoli comes from which family of plants?

12 In relation to technology, for what do the letters PC stand?

13 What type of cheese is traditionally used on a pizza?

14 To which US state is the island of Jamaica closest?

15 The 2010 film *Clash of the Titans* was based on characters from which branch of mythology?

16 In which venue were the Brit Awards held in 2019?

17 The word "tsunami" comes from which language?

18 Australia is divided into how many states?

19 Which sport involves players sliding a stone across a sheet of ice?

20 Which character in *Friends* was associated with the phrase "How you doin'?"?

Answers to QUIZ 333 – Pot Luck

1	*Immaculate*	11	Tubby Toast
2	Purple	12	Ten
3	*Home and Away*	13	1950s (1955)
4	The Osmonds	14	Pants
5	Microsoft Network®	15	Jim Carrey
6	Cricket	16	21 (1997)
7	Calendar	17	Hollyoaks
8	*Sorry Seems to Be the Hardest Word*	18	Manchester City and Watford
9	Wings	19	Asymmetrical
10	The limit	20	Friday's

Easy

1 What does a vertebrate have that an invertebrate does not?

2 What term is given to a group of bats?

3 Is a cedar tree deciduous or evergreen?

4 What colour are the flowers of the lily of the valley?

5 The gerbera flower originates from which continent?

6 What is the name for very fine rain?

7 Which continent has no native trees?

8 Shoots from which plant are the main constituent of a giant panda's diet?

9 What two-word term is given to a sudden rush of water over dry land after heavy rain?

10 What colour plumage does a ptarmigan have in winter?

11 Which creature produces royal jelly?

12 In which direction would you look to see the sun set?

Medium

13 A tadpole is the name given to the young of a frog and what other creature?

14 The anaconda snake is native to which continent?

15 What type of flowers are lady's slippers?

16 What are planted in an arboretum?

17 The maple tree belongs to which genus?

18 What colour is the skin of a Désirée potato?

19 Which weather feature might be fork or sheet?

20 Which large body of water has a name that means "peaceful"?

Hard

ANSWERS ON PAGE 339

1   What is the term for a substance prescribed to a patient instead of a drug, that is known to have no active constituents?

2   With which country did the UK enter into a dispute known as the "Cod War"?

3   In which year was *The Empire Strikes Back* released in cinemas?

4   Zinfandel is what type of fruit?

5   Who hosts the game show *Impossible Celebrities*?

6   In which country did tea originate?

7   Which organisation decides on storm names in the UK?

8   Marc Jacobs is a famous name in which profession?

9   Who played the protagonist of the 2001 film *A Knight's Tale*?

10 Up to the reign of Elizabeth II, how many English kings were called Edward?

11 In which year was the first series of *Big Brother* broadcast?

12 In Greek mythology, what type of animal is Pegasus?

13 Which fast-food chain shares its name with an American underground form of transport?

14 "Olfactory" relates to which of the senses?

15 "Don't ask my opinion, Don't ask me to lie" are lyrics from which 2016 song?

16 What is the name of the yellow piece in Cluedo®?

17 Who resigned as Leader of the House of Commons in May 2019?

18 What is the term given to a consecutive series of point-scoring shots in snooker?

19 In which century was the explorer Ferdinand Magellan born?

20 The town of Walton-on-the-Naze lies in which county in the east of England?

Answers to QUIZ 335 – Pot Luck

1	Sand	11	Cabbage
2	Sherlock Holmes	12	Personal computer
3	Confidence	13	Mozzarella
4	Niki Lauda (Lauda Air)	14	Florida
5	Two	15	Greek mythology
6	National Debt	16	O2 Arena
7	At night	17	Japanese
8	Metropolitan Line	18	Six
9	The skin or peel	19	Curling
10	Ship	20	Joey Tribbiani

1   What is the score in a game of tennis if both players have 40 points?

2   How many decades are there in 40 years?

3   Which precious stone is associated with a 40th wedding anniversary?

4   Is an angle of 40 degrees an acute angle or an obtuse angle?

5   According to Douglas Adams, what number was the answer to "the Ultimate Question of Life, the Universe, and Everything"?

6   What is 48 divided by six?

7   The 49th parallel is the name given to the unguarded border between the USA and which other country?

8   What term is given to the 40 days preceding Easter?

9   The nickname "forty-niner" was given to a gold prospector in which US state during the "gold rush"?

10   Which is the next prime number after 43?

11   *Lullaby of Broadway* is a song from which musical?

12   Who was the 43rd president of the USA?

13   Generally found between the latitude of 40 and 50 degrees, what are the Roaring Forties?

14   In which year did WWII end?

15   How is 40 represented in Roman numerals?

16   "Droopy drawers" is the traditional bingo call for which number?

17   What is the square root of 49?

18   Which two actors co-starred in the 1982 film *48 Hrs*?

19   Which character from a folk tale is associated with 40 thieves?

20   How many people crew a 49er sailing ship?

Answers to QUIZ 336 – Planet Earth

1	Backbone	11	Bee
2	Colony	12	West
3	Evergreen	13	Toad
4	White	14	South America
5	Africa	15	Orchids
6	Drizzle	16	Trees
7	Antarctica	17	Acer
8	Bamboo	18	Pinky-red
9	Flash flood	19	Lightning
10	White	20	Pacific Ocean

1   Who served as US National Security Advisor from 2001 to 2005, then as Secretary of State until 2009?

2   What are the three earth signs of the zodiac?

3   What type of creature is a hoopoe?

4   Moving anti-clockwise on a dartboard, what number is next to 7?

5   What is the name given to the stone at the top of a wall?

6   In what decade did Alain Prost win his first Formula 1 World Championship?

7   What word can mean both "size" and "to climb"?

8   Who directed the 2003 film *Hulk*?

9   What colour is the liqueur advocaat?

10 Prince Charmont, played by Hugh Dancy, is a character in which 2004 fantasy film starring Anne Hathaway?

11 *I Believe in a Thing Called Love* was a 2003 hit for which band?

12 How many vowels are there on the top row of a standard computer keyboard?

13 What part of ginger is used in cooking?

14 What does it mean in tennis to "break" a serve in a game?

15 Minsk is the capital of which Eastern European country?

16 What small boat is used to tow larger ships in a harbour?

17 What type of lace did the Big Bopper sing about in 1958?

18 Which is Japan's largest city by population?

19 The FaceTime video telephony service is owned by which company?

20 Who wrote the 2018 novel *Paris Echo*?

Easy

Medium

Hard

Answers to QUIZ 337 – Pot Luck

1	Placebo	11	2000
2	Iceland	12	(Winged) horse
3	1980	13	Subway
4	Grape	14	Smell
5	Rick Edwards	15	*Human* (Rag'n'Bone Man)
6	China	16	Colonel Mustard
7	The Met Office	17	Andrea Leadsom
8	Fashion design	18	Break
9	Heath Ledger	19	15th century (c.1480)
10	Eight	20	Essex

1. *Danse Macabre* was written by which composer?

2. *The Five* were a group of 18th century composers from which country?

3. How many musicians play in a string quartet?

4. *Tristan und Isolde* was a work by which German composer?

5. In what century was Gustav Mahler born?

6. *Klavier* is the German word for what instrument?

7. Pablo Casals was famous for playing which instrument?

8. What does the word "rallentando" instruct a musician to do?

9. What nationality was the composer Kurt Weill?

10. *Pathétique* is the common name of which of Beethoven's piano sonatas?

11. *The Blue Danube Waltz* was composed by which Strauss?

12. The musical term *toccata* is taken from the Italian verb *toccare*. What is the English translation of *toccare*?

13. *Pizzicato* is a term associated with which group of instruments?

14. *The Bridal Chorus*, more famous today as *Here Come The Bride*, is from which opera?

15. What term is given to the act of playing a musical piece in a key other than the one in which it was written?

16. What does "andante" mean?

17. Which Austrian composer died in 1791 at the age of 35?

18. The *Saturday Night Fever* track *Night on Disco Mountain* was based on a work by which Russian composer?

19. What does *Nessun Dorma* mean in English?

20. What nationality was the composer Sibelius?

Answers to QUIZ 338 – Life Begins

1	Deuce	11	*42nd Street*
2	Four	12	George W Bush
3	Ruby	13	Strong winds
4	Acute angle	14	1945
5	42	15	XL
6	Eight	16	44
7	Canada	17	Seven
8	Lent	18	Eddie Murphy and Nick Nolte
9	California	19	Ali Baba
10	47	20	Two

1 The sitcom *'Allo 'Allo!* was set in which country?

2 Which football team plays home games at Pride Park?

3 What colour is a standard second class stamp in the UK?

4 What is the name of the area in front of a fireplace?

5 Who played Bert the chimney sweep in the 1964 film *Mary Poppins*?

6 Which company manufactures the Cactus car model?

7 Sir Malcolm Rifkind and Michael Portillo both served as Defence Secretary in which decade?

8 Which condiment is mentioned in *Jack and Jill*?

9 What are the international car registration letters for the Netherlands?

10 A video to which Dire Straits song was the first to be featured on MTV Europe in 1987?

11 Mauricio Pochettino was appointed manager of which football club in 2014?

12 The Freddo chocolate bar is in the shape of what creature?

13 What is opposite "nature" in the phrase referring to the debate about the basis of behaviour?

14 easyJet is based at which English airport?

15 Which variety of American whiskey shares its name with a chocolate biscuit?

16 How many rounds are there in the US Open golf tournament?

17 The Reverend Edward Casaubon appears in which novel by George Eliot?

18 Samia Longchambon plays which character in *Coronation Street*?

19 What type of event is the Daytona 500?

20 What nationality is tennis player Kei Nishikori?

Easy

Medium

Hard

Answers to QUIZ 339 – Pot Luck

1	Condoleezza Rice	11	The Darkness
2	Capricorn, Taurus and Virgo	12	Four (E, U, I, O)
3	A (crested) bird	13	The root
4	19	14	The server loses the game
5	Coping stone	15	Belarus
6	1980s (1985)	16	Tug
7	Scale	17	*Chantilly Lace*
8	Ang Lee	18	Tokyo
9	Yellow	19	Apple
10	*Ella Enchanted*	20	Sebastian Faulks

1   In the well-known tongue-twister, where does "she sell sea shells"?

2   Who played the title role in the 1998 film *The Wedding Singer*?

3   What is the basic measure used in calculating the height of land?

4   In which decade was Piers Morgan born?

5   What was the basis for the 2010 film *Prince of Persia: Sands of Time*?

6   What name is given to a traditional sailor's song?

7   Former footballer David Seaman played in which position?

8   Which seaside resort in East Sussex was favoured by George IV?

9   In which country was the band The Seahorses founded?

10 What name do Americans give to the land next to the sea?

11 Clacton-on-Sea lies in which county?

12 Which group had a 1980 hit with *Echo Beach*?

13 Grunge music originated in which Pacific Coast US city?

14 Who played Sam Seaborn in the TV series *The West Wing*?

15 What is a seascape?

16 Which classic TV series was set in Walmington-on-Sea?

17 In which country is the freshwater lake known as the Sea of Galilee?

18 What is the alcoholic ingredient in a Sea Breeze cocktail?

19 Which company made the Sea Jade fragrance?

20 What was the surname of Sandy, Olivia Newton-John's character, in the 1978 film *Grease*?

Answers to QUIZ 340 – Classical Music

1	Saint-Saëns	11	Johann
2	Russia	12	To touch
3	Four	13	Stringed instruments
4	Wagner	14	*Lohengrin* (Wagner)
5	19th century (1860)	15	Transposing
6	Piano	16	Walking pace
7	Cello	17	Mozart
8	Gradually decrease tempo	18	Mussorgsky
9	German	19	None shall sleep
10	The eighth	20	Finnish

1   What type of fabric is chintz?

2   Who is the cook in *The Wombles*?

3   In which decade was the Empire State Building completed?

4   Which of these cities is most easterly, Coventry, Hereford or York?

5   Who presented *Question Time* from 1989 to 1993?

6   Which TV presenter and chat show host published the 2004 autobiography *So Me*?

7   Lord Belborough and his butler Brackett were characters in which 1960s stop-motion animation series?

8   Who was appointed head coach of the Scotland national football team in May 2019?

9   Which French car company has a diamond-shaped logo?

10 Proverbially, which part of the body do you keep to the grindstone, if you are working hard?

11 What word can mean both "a piece of meat" and "shared"?

12 Which singer co-starred with Matthew McConaughey in the 2001 film *The Wedding Planner*?

13 How many minutes are there in four hours?

14 What is a fly agaric?

15 What nationality is snooker player Stephen Maguire?

16 *Space Oddity* was a UK no.1 for which singer?

17 Which country won the FIFA World Cup for the fifth time in 2002?

18 For what do the letters MP stand in relation to politics in the UK?

19 What adjective relates to the heart and blood vessels?

20 Who plays the older Professor Charles Xavier in the X-Men films?

Easy

Medium

Hard

Answers to QUIZ 341 – Pot Luck

1	France	11	Tottenham Hotspur FC
2	Derby County FC	12	A frog
3	Blue	13	Nurture
4	Hearth	14	Luton
5	Dick Van Dyke	15	Bourbon
6	Citroën	16	Four
7	1990s	17	*Middlemarch*
8	Vinegar	18	Maria Connor
9	NL	19	Motor race
10	*Money for Nothing*	20	Japanese

Easy

1   How is 21 represented in Roman numerals?

2   A "pony" refers to how many pounds?

3   How many languages does a bilingual person speak?

4   On a standard snooker table, how many pockets are there?

5   What number comes next in the Fibonacci sequence: 3, 5, 8, 13, ___?

6   What three numbers do directory enquiry services begin with in the UK?

7   What distance is equal to 25.4 mm?

8   A dodecagon has how many sides?

9   Which metric distance is equivalent to approximately 3280 feet?

10 A quart is a quarter of what measure of volume?

11 An acute angle is one which is less than how many degrees?

12 Other than Rudolph, how many reindeer pull Santa's sleigh in the song *Rudolph the Red-Nosed Reindeer*?

Medium

13 What metric weight is equal to 2.205 pounds?

14 How many degrees are there in three-quarters of a circle?

15 How many French hens are there in *The Twelve Days of Christmas*?

16 What name is given to the middle number in a set of numbers arranged by value?

17 How many days are there in February in a leap year?

18 What indefinite number is represented by the symbol ∞?

19 How many pints are there in three quarts?

20 How many queens are on the board at the start of a game of chess?

Hard

Answers to QUIZ 342 – Seaside

1	On the sea shore	11	Essex
2	Adam Sandler	12	Martha and the Muffins
3	Sea level	13	Seattle
4	1960s (1965)	14	Rob Lowe
5	A video game	15	A painting or photograph of the sea
6	Sea shanty	16	*Dad's Army*
7	Goalkeeper	17	Israel
8	Brighton	18	Vodka
9	England	19	Yardley
10	Seaboard	20	Olsson

1   The song *Big Spender* is from which musical?

2   Which 1980s crime-fighting duo were played by Sharon Gless and Tyne Daly?

3   Which team did England beat in the 1966 FIFA World Cup final?

4   The city of Bristol lies on which river?

5   Which Christopher Nolan film was released first, *Inception*, *Insomnia* or *Memento*?

6   What name is given to the group of people attending a church service?

7   What word can refer to both "a method of knitting" and "to tease"?

8   Grey Gables and Arkwright Hall are common locations found in which soap?

9   In 2014, Salford City FC was bought by a business together with six former players from which club?

10   What name, beginning with "Z", is used to describe the biblical land of Israel?

11   Which city is further south, Perth or Stirling?

12   In which year was the first series of *I'm a Celebrity...Get Me Out of Here!* aired?

13   In *EastEnders*, who killed Den Watts?

14   In which country was chef Atul Kochhar born?

15   The 2018 film *Widows* was based on a 1980s TV series by which writer?

16   What is omega-3?

17   Which children's toy is a tube with coloured patterns at one end that change as the tube is rotated?

18   *Look What You Made Me Do* was a 2017 no.1 single by which singer?

19   Which flower was named after botanist Leonhard Fuchs?

20   How many general elections were held in the UK in the 1980s?

Answers to QUIZ 343 – Pot Luck

1	Cotton	11	Joint
2	Madame Cholet	12	Jennifer Lopez
3	1930s (1931)	13	240
4	York	14	A (poisonous) fungus
5	Peter Sissons	15	Scottish
6	Graham Norton	16	David Bowie
7	*Chigley*	17	Brazil
8	Steve Clarke	18	Member of Parliament
9	Renault	19	Cardiovascular
10	Your nose	20	Sir Patrick Stewart

Easy

1. What was Ross and Monica's surname in *Friends*?
2. Howard Wolowitz was a character in which series?
3. Which series went behind the scenes of the comedy sketch series *TGS*?
4. What relation was Charlie Harper to Alan Harper in *Two and a Half Men*?
5. Jess Day, played by Zooey Deschanel, was the central character in which sitcom?
6. Which numbers follow *Brooklyn* in the title of a sitcom set in a police precinct?
7. What was the name of the dog in *Frasier*?
8. Amy Poehler won a Golden Globe for playing Leslie Knope in which sitcom?
9. Which star of *Mary Poppins* had his own comedy series in the 1960s?
10. The Bluth family feature in which series?
11. *Rhoda* was a spin-off from which series?

Medium

12. Bree Van de Kamp, played by Marcia Cross, was a main character in which series?
13. In which decade was *The Fresh Prince of Bel-Air* originally broadcast?
14. *Seinfeld* was set in which city?
15. In which sitcom did Shelley Long play Diane Chambers?
16. Frankie Muniz played which title character in a 2000s sitcom?
17. The *Modern Family* characters live in the suburb of which city?
18. The US TV series *Benson* was a spin-off from which sitcom?
19. Charlotte's surname in *Sex and the City* is the same as which UK city?
20. What was Frasier's surname in the show *Frasier*?

Hard

ANSWERS ON PAGE 349

1 Burlington Bertie is a slang term for which racing odds?

2 Marcus Bentley gained fame narrating which TV series?

3 According to the saying, what season does one swallow not make?

4 Which desert animal lends its name to a brand of US cigarettes, first marketed in 1913?

5 Patrick and Pippa Trench were characters in which sitcom?

6 Vouvray wine originates from which country?

7 In which English county is the stately home of Holkham Hall?

8 What was the name of the group of policeman which featured in slapstick silent movies of the 1910s?

9 In the *Godfather* films, who played the older Vito Corleone?

10 What type of window is opened by sliding one frame vertically over the other?

11 In which city does the Australian Formula 1 Grand Prix take place?

12 As at 2019, how many World Championship titles had snooker player Mark Selby won?

13 What word can mean both a warning device and an alluring sea nymph?

14 Which part of the body produces serotonin?

15 Ragu is a meat and tomato sauce originating from which country?

16 What is the third event in a triathlon?

17 U is the chemical symbol for which element?

18 What name links Blenheim Palace with the *Peanuts* cartoon strip?

19 Which two pop stars organised the Live Aid concert in 1985?

20 Plans to build which bridge across the River Thames in central London were abandoned in 2017?

Easy

Medium

Hard

Answers to QUIZ 345 – Pot Luck

1	*Sweet Charity*	11	Stirling
2	Cagney and Lacey	12	2002
3	West Germany	13	Chrissie Watts
4	River Avon	14	India
5	*Memento* (2000)	15	Lynda La Plante
6	Congregation	16	A fatty acid (in fish oils)
7	Rib	17	Kaleidoscope
8	*The Archers*	18	Taylor Swift
9	Manchester United FC	19	Fuchsia
10	Zion	20	Two (1983 and 1987)

1   What was the name of Ron's fiancée in the radio sketch series *The Glums,* which was adapted for TV in the late 1970s?

2   Which musical is nicknamed *The Glums?*

3   Low Sunday is the name given to the Sunday following which event in the Christian calendar?

4   Downing Street lies off which major road?

5   Which band had a hit in 1979 with *Every Day Hurts?*

6   Which tree, in the *Salix* genus, has a variety known as "weeping"?

7   Who directed the film *Cry Freedom?*

8   "Cry in the night if it helps" is a line from which song by Sir Elton John?

9   Who composed the rock song *Read 'em and Weep,* originally recorded by Meat Loaf?

10 Proverbially, what fruit-carrying vehicle should you not upset?

11 *Trouble* was a 2000 hit for which band?

12 What is the name of a shop that sells horse-riding equpiment?

13 What investment product might be described as blue chip?

14 In which two seasons of the year might someone suffer from SAD?

15 The vale of Glendalough lies in which Irish county?

16 In which decade was Robert Downey Jr born?

17 Which band had a 1983 hit with *Blue Monday?*

18 "Splashdown" is the term for the landing of what type of craft?

19 *Tragedy* was a 1979 hit for which group?

20 What was the name of Lord Grantham's wife in the TV series *Downton Abbey?*

Answers to QUIZ 346 – US Sitcoms

1	Geller	11	*The Mary Tyler Moore Show*
2	*The Big Bang Theory*	12	*Desperate Houswives*
3	*30 Rock*	13	1990s (1990)
4	Brother	14	New York
5	*New Girl*	15	*Cheers*
6	Nine-Nine	16	Malcolm (*Malcolm in the Middle*)
7	Eddie (played by Moose)	17	Los Angeles
8	*Parks and Recreation*	18	*Soap*
9	Dick Van Dyke	19	York
10	*Arrested Development*	20	Crane

1. "Old friend, why are you so shy" is a lyric from which song?

2. On a standard keyboard, which letter is immediately to the left of T?

3. Which company made the first Accord model in 1976?

4. Which is the next prime number after seven?

5. Whom did Sir Nick Clegg succeed in 2007 as Leader of the Liberal Democrats?

6. Ragdale Hall spa is in which county?

7. How many points is the letter Q worth in Scrabble®?

8. Which comedy series, first broadcast in 1999, featured a dysfunctional family living in Dudley?

9. What type of poem is an anagram of the word for a female deer?

10. Which animated film of 2014 features President Business?

11. The 1994-95 show *Don't Forget Your Toothbrush* aired on which channel in the UK?

12. *Nothing Ever Happens* was a single in the charts in 1990 by which Scottish band?

13. What vegetable gives green pasta its colour?

14. Which sports equipment company has a panther as its logo?

15. The Pease Pottage services are on the M23 in which county?

16. Is Bloomsbury in east London or west London?

17. If a chef describes a dish's ingredients as foraged, what does that indicate?

18. Who hosted *Who Wants to Be a Millionaire* on its return in 2018?

19. What type of vehicle is a Black Maria?

20. What was the title of the 2003 song that was a hit for Kelly and Ozzy Osbourne?

Easy

Medium

Hard

Answers to QUIZ 347 – Pot Luck

1	100-30	11	Melbourne
2	*Big Brother*	12	Three
3	A summer	13	Siren
4	Camel	14	The brain
5	*One Foot in the Grave*	15	Italy
6	France	16	Running
7	Norfolk	17	Uranium
8	The Keystone Cops	18	Woodstock
9	Marlon Brando	19	Bob Geldof and Midge Ure
10	Sash window	20	Garden Bridge

Easy

1 What is Bentley famous for making?

2 The BVLGARI company was founded in which country?

3 Which London department store is particularly noted for its prints?

4 What does *haute couture* mean in English?

5 Monte Carlo lies in which principality?

6 What precious stone does the De Beers company specialise in?

7 Harrods is located in which area of London?

8 Moët & Chandon is a famous brand of which drink?

9 What is the first name of the designer Armani?

10 Fifth Avenue is in which area of New York?

11 Which design company's goods carry the monogram LV?

12 Which area of West London is the most expensive property on a Monopoly™ board?

Medium

13 The Swiss company Rolex specialises in what type of product?

14 Milan is the capital of which Italian region?

15 What did Fortnum & Mason originally sell?

16 In 1996, in which English city did Harvey Nichols open its first store outside London?

17 Which London hotel lends its name to a brand of snack biscuit?

18 Which Agatha Christie novel was set on a luxury train?

19 The Avenue des Champs-Elysées is a fashionable shopping street in which European city?

20 In which country was the original Raffles Hotel opened?

Hard

Answers to QUIZ 348 – Unhappy

1 Eth
2 *Les Misérables*
3 Easter Sunday
4 Whitehall
5 Sad Café
6 Willow
7 Sir Richard Attenborough
8 *I Guess That's Why They Call It the Blues*
9 Jim Steinman
10 Apple-cart
11 Coldplay
12 Saddlery
13 Stocks and shares
14 Autumn and winter (Seasonal Affective Disorder)
15 County Wicklow
16 1960s (1965)
17 New Order
18 Spacecraft
19 The Bee Gees
20 Cora

1 What word completes the title of Coldplay's second album *A Rush of Blood to the __*?

2 In which sport would you see a lutz?

3 What is the name of James Bye's character in *EastEnders*?

4 What name is given to the practising of a play before its first performance?

5 The Thought Police feature in which famous novel?

6 What number is represented by the Roman numerals XLIV?

7 Abu Bakr is a key figure in which religion's history?

8 Which decade does Nicholas Lyndhurst's character travel back to in *Goodnight Sweetheart*?

9 What word can mean both a "work of fiction" and "new"?

10 Swarovski is famous for ornaments made from what substance?

11 What flavouring is used to describe something that has no extra or special features?

12 Which singer played Deena Jones in the 2006 film *Dreamgirls*?

13 Which was the only Grand Slam tournament in which Björn Borg failed to reach the final?

14 An annual Festival of Remembrance is held in which London venue?

15 What colour is the background of the Snapchat logo?

16 Who had a hit single in 2012 with *Somebody That I Used to Know*?

17 The town of Falmouth lies in which English county?

18 What is the name of the round window in the cabin of a ship?

19 What type of plant is a clematis?

20 Who is Bryce Dallas Howard's film director father?

Answers to QUIZ 349 – Pot Luck

1	*Someone Like You* (Adele)	11	Channel 4
2	R	12	Del Amitri
3	Honda	13	Spinach
4	11	14	Slazenger
5	Sir Vince Cable	15	West Sussex
6	Leicestershire	16	West London
7	Ten	17	They have been obtained from the wild
8	*The Grimleys*	18	Jeremy Clarkson
9	Ode (doe)	19	Police van for transporting prisoners
10	*The Lego Movie*	20	*Changes*

ANSWERS ON PAGE 354

Easy

1. Who played Tony Clark in the series *Between the Lines*?

2. Which former *Neighbours* actor was a presenter on *The Big Breakfast* in the mid-1990s?

3. Who was the builder on the *Ground Force* team?

4. Garry Shandling created which fictional talk-show host?

5. What was the name of the captain in the *Star Trek: Voyager* series?

6. What was the title of Ray Romano's sitcom featuring a sportswriter?

7. Newsreaders Henry Davenport and Sally Smedley appeared in which satirical comedy series?

8. Which engineering competition first broadcast in 1998 was presented by Craig Charles?

9. In which series did a policeman have a deaf half-wolf called Diefenbaker as a companion?

10. Played by Kathy Burke, what was the name of Wayne Slob's wife?

Medium

11. Eric McCormack and Debra Messing played the title characters in which US sitcom?

12. Who played Sergeant Nick Rowan in *Heartbeat*?

13. *The Camomile Lawn* was adapted from a book by which author?

14. Who played Detective Superintendent Andy Dalziel in the series *Dalziel and Pascoe*?

15. Which TV presenter experienced *Weird Weekends* in the late 1990s?

16. In which crime series, set in Newcastle-upon-Tyne, did Jimmy Nail play the title character?

17. Which series was set in the fictional women's prison of Larkhall?

18. What was the first name of the daughter of the Royles' next door neighbour in the sitcom *The Royle Family*?

19. Designers on which makeover show, first broadcast in 1996, included Graham Wynne and Linda Barker?

20. What type of shop featured in *Desmond's*?

Hard

Answers to QUIZ 350 – Luxury

1	Cars	11	Louis Vuitton
2	Italy	12	Mayfair
3	Liberty	13	Watch
4	High fashion	14	Lombardy
5	Monaco	15	Groceries
6	Diamond	16	Leeds
7	Knightsbridge	17	The Ritz
8	Champagne	18	*Murder on the Orient Express*
9	Giorgio	19	Paris
10	Manhattan	20	Singapore

1   From which country does the spirit Metaxa® originate?

2   Which actor is nicknamed "The Muscles from Brussels"?

3   What was the name of Howard Charles' character in the TV series *The Musketeers*?

4   Proverbially, what is greener on the other side of the fence?

5   Which weather phenomenon is used to describe something that happens quickly?

6   How many holes are there on a standard golf course?

7   Who played gangster John Rooney in the 2002 film *The Road to Perdition*?

8   What word can mean both something of little significance and a board game using small balls or marbles?

9   Tennis player Caroline Wozniacki has what nationality?

10 Who played the title role in the 2017 film *The Wife*?

11 In which month of 2019 did Theresa May announce her resignation as prime minister of the UK?

12 Oldham is a town in which metropolitan county?

13 What is the name of Channel 4's video-on-demand service?

14 Which was the eighth month in the old Roman calendar?

15 Sylvester Stallone is the star of which boxing series of films?

16 What is the sum of the even numbers from two to eight?

17 What type of animal was *Digby, the Biggest Dog in the World* in the title of a 1973 film?

18 What is the chemical symbol for zinc?

19 Who had a hit album in 2014 with *X*?

20 How many sealed boxes were there at the start of a game of *Deal or No Deal*?

Easy

Medium

Hard

Answers to QUIZ 351 – Pot Luck

1	*Head*	11	Vanilla
2	Figure skating	12	Beyoncé
3	Martin Fowler	13	Australian Open
4	Rehearsal	14	Royal Albert Hall
5	*Nineteen Eighty-Four*	15	Yellow
6	44	16	Gotye
7	Islam	17	Cornwall
8	1940s	18	Porthole
9	Novel	19	Climbing plant
10	Crystal (lead glass)	20	Ron Howard

Easy

1 Which Prokofiev ballet shares its name with a well-known Disney film?

2 Who is responsible for arranging dance moves?

3 Which traditional dance from the north of England is performed wearing a wooden-soled shoe?

4 *Casse-noisette* is the French name for which ballet?

5 Which trio had a 1975 hit with *Jive Talkin'*?

6 The hornpipe dance is traditionally associated with which group of people?

7 Which group reached the UK top ten in 1984 with *Do the Conga*?

8 What was the subtitle of the 2014 film in the *Step Up* series?

9 Which creatures perform a waggle dance?

10 The song *Born to Hand Jive* features in which musical?

11 What is the meaning of the word "demi", as in the ballet term "demi-plié"?

12 Who had a 1999 hit with *Mambo No.5*?

Medium

13 In which traditional English folk dance do the participants wave handkerchiefs?

14 Bhangra dance originated on which continent?

15 Who played Billy Elliot's dance teacher, Mrs Wilkinson, in the 2000 film?

16 Which dance is mentioned in the phrase meaning that both parties are equally to blame for an incident or situation?

17 Which singer released the 2003 album *Dance with My Father*?

18 In which decade was the 2013 TV series *Dancing on the Edge* set?

19 Which dance, originating in the 1920s, was named after aviator Charles Lindbergh?

20 Which footballer famously performed a robot dance in 2006 after scoring a goal for England?

Hard

1   Which is the correct spelling: comitted, commited, or committed?

2   What nation has Dana International twice represented in Eurovision?

3   The town of Bracknell lies in which county?

4   Who swam the English Channel in 2006 to raise money for Comic Relief?

5   In the fable of the Three Little Pigs, of what material does the first pig build his house?

6   What type of motor racing takes place at Santa Pod Raceway?

7   What colour is the "y" in the eBay logo?

8   In which Bond film does Dr Christmas Jones appear?

9   What name is given to the scenic painting at the rear of a stage?

10 What is the radio code word for the last vowel in the alphabet?

11 In which 1994 film did the main character goes out for a run that became a three-and-a-half year journey?

12 The football ground of Selhurst Park lies within which London borough?

13 Whom did Ed Balls marry in 1998?

14 Primrose Everdeen is a character in which series of novels?

15 What type of creature is a corncrake?

16 In which country did the Corinthian War take place?

17 Who directed the 2019 version of *Dumbo*?

18 Which dried fruit shares its name with a verb meaning "to cut back"?

19 Cantonese and Sichuan are types of regional cuisine in which country?

20 Who was TV's *Supernanny*?

Answers to QUIZ 353 – Pot Luck

1	Greece	11	May 2019
2	Jean-Claude Van Damme	12	Greater Manchester
3	Porthos	13	All 4
4	Grass	14	October
5	Whirlwind	15	*Rocky*
6	18	16	20
7	Paul Newman	17	Old English sheepdog
8	Bagatelle	18	Zn
9	Danish	19	Ed Sheeran
10	Glenn Close	20	22

ANSWERS ON PAGE 358

1   The phrase "Oh, dearie me" is associated with which 1994 Scottish sitcom?

2   What colour is a West Highland terrier?

3   *Ain't No Mountain High Enough* was a hit for which US singer in 1970?

4   In the Christmas carol *Ding Dong Merrily on High*, where are the bells ringing?

5   The royal residence of Highgrove House lies in which English county?

6   "I'm the dandy highwayman" are the opening words to which 1981 song?

7   What is the usual short form of the term "high fidelity"?

8   Who wrote the novel on which the film *The Talented Mr Ripley* was based?

9   To what form of travel does the English High Speed 2 (HS2) development relate?

10 In what are radio waves measured, with high frequency being between three and 30?

11 Who formed the band the High Flying Birds in 2010?

12 Something small might be described as knee-high to which insect?

13 Is the sea closest to the shore or furthest away from the shore at high tide?

14 High Barnet is a terminus of which London Underground line?

15 In which 1986 film did Sir Sean Connery play an Egyptian immortal?

16 Highbury is the former stadium of which London football club?

17 What "high" animal would you be on if you were being arrogant, or over-principled?

18 What is the medical term for high blood pressure?

19 For what do the letters HD stand in relation to televisions?

20 How many Oscars did the 1952 film *High Noon* win?

Answers to QUIZ 354 – Dance

1	*Cinderella*	11	Half
2	Choreographer	12	Lou Bega
3	Clog dance	13	Morris dance
4	*The Nutcracker*	14	Asia
5	The Bee Gees	15	Dame Julie Walters
6	Sailors	16	Tango (It takes two to tango)
7	Black Lace	17	Luther Vandross
8	*All In*	18	1930s
9	Bees	19	Lindy Hop
10	*Grease*	20	Peter Crouch

QUIZ 357 – Pot Luck

ANSWERS ON PAGE **359**

1 Tej Lalvani replaced Nick Jenkins on which long-running TV series?

2 Who took over from Anneka Rice as the "hunter" on *Treasure Hunt* for the 1989 series?

3 Suzuka is the home to the Grand Prix of which country?

4 What word can mean a group of theatre performers and "to throw"?

5 Which small vegetable lends its name to a short, double-breasted overcoat?

6 Olympiacos FC is a football team based in which country?

7 Which children's author and illustrator (d.2019) created the character of Mog the cat?

8 Which French car company has two chevrons as its logo?

9 When did conscription first come into effect in Great Britain?

10 Dunster Castle lies in which county?

11 What colour was the tide in the title of a 1995 thriller?

12 In which decade was *Back to the Future Part II* released?

13 On a standard keyboard, which is the right-most letter on the top row?

14 What name is given to an animal that only eats plants?

15 What is the official language of Israel?

16 What rank is immediately below warrant officer in the British Army?

17 The musical *Blood Brothers* is set in which city?

18 Which six words follow "We plough the fields and scatter" in the harvest festival hymn?

19 What colour is the background of the *National Geographic* magazine?

20 Which underground creature gives its name to a spy?

Answers to QUIZ 355 – Pot Luck

1 Committed
2 Israel
3 Berkshire
4 David Walliams
5 Straw
6 Drag racing
7 Green
8 *The World is Not Enough*
9 Backcloth or backdrop
10 Uniform
11 *Forrest Gump*
12 Croydon
13 Yvette Cooper
14 *The Hunger Games*
15 A bird
16 Greece
17 Tim Burton
18 Prune
19 China
20 Jo Frost

357

1 Who wrote the screenplay for *The Social Network* (2010)?

2 Which actress played Jackie Kennedy in the 2016 film *Jackie*?

3 *The King's Speech* (2010) was nominated for 12 Oscars. How many did it win?

4 Which band was the subject of a 1991 film starring Val Kilmer?

5 Who played John Reid in the 2019 film *Rocketman*?

6 Which silent-film star was portrayed on screen by Robert Downey Jr in 1992?

7 In which 2011 film did Jim Broadbent play Denis Thatcher?

8 Who won an Oscar for his portrayal of pianist David Helfgott in the 1996 film *Shine*?

9 In the title of a 1997 film, which royal figure was referred to as *Mrs Brown*?

10 *Anne of the Thousand Days* (1969) was about which historical figure?

11 Which artist did Guy Pearce portray in the 2006 film *Factory Girl*?

12 Who directed the 1992 film *Malcolm X*?

13 *In the Name of the Father* (1993) was a courtroom drama about which group of people?

14 Who played PL Travers in the 2013 film *Saving Mr Banks*?

15 Which bushranger was played by Heath Ledger in a 2003 film?

16 Which writer was the subject of the 2017 biopic *Goodbye Christopher Robin*?

17 In the 1980 film *Coal Miner's Daughter*, who played Loretta Lynn?

18 Which 1995 film starred Tom Hanks as astronaut Jim Lovell?

19 Who directed and starred in the 1989 film Henry V?

20 Which actor starred as Benjamin Mee in the 2011 film *We Bought a Zoo*?

Answers to QUIZ 356 – High Time

1	*The High Life*	11	Noel Gallagher
2	White	12	A grasshopper
3	Diana Ross	13	Closest to the shore
4	Heaven	14	Northern Line
5	Gloucestershire	15	*Highlander*
6	*Stand and Deliver* (Adam and the Ants)	16	Arsenal FC
7	Hi-fi	17	Horse
8	Patricia Highsmith	18	Hypertension
9	Train travel	19	High definition
10	Megahertz (Mhz)	20	Four

1   How is 68 represented in Roman numerals?

2   What is the correct spelling: internal, internnal or interrnal?

3   Which actor starred in *Doctor Who* first, Christopher Eccleston or Matt Smith?

4   What word can mean both a type of cooking hob and an introductory procedure?

5   In the initials of the trade union RMT, for what does the "R" stand?

6   Who played Alfred in *Batman Begins*?

7   What does a contortionist do?

8   Which of these cities is most easterly: Edinburgh, Glasgow or Stirling?

9   Magny-Cours is a racing circuit in which country?

10   Which *Coronation Street* actor is the father of actor Linus Roache?

11   How many acts are there in the ballet *The Nutcracker*?

12   What was the name of Keeley Hawes' character in the TV series *Bodyguard*?

13   Which sci-fi film of 2016 shares its name with the title of a 1976 album by Abba?

14   Harlow in Essex lies on the border of which other county?

15   The National Water Sports Centre lies in which English county?

16   Which country hosted the 2019 FIFA Women's World Cup?

17   Which part of the body is affected by Raynaud's disease?

18   Which historical leader did Colin Farrell play in a 2004 film?

19   Who do you favour if you practise nepotism?

20   The pursuit features in competition in cycling and which winter sport?

Easy

Medium

Hard

Answers to QUIZ 357 – Pot Luck

1	*Dragons' Den*	11	*Crimson*
2	Annabel Croft	12	1980s (1989)
3	Japan	13	P
4	Cast	14	Herbivore
5	Pea (coat)	15	Hebrew
6	Greece	16	Staff sergeant
7	Judith Kerr	17	Liverpool
8	Citroën	18	The good seed on the land
9	1916	19	Yellow
10	Somerset	20	Mole

1 Which instrument shares its name with an historic region of Scotland?

2 What term is given to all the works that a musician can perform?

3 What musical instrument is mentioned in the rhyme *Hey Diddle Diddle*?

4 *Deeper Underground* was a 1998 song by which band?

5 What is the lowest pitched string on a violin?

6 Which singer featured on Dire Straits' *Money for Nothing*?

7 *Parallel Lines* was a 1978 album by which group?

8 Which singer was nicknamed "the Thin White Duke"?

9 "Just the memory of your face" is a line from which song originally recorded in 1984?

10 Who had a 1989 hit with *Right Here Waiting*?

11 What word can mean both a church instrument and a vital part of the body?

12 With which tenor did Michael Ball team up to release the albums *Together* and *Together Again*?

13 What musical term is given to a seamless join between phrases?

14 *One Night in Bangkok* is a song from which musical?

15 In music, a triple is three notes played in the time of how many notes?

16 Which 2001 Kylie Minogue song begins with the word "La" 32 times?

17 How many strings does a guitar usually have?

18 Madonna had two UK no.1 hits in 2000, *American Pie* and which other single?

19 What is the name of the half-sized orchestral flute, the name of which is the Italian for "small"?

20 *You Don't Have to Say You Love Me* was a hit for which 1960s singer?

Answers to QUIZ 358 – Biopics

1	Aaron Sorkin	11	Andy Warhol
2	Natalie Portman	12	Spike Lee
3	Four	13	Guildford Four
4	The Doors	14	Dame Emma Thompson
5	Richard Madden	15	Ned Kelly
6	Sir Charlie Chaplin (*Chaplin*)	16	AA Milne
7	*The Iron Lady*	17	Sissy Spacek
8	Geoffrey Rush	18	*Apollo 13*
9	Queen Victoria	19	Sir Kenneth Branagh
10	Anne Boleyn	20	Matt Damon

1 Who had a 1958 hit with *Rave On*?

2 Zoology is the study of what?

3 John Cleese was born in which decade?

4 Zawe Ashton and Joe Thomas starred in which Channel 4 sitcom first broadcast in 2011?

5 Giant Haystacks was a famous name in which sport during the 1970s and 1980s?

6 What French word is given to the conclusion of a book, film or play?

7 What is the first name of Mrs Brown in the sitcom *Mrs Brown's Boys*?

8 Proverbially, what is a little learning?

9 Which football team does Sir Elton John support?

10 Which brother of John F Kennedy was assassinated in 1968?

11 What had inventor Wayne Szalinski, played by Rick Moranis, accidentally done in the title of a 1989 film?

12 Robin Cousins appeared as a judge on which reality TV show from 2006 to 2014?

13 Is the town of Barnstaple in North Devon or South Devon?

14 Whom did Michael Howard (Baron Howard of Lympne) succeed as Leader of the Conservative Party?

15 The Ffestiniog Railway lies mostly in which National Park?

16 0.25 is equivalent to what fraction?

17 In 2012, the skeleton of Richard III was found under a car park in which city?

18 Hannukah is an occasion in which religion?

19 What name is given to the fruit of the rose?

20 Which French football manager was in charge of Liverpool FC from 1998 to 2004?

Easy

Medium

Hard

Answers to QUIZ 359 – Pot Luck

1	LXVIII	11	Two
2	Internal	12	Julia Montague
3	Christopher Eccleston	13	*Arrival*
4	Induction	14	Hertfordshire
5	Rail	15	Nottinghamshire
6	Sir Michael Caine	16	France
7	Twist their body into shapes	17	Fingers or toes
8	Edinburgh	18	Alexander the Great (*Alexander*)
9	France	19	Members of your family
10	William Roache	20	Speed skating

1 What term has emerged in recent years to describe the act of unexpectedly appearing in a photograph?

2 Which member of the Sex Pistols went on to found Public Image Ltd?

3 "Picture palace" is an old term for what type of building?

4 Which comedian's routines are based around the PowerPoint application?

5 "All I want is a photo in my wallet" is a line from which 1978 song?

6 The National Portrait Gallery is just off which London square?

7 Which member of the Beatles released the 1973 album *Photograph*?

8 What nationality was *Pictures at an Exhibition* composer Mussorgsky?

9 Which group of people make use of photofit pictures?

10 *Wishing (If I Had a Photograph of You)* was a 1982 song by which band?

11 Which group released *Picture of You* in 1997?

12 Proverbially, how many words is a picture worth?

13 Who released the 2015 song *Photograph*?

14 "Got a picture of you beside me, got your lipstick mark still on your coffee cup" are lyrics from which 1995 song?

15 For what do the initials CGI stand in relation to film and television?

16 Who wrote the 1881 novel *The Portrait of a Lady*?

17 What type of publication was *The Daily Sketch*?

18 Lucy Sketch was a character in which teen series based in Bristol?

19 What nationality is photographer Annie Leibovitz?

20 What artist's requisite are you said to go back to, if you have to start again?

Answers to QUIZ 360 – Music

1	Fife	11	Organ
2	Repertoire	12	Alfie Boe
3	A fiddle	13	Segue
4	Jamiroquai	14	*Chess*
5	G	15	Two
6	Sting	16	*Can't Get You Out of My Head*
7	Blondie	17	Six
8	David Bowie	18	*Music*
9	*Against All Odds*	19	Piccolo
10	Richard Marx	20	Dusty Springfield

1   Which Harry Potter film was released first, *The Goblet of Fire* or *The Half-Blood Prince*?

2   Grand Central Station is the main railway terminus in which US city?

3   What name is shared by the area above a stage and a group of insects?

4   What is the name of Malcolm Hebden's *Coronation Street* character?

5   Oxon is an abbrevation for which English county?

6   Which children's author created the Bandersnatch?

7   Which former Eurovision winner recorded a version of *Hand in Glove* in 1984?

8   Who wrote the 1895 play *An Ideal Husband*?

9   Pecorino cheese originates from which country?

10 What is the chemical symbol for aluminium?

11 What name is given to a luxurious flat at the top of a building?

12 What is the main ingredient of a frittata?

13 The island of Antigua lies in which body of water?

14 Which actor co-wrote and starred in the 2019 TV series *Don't Forget the Driver*?

15 What items of furniture do you proverbially fall between two of, if you fail to satisfy either of two competing demands?

16 Vera Wang is a well-known name in which profession?

17 What is a Belted Galloway?

18 What is the English meaning of the name "Montenegro"?

19 What vegetable is called "aloo" in Indian cookery?

20 In the nursery rhyme, where did Polly Flinders sit?

Easy

Medium

Hard

Answers to QUIZ 361 – Pot Luck

1	Buddy Holly	11	Shrunk the kids (*Honey, I Shrunk the Kids*)
2	Animals	12	*Dancing on Ice*
3	1930s (1939)	13	North Devon
4	*Fresh Meat*	14	Iain Duncan Smith
5	Wrestling	15	Snowdonia
6	Dénouement	16	One quarter
7	Agnes	17	Leicester
8	A dangerous thing	18	Judaism
9	Watford FC	19	Hip
10	Robert F Kennedy	20	Gérard Houllier

1 Which *Wacky Races* character had the catchphrase: "Drat, drat and double drat!"

2 What is the name of the teddy bear owned by the cartoon cat Garfield?

3 In *Lady and the Tramp*, what is the English translation of the song *Bella Notte*?

4 Peppermint Patty appears in which cartoon strip?

5 Who accompanied Jive Bunny on the novelty records of the late 1980s and early 1990s?

6 Which cartoon character did Robin Williams play in a 1980 film?

7 In which animated comedy do characters drink Duff beer?

8 What is the name of Popeye's enemy?

9 In the 2015 film *Inside Out*, what is the name of the girl?

10 Which Disney characters sang *Whistle While You Work*?

11 Who created the character of Budgie, an animated blue helicopter?

12 How is Roy Race known in the title of a comic first printed in 1954?

13 Which feline TV cartoon character lives in a dustbin?

14 What type of creature is Angelina Ballerina in the children's books and TV series?

15 Which breakfast cereal is advertised by the cartoon character Tony the Tiger?

16 Bugs Bunny is often seen chewing on which vegetable?

17 What type of dog is Scooby-Doo?

18 How are Hunca Munca and Tom Thumb referred to in the title of a Beatrix Potter tale?

19 Professor Calculus appears in the adventures of which character?

20 Kanga is a friend of which cartoon bear?

Answers to QUIZ 362 – Picture Perfect

1 Photobombing
2 John Lydon (Johnny Rotten)
3 Cinema
4 Dave Gorman
5 *Picture This* (Blondie)
6 Trafalgar Square
7 Ringo Starr (Sir Richard Starkey)
8 Russian
9 Police
10 A Flock of Seagulls
11 Boyzone
12 1000
13 Ed Sheeran
14 *Back for Good* (Take That)
15 Computer-generated image
16 Henry James
17 Newspaper
18 *Skins*
19 American
20 Drawing board

1 Walter White was the main character in which series, first broadcast in 2008?

2 In social circles, for what do the letters FOMO stand?

3 What word can mean a ball of small fibres and "to get one's lines wrong on stage"?

4 A mosque is a building of worship in which religion?

5 In the 1980s, who was Pepsi's singing partner?

6 At which cricket ground does Middlesex play home games?

7 What colour light does a ship have on its starboard side at night?

8 How many squares are there in a Sudoku puzzle that uses the digits 1 to 9?

9 Which actress won a Best Actress Oscar first, Dame Julie Andrews or Dame Maggie Smith?

10 Which "ology" is the study of society?

11 Princess Jasmine appears in which 1992 Disney film?

12 Which poet was born in Alloway in Ayrshire in 1759?

13 The aerial campaign known as the Blitz took place during which war?

14 Which square lies at the bottom of the Spanish Steps in Rome?

15 Which Swiss chocolate bar is famously triangular?

16 In which 1955 film did Marilyn Monroe wear an iconic white dress?

17 Ragnar Lothbrok is the main character in which TV costume drama?

18 Which planet in the solar system takes the least time to orbit the Sun?

19 Which 19th-century English naturalist and biologist was influenced by his visit to the Galapagos Islands on *HMS Beagle*?

20 Which football team has the nickname "The Blades"?

Answers to QUIZ 363 – Pot Luck

1	*The Goblet of Fire* (2005)	11	Penthouse
2	New York	12	Eggs
3	Flies	13	Caribbean Sea
4	Norris Cole	14	Toby Jones
5	Oxfordshire	15	Two stools
6	Lewis Carroll	16	Fashion design
7	Sandie Shaw	17	Breed of cattle
8	Oscar Wilde	18	Black mountain
9	Italy	19	Potato
10	AI	20	Among the cinders

1 Nestlé is based in which country?

2 For what does the charity the Howard League campaign?

3 What do the organisations in a cartel seek to do?

4 Which car company has a circle with a horizontal lightning bolt as its logo?

5 In 1994, Norwegians voted in a referendum not to join which organisation?

6 Tony Blair was famously heckled at the national conference of which organisation in 2000?

7 What does the retail chain Hamleys sell?

8 For what did the initials GLC stand in the name of an administrative body abolished in 1986?

9 Who was appointed head coach of the England rugby union team in 2015?

10 In which year was the British company Deliveroo founded?

11 How is the International Criminal Police Organisation more usually referred to?

12 The institution Opus Dei is part of which church?

13 Which body organises the annual Tatton Park Flower Show?

14 What colour is the background of the Salvation Army logo?

15 Who was elected as General Secretary of the Unite trade union in 2010?

16 Lindisfarne Castle in Northumberland is maintained by which organisation?

17 In which year of the 2010s was the Northern Ireland Assembly suspended?

18 AT&T is a major US company in which industry?

19 What did Amazon sell when it was first established in 1994?

20 The RSPB reserve of Rainham Marshes is part of which estuary?

Answers to QUIZ 364 – Cartoon Characters

1	Dick Dastardly	11	Sarah, Duchess of York
2	Pooky	12	*Roy of the Rovers*
3	Beautiful night	13	Top Cat
4	*Peanuts*	14	A mouse
5	The Mastermixers	15	Frosties
6	Popeye	16	Carrot
7	*The Simpsons*	17	Great Dane
8	Bluto	18	*The Tale of Two Bad Mice*
9	Riley	19	Tintin
10	The Seven Dwarfs	20	Winnie-the-Pooh

1 Who was leader of the Soviet Union first, Lenin or Stalin?

2 The TV series *Cold Feet* is set in which city?

3 What is someone who falsifies accounts said to be cooking?

4 The city of Liverpool lies on which river?

5 Which of these cities is furthest south: Nottingham, Sheffield or Wakefield?

6 What nationality is golfer Corey Pavin?

7 Who played Teddy Daniels in the 2010 film *Shutter Island*?

8 In Cockney rhyming slang, what is a "two and eight"?

9 Who plays Commander Fred Waterford in the TV series *The Handmaid's Tale*?

10 Which comedian (d.2005) signed off his TV show with the words "May your God go with you"?

11 In the wartime song, in what should you pack up your troubles?

12 Who played Bridget's boss Daniel Cleaver in the film *Bridget Jones's Diary*?

13 Who provided the voice of the baby in the first two *Look Who's Talking* films?

14 The cake decoration angelica is what colour?

15 What word can mean both an accidental happening and a parasitic worm?

16 Which sea lies north of Iran?

17 On the map of the London Underground, which line is coloured pink?

18 Who wrote the 1974 horror novel *Carrie*?

19 Who was named the 2019 BBC Women's Footballer of the Year?

20 What number is given to a fresh breeze on the Beaufort Scale?

Easy

Medium

Hard

Easy

1. What was the name of James Marsters' character in the TV series *Buffy the Vampire Slayer*?

2. Which HG Wells novel was famously broadcast as a radio drama in America in 1938, supposedly causing panic?

3. Who had a 1972 hit with *Superstition*?

4. 1982's *Ghosts* was the highest-charting single for which group?

5. Spook was a member of which TV feline's gang?

6. *Ghost Protocol* was the subtitle of the 2011 film in which series?

7. What name is given to a witch's large pot?

8. The Great Pumpkin is a Hallowe'en figure mentioned in which cartoon strip?

9. Who directed the 1974 film *Young Frankenstein*?

10. In which cartoon series do the characters travel in the Mystery Machine?

11. Who played psychic Oda Mae Brown in the 1990 film *Ghost*?

12. Which TV series introduced "the Weeping Angels"?

Medium

13. *Ghost Stories* was a 2014 album released by which band?

14. What is missing from the tag line from the TV series *Spooks*, "___ not nine to five"?

15. What was the title of the 1973 hit by Bobby Pickett and the Crypt-Kickers?

16. In which 1981 horror film does the pub *The Slaughtered Lamb* feature?

17. "If there's something strange in your neighbourhood" is the opening line from the theme tune to which 1984 film?

18. Which English film company, founded in 1934, is famous for its horror films?

19. Witchiepoo was a character in which children's series, originally broadcast in 1969?

20. Which of *The X-Files* characters was nicknamed "Spooky"?

Hard

Answers to QUIZ 366 – Organisations

1	Switzerland (Vevey)	11	Interpol
2	Penal reform	12	Catholic church
3	Control prices and competition	13	RHS (Royal Horticultural Society)
4	Opel	14	Red
5	European Union	15	Len McCluskey
6	Women's Institute	16	National Trust
7	Toys	17	2017
8	Greater London Council	18	Telecommunications
9	Eddie Jones	19	Books
10	2013	20	Thames Estuary

1 According to the song, where did Puff the Magic Dragon live?

2 Raymond van Barneveld is a famous competitor in which sport?

3 Which US political party has traditionally had an elephant as its mascot, the Democrats or the Republicans?

4 Who had a 1982 hit with *Love Plus One*?

5 Moving anti-clockwise on a dartboard, what number is next to 2?

6 What is added to soda water to make tonic water?

7 Which alien race in *Doctor Who* is associated with the word "exterminate"?

8 For which 1993 film did Steven Spielberg win his first Best Director Oscar?

9 The sitcom *Cheers* was set in which US city?

10 Which small bird of prey is also known as a windhover?

11 Who won *Britain's Got Talent* first, George Sampson or Jai McDowall?

12 Which is the smallest state of Australia?

13 In 2012, which Chancellor of the Exchequer announced plans to tax takeaway food, dubbed the "pasty tax"?

14 What nationality was the poet Ted Hughes?

15 In the European Union, what size of egg must have a minimum weight of 53g?

16 Which actress incorrectly announced the winner of the Best Picture Oscar at the 2017 award ceremony?

17 Which England manager was in charge for only one game, which took place in September 2016?

18 The Nikkei is the financial index in which country?

19 What nationality is tennis player Kevin Anderson?

20 Which musical instrument is also the name of a champagne glass?

Easy

Medium

Hard

Answers to QUIZ 367 – Pot Luck

1	Lenin (1924)	11	Your old kit bag
2	Manchester	12	Hugh Grant
3	The books	13	Bruce Willis
4	River Mersey	14	Green
5	Nottingham	15	Fluke
6	American	16	Caspian Sea
7	Leonardo DiCaprio	17	Hammersmith and City Line
8	State	18	Stephen King
9	Joseph Fiennes	19	Ada Hegerberg
10	Dave Allen	20	Five

Easy

1. Native to Africa, what type of creature is a serval?

2. To the nearest 10%, what percentage of the Earth's land area is in Africa?

3. Does Burkino Faso have a coast or is it a landlocked country?

4. Which is the second-largest city in South Africa, by population?

5. What colour is the background of the flag of Morocco?

6. The township of Soweto is part of which South African city?

7. "As sure as Kilimanjaro rises like Olympus above the Serengeti" is a line from *Africa* by which band?

8. In which Kenyan hotel was Elizabeth II staying when she acceded to the throne?

9. The mouth of the Congo River is in which ocean?

10. Dar es Salaam is the largest city in which African country?

11. Is Mauritania on the east coast or west coast of Africa?

12. In which country is the Aswan Dam?

13. Who received her sixth Oscar nomination for the 1985 film *Out of Africa*?

14. Which African capital city is an anagram of I ROB IAN?

15. The ancient city of Carthage lies in which modern-day country?

16. *Living Free* and *Forever Free* were sequels to which 1960 non-fiction book, set in Kenya?

17. In which country is Table Mountain National Park?

18. *Escape 2 Africa* is a sequel to which Disney film?

19. Which capital city lies at the confluence of the Blue Nile and the White Nile?

20. Which two African countries begin with "Z"?

Medium

Hard

Answers to QUIZ 368 – Spooky

1	Spike	11	Whoopi Goldberg
2	*The War of the Worlds*	12	*Doctor Who*
3	Stevie Wonder	13	Coldplay
4	Japan	14	MI5
5	Top Cat	15	*Monster Mash*
6	*Mission: Impossible*	16	*An American Werewolf in London*
7	Cauldron	17	*Ghostbusters*
8	*Peanuts*	18	Hammer
9	Mel Brooks	19	*HR Pufnstuf*
10	*Scooby-Doo*	20	Fox Mulder

1 "One taught me love, one taught me patience" is a lyric from which 2018 song?

2 Which of these cities lies furthest west: Bangor, St Asaph or Swansea?

3 Who was the UK Home Secretary from 2001 to 2004?

4 Which of the characters in *Friends* had the surname Bing?

5 What type of bird is a goosander?

6 According to the proverb, what is there no smoke without?

7 How was Louisa Trotter referred to in the title of a 1970s TV series?

8 What is the name of the city of Turin in Italian?

9 What five-letter word is the opposite of "rural"?

10 In which country was the manufacturing company Olivetti founded?

11 What do the letters "R" and "A" stand for in the name of the world's oldest golf club?

12 How many minutes are there in three hours?

13 Which football team won the Championship play-offs in 2019 to obtain promotion to the Premier League?

14 In which 2005 animated film did Helena Bonham Carter provide the voice of Lady Tottington?

15 Traditionally, to which side is port passed?

16 *Whatever People Say I Am, That's What I'm Not* was the 2006 debut album by which band?

17 Which country has the internet code .it?

18 Sir Andy Murray teamed up with which player to win the men's doubles at the 2019 tennis tournament at Queen's Club?

19 Who hosted *Pop Idol*?

20 International Workers' Day is celebrated on the first day of which month?

Answers to QUIZ 369 – Pot Luck

1	Honahlee	11	George Sampson (2008)
2	Darts	12	Tasmania
3	Republicans	13	George Osborne
4	Haircut 100	14	English
5	15	15	Medium
6	Quinine	16	Faye Dunaway
7	Daleks	17	Sam Allardyce
8	*Schindler's List*	18	Japan
9	Boston	19	South African
10	Kestrel	20	Flute

Easy

1 In which decade was the Hard Rock Cafe founded in London?

2 Which stage musical features a roller-skating robot called Ariel?

3 When a choice has to be made between two unpleasant alternatives, the chooser is said to be between a rock and what else?

4 What name is given in the UK to the register of people entitled to vote in elections?

5 Which Australian rock formation is also known as Ayres Rock?

6 In which UK resort is The Big One roller coaster located?

7 Who were the enemies of the rockers in the 1960s?

8 What type of vehicle would perform a barrel roll?

9 "One, two, three o'clock, four o'clock, rock" is the opening line to which 1954 song?

10 What is a French roll?

Medium

11 Which "rock" was created by puppeteer Jim Henson?

12 What is wrapped in a layer of sponge cake in an Arctic roll dessert?

13 How was Hollywood actor Roy Harold Scherer, Jr (d.1985) better known?

14 Who had a 1982 hit with *I Love Rock 'n' Roll*?

15 Which band released the 1980 song *Sgt. Rock (Is Going to Help Me)*?

16 Austrian, roller and Venetian are types of what household item?

17 What substance is boiled with glucose syrup to make seaside rock?

18 Which long-running series features Roy's Rolls café?

19 A rockhopper is what type of bird?

20 How is a herring treated to make a rollmop?

Hard

Answers to QUIZ 370 – Africa

1	A wildcat	11	West coast
2	20% (20.4%)	12	Egypt
3	Landlocked	13	Meryl Streep
4	Cape Town	14	Nairobi (Kenya)
5	Red	15	Tunisia
6	Johannesburg	16	*Born Free* (Joy Adamson)
7	Toto	17	South Africa
8	Treetops Hotel	18	*Madagascar*
9	Atlantic Ocean	19	Khartoum
10	Tanzania	20	Zambia and Zimbabwe

1   Which is the only city in West Sussex?

2   How is 76 represented in Roman numerals?

3   Mikhail Baryshnikov starred in the last series of which TV programme?

4   What word describes something that spreads rapidly via social media?

5   In which county is the stately home of Althorp?

6   Who was the first US president to resign?

7   In what year was the first Hunger Games book published?

8   Which TV competition includes the technical challenge and the showstopper?

9   In which city was the film *Slumdog Millionaire* set?

10 Which rank in the British Army is immediately above captain?

11 In computing, how many bits are there in a byte?

12 What is the atomic number of hydrogen?

13 In what year did Madonna have a hit with *Vogue*?

14 "Life Begins" is a traditional bingo call for which number?

15 What is the national bird of India?

16 Which author's characters drink Butterbeer?

17 In which decade was the old 5p piece withdrawn from circulation?

18 What is the correct spelling for a dam across a stream: weer, weir, or wier?

19 In the New Testament, what relation was John the Baptist to Jesus?

20 Which body of water lies to the north of Brittany?

Easy

Medium

Hard

Answers to QUIZ 371 – Pot Luck

1	*Thank U, Next* (Ariane Grande)	11	Royal and Ancient
2	Bangor	12	180
3	David Blunkett (Baron Blunkett)	13	Aston Villa FC
4	Chandler	14	*Wallace and Gromit: The Curse of the Were-Rabbit*
5	A duck	15	The left
6	Fire	16	The Arctic Monkeys
7	*The Duchess of Duke Street*	17	Italy
8	Torino	18	Feliciano López
9	Urban	19	Ant and Dec
10	Italy	20	May

ANSWERS ON PAGE 376

Easy

1   What name is given to the building in which Jewish people worship?

2   In which Russian city is the Hermitage Museum?

3   One of Europe's longest bridges, the Vasco da Gama bridge, lies in which country?

4   Which cathedral stands in Red Square in Moscow?

5   The Hoover Building in Ealing, opened in 1933, is an example of what type of architecture?

6   What is the full name of the area within a building known as a quad?

7   In what type of building does the 1979 film *The China Syndrome* take place?

8   "When you're weary, feeling small" are the opening lines to which 1970 song?

9   Which main London railway terminus is named after a 19th-century battle?

10   What do the initials CN stand for in the name of the tower in Toronto?

11   What building is associated with children's presenters Dick and Dom?

Medium

12   In which century were Martello towers built in the UK?

13   What two-word term is used to describe an array of wind turbines?

14   The Pharos of Alexandria, one of the Seven Wonders of the Ancient World, was what type of structure?

15   In which garden in south-west London is there a 50m high 18th-century pagoda?

16   What is a transmission tower called in the UK?

17   What is stored in a granary on a farm?

18   On an Ordnance Survey map, what type of building is indicated by a black circle with a cross on top?

19   In what type of building was Elvis Presley crying, in the title of a 1965 single?

20   Which two languages were used in the TV series *The Bridge*?

Hard

Answers to QUIZ 372 – Rock and Roll

1	1970s (1971)	11	*Fraggle Rock*
2	*Return to the Forbidden Planet*	12	Ice cream
3	A hard place	13	Rock Hudson
4	Electoral roll	14	Joan Jett & the Blackhearts
5	Uluru	15	XTC
6	Blackpool	16	Blind
7	The mods	17	Sugar
8	An aeroplane	18	*Coronation Street*
9	*Rock Around the Clock* (Bill Haley and his Comets))	19	A penguin
10	A hairstyle	20	Pickled

1. Which ancient philosopher is associated with a theory relating to triangles?

2. The film *In Which We Serve* was set during which war?

3. There are three US states with five-letter names: Idaho, Maine and which other?

4. Kr is the chemical symbol for which element?

5. Who won FIFA's Ballon d'Or award for four consecutive years from 2009 to 2012 and again in 2015?

6. In which Queen video are the band seen doing housework?

7. Which four-letter word beginning with "v" means "I forbid" in Latin?

8. Dolly and Cissy were the sisters of which *Dad's Army* character?

9. Which Tom Cruise film was released first, *Rain Man* or *The Firm*?

10. In ten-pin bowling, what term is given to the score when all the skittles are knocked over once the second ball of a turn has been thrown?

11. What number do opposites sides of a die add up to?

12. In which county is East Midlands Airport?

13. Which number is *tres* in Spanish?

14. David Prowse was one of the actors to portray which character in the Star Wars films?

15. Which female writer created the character of Rupert Campbell-Black?

16. How many recordings are "castaways" allowed on *Desert Island Discs*?

17. Bushmills in Northern Ireland is famous for producing which drink?

18. What word follows "Apostles'" and "Nicene" to make the names of statements of Christian belief?

19. On which quiz show does Pat Gibson regularly appear?

20. Which group had a hit in 1997 with *D'You Know What I Mean*?

Answers to QUIZ 373 – Pot Luck

1	Chichester	11	Eight
2	LXXVI	12	1
3	*Sex and the City*	13	1990
4	Viral	14	40
5	Northamptonshire	15	Peacock
6	Richard Nixon	16	JK Rowling (in the Harry Potter books)
7	2008	17	1990s (1990)
8	*The Great British Bake Off*	18	Weir
9	Mumbai	19	Cousin
10	Major	20	English Channel

1   How many years were there in the title of a 2008 Will Smith film?

2   Which Sir Alfred Hitchcock film was released first, *Rebecca* or *The 39 Steps*?

3   Who sang the theme song to the 1980 film *9 to 5*?

4   Steve Guttenberg, Tom Selleck and which other actor played the three men in *Three Men and a Baby*?

5   Who played the mother of Haley Joel Osment's character in *The Sixth Sense*?

6   Which Shakespeare play was the inspiration for the 1999 film *10 Things I Hate About You*?

7   Who played Rusty Ryan in the *Ocean's Eleven* film and its sequels?

8   How many realms were associated with *The Nutcracker* in the title of the 2018 film?

9   Which member of the Monty Python team directed the 1995 film *Twelve Monkeys*?

10 In which 2012 film did Channing Tatum and Jonah Hill play two policemen who go undercover in a high school?

11 On which precinct was there an assault, according to the title of a 1976 film?

12 Who starred as Jane in the 2008 film *27 Dresses*?

13 In what type of transport did the main action take place in *The Taking of Pelham 123* (2009)?

14 Which rapper starred in the 2002 film *8 Mile*?

15 Who starred as Korben Dallas in the 1997 film *The Fifth Element*?

16 Which TV quiz featured in the 2006 film *Starter for 10*?

17 In which year was the first *Fantastic Four* film released?

18 The 2007 horror film *28 Weeks Later* was set in which capital city?

19 Who played Lucy in the 2004 film *50 First Dates*?

20 In which country was the sci-fi film *District 9* set?

Answers to QUIZ 374 – Buildings and Structures

1	Synagogue	11	Bungalow
2	St Petersburg	12	19th century
3	Portugal (Lisbon)	13	Wind farm
4	St Basil's Cathedral	14	Lighthouse
5	Art Deco	15	Kew Gardens
6	Quadrangle	16	(Electricity) pylon
7	Nuclear power plant	17	Grain or animal feed
8	*Bridge Over Troubled Water* (Simon and Garfunkel)	18	Church with a spire or steeple
9	Waterloo	19	The chapel
10	Canadian National	20	Danish and Swedish

1   What was the nickname of James Doohan's character in the original *Star Trek* series?

2   On which day of the year are hot cross buns traditionally eaten?

3   Who had a 1990 hit with *Show Me Heaven*?

4   Myleene Klass found fame on which reality show?

5   Who composed *The Wedding March*?

6   Which European capital city did George Ezra sing about in 2014?

7   Which capital city was the first to host the Summer Olympic Games for a third time?

8   "Every little helps" is the advertising slogan for which supermarket?

9   What has an intestate person not done?

10   What term is given to the promenade between Blackpool's two piers?

11   Which European country has the international dialling code 0039?

12   In the play by Shakespeare, what is the name of Hamlet's uncle who becomes the new king?

13   Which large musical instrument is a symbol of Ireland?

14   Which two compass directions are used in rhyming slang for the mouth?

15   In 2019, which company introduced the Fold mobile phone?

16   What title is given to the head of government in Germany?

17   Who were *Most Wanted* in the title of a 2014 film?

18   How many yards is the penalty spot from the goal in football?

19   The town of Saltash lies in which English county?

20   In the UK, who announces the results of a local election?

Easy

Medium

Hard

Answers to QUIZ 375 – Pot Luck

1	Pythagoras	11	Seven
2	WWII	12	Leicestershire
3	Texas	13	Three
4	Krypton	14	Darth Vader
5	Lionel Messi	15	Jilly Cooper
6	*I Want to Break Free*	16	Eight
7	Veto	17	Whiskey
8	Private Godfrey	18	Creed
9	*Rain Man* (1988)	19	*Eggheads*
10	Spare	20	Oasis

1   Where does a puffin make its nest?

2   Which large member of the family that includes weasels and stoats is primarily found in Scotland in the UK?

3   How long does it take a biennial plant to flower?

4   What is the stage of an insect between larva and adult?

5   What is the fruit of an oak tree?

6   Does moss grow in damp conditions or dry conditions?

7   Which squirrel is native to the UK, the grey squirrel or the red squirrel?

8   What colour is chlorophyll in plants?

9   Bottlenose and long-beaked are species of which marine creature?

10   How many compartments does the stomach of a cow have?

11   What is the national flower of Scotland?

12   Which type of insect has species called "hairy-footed flower" and "mason"?

13   A stickleback is what type of creature?

14   What colour is a female sparrowhawk?

15   In the term "flora and fauna", which of the words describes plant life?

16   What type of bird is a mallard?

17   What does water contain if it is described as "brackish"?

18   What is the term given to the biological community of plants and creatures of a particular area?

19   The rhea is native to which continent?

20   What term is given to a creature whose body temperature is not much affected by the surrounding temperature?

Answers to QUIZ 376 – Film in Numbers

1	Seven	11	13 (*Assault on Precinct 13*)
2	*The 39 Steps* (1935)	12	Katherine Heigl
3	Dolly Parton	13	A subway car
4	Ted Danson	14	Eminem
5	Toni Collette	15	Bruce Willis
6	*The Taming of the Shrew*	16	*University Challenge*
7	Brad Pitt	17	2005
8	Four	18	London
9	Terry Gilliam	19	Drew Barrymore
10	*21 Jump Street*	20	South Africa

1   Which *Pop Idol* winner covered the song *Light My Fire*?

2   In what month of 1914 did WWI commence?

3   The town of Biggleswade lies in which English county?

4   Which nation did 2014 Eurovision winner Conchita Wurst represent?

5   How many legs does a biped have?

6   What colour flag signals a premature end to a Formula 1 race?

7   Which US talk show host had an opera written about his show?

8   Which actress starred in the film *Annie Hall*?

9   In which decade did Kampuchea change its name to Cambodia?

10   Who presented the TV series *The Biggest Loser* in 2011 and 2012?

11   *The Little Mermaid* statue in Copehagen harbour is a tribute to which author?

12   Victoria Beckham was born in which decade?

13   *Shine On You Crazy Diamond* appears on which Pink Floyd album?

14   The Sugden family appear in which long-running TV series?

15   In the children's novel *My Friend Flicka*, what type of animal is Flicka?

16   Who was the lead singer of Bronski Beat?

17   On what side of the road do Germans drive?

18   In stones, what is the maximum weight of a featherweight boxer?

19   Which day of the week is alphabetically first?

20   Which UK country reached the semi-finals of the Euro 2016 football tournament, losing to Portugal?

Easy

Medium

Hard

Answers to QUIZ 377 – Pot Luck

1	Scotty	11	Italy
2	Good Friday	12	Claudius
3	Maria McKee	13	The harp
4	*Popstars*	14	North and south
5	Mendelssohn	15	Samsung
6	Budapest	16	Chancellor
7	London (2012)	17	Muppets
8	Tesco	18	12 yards
9	Made a will	19	Cornwall
10	The Golden Mile	20	Returning officer

1   "En garde" is a phrase used in which sport?

2   In which winter sport do participants perform a "step sequence"?

3   Under whose orders are you, if you are waiting to start a race?

4   "King or Queen of the Mountains" is a title used in which road-based sport?

5   In which sport do men perform the Iron Cross and Maltese Cross?

6   What three-word term is given to the achievement of winning all four major tennis tournaments between January and December in the same year?

7   In what sport might you use a dolphin kick?

8   A participant in which sport might "catch a crab"?

9   In which sport would a player encounter the rub of the green?

10 Which sport produces "the sound of leather on willow"?

11 What sporting piece of equipment is someone said to have moved if they redefine a task?

12 Which phrase from the final of the 1966 FIFA World Cup was used as the title for a 1990s sports-based game show?

13 In which indoor sport might you score a "bed and breakfast" of 26 points?

14 A player who is dismissed or substituted from a match is said to be taking an early what?

15 What boxing term is used to describe someone who is close to being defeated?

16 Which US sport gives rise to the phrase "to come from left field"?

17 What informal three-word name is given to a round of a tournament where the teams are all potential qualifiers?

18 The term "first past the post" to describe an election is taken from which sport?

19 What vessel are you said to paddle if you do something independently?

20 What type of sporting surface might be mentioned in a situation where everyone has an equal chance of winning?

Answers to QUIZ 378 – Natural World

1	In a burrow	11	Thistle
2	Pine marten	12	Bee
3	Two years	13	A fish
4	Pupa (or chrysalis)	14	(Dark) brown
5	Acorn	15	Flora
6	Damp conditions	16	A duck
7	Red squirrel	17	Salt
8	Green	18	Ecosystem
9	Dolphin	19	South America
10	Four	20	Warm-blooded

QUIZ 381 – Pot Luck

1 Was the former county of Cleveland in the north-east or the north-west of England?

2 Which is the first prime number higher than 100?

3 Peroni beer originated in which country?

4 How is 89 represented in Roman numerals?

5 In the name of the former investment account, for what did PEP stand?

6 Which royal residence suffered a major fire in 1992?

7 What is the Italian name for an open square?

8 Patrick Vieira played Premier League football for Arsenal and which other club?

9 Which telecommunications company uses the advertising slogan "Believe in better"?

10 Which US state lends its name to a dessert of ice cream, meringue and sponge?

11 In which decade was the powerful television play *Cathy Come Home* first broadcast?

12 What word can mean both a study and a wild animal's lair?

13 The single *Everything Changes* was a 1994 hit for which group?

14 How many lanes are usually used in an Olympic swimming pool?

15 What was the name of Ruth Wilson's character in the TV series *Luther*?

16 Which country is bordered by Guatemala and Belize to the south and the USA to the north?

17 Who played Moses in the 1956 film *The Ten Commandments*?

18 What word meaning a cross between species is also used to refer to a vehicle that uses more than one source of power?

19 Orly Airport lies near which French city?

20 Used in Asia, what type of transport is a sampan?

Easy

Medium

Hard

Answers to QUIZ 379 – Pot Luck

1	Will Young	11	Hans Christian Andersen
2	July (28th)	12	1970s (1974)
3	Bedfordshire	13	*Wish You Were Here*
4	Austria	14	*Emmerdale*
5	Two	15	A horse
6	Red	16	Jimmy Somerville
7	Jerry Springer	17	The right-hand side
8	Diane Keaton	18	Nine stone
9	1990s (1993)	19	Friday
10	Davina McCall	20	Wales

1   Which fictional bear is associated with the Hundred Acre Wood?

2   Elijah Wood played which character in *The Lord of the Rings* films?

3   In which English county is the coastal town of Fleetwood?

4   Mark Wood (b.1990) plays which sport for England?

5   Who was Kim Woodburn's cleaning partner in the TV series *How Clean is Your House*?

6   Who narrated the 1960s children's series *Pogles' Wood*?

7   "Why don't you ask him if he's going to stay?" is the opening line of which 1979 Fleetwood Mac song?

8   St John's Wood is in which borough of London?

9   *Mens Sana in Thingummy Doodah* (1991) was the title of a book of TV scripts by which comedienne?

10 What was the name of Natalie Wood's character in the film *West Side Story*?

11 Proverbially, what can you not see the wood for?

12 What is the plural of "woodlouse"?

13 Josiah Wedgwood was born in which century?

14 Which colour shirt does Tiger Woods usually wear on the last day of a golf tournament?

15 What is another name for the sequoia tree?

16 "I don't want to lose you, this good thing that I got" are the opening lines to which 1979 song?

17 Which cartoon bird was famous for his laugh?

18 What are the first names of the two brothers Underwood who played rugby for England in the 1990s?

19 The name of which tree, used for furniture wood, is an anagram of "Hogmanay"?

20 Who directed the 2019 film *Once Upon a Time in Hollywood*?

Answers to QUIZ 380 – Sporting Phrases

1	Fencing	11	Goalposts
2	Figure skating	12	They think it's all over
3	Starter's	13	Darts
4	Cycling	14	Bath
5	Gymnastics (on the rings)	15	On the ropes
6	Calendar Grand Slam	16	Baseball
7	Swimming	17	Group of death
8	Rowing	18	Horse racing
9	Golf or bowls	19	Your own canoe
10	Cricket	20	Level playing field

1 What type of creature is a hartebeest?

2 Which member of Genesis had a solo hit with *I Missed Again*?

3 In 2019, who won the Best Supporting Actress BAFTA award for her role in the series *Killing Eve*?

4 Which yeast extract's name has come to mean something that divides opinion?

5 The Islamic prayer service of Jumu'ah occurs how often?

6 What is seersucker?

7 Which foodstuff made from pork and jelly shares its name with a term for strength?

8 Which word for a short sleep spells out a kitchen item when read backwards?

9 Hants is an abbrevation for which English county?

10 What was Ron's surname in the Harry Potter novels and films?

11 What does Manolo Blahnik famously design?

12 The character of Mary Alice Young narrated which TV series?

13 Which chocolate bar takes its name from Earth's galaxy?

14 Complete the title of the famous work by Douglas Adams, *So Long and Thanks for All the ___*?

15 What colour is the piece for Mrs Peacock in Cluedo®?

16 Which Bond film was released first, *The Living Daylights* or *Thunderball*?

17 What is 3/5ths expressed as a decimal amount?

18 Which of the four major golf tournaments did Rory McIlroy win first?

19 Who lost the Conservative Party leadership election to David Cameron?

20 The 1993 sequel to which film was subtitled *Back in the Habit*?

Answers to QUIZ 381 – Pot Luck

1	North-east	11	1960s (1966)
2	101	12	Den
3	Italy	13	Take That
4	LXXXIX	14	Eight
5	Personal Equity Plan	15	Alice Morgan
6	Windsor Castle	16	Mexico
7	Piazza	17	Charlton Heston
8	Manchester City (2010-11)	18	Hybrid
9	Sky	19	Paris
10	Alaska (baked Alaska)	20	A boat

1   Who presents the 2019 game show *In for a Penny*?

2   What is TV presenter Simon Rimmer's occupation?

3   *Mr MacGregor* is a 2004 novel by which TV gardener?

4   Who was the original presenter of the children's TV series *Record Breakers*?

5   Which former footballer was one of the original presenters on the 1990s gameshow *Gladiators*?

6   Which couple present the 2019 music game show *The Hit List*?

7   Jeremy Clarkson, James May and which other presenter appear on *The Grand Tour*?

8   Which TV scientist presented the 2019 series *The Planets*?

9   Which TV naturalist co-founded the campaigning group Wild Justice in 2019?

10 Who co-presents *Eat Well for Less* with Chris Bavin?

11 The phrase "cheap as chips" is associated with which presenter?

12 ITV's *World of Sport* was presented by whom from 1968 until it ended in 1985?

13 Which couple famously started a book club on their show in 2004?

14 Which two new presenters took over *Top Gear* in June 2019?

15 Carol Klein presents programmes on what subject?

16 Who co-presents *Long Lost Family* with Nicky Campbell?

17 Which BBC business presenter began presenting on *Watchdog* in 2016?

18 In which year did Gillian Burke first appear on BBC2's *Springwatch*?

19 Which comedian co-hosts *Bake Off: the Professionals* alongside Liam Charles?

20 Julia Bradbury is famous for presenting programmes featuring which outdoor pursuit?

Answers to QUIZ 382 – Wood

1	Winnie-the-Pooh	11	The trees
2	Frodo Baggins	12	Woodlice
3	Lancashire	13	18th century (1730)
4	Cricket	14	Red
5	Aggie MacKenzie	15	Redwood
6	Oliver Postgate	16	*Knock on Wood* (Amii Stewart)
7	*Tusk*	17	Woody Woodpecker
8	City of Westminster	18	Rory and Tony
9	Victoria Wood	19	Mahogany
10	Maria	20	Quentin Tarantino

1   What item of make-up is named after the French word for "red"?

2   Who played Elizabeth R in the 1971 TV series?

3   Which is the correct spelling for a system of voting: balott, ballot or ballott?

4   Proverbially, what do you gain on, if you lose on the swings?

5   Barclays Bank has its headquarters in which city?

6   Bill McLaren (d.2010) was a commentator on which sport?

7   Which English county lies furthest north?

8   In which city was the TV series *Sex and the City* set?

9   How many degrees are there in a semi-circle?

10 What is ciabatta?

11 Braintree lies in which English county?

12 What word describes foliage that has more than one colour?

14 What colour is the liqueur crème de menthe?

13 Which TV chef has encountered many *Kitchen Nightmares*?

15 In which branch of the services did Prince Harry serve?

16 Did a gill measure volume or weight?

17 What name is given to the toxin in a snake?

18 Which football team came second in the 2019 Scottish Premiership?

19 Who won the Best Actress Oscar for playing the title role in the 1982 film *Sophie's Choice*?

20 Which planet in the solar system has the shortest name?

Answers to QUIZ 383 – Pot Luck

1	An antelope	11	Shoes
2	Phil Collins	12	*Desperate Housewives*
3	Fiona Shaw	13	Milky Way
4	Marmite®	14	*Fish*
5	Weekly	15	Blue
6	A cotton fabric	16	*Thunderball* (1965)
7	Brawn	17	0.6
8	Nap (pan)	18	US Open (2011)
9	Hampshire	19	David Davis
10	Weasley	20	*Sister Act*

Easy

Medium

Hard

1   *The Boxer* was a 1970 song by which duo?

2   Theologians have studied what subject?

3   *The Odyssey* was an epic poem written by whom?

4   The Edge plays guitar in which band?

5   Thespians are employed in which profession?

6   *The Guardian* newspaper was founded in which city?

7   The band The Killers were formed in which country?

8   The Epsom Derby is run in which month?

9   Theo Paphitis appeared on which TV series from 2005 to 2012?

10 *The Martian*, starring Matt Damon, was released in which year?

11 The Needles lie off which UK island?

12 Thelma Barlow played which *Coronation Street* character?

13 *The First Nowell* is sung at what time of year?

14 Thessaloniki is a city in which European country?

15 *The Chrysalids* is a 1955 sci-fi novel by which author?

16 The last straw proverbially broke which creature's back?

17 *The Firebird* ballet was written by which composer?

18 Theresa May was born in which decade?

19 Thebes was the name of an ancient city in Greece and which other modern-day country?

20 *The Lost World* was a 1912 novel by which author?

Answers to QUIZ 384 – TV Presenters

1	Stephen Mulhern	11	David Dickinson
2	Chef	12	Dickie Davies
3	Alan Titchmarsh	13	Richard Madeley and Judy Finnigan
4	Roy Castle	14	Andrew Flintoff and Paddy McGuinness
5	John Fashanu	15	Gardening
6	Marvin and Rochelle Humes	16	Davina McCall
7	Richard Hammond	17	Steph McGovern
8	Brian Cox	18	2017
9	Chris Packham	19	Tom Allen
10	Gregg Wallace	20	Walking

1. On a standard keyboard, which letter is immediately to the left of P?

2. What type of animal was Uggie, who featured in the 2011 film *The Artist*?

3. How many sides does a decagon have?

4. What word describes a surface that curves outwards in the centre?

5. In which country was singer Peter Andre born?

6. Is France ahead of, or behind Greenwich Mean Time?

7. According to the proverb, what type of waters run deep?

8. In which decade was the word "yuppie" invented?

9. How many seconds do contestants get to make words in a round of *Countdown*?

10. Which two colours feature on the Austrian flag?

11. What is a Little Gem?

12. *Boom Boom Pow* and *I Gotta Feeling* were UK no.1 hits for which group in 2009?

13. What is the term given to first place on a Formula 1 grid at the start of a race?

14. The name of what company completes the former marketing slogan: "Ding Dong, ___ Calling"?

15. Sauerkraut originated in which country?

16. *Sylvia's Mother* was a 1972 hit for which US group?

17. Which body of water lies off the north-west coast of Belgium?

18. *Songs of Praise* was first broadcast in which decade?

19. Which fictional detective was portrayed on TV by Jeremy Brett between 1984 and 1994?

20. In *The Wizard of Oz*, which character wanted a brain?

Answers to QUIZ 385 – Pot Luck

1	Rouge	11	Essex
2	Glenda Jackson	12	Variegated
3	Ballot	14	Green
4	The roundabouts	13	Gordon Ramsay
5	London	15	The army
6	Rugby Union	16	Volume (quarter of a pint)
7	Northumberland	17	Venom
8	New York City	18	Rangers
9	180	19	Meryl Streep
10	Italian bread	20	Mars

Easy

Medium

Hard

Easy

1 What is the plural of "genius"?

2 "Able Was I Ere I Saw Elba" is an example of what type of phrase?

3 Who plays Chief Superintendent Bright in *Endeavour*?

4 For what do the letters IQ stand?

5 Which comedian hosted the BBC2 comedy game show *Genius*?

6 On which radio station is the *Brain of Britain* quiz broadcast?

7 What man's name follows "smart" in the nickname of an annoyingly clever person?

8 *Child Genius* is broadcast on which channel in the UK?

9 Who was the original presenter of the quiz show *Eggheads*?

10 What was Sarah Brightman's debut single, released in 1978?

11 By what nickname is the *Thunderbirds* character Mr Hackenbacker better known?

12 Who is reputed to have said "I have nothing to declare except my genius"?

13 The name Billy Smart was associated with which form of entertainment?

14 Which two actors co-starred in the 2016 film *Central Intelligence*?

Medium

15 Sarah Smart played Anne-Britt Hoglund in the English version of which Swedish crime drama?

16 In which decade was the Val Kilmer film *Real Genius* released?

17 Nick Bright hosts which daytime Sunday show on Radio 5 Live?

18 What is eyebright?

19 What footwear follows "clever" in the nickname of someone who thinks they know everything?

20 By what abbreviation is the UK's Secret Intelligence Service better known?

Hard

1 Which Nicole Kidman film was released first, *Bewitched* or *Margot at the Wedding*?

2 Who partnered Chris Hollins when he won *Strictly Come Dancing*?

3 Harry Ramsden's is famous for which takeaway food?

4 Proverbially, which part of the body do you put to the wheel to make a determined effort?

5 The character of Mrs Mangel appeared in which long-running series?

6 What term is traditionally given to an unmarried woman in France?

7 Who played Dennis Rickman in *EastEnders*?

8 What is heated to make caramel?

9 A natterjack is what type of creature?

10 Dipsophobia is a fear of drinking what?

11 Kenny Ball (d.2013) was most associated with what musical instrument?

12 In which decade did the Wright Brothers achieve the first powered sustained flight of an aircraft?

13 What is the opposite of a pessimist?

14 What name is given to a short tune used in an advertisement?

15 Who had a 1989 hit with *Song for Whoever*?

16 In which city was the American Werewolf in the 1997 sequel?

17 What is two gross?

18 Who played the chauffeur in the 1989 film *Driving Miss Daisy*?

19 Agar is used as a vegetarian alternative to what substance?

20 In the novel by Anna Sewell, what was *Black Beauty*?

Answers to QUIZ 387 – Pot Luck

1	O	11	A lettuce
2	A dog	12	The Black Eyed Peas
3	Ten	13	Pole position
4	Convex	14	Avon
5	England	15	Germany
6	Ahead	16	Dr Hook (and the Medicine Show)
7	Still waters	17	North Sea
8	1980s	18	1960s (1961)
9	30 seconds	19	Sherlock Holmes
10	Red and white	20	Scarecrow

ANSWERS ON PAGE 392

1 *Atlantic Crossing* was a 1975 album by which singer?

2 What was the only UK no.1 for Wings?

3 *Anarchy in the UK* (1976) was the first single released by which group?

4 *Rock Me Baby* was a 1972 album by which teen idol?

5 In which Sir Elton John song was he going "Back to the howling old owl in the woods"?

6 The 1972 album *Thick as a Brick* was released by which group, named after the inventor of the seed drill?

7 What was the title of the 1977 double album released by the Electric Light Orchestra?

8 Rick Wakeman played what instrument in the prog-rock band Yes?

9 What was the title of the England World Cup Squad's no.1 in 1970?

10 What part of London did Elvis Costello not want to go to, in the title of a 1978 single?

11 In which 1979 song by Squeeze were the "Sweeney doing ninety"?

12 Steve Harley was backed by which band?

13 What was the title of Abba's last no.1 of the 1970s?

14 Where did Supertramp have breakfast in the title of a 1979 single and album?

15 Charles Aznavour (d.2018) was born in which country?

16 *Whispering Grass* was a no.1 for which two *It Ain't Half Hot Mum* actors?

17 Dave Bartram was the lead singer with which group?

18 Which singer died on August 16, 1977?

19 Brian and Michael's *Matchstalk Men and Matchstalk Cats and Dogs* was a tribute to which artist?

20 Siouxsie Sioux was backed by which band?

Answers to QUIZ 388 – Clever

1	Geniuses	11	Brains
2	Palindrome (reads both ways)	12	Oscar Wilde
3	Anton Lesser	13	Circus
4	Intelligence quotient	14	Dwayne Johnson and Kevin Hart
5	Dave Gorman	15	*Wallander*
6	Radio 4	16	1980s (1985)
7	Alec	17	*The Squad*
8	Channel 4	18	A flowering plant
9	Dermot Murnaghan	19	Clogs
10	*I Lost My Heart to a Starship Trooper*	20	MI6

Easy

Medium

Hard

Easy

Medium

Hard

1   What was the name of the mouse who was Dumbo's best friend in the 1941 Disney film?

2   What nationality is golfer Dustin Johnson?

3   *Mercy* was a 2008 UK hit for which singer?

4   Which singer had a band called The Spiders from Mars?

5   Which company advertises with the slogan "Should have gone to"?

6   Who was the youngest of the Brontë sisters?

7   In which decade was *Gangs of New York* released?

8   Cheltenham is in which English county?

9   Whom did Sir John Major succeed as Chancellor of the Exchequer?

10   "Sunset Strip" is a traditional bingo call for which number?

11   What nautical symbol does Popeye have tattooed on his arm?

12   What is the sum of the whole numbers from one to five?

13   Which retired Formula 1 driver died in May 2019 at the age of 70?

14   Which teeth-straightening device shares its name with a strengthening piece?

15   What colour Jaguar did Inspector Morse drive in the TV series?

16   In which country did Primark originate?

17   Which month is first alphabetically?

18   Which blue colour is used in printing ink?

19   How many minutes are there in one-and-a-half hours?

20   I is the chemical symbol for which element?

Answers to QUIZ 389 – Pot Luck

1	*Bewitched* (2005)	11	Trumpet
2	Ola Jordan	12	1900s (1903)
3	Fish and chips	13	An optimist
4	Your shoulder	14	Jingle
5	*Neighbours*	15	The Beautiful South
6	Mademoiselle	16	Paris
7	Nigel Harman	17	288
8	Sugar	18	Morgan Freeman
9	Toad	19	Gelatin
10	Alcohol	20	A horse

Easy

1. In which cell block was the prisoner in the title of the Australian drama series?

2. How many points is the letter Z worth in Scrabble®?

3. What is the third note in the scale of C major?

4. What colour is the letter "P" on the plate that can optionally be displayed by a driver who has recently passed their driving test?

5. For what did "V" stand in the title of a 2005 film?

6. Which letters provided the title of a 2006 hit for Rihanna?

7. In the James Bond films, for what does Q stand in the name of the gadget-supplying character?

8. What is indicated by a small "c" in a circle in a text?

9. The force resulting from acceleration is denoted by which letter?

10. What letter does the shape of a horseshoe resemble?

11. In which winter sport might competitors use the V technique?

12. The first person singular pronoun is indicated by which letter?

Medium

13. What letter is used to denote a secondary road on UK maps?

14. What is the 18th letter of the alphabet?

15. Which chess piece is identified by the letter B?

16. K is the chemical symbol for which element?

17. Which letter "marks the spot" on a map?

18. Which constellation forms the shape of a W?

19. What seven-letter word beginning with "P" is a name for a remedy for all ills?

20. A is the international car registration letter for which country?

Hard

Answers to QUIZ 390 – 1970s Music

1. Sir Rod Stewart
2. *Mull of Kintyre/(Girls' School)*
3. The Sex Pistols
4. David Cassidy
5. *Goodbye Yellow Brick Road*
6. Jethro Tull
7. *Out of the Blue*
8. Keyboards
9. *Back Home*
10. Chelsea (*(I Don't Want to Go to) Chelsea*)
11. *Cool for Cats*
12. Cockney Rebel
13. *Take a Chance on Me* (1978)
14. America (*Breakfast in America*)
15. France
16. Don Estelle and Windsor Davies
17. Showaddywaddy
18. Elvis Presley
19. LS Lowry
20. The Banshees

1 Which of these is the correct spelling: acheeve, acheive or achieve?

2 Which boxing weight has a maximum of ten and a half stone?

3 Who was the UK foreign secretary from 1989 to 1995?

4 How many days are there in April?

5 Which organ of the body is affected by atrial fibrillation?

6 In which county is the town of Warrington?

7 What name is given to a wind of force 12 or above on the Beaufort Scale?

8 What term is given to a musical note that is neither sharp nor flat?

9 Taittinger is famous for what type of drink?

10 Mohammed Al-Fayed owned which London football club from 1997 to 2013?

11 Snooker player Mark Allen is from which country?

12 The letter F is on which row of a computer keyboard?

13 How many times did Slade top the UK charts in the 1970s?

14 According to the proverb, what will the mice do when the cat's away?

15 Gordon Jackson played which character in the 1970s series *Upstairs, Downstairs*?

16 How many inches are there in five feet?

17 Who voiced Detective Pikachu in the 2019 *Pokémon* film?

18 What nationality is singer/songwriter Lewis Capaldi?

19 In which decade did Terminal 5 open at Heathrow?

20 What colour is the mineral jade?

Easy

Medium

Hard

Answers to QUIZ 391 – Pot Luck

1	Timothy	11	An anchor
2	American	12	15
3	Duffy	13	Niki Lauda
4	David Bowie	14	Brace
5	Specsavers	15	Red
6	Anne	16	Republic of Ireland
7	2000s (2002)	17	April
8	Gloucestershire	18	Cyan
9	Nigel Lawson (Baron Lawson of Blaby)	19	90
10	77	20	Iodine

Easy

1   What is the Italian word for "red"?

2   What type of institution may be described as "red-brick"?

3   Who wrote the 1981 novel *Red Dragon*?

4   The ladybird belongs to which group of insects?

5   Which socialist anthem is sung to the tune of the German carol *O Tannenbaum*?

6   Which sauce, based on redcurrants, takes its name from a traditional English county?

7   *Red Light Spells Danger* was a 1977 hit for which singer?

8   What type of food is Red Leicester?

9   A ship displays a red light on which side at night?

10 The cabernet sauvignon grape originated in which country?

11 Who starred as Frank Moses in the 2010 film *RED*?

12 What is a red snapper?

13 What colour paint is obtained by mixing blue and red?

Medium

14 *Red and Black* is a song sung by revolutionaries in which musical?

15 Redhill Aerodrome lies in which southern English county?

16 The Red Ensign has what national flag on a red background?

17 Which type of tomato, commonly tinned, starts with the name of a fruit?

18 Which famously red item of street furniture was designed by Sir Giles Gilbert Scott in the 1920s?

19 The band the Red Hot Chili Peppers was formed in which country?

20 Which football team did Harry Redknapp manage from 2008 to 2012?

Hard

Answers to QUIZ 392 – Letters

1	H (*Prisoner: Cell Block H*)	11	Ski jumping
2	Ten	12	I
3	E	13	B
4	Green	14	R
5	Vendetta (*V for Vendetta*)	15	Bishop
6	*SOS*	16	Potassium
7	Quartermaster	17	X
8	Copyright	18	Cassiopeia
9	G	19	Panacea
10	U	20	Austria

1 What type of creature is a guillemot?

2 In which year was Baroness Margaret Thatcher ousted from the office of UK prime minister?

3 *You're Fired* is a spin-off from which reality show?

4 Hannah Spearritt was an original member of which group, formed in 1999?

5 *If You Tolerate This Then Your Children Will Be Next* was a hit for which group?

6 The radio code word for which letter of the alphabet is the name of a Canadian province?

7 David Coulthard made his Formula 1 debut in which decade?

8 Which winter sport was inspired by skateboarding?

9 In which country was the Bayeux Tapestry created?

10 How is 60 represented in Roman numerals?

11 Which 1970s detective famously enjoyed lollipops?

12 With what is a steak coated if it served *au poivre*?

13 Which day of the week has the most letters in its name?

14 The River Po is the longest river in which European country?

15 In what decade did Leeds Rhinos become known under their present name?

16 Moving anti-clockwise on a dartboard, what number is next to 14?

17 "Are you ready for this, are you hanging on the edge of your seat?" are lines from which Queen song?

18 What colour smoke is seen at the Vatican when the cardinals have failed to agree on the election of a new pope?

19 Which 2019 film starred Anne Hathaway and Rebel Wilson as con artists?

20 In the nursery rhyme, which bells said "Oranges and Lemons"?

Easy

Medium

Hard

Answers to QUIZ 393 – Pot Luck

1	Achieve	11	Northern Ireland
2	Welterweight	12	Middle row
3	Douglas Hurd (Baron Hurd of Westwell)	13	Six
4	30	14	Play
5	The heart	15	Mr Hudson
6	Cheshire	16	60
7	Hurricane	17	Ryan Reynolds
8	Natural	18	Scottish
9	Champagne	19	2000s (2008)
10	Fulham FC	20	Green

Easy

1 Who played Professor Henry Jones Sr in *Indiana Jones and the Last Crusade*?

2 In the *Men in Black* trilogy, who plays Kevin Brown, known as Agent K?

3 Who provides the voice of Gru in the *Despicable Me* films?

4 The 2019 film *Dark Phoenix* is part of which franchise?

5 Which 1991 film popularised the phrase "Hasta la vista, baby"?

6 Who played Cedric Diggory in *Harry Potter and the Goblet of Fire*?

7 Which character did Chris O'Donnell play in the 1995 and 1997 Batman films?

8 What was the title of the James Bond film in which George Lazenby played the lead role?

9 In which fictional land were *The Lord of the Rings* and *The Hobbit* films set?

10 *The Last Knight* was the 2017 episode in which franchise?

Medium

11 Who plays Caesar in the Planet of the Apes films?

12 Which country completes the title of the 2014 animated film *Penguins of ___*?

13 The Scorpion King series of films were spin-offs from which 1999 film?

14 Which superhero character did Tom Holland play for the first time in a 2016 film?

15 Which company owns Marvel Studios?

16 Lightning McQueen, voiced by Owen Wilson, is a character in which series of animated films?

17 What was *Prometheus* in the title of the 2012 film in the Alien series?

18 In which decade was the first Shrek film released?

19 Which animated characters had a *Squeakquel* in 2009?

20 Who voiced Aslan in the Chronicles of Narnia films?

Hard

Answers to QUIZ 394 – Red

1	Rosso	11	Bruce Willis
2	University	12	A fish
3	Thomas Harris	13	Purple
4	Beetles	14	*Les Misérables*
5	*The Red Flag*	15	Surrey
6	Cumberland sauce	16	Union Jack
7	Billy Ocean	17	Plum tomato
8	Cheese	18	Telephone box
9	Port	19	USA (Los Angeles)
10	France	20	Tottenham Hotspur FC

1 Whom did Sam Cooke ask to "draw back your bow" in a 1961 song?

2 "Ghost gum" is a nickname for a eucalyptus tree in which country?

3 How many eighths are there in three-quarters?

4 What is the profession of Billy Flynn in the musical *Chicago*?

5 Where would you find a gargoyle?

6 What was Patsy's surname in the series *Absolutely Fabulous*?

7 The initials DDR were used to denote which former country?

8 What colour belt is the highest rank in judo?

9 In which decade did Jimmy Carter become US president?

10 Which dramatist wrote and directed the 2019 TV series *Summer of Rockets*?

11 What is the official language of Qatar?

12 Which British police department is concerned with political security?

13 In cookery, what measure is abbreviated to "dsp"?

14 *Trick or Treat* was a 2007 TV series featuring which illusionist?

15 The Belfry is a golf course on the outskirts of which major city?

16 In which country was the short-lived series *Eldorado* set?

17 What is the name of Miami's American football team?

18 In which decade was *Panorama* first broadcast?

19 What is the name of the hand-signalling system used by bookmakers to convey horses' odds?

20 Which twin island country has Port of Spain as its capital?

Easy

Medium

Hard

Answers to QUIZ 395 – Pot Luck

1	A bird	11	Kojak
2	1990	12	Peppercorns
3	*The Apprentice*	13	Wednesday
4	S Club 7	14	Italy
5	The Manic Street Preachers	15	1990s (1997)
6	Q (Quebec)	16	11
7	1990s (1994)	17	*Another One Bites the Dust*
8	Snowboarding	18	Black
9	France	19	*The Hustle*
10	LX	20	St Clement's

Easy

1   GCHQ is based in which English town?

2   *Surf's Up* (2007) featured the adventures of what type of bird called Cody Maverick?

3   Olney, famed for its pancake race, is in which English county?

4   *Hedda Gabler* was written by which playwright?

5   Gaia is the personification of Earth in which branch of classical mythology?

6   Sepia is a shade of what colour?

7   Omega, the Swiss company, is a famous maker of what accessory?

8   Haggis is a traditional dish from which country?

9   Gozo is a small island off the coast of which state?

10 Salma Hayek was born in which decade?

11 Oberon appears in which Shakespeare play?

12 Harlech Castle is in which country of the UK?

13 Gavin Maxwell wrote which 1960 book about the wild otters that he kept as pets?

14 Salopians come from which county?

15 Okinawa is a region in which country?

16 Hoylake on the Wirral is a famous venue for which sport?

17 Gouda cheese usually has what colour rind?

18 Seoul hosted the Summer Olympic Games in which year?

19 Olivia Colman played secretary Sally Owen in which TV series?

20 Hibernian FC is usually known by what shorter name?

Medium

Hard

Answers to QUIZ 396 – Film Franchises

1	Sir Sean Connery	11	Andy Serkis
2	Tommy Lee Jones	12	*Madagascar*
3	Steve Carell	13	*The Mummy*
4	X-Men	14	Spider-Man
5	*Terminator 2: Judgment Day*	15	Walt Disney (Studios)
6	Robert Pattinson	16	Cars
7	Robin	17	A spaceship
8	*On Her Majesty's Secret Service*	18	2000s (2001)
9	Middle-Earth	19	Alvin and the Chipmunks
10	Transformers	20	Liam Neeson

1   What part of a lentil plant is used in cooking?

2   Proverbially, what do little things please?

3   What is the name of Sue Cleaver's *Coronation Street* character?

4   Which UK prime minister was the MP for Huntingdon when he became leader of his party?

5   The Ant Hill Mob appeared in which cartoon series?

6   Which country does tennis player Garbiñe Muguruza represent?

7   Did a bushel measure volume or weight?

8   In Mexican cooking, what is mole?

9   0.75 is equivalent to what fraction?

10 Paul Sinha, stand-up comedian, is also a star of which quiz show?

11 What relationship is Formula 1 World Champion Jacques Villeneuve to Gilles Villeneuve?

12 Which actor had a 1987 hit with *Under the Boardwalk*?

13 Which football team plays home games at the Etihad Stadium?

14 *Back to Bedlam* was a 2004 album by which singer/songwriter?

15 What does the ampersand symbol mean?

16 Which cartoon bear is particularly fond of picnic baskets?

17 Where in London is the Woolsack?

18 What is the name of the only star in our solar system?

19 Budgens is a well-known name in which branch of retail?

20 What word can mean both a building support and a big smile?

Answers to QUIZ 397 – Pot Luck

1	Cupid	11	Arabic
2	Australia	12	Special Branch
3	Six	13	Dessertspoonful
4	Lawyer	14	Derren Brown
5	On an (old) building (grotesque water spout)	15	Birmingham
6	Stone	16	Spain
7	East Germany	17	Miami Dolphins
8	Black belt	18	1950s (1953)
9	1970s (1977)	19	Tic-tac
10	Stephen Poliakoff	20	Trinidad and Tobago

Easy

1 Which type of lock shares its name with an American university?

2 What word ending in "lock" is a term for a pressure chamber?

3 In the nursery rhyme, what did Lucy Locket lose?

4 Lockjaw is the common name for what medical condition?

5 What was a flintlock?

6 John Locke, played by Terry O'Quinn, was a character in which TV series?

7 What term ending in "lock" is given for traffic at a standstill?

8 What is the name for someone who makes or repairs locks?

9 How many bears did Goldilocks meet?

10 With what type of machine would you use an overlocker?

11 What type of animal has fetlocks?

12 What nationality is comedian Sean Lock?

13 On a rowing boat, what is the name of the holders for the oars?

14 What does a warlock practise?

Medium

15 Who played the title role in the TV series *Sherlock*?

16 Pollock is what type of creature?

17 Matlock is the county town of which county?

18 What word ending in "lock" is a term for an impasse?

19 Which TV quiz refers to a tie-break situation as a "lockdown"?

20 What is a young male bovine animal called?

Hard

Answers to QUIZ 398 – GSOH

1	Cheltenham	11	*A Midsummer Night's Dream*
2	(Rockhopper) Penguin	12	Wales
3	Buckinghamshire	13	*Ring of Bright Water*
4	Henrik Ibsen	14	Shropshire
5	Greek	15	*Japan*
6	Brown	16	Golf
7	Watch	17	Yellow
8	Scotland	18	1988
9	Malta	19	*Twenty Twelve*
10	1960s (1966)	20	Hibs

1   In what decade did Nicholas II order the fourth Duma to be dissolved?

2   *Spellbound* was a 1991 album by which female artist?

3   Dione is a moon of which planet?

4   In the film *Kung Fu Panda*, what type of creature is Tai Lung, the evil prison escapee?

5   Which Croatian footballer signed for Real Madrid in 2012?

6   Which word means both "suitable" and "to take something that does not belong to you"?

7   What caused the collapse of the Colossus of Rhodes in 226 AD?

8   Which 1966 film was inspired by the life of photographer David Bailey?

9   In which Olympic sport is "clipping" a major foul?

10 In 1935 in the UK, what did Mr R Beere become the first person to do?

11 The forest-dwelling indri is native to which island?

12 In which county is the parliamentary constituency of Berwick-upon-Tweed?

13 *Foeniculum vulgare* is the Latin name for which culinary plant?

14 Jeremiah Flintwich appears in which novel by Charles Dickens?

15 In Olympic archery, how far is the competitor from the target in metres?

16 The Spinnaker Tower is found in which UK city?

17 In Holst's *The Planets* suite, how is Mercury described?

18 Makka Pakka was a character in which children's TV series?

19 Carey Mulligan received a Best Actress Oscar nomination for her role in which 2009 film?

20 Ivan Mauger was a multiple world champion in which sport?

Easy

Medium

Hard

Answers to QUIZ 399 – Pot Luck

1	The seeds	11	Son
2	Little minds	12	Bruce Willis
3	Eileen Grimshaw	13	Manchester City FC
4	Sir John Major	14	James Blunt
5	*Wacky Races*	15	And
6	Spain	16	Yogi Bear
7	Volume	17	In the House of Lords
8	A sauce	18	The Sun
9	Three-quarters	19	Groceries
10	*The Chase*	20	Beam

1 What is the body's largest internal organ?

2 Which vitamin is also known as biotin?

3 Where on the body is the frontalis muscle?

4 The mitral valve is part of which human organ?

5 Chromhidrosis is a rare condition that causes what to turn different colours?

6 The latissimus dorsi lies in which part of the body?

7 Lacrimal bones can be found in which part of the human body?

8 Which word, a part of the body, comes from the Latin for "little mouse"?

9 There is one pair of palatine bones in which part of the human body?

10 What does the term "ossicle" mean?

11 What effect do higher temperatures have on nails?

12 Which two organs does the pylorus connect?

13 What name is given to the white part of the eye?

14 By what name is Hansen's disease also known?

15 What is the literal English meaning of *spina bifida*?

16 What is the more common name for the pharyngeal tonsils?

17 Leucoderma affects which part of the human body?

18 The part of the brain known as the amygdala takes its name from which nut?

19 What is the Latin word for the brain?

20 What percentage of the human body is oxygen?

Answers to QUIZ 400 – Lock Up

1	Yale	11	A horse
2	Airlock	12	English
3	Her pocket	13	Rowlocks
4	Tetanus	14	Magic (sorcery)
5	A gun or rifle	15	Benedict Cumberbatch
6	*Lost*	16	A fish
7	Gridlock	17	Derbyshire
8	Locksmith	18	Deadlock
9	Three	19	*Pointless*
10	Sewing machine	20	Bullock

QUIZ 403 – Pot Luck

ANSWERS ON PAGE 405

1   Who was the Greek equivalent of the Egyptian god Ra?

2   What is an escarpment on a hill or mountain?

3   In which major French city would you find Blagnac Airport?

4   Which actor won the Best Actor Oscar first, Colin Firth or Sean Penn?

5   In what decade did the Ryder Cup become open to players from continental Europe rather than just Great Britain?

6   What letter follows psi in the Greek alphabet?

7   Grimethorpe in South Yorkshire is famous for what type of musical group?

8   How many noble truths are there in Buddhism?

9   What type of vehicle is a curricle?

10 Who directed the 1964 film *A Hard Day's Night*?

11 *Four* was the title of a 2014 album released by which boy band?

12 In heraldy, is an item described as "dexter" on the right or the left as you look at the image?

13 What colour is the semi-precious stone carnelian?

14 What is the maximum number of runners in the Grand National?

15 In which 1988 film did Bill Murray play TV executive Frank Cross?

16 Which cartoon brother and sister were created by Lauren Child?

17 "If you shall chance, Camillo, to visit Bohemia" is the opening line in which Shakespeare play?

18 What is pennywort?

19 Which group recorded the 1964 version of *Dancing in the Street*?

20 What is the cube root of 125?

Easy

Medium

Hard

Answers to QUIZ 401 – Pot Luck

1	1910s (1917)	11	Madagascar
2	Paula Abdul	12	Northumberland
3	Saturn	13	Fennel
4	Snow leopard	14	*Little Dorrit*
5	Luka Modrić	15	70m
6	Appropriate	16	Portsmouth
7	Earthquake	17	The Winged Messenger
8	*Blow-Up*	18	*In the Night Garden*
9	Ice hockey	19	*An Education*
10	Pass the driving test	20	Speedway

1   In its own language, which African country refers to itself as Misr?

2   Argentina shares a border with how many other nations?

3   On which Scottish island is the RSPB reserve of Balranald?

4   Which country's flag is the oldest continually used national flag in the world?

5   Which English city lies on the River Witham?

6   In which African country are the Tugela Falls?

7   What is the name of the highest volcano in America?

8   In which modern day country is the prehistoric site of Colchis?

9   The Golden Horn, or Haliç, is a major waterway in which Turkish city?

10 At nearly 54 km (33½ miles) long the Seikan Tunnel is the world's longest. In which country does it lie?

11 The city of Antwerp lies on which river?

12 Outside of Europe, in which country does the Southern Alps mountain range lie?

13 The area known as "Waterfall Country" lies in which UK National Park?

14 Which two countries lie either side of the Gulf of Bothnia?

15 By area, which of these countries is larger, Chile or Kenya?

16 What is the current name of the area that used to be known as the Cape of Storms?

17 Which mathematical term is a synonym for all lines of latitude?

18 Which US state lies immediately south of Utah?

19 The site of Arkaim, key to prehistoric finds, lies on the border between Russia and which other country?

20 Which animal appears on the flag of the Falkland Islands?

1 Which of Jane Austen's novels was the first to be published?

2 *Fratercula Arctica* is the taxonomical name for which recognisable seabird?

3 What is the unit of currency in Andorra?

4 In which decade did *The Vicar of Dibley* first air?

5 "You'll succeed at last" is a lyric from which song by Jimmy Cliff?

6 During WWII, the Rugby League Challenge Cup was played over how many legs?

7 *Disc-Overy* was the title of the 2010 breakthrough album by which rapper?

8 In the memory chip EPROM, for what does the "E" stand?

9 Which Swedish city hosted the Eurovision Song Contest in 1992?

10 Zanzibar is part of which African country?

11 What is the more common name of the gean tree?

12 Who plays Lucy in the sitcom *Not Going Out*?

13 Matera is a province of which European country?

14 The word for which singing voice can also mean "the general mood"?

15 Which 1950s film tells the true story of Operation Chastise?

16 Tim Booth is the lead singer of which band?

17 *War and Peace* was published in which decade?

18 Falukorv is a type of sausage from which European country?

19 Which film was awarded the Best Picture Oscar first, *My Fair Lady* or *West Side Story*?

20 Jack Nicklaus won the US Masters on how many occasions?

Easy

Medium

Hard

Answers to QUIZ 403 – Pot Luck

1	Helios	11	One Direction
2	A wide, steep slope	12	On the right
3	Toulouse	13	Red (or reddish-yellow)
4	Sean Penn (2004)	14	Forty
5	1970s (1979)	15	*Scrooged*
6	Omega	16	Charlie and Lola
7	Brass band	17	*The Winter's Tale*
8	Four	18	A (low-growing) plant
9	A two-wheeled carriage	19	Martha and the Vandellas
10	Richard Lester	20	Five

Easy

1   Boris Yeltsin became the first president of the Russian Federation in which year?

2   What was the minimum voting age in Japan before it was lowered to 18 in 2016?

3   In which decade did Singapore gain full independence?

4   Who was the 41st president of the USA?

5   Whom did Georges Pompidou succeed as President of France?

6   *My Life, Our Times* is a memoir by which former UK Prime Minister?

7   Former President Carlos Menem was arrested in which country in 2004 on allegations of fraud?

8   General Trujillo established a dictatorship in which Caribbean country in the 20th century?

9   In what year did Raúl Castro take over as president of Cuba?

10 Who was the UK Foreign Secretary from 1935 to 1938, a post he returned to in 1940-45 and 1951-55?

Medium

11 As at 2019, who was the youngest US president at the time of his inauguration?

12 In 2018, who became the first woman to hold the post of Black Rod, being known as the Lady Usher of the Black Rod?

13 How many of the US presidents of the 20th century were Republicans, five, seven or ten?

14 Jair Bolsonaro became president of which country in January 2019?

15 Latvia declared its independence from the Soviet Union in which year?

16 In which year did Vladimir Putin first become president of Russia?

17 Who was the last UK Governor of Hong Kong, serving from 1992 to 1997?

18 Who led the Expedition of the Thousand against the Kingdom of the Two Sicilies in 1860?

19 In 1974, who succeeded Golda Meir as the prime minister of Israel?

20 Who was elected as the Prime Minister of Canada in 1980?

Hard

Answers to QUIZ 404 – Geography

1	Egypt	11	Scheldt
2	Five (Chile, Bolivia, Paraguay, Brazil, Uruguay)	12	New Zealand
3	North Uist	13	Brecon Beacons
4	Denmark	14	Finland and Sweden
5	Lincoln	15	Chile
6	South Africa	16	The Cape of Good Hope
7	Mount Rainier	17	Parallel
8	Georgia	18	Arizona
9	Istanbul	19	Kazakhstan
10	Japan	20	Sheep

1   Magnus Pym is a spy created by which author?

2   What is the meaning of the verb "roil"?

3   How many countries border Belarus?

4   Who was the mother of Emperor Constantine?

5   The Aire Gap is a pass through which range of hills?

6   The Indian Premier League's first cricket tournament was held in which year?

7   In which country was the group Catfish and the Bottlemen formed?

8   On which side of the road do cars drive in Monaco?

9   *The Lion King* is loosely based on which Shakespeare play?

10 Used often in relation to music and ballet performances, what is the meaning of *divertissement*?

11 Which Tom Hanks film was released first, *The Green Mile* or *Saving Private Ryan*?

12 How is the Southern Ocean also referred to?

13 What is the airport code of Dallas/Fort Worth International Airport?

14 What nationality is UK-based composer Barrington Pheloung?

15 Jimmy Rabbitte is the leading character in which 1991 film directed by Alan Parker?

16 Which country lost in both the 1974 and 1978 FIFA World Cup finals?

17 What is the name of Rab C Nesbitt's wife?

18 Published in 1954, what was the title of the second of Ian Fleming's James Bond novels?

19 What sport does the American Webb Simpson (b.1985) play?

20 The Specials were formed in which English city?

Easy

Medium

Hard

Easy

1   What Asian mammal is the heaviest living tree-dwelling creature?

2   The cavy is native to which continent?

3   Which animal has species called elephant, crabeater and fur?

4   Which is the largest living member of the deer family?

5   How many toes does a rhinoceros have on each foot?

6   What type of creature is a crown-of-thorns?

7   What bird is also known as a gooney?

8   Making a yodelling sound called a "barroo", which African-originating dog breed does not bark?

9   Native to North America, prairie dogs belong to which family of animals?

10 What is another name for a hedgehog's spines?

11 Which relative of the antelope shares its name with a percussion instrument?

12 American Curl and Australian Mist are breeds of which household pet?

13 Which creature that lives in the Galapagos Islands is the only reptile adapted to life in the sea?

Medium

14 What dog is the largest of the terrier breeds?

15 The roadrunner is a member of which bird family?

16 In which century did the dodo become extinct?

17 Inhabiting the Tibetan Plateau, what type of creature is a kiang?

18 What makes the kakapo unique amongst parrots?

19 The adjective "leporine" means relating to or resembling which animal?

20 The fossa is a cat-like mammal native to which island?

Hard

Answers to QUIZ 406 – Politics

1	1991	11	Theodore Roosevelt (42)
2	20	12	Sarah Clarke
3	1960s (1965)	13	Ten
4	George HW Bush	14	Brazil
5	Charles de Gaulle	15	1991
6	Gordon Brown	16	2000
7	Argentina	17	Chris Patten (Baron Patten of Barnes)
8	Dominican Republic	18	Garibaldi
9	2008	19	Yitzhak Rabin
10	Anthony Eden (First Earl of Avon)	20	Pierre Trudeau

1   Which Tom Cruise film was released first, *Collateral* or *Minority Report*?

2   The Triple Crown of Irish racing comprises the 1,000 Guineas, Derby, and which other?

3   Which band had a 1995 hit with *Macarena*?

4   Roland Joffé directed which 1984 film set in Cambodia?

5   Stephen Blackpool appears in which Dickens novel?

6   The first Rugby League World Cup was held in which decade?

7   Which former *Parks and Recreation* actor co-created and stars in the TV series *Master of None*?

8   Which 1994 film is based on the Regency Crisis of 1788?

9   Who won the 2018 BBC Sports Personality Coach of the Year award?

10 1973's *Ball Park Incident* was the first single for which British band?

11 Marcus Collins was runner-up to which *The X Factor* winning act?

12 Napoleon crowned himself Emperor of France in what decade?

13 What is the decimal equivalent of the binary number 1101?

14 Who was appointed manager of Oldham Athletic FC in February 2019, only to resign the following month?

15 Handel's *The Arrival of the Queen of Sheba* is part of which oratorio?

16 Hortense is a main character in which 1996 Mike Leigh film?

17 In feet, what is the full length of an ice hockey rink?

18 Which part of the hand is the pollex?

19 In which decade did Albert Einstein publish his theory of general relativity?

20 Which breed of dog won Best in Show at Crufts in 2019?

Easy

Medium

Hard

Answers to QUIZ 407 – Pot Luck

1	John le Carré	11	*Saving Private Ryan*
2	Disturb	12	Antarctic Ocean
3	Five (Latvia, Lithuania, Poland, Russia, Ukraine)	13	DFW
4	Helena	14	Australian
5	The Pennines	15	*The Commitments*
6	2008	16	The Netherlands
7	Wales	17	Mary
8	The right	18	*Live and Let Die*
9	*Hamlet*	19	Golf
10	Minor entertainment	20	Coventry

1 Swanhilda is a villager in which comic ballet?

2 Which ballet centres on the story of its hero Prince Ivan entering the realm of Koschei the Immortal?

3 What nationality was Manuel de Falla, composer of *El Amor Brujo*?

4 In which country is *La Bayadère* set?

5 Which 1789 ballet contains the characters Lise, Alain and Colas?

6 What does the ballet term "cabriole" mean?

7 What name is given to the codified system of arm positions and movements?

8 Lord Rothbart is a villain in which Tchaikovsky ballet?

9 The 2018 film *The White Crow* was based on the life of which ballet dancer?

10 In which major city was the Teatro San Benedetto?

11 The "second position" of the feet in ballet suggests that feet should be spaced approximately how many inches apart?

12 What does the word Bolshoi mean in English?

13 Which French word is the official term for a male ballet dancer?

14 Who is Princess Florine's partner in *Sleeping Beauty*?

15 In which country did ballet originate?

16 What is the name of Don Quixote's squire, who appears in the ballet and the source text?

17 What nationality was the man who devised the Cecchetti method of ballet training?

18 Which ballet movement means "Step of the Cat"?

19 Who composed *Orpheus* (1947)?

20 What nationality is ballet dancer Vadim Muntagirov?

Answers to QUIZ 408 – Animal World

1	Orang-utan	11	Bongo
2	South America	12	Cat
3	Seal	13	Marine iguana
4	Moose (called elk in the UK)	14	Airedale
5	Three	15	Cuckoo
6	Starfish	16	17th century (c.1662)
7	Albatross	17	Wild ass
8	Basenji	18	It cannot fly
9	Rodents	19	Hare
10	Quills	20	Madagascar

Easy

Medium

Hard

1   How was singer Jamesetta Hawkins (d.2012) better known?

2   In which South of England town does Virgin Atlantic have its headquarters?

3   Which Scottish chemist discovered nitrogen?

4   Cambodia shares a border with how many countries?

5   For what kind of work was the Greek writer Hesiod known?

6   What does the name of the Indian state Rajasthan mean in English?

7   Zoologist Jane Goodall is a pioneer in the study of which animals?

8   To the nearest 10 kg, what is the maximum weight of the men's sled in the skeleton event?

9   A loganberry is a cross between a raspberry and which other fruit?

10 Which are the only two South American countries that do not share a border with Brazil?

11 In which US state is the city of Long Beach?

12 Which car manufacturer made the Ranchero?

13 *In the City* was a brief spin-off from which long-running TV series?

14 Who wrote the song *Who Wants to Be a Millionaire*?

15 Ronnie James Dio and Graham Bonnet both sang with which band?

16 In the Harry Potter books and films, what type of tree in the Hogwarts grounds is described as "Whomping"?

17 Which author wrote the award-winning thriller *The Ghost* in 2007?

18 Which country experiences the wind known as "the Brickfielder"?

19 The Formula 1 team Sauber competed under what name in the 2019 season?

20 Which part of the body is affected by periodontal disease?

Answers to QUIZ 409 – Pot Luck

1	*Minority Report*	11	Little Mix
2	St Leger	12	1800 (1804)
3	Los Del Río	13	13
4	*The Killing Fields*	14	Paul Scholes
5	*Hard Times*	15	Solomon
6	1950s (1954)	16	*Secrets and Lies*
7	Aziz Ansari	17	200 feet
8	*The Madness of King George*	18	The thumb
9	Gareth Southgate	19	1910s (1915)
10	Wizzard	20	Papillon

Easy

1. Who wrote the 1942 report *Social Insurance and Allied Services*, which formed the basis for the welfare state in the UK?

2. Which city gives Skye its postal code?

3. Which UK city is nicknamed "Warehouse City"?

4. As at 2019, how many National Parks were there in England?

5. If someone is described as a "Mackem", from where do they hail?

6. *Ich dien* is the motto of which British royal?

7. The Welsh village of Beddgelert was named after a legendary animal of which type?

8. Which emperor built a second wall north of Hadrian's Wall?

9. St Machar's Cathedral is located in which Scottish city?

10. HNMB Devonport lies in which UK city?

11. Which city was previously known as New Sarum?

12. In which year following WWII was petrol rationing abolished in the UK?

13. Which is Britain's only "island city"?

14. Which anniversary did the Open University celebrate in 2019?

15. Valentine's Brook is the name of a fence on which English racecourse?

16. Built for the Great Exhibition, in which decade was the Crystal Palace in south London destroyed by fire?

17. Which West Country city became a World Heritage site in 1987?

18. Which building is the main meeting place of the Northern Ireland executive?

19. With what material is Bradford particularly associated?

20. In which year of the 2010s did Scotland hold its first referendum on independence?

1   Lesquin Airport is located in which French city?

2   Which actress was awarded the Best Actress Oscar award first, Faye Dunaway or Glenda Jackson?

3   Who composed the music for the stage musical of *Billy Elliot*?

4   Darius Campbell won the first series of which TV talent show?

5   In which decade was the stock car body NASCAR founded?

6   The Gulf of Roses lies off the coast of which European country?

7   Which group had a 1973 hit with *Cindy Incidentally*?

8   The steamship *Sir Walter Scott* sails on which Scottish loch?

9   What is the first name of Nobel laureate Robert Hofstadter's son, author of *I Am a Strange Loop*?

10 How many Oscars did the 1966 film *A Man for All Seasons* win?

11 Which of the Great Lakes is the location of Manitoulin Island?

12 Who presents the TV series *Hidden Britain by Drone*?

13 What is the literal meaning of the Latin term *in excelsis*?

14 On which horse did AP McCoy win his only Grand National?

15 Who directed the award-winning film *The King's Speech*?

16 Lake Orta lies in which European country?

17 To the nearest ten, how many planes of existence exist according to Buddhism?

18 In Holst's *The Planets* suite, of what is Saturn the bringer?

19 In which year was George I crowned King of Great Britain and Ireland?

20 Philosopher Friedrich Nietzsche was born in what decade?

Easy

Medium

Hard

Answers to QUIZ 411 – Pot Luck

1	Etta James	11	California
2	Crawley	12	Ford
3	Daniel Rutherford	13	*Hollyoaks*
4	Three (Laos, Thailand and Vietnam)	14	Cole Porter
5	Poetry	15	Rainbow
6	Land of Kings	16	Willow
7	Chimpanzees	17	Robert Harris
8	40 kg (43 kg)	18	Australia
9	Blackberry	19	Alfa Romeo Racing
10	Chile and Ecuador	20	The gums

1 A dish served à la Crécy is made from or accompanied by which vegetable?

2 *Malus sylvestris* is the technical name of which fruit?

3 Loch Ness and Loch Tay are types of which berry?

4 What is cooked with olives, tomatoes, garlic and olive oil to make the Turkish dish *Imam bayildi*?

5 What is the American name for a beer to which a shot of whiskey is added?

6 Which Italian region is nicknamed "the wine cellar of Italy"?

7 Fix and Mythos lagers are from which country?

8 How many standard litres of champagne fit in a Methuselah?

9 In the UK, what is the maximum adult daily recommended intake of fat, in grams?

10 What family of plants does the globe artichoke belong to?

11 The herb basil takes its name from the Greek for what word?

12 What are the two main ingredients of butterscotch?

13 In which South American country were Angostura bitters first produced?

14 A pastizz is a small pastry filled with ricotta or mushy peas and is the national dish of which country?

15 What does the name of the French pastry *religieuse* translate to in English?

16 The word "crouton" derives from the French for what word?

17 Which meat is typically used in Mexican carnitas?

18 An Arthur Turner plant produces which kind of fruit?

19 A firkin of beer consists of how many gallons?

20 Budweiser® beer was originally brewed in which country?

Answers to QUIZ 412 – The UK

1	William Beveridge (First Baron Beveridge)	11	Salisbury
2	Inverness (IV)	12	1950
3	Manchester	13	Portsmouth (on Portsea Island)
4	Ten	14	50th anniversary
5	Sunderland	15	Aintree
6	Prince of Wales	16	1930s (1936)
7	Hound	17	Bath
8	Antoninus Pius (the Antonine Wall)	18	Stormont Castle
9	Aberdeen	19	Wool
10	Plymouth	20	2014

1   Randy Jackson (b.1956) was the longest-serving judge on which TV talent show?

2   Over what distance is the 2,000 Guineas Stakes run?

3   What does the "B" stand for in the name of the poet WB Yeats?

4   In the TV show *The Littlest Hobo*, the title character was which kind of animal?

5   Mary O'Brien was the birth name of which British singer (d.1999)?

6   In which year did the Republic of Ireland football team first qualify for the World Cup Finals?

7   Which hospital owns the copyright to *Peter Pan*?

8   Launched in 1989, the *Magellan* spacecraft mapped the surface of which planet?

9   Rachel Stevens was the runner-up to which fellow competitor on *Strictly Come Dancing*?

10 *Metaphysics* and *On The Soul* are works by which philosopher?

11 Arrecife Airport can be found in which popular European holiday destination?

12 Herdwick and Rough Dale are sheep breeds most associated with which area of the UK?

13 In which year was the Ryder Cup referred to as the Battle of Brookline?

14 "I keep a close watch on this heart of mine, I keep my eyes wide open all the time" are the opening lines of which 1956 song?

15 In what year did Japan first host the Olympic games?

16 For how many years did Leonid Brezhnev preside over the Communist Party?

17 Of what is ethnography the study?

18 What nationality was the artist Georges Braque?

19 The Colombo Plan, implemented in 1951, was designed to strengthen economic and social ties between members of which continent and which ocean?

20 Where on the body can lunulae be found?

Answers to QUIZ 413 – Pot Luck

1	Lille	11	Lake Huron
2	Glenda Jackson (1971)	12	Sir Tony Robinson
3	Sir Elton John	13	In the highest
4	*Popstar to Operastar*	14	Don't Push It
5	1940s (1948)	15	Tom Hooper
6	Spain	16	Italy
7	Faces	17	30 (31)
8	Loch Katrine	18	Old age
9	Douglas	19	1714
10	Six	20	1840s (1844)

1 The film *Don't Look Now* was adapted from a novel by which author?

2 Victoria Page is the leading character in which 1948 film?

3 Who won the Best Director Oscar for the 2018 film *Roma*?

4 What is the name of the wrecked ship in the 1949 film *Whisky Galore!*?

5 Cathy Tyson played Simone and Bob Hoskins played George in which 1986 film?

6 What decade provides the setting for the 1959 film *Room at the Top*?

7 For which 1968 film did Carol Reed win his only Oscar for Best Director?

8 Who played the lead role in the 2013 remake of *The Secret Life of Walter Mitty*?

9 What prize is awarded to the best film at the Venice Film festival?

10 Who won his only Oscar for the 1958 film *Separate Tables*?

11 Adam Driver played which character in *Star Wars: The Force Awakens*?

12 How many years were there in the title of a 2015 film starring Charlotte Rampling and Sir Tom Courtenay?

13 Who played the character of Nebula in *Guardians of the Galaxy* and its sequel?

14 Which two actors starred in the "Cornetto trilogy" series of films?

15 What is the name of Carol Danvers' alter-ego in a 2019 film?

16 Darlington Hall was the setting for which 1993 film?

17 *The Shawshank Redemption* was released in which year?

18 What was the first name of the character played by James Caan in *The Godfather*?

19 *Saturday Night and Sunday Morning* was set in which city?

20 Which 2013 film won the Best Picture Oscar?

Answers to QUIZ 414 – Food and Drink

1	Carrots	11	King
2	(Crab) apple	12	Butter and sugar
3	Blackberry	13	Venezuela
4	Aubergines	14	Malta
5	Boilermaker	15	Nun
6	Puglia	16	Crust
7	Greece	17	Pork
8	Six	18	Apple
9	70g	19	Nine
10	Thistle	20	Czechia/Czech Republic

ANSWERS ON PAGE 419

1 Who played Sir Lancelot in *Monty Python and The Holy Grail* (1975)?

2 The name of which alcoholic drink comes from the Latin for "bitter"?

3 How old was Buddha when he died?

4 How many wheels does a phaeton have?

5 *Homage to Catalonia* was a 1938 work by which author?

6 Which band released the 1994 album *Dog Man Star*?

7 Joan Gamper founded which Spanish football club?

8 In what year was NATO created?

9 What is the stage name of comedian Lee Ridley (b.1980)?

10 What colour belt do beginners start with in karate?

11 What is the name of Nottinghamshire's limited-overs team?

12 At which racecourse is the Ladbroke's Trophy run?

13 What is the common name of the plant group *Sempervivum*?

14 Asia Minor is a biblical region in which modern-day country?

15 Franklin D Roosevelt was what number president of the USA?

16 The Whitworth Art Gallery is located in which English city?

17 What was the real first name of Bing Crosby?

18 What did the French company Delage manufacture?

19 "You've got me wrapped around your finger" is a lyric from which 1993 song?

20 How many African nations achieved independence in 1960, dubbed "the year of Africa"?

Easy

Medium

Hard

Answers to QUIZ 415 – Pot Luck

1	*American Idol*	11	Lanzarote
2	One mile	12	Lake District
3	Butler	13	1999
4	A dog	14	*I Walk the Line* (Johnny Cash)
5	Dusty Springfield	15	1964
6	1990	16	18 (1964 to 1982)
7	Great Ormond Street	17	Different cultures or human societies
8	Venus	18	French
9	Tom Chambers	19	Asia and Pacific
10	Aristotle	20	On the finger-nails

Easy

1. The world's first powered flight took place in which decade?
2. How many years did it take to construct the Suez Canal?
3. In what year did Gandhi make his famous Salt March?
4. The Second Sino-Japanese War merged into which war?
5. In what century did the Aztecs found the city of Tenochtitlan?
6. US president Woodrow Wilson was awarded the Nobel Peace Prize for his role in founding which organisation?
7. In 1804 the world's population reached what milestone?
8. Who became Queen of England in 1533?
9. In which decade was the Kingdom of Italy created?
10. Who signed the October Manifesto in 1905?

Medium

11. The 1944 Dumbarton Oaks conference was an important step in the formation of which organisation?
12. Which happened earlier, the discovery of penicillin or the creation of Pasteur's vaccine against rabies?
13. Why was Royal Ascot postponed for a month in 1955?
14. With which nation did Rome go to war in 211 AD?
15. The spinning mule was the creation of which 18th-century inventor?
16. In what year did Stalin die?
17. In which decade did California join the United States of America?
18. Who was the father of Henry I of England?
19. In which decade did Algeria gain independence from France?
20. Which organisation instituted the Florence Nightingale Medal in 1912 to recognise outstanding nursing?

Hard

Answers to QUIZ 416 – Film

1. Daphne du Maurier
2. *The Red Shoes*
3. Alfonso Cuarón
4. *SS Cabinet Minister*
5. *Mona Lisa*
6. 1940s
7. *Oliver!*
8. Ben Stiller
9. Golden Lion (Leone d'Oro)
10. David Niven
11. Kylo Ren
12. 45 (*45 Years*)
13. Karen Gillan
14. Simon Pegg and Nick Frost
15. Captain Marvel
16. *The Remains of the Day*
17. 1994
18. Sonny
19. Nottingham
20. *12 Years A Slave*

1   Who played Napoleon Solo in the 2015 film *The Man from UNCLE*?

2   Which desert is larger in terms of area, the Gobi Desert or the Great Basin?

3   Martin Bryce was the lead character in which sitcom?

4   The 1962 event known as the Cuban Missile Crisis lasted for how many days?

5   Pablo Neruda, who won the 1971 Nobel Prize for Literature, was from which country?

6   Joe Louis first became boxing World Champion in which decade?

7   Which French player was famously sent off in the 2006 FIFA World Cup final?

8   In which decade was Irish jockey Ruby Walsh born?

9   Which Lastminute.com founder joined the board of Twitter in 2016?

10 The airport with the code BWI can be found in which US city?

11 Which football club plays its home games at the Estádio da Luz?

12 Prior to Sir Andy Murray in 2013, who was the last British man to win the Wimbledon singles title?

13 Who played Fran in the sitcom *Black Books*?

14 What is the name of Lady's owner in *Lady and The Tramp*?

15 Mad house, leg and bed are terms found in which sport?

16 Which nation restored its independence on August 20, 1991?

17 The former Kimmeridge clay quarry is located in which East Anglian city?

18 Which king led the English to victory at the Battle of Crécy ?

19 In Mexico, what are frijoles?

20 Which candidate was fired in 2019's *Comic Relief Does the Apprentice*?

Easy

Medium

Hard

Easy

1 In Herman Melville's novel, what type of whale is Moby Dick?

2 *Parade's End* is a famous series of novels by which writer?

3 Who wrote the 1898 short story *The Reluctant Dragon*?

4 John Wycliffe famously translated the Bible into English in what century?

5 *Childe Harold's Pilgrimage* was written by which poet?

6 Vladimir Sirin was another name given to which writer (d.1977)?

7 Barliman Butterbur is the owner of which fictional inn?

8 What was the title of Hilary Mantel's 2012 sequel to *Wolf Hall*?

9 Which author wrote an 1946 essay entitled *A Nice Cup of Tea*, in which he described his 11 rules for making the perfect cup?

10 *Anna of the Five Towns* was a 1902 work by which author?

11 What was Lewis Carroll's real name?

12 The 1983 film *The Dead Zone* was based on the work of which writer?

13 Daniel Quilp features in which novel by Charles Dickens?

14 Who wrote the 1905 novel *Where Angels Fear To Tread*?

15 In what country was Rudyard Kipling born?

16 The Costa Short Story Award was created in which year?

17 What word completes the title of a novel by Horace Walpole, *The Castle of ___*?

18 Mary Crawford appears in which novel of 1814?

19 What does the "S" stand for in the name of TS Eliot?

20 The literary and film characters Shelob, Aragog and Charlotte are all what type of creatures?

Medium

Hard

Answers to QUIZ 418 – History

1	1900s (1903)	11	The United Nations
2	Ten years	12	Pasteur's vaccination for rabies
3	1930	13	Rail strike
4	WWII	14	Macedonia
5	14th century (1325)	15	Samuel Crompton
6	The League of Nations	16	1953
7	One billion	17	1850s (1850)
8	Anne Boleyn	18	William the Conqueror
9	1860s (1861)	19	1960s (1962)
10	Tsar Nicholas II	20	The Red Cross

1 In what decade did *Hancock's Half Hour* first air on TV?

2 Wheldon Road is the home of which Rugby League team?

3 Which Steven Spielberg film was released first, *Amistad* or *Minority Report*?

4 *The Sand Reckoner* was a work by which Greek mathematician?

5 What is the name of the teaching hospital featured in the TV series *Scrubs*?

6 Alfred Mosher Butts invented what game in the 1930s?

7 The city of Kazan lies on which river?

8 Who was the first footballer to be honoured with an English Heritage blue plaque?

9 The Venus Rosewater Dish is awarded to the winners of which tennis event?

10 Which English city is nicknamed "The City of Six Towns"?

11 Who played Lady Edith in the TV series *Downton Abbey*?

12 King Edward I granted which city royal status in 1299?

13 Who starred as Tom Farrell in the 1987 film *No Way Out*?

14 Which sports presenter hosted *Countdown* from 2009 to 2011?

15 In which decade was Greenpeace founded?

16 Which natural history broadcaster was controller of BBC2 from 1965 to 1969?

17 What word can follow "Arctic" and "roseate" in the name of birds?

18 Tacitus was famous in Roman times in which profession?

19 Which *Lord of the Rings* actor played the part of Hetty Wainthropp's assistant in the 1990s TV series?

20 Saïd Aouita was the first person to run what race in under three minutes 30 seconds?

Easy

Medium

Hard

Easy

1 Who won five British Open titles between 1975 and 1983?

2 What nationality is Martin Kaymer?

3 In which year were the women's world rankings introduced?

4 How many points are available in each Ryder Cup tournament?

5 Amen Corner can be found at which major golf course?

6 What is the name of the amateur equivalent of the Ryder Cup?

7 In which year did Tiger Woods first win the US Masters?

8 Who defeated Greg Norman in a play-off to win the 1984 US Open?

9 In which US state is the World Golf Hall of Fame located?

10 Vijay Singh was born in which country?

11 At the end of every year, an award named after which golfer is given to the most sportmanslike player on the PGA Tour?

12 What is the term for scoring four under par on any given hole?

13 Who captained the European team to victory in the 2018 Ryder Cup?

14 Which US golfer topped the world rankings for the first time in October 2018?

Medium

15 If a right-handed golfer hits a fade shot, in which direction does the ball eventually head?

16 Who first won The Open Championship in 2002 and followed it up with a second win in 2012?

17 In 2010 who became the first British golfer since 1994 to top the world rankings?

18 What is the middle name of US golfer Phil Mickelson?

19 In what year was Rory McIlroy born?

20 In which US state is the Northwood Club course?

Hard

Answers to QUIZ 420 – Literature

1	Sperm whale	11	Charles Lutwidge Dodgson
2	Ford Madox Ford	12	Stephen King
3	Kenneth Grahame	13	*The Old Curiosity Shop*
4	14th century (1382)	14	EM Forster
5	Lord Byron	15	India
6	Vladimir Nabokov	16	2012
7	The Prancing Pony (*The Lord of the Rings*)	17	*Otranto*
8	*Bring Up the Bodies*	18	*Mansfield Park*
9	George Orwell	19	Stearns
10	Arnold Bennett	20	Spiders

ANSWERS ON PAGE 425

1   What nationality is footballer Dimitar Berbatov?

2   In which century is the animated film *Pocahontas* set?

3   The Three Choirs festival originally featured the choirs of which three cities?

4   To the nearest thousand metres, how high is Mount Everest?

5   County Kerry is in which province of Ireland?

6   Who directed the 2002 film *Road to Perdition*?

7   In what year did Cassius Clay win Olympic Gold in boxing?

8   What was the name of the award-winning Amazon TV series starring Jeffrey Tambor as Maura?

9   In relation to finance, what type of website is Kickstarter?

10 Which girl group released the 1999 song *Bills, Bills, Bills*?

11 Which 1989 film directed by Oliver Stone was based on a book by war veteran Ron Kovic?

12 *Lose Yourself* and *Without Me* were 2002 hits by which rapper?

13 Which group had a top ten single with *Slow Hand* in 1981?

14 What name is given to the larva of a mayfly?

15 International Dawn Chorus Day is marked annually on the first Sunday in which month?

16 For which Formula 1 team did Ralf Schumacher and Juan Pablo Montoya drive in 2004?

17 The River Leven links Loch Lomond with which major river?

18 Which actress starred as Camille Preaker in the TV series *Sharp Objects*?

19 What is the name of the girl who is unafraid of all monsters except Randall in the film *Monsters, Inc.*?

20 How many fences are jumped during the Cheltenham Gold Cup race?

Easy

Medium

Hard

Answers to QUIZ 421 – Pot Luck

1	1950s (1956)	11	Laura Carmichael
2	Castleford Tigers	12	Kingston-upon-Hull
3	*Amistad* (1997)	13	Kevin Costner
4	Archimedes	14	Jeff Stelling
5	Sacred Heart	15	1970s (1971)
6	Scrabble®	16	Sir David Attenborough
7	River Volga	17	Tern
8	Bobby Moore	18	Historian and senator
9	Wimbledon Ladies' singles	19	Dominic Monaghan
10	Stoke-on-Trent	20	1500m

1   *Oedipus Rex* was a tragedy by which Greek playwright?

2   Who wrote *The American Clock* (1980), set during the 1930s Depression?

3   In which country is the play *Stones in His Pockets* set?

4   Which playwright said "Youth is wasted on the young"?

5   In which year did London's National Theatre begin broadcasting live to cinemas?

6   Blanche DuBois is the central character in which 1947 play?

7   The 1884 play *The Wild Duck* was written by which dramatist?

8   Which show won the Olivier Award for Best New Musical in 2018?

9   What nationality is playwright Yazmina Reza?

10 Vittoria Corombona is a central character in which 1612 play by John Webster?

11 Which word of Greek origin is given to the area of a theatre surrounding the stage opening?

12 How is an Antoinette Perry Award for Excellence in Broadway Theatre better known?

13 Which play contains the famous stage direction "Exit, pursued by a bear"?

14 Who wrote the 1959 play *The Night of the Iguana*?

15 What term is used for the process of giving actors their moves on stage?

16 *Doctor Faustus* was a 16th-century play by which writer?

17 Who produced the musical *Miss Saigon* in the West End?

18 Which theatre hosted the Royal Variety Performance in 2017 and 2018?

19 Judith Bliss is a character in which play by Sir Noël Coward?

20 In which part of a theatre would you find the cyclorama?

Easy

Medium

Hard

Answers to QUIZ 422 – Golf

1	Tom Watson	11	Payne Stewart
2	German	12	Condor
3	2006	13	Thomas Bjørn
4	28	14	Brooks Koepka
5	Augusta	15	Right
6	Walker Cup	16	Ernie Els
7	1997	17	Lee Westwood
8	Fuzzy Zoeller	18	Alfred
9	Florida (St Augustine)	19	1989
10	Fiji	20	Texas (Dallas)

1 Which member of One Direction made his debut for Doncaster Rovers FC in 2014?

2 In relation to shopping, for what do the initials of the organisation CMA stand?

3 Which Italian football club is often called "The Old Lady"?

4 What subject did Herodotus write about?

5 What type of animal is a bontebok?

6 *My Simple Heart* and *Woman in Love* were 1979 hits for which group?

7 What colour horse represents Famine in the Four Horsemen of the Apocalypse?

8 Who played Pippin in Peter Jackson's *The Lord of the Rings* trilogy?

9 Charnwood is a parliamentary constituency in which English county?

10 To the nearest ten percent, approximately how much of the Earth's surface water is in the Indian Ocean?

11 Walter Gay features in which Dickens novel?

12 Who directed the 1942 film *In Which We Serve*?

13 In which decade did Martin Van Buren become US president?

14 The Parkinson family featured in which TV sitcom?

15 Steve Davis first became World Snooker Champion in which year?

16 *Joan of Arc* and *Souvenir* were 1981 singles by which band?

17 The Abdabs was the original name of which major band?

18 What is the second-largest species of shark?

19 In what year did the last-ever episode of *Brookside* air?

20 Which actor was awarded the Best Actor Oscar award first, Al Pacino or Sir Daniel Day-Lewis?

Easy

Medium

Hard

Answers to QUIZ 423 – Pot Luck

1	Bulgarian	11	*Born on the Fourth of July*
2	17th century	12	Eminem
3	Gloucester, Hereford and Worcester	13	Pointer Sisters
4	9000m (8848)	14	Nymph
5	Munster	15	May
6	Sam Mendes	16	Williams
7	1960	17	River Clyde
8	*Transparent*	18	Amy Adams
9	Crowdfunding	19	Boo
10	Destiny's Child	20	22

Easy

1   Chişinău is the capital of which Eastern European republic?

2   In which country do names generally take the suffix "son" or "dóttir" to indicate parentage?

3   Poland joined the European Union in which decade?

4   The Brissago Islands are located in which lake shared by two countries?

5   Which 2013 Swedish TV drama series featured the Waldermar family?

6   What is the second-largest city in Spain?

7   In which decade did the Republic of Ireland come into being?

8   Which three colours appear on the Hungarian national flag?

9   The Temple of Hephaestus is located in which Greek city?

10 Alfama and Chiado are neighbourhoods of which capital city?

Medium

11 In which city were the 1928 Olympics held?

12 The Vosges Mountains lie in which country?

13 In which country is the Plitvice National Park?

14 *Presidente del Consiglio* is the title of the Prime Minister in which country?

15 Le Bourget airport lies seven miles north-west of which French city?

16 What are the three official languages of Belgium?

17 In which decade was Konrad Adenaeur appointed Chancellor of Germany?

18 Which river flows through Prague?

19 Triodos Bank has its headquarters in which country?

20 In which capital city would you see the Schönbrunn Palace?

Hard

Answers to QUIZ 424 – The Theatre

1	Sophocles	11	Proscenium (arch)
2	Arthur Miller	12	Tony Award
3	Ireland	13	*The Winter's Tale*
4	George Bernard Shaw	14	Tennessee Williams
5	2009	15	Blocking
6	*A Streetcar Named Desire*	16	Christopher Marlowe
7	Henrik Ibsen	17	Sir Cameron Mackintosh
8	*Hamilton*	18	London Palladium
9	French	19	*Hay Fever*
10	*The White Devil*	20	At the back of the stage

ANSWERS ON PAGE **429**

Easy

1 Who finished third in the first series of *Pop Idol*?

2 How were the characters of John Beckwith and Jeremy Grey known in the title of a 2005 film?

3 Mr Seth Pecksniff features in which Dickens novel?

4 Atatürk Airport is in which city?

5 Boxer Joe Frazier won an Olympic gold medal in which decade?

6 *Solanum tuberosum* is the Latin name for which vegetable?

7 Which actress co-starred with Sir Laurence Olivier in the 1957 film *The Prince and the Showgirl*?

8 Who was appointed captain of Britain's Federation Cup tennis squad in 2017?

9 Herse and Kale are moons of which planet?

10 In which US state is the TV series *True Detective* set?

11 Who became Emperor of Japan in April 2019?

12 In which year was the first Nobel Peace Prize awarded?

13 What was the first UK no.1 hit for the boy band 5ive, which topped the charts in 1999?

14 Herbie Flowers, John Williams and Tristan Fry were members of which rock group?

15 In relation to communications, for what does the "S" stand in ISDN?

16 Who played Emily Waltham in the TV series *Friends*?

17 The River Camel flows through which English county?

18 Pakistan achieved full independence in which decade?

19 Instagram™ was launched in which year?

20 For what does the "K" stand in the music genre K-pop?

Medium

Hard

Answers to QUIZ 425 – Pot Luck

1	Louis Tomlinson	11	*Dombey and Son*
2	Competition and Markets Authority	12	Sir Noël Coward
3	Juventus	13	1830s (1837)
4	History	14	*Butterflies*
5	An antelope	15	1981
6	The Three Degrees	16	Orchestral Manoeuvres in the Dark
7	Black	17	Pink Floyd
8	Billy Boyd	18	Basking shark
9	Leicestershire	19	2003
10	20%	20	Sir Daniel Day-Lewis (1989)

Easy

1   In which area of London are the Bernie Spain Gardens and Gabriel's Wharf?

2   The Treehouse Restaurant is a feature of which Northumberland garden?

3   Which English airport is located at Lulsgate Bottom?

4   Which National Trail runs from Overton Hill near Avebury to Ivinghoe Beacon in Buckinghamshire?

5   The site of Stonehenge is managed by which organisation?

6   In which Scottish city is the Stagecoach franchise based?

7   The Royal Cornwall Museum can be found in which city?

8   How many wheels are there on a pedicab?

9   Folkestone lies at the eastern end of which hills?

10 In which decade did Exmoor become a National Park?

11 The seaside resort of Cleethorpes is in which English county?

12 Burghley House is located ten miles north-west of which English city?

13 Golders Green is a station on which London Underground line?

14 In which decade was the Motability charity formed to assist disabled people with transport?

15 Stowe Landscape Gardens are situated in which county?

16 For what do the initials PT stand in the name of the Segway PT?

17 Moel Siabod is a mountain situated in which National Park?

18 Which rail franchise, owned by Arriva, runs services from Marylebone Station?

19 In which city is the northern terminus of the East Coast Main Line?

20 The Dreamland amusement park is situated in which Kent town?

Medium

Hard

Answers to QUIZ 426 – Europe

1	Moldova	11	Amsterdam
2	Iceland	12	France
3	2000s (2004)	13	Croatia
4	Lake Maggiore	14	Italy
5	*Thicker Than Water*	15	Paris
6	Barcelona	16	Dutch, French and German
7	1940s (1949)	17	1940s (1949)
8	Red, white and green	18	Vltava River
9	Athens	19	The Netherlands
10	Lisbon	20	Vienna

QUIZ 429 – Pot Luck

ANSWERS ON PAGE 431

1   Who had a hit with a cover of *Take on Me* in 2000?

2   Who won The Open golf title in both 2007 and 2008?

3   Which Star Wars villain's voice was provided by Peter Serafinowicz?

4   How many tribes of Israel were descended from Jacob's sons?

5   Which tiny projections remove mucus from the bronchial tubes?

6   In which country did the series *Dragons' Den* originate?

7   Diego Forlán is a record football cap winner for which nation?

8   Dulce de leche, the traditional Argentinian dessert, roughly translates as what?

9   What two-word term is given to a written promise to pay a specific sum of money to a particular person?

10 How many times did Juan Manuel Fangio win the F1 World Championship?

11 Who was the Greek equivalent of the Roman god Neptune?

12 *Sail on* and *Still* were 1979 hits for which group?

13 Who wrote the 1976 novel *The Deep*?

14 To which group of amphibians do newts belong?

15 Raasay and Tiree are part of which group of islands?

16 The Weddell seal is found on which continent?

17 What name is given to the practice of growing rhubarb without light?

18 Which ballet term means "behind"?

19 Who recorded the 2015 album *Rebel Heart*?

20 Which 1970s TV series starring Yul Brynner was a non-musical version of *The King and I*?

Easy

Medium

Hard

Answers to QUIZ 427 – Pot Luck

1   Darius Campbell (as Darius Danesh)
2   *The Wedding Crashers*
3   *Martin Chuzzlewit*
4   Istanbul
5   1960s (1964)
6   Potato
7   Marilyn Monroe
8   Anne Keothavong
9   Jupiter
10 Louisiana
11 Naruhito
12 1901
13 *Keep on Movin'*
14 Sky
15 Services
16 Helen Baxendale
17 Cornwall
18 1940s (1947)
19 2010
20 Korean

1 In which decade did Radio Caroline begin broadcasting?

2 Which former *Gogglebox* viewer co-presents *Good Morning Sunday* on Radio 2?

3 What is the name of the classical digital radio station that began broadcasting in March 2019?

4 "You're not really here, it's just the radio" is a line from which song by the Carpenters?

5 Released in 1993, what was the title of Radiohead's debut album?

6 What was the name of the radio station in the 2009 film *The Boat That Rocked*?

7 Which former radio station based in Europe broadcast on 208 medium wave?

8 In the sitcom *Frasier*, who played radio producer Roz Doyle?

9 Which future film score composer appeared in the video for The Buggles' *Video Killed the Radio Star*?

10 Who played the talk-show host Jack Killian in the TV series *Midnight Caller*?

11 *On My Radio* was a 1979 single by which group?

12 Which long-running radio quiz has a movement from *Eine Kleine Nachtmusik* as its theme tune?

13 Which organisation has its own radio station called Third Rock?

14 In which decade was the radio show *Just a Minute* first broadcast?

15 What was the real name of Lord Haw-Haw who broadcast propaganda from Germany during WWII?

16 Lakey Hill is a location often mentioned in which long-running radio series?

17 "Invisible airwaves crackle with light" is a line from which 1980 single?

18 In 2019, in a poll for *Radio Times*, what did a panel of experts vote the best ever UK radio show?

19 During which war did the BBC Forces Programme broadcast?

20 Which radio presenter published *Mad Blood Stirring* in 2018, his first book written for adults?

Answers to QUIZ 428 – Out and About

1	The South Bank	11	Lincolnshire
2	Alnwick Garden	12	Peterborough
3	Bristol	13	Northern Line
4	The Ridgeway	14	1970s (1977)
5	English Heritage	15	Buckinghamshire
6	Perth	16	Personal transporter
7	Truro	17	Snowdonia
8	Three (also called a cycle rickshaw)	18	Chiltern Railways
9	North Downs	19	Edinburgh
10	1950s (1954)	20	Margate

1. In which decade was *Dad's Army* first broadcast on TV?

2. How many volcanic cones are there on Mount Kilimanjaro?

3. What is the most northerly National Hunt racecourse in England?

4. The Australian Open tournament has traditionally been played in which of the country's major cities?

5. In which decade was the world's first quartz clock invented?

6. What was the first name of the composer Shostakovich (d.1975)?

7. In 2008, the next Russian president's term was increased to how many years?

8. Where in Switzerland was the first ever Eurovision final held?

9. Which Star Wars villain was played by the legendary Christopher Lee?

10. Which actor co-starred with Jennifer Lopez in the 2002 film *Maid in Manhattan*?

11. *L'Oiseau de Feu* is the French title of which ballet?

12. Santander Bank has its headquarters in which European country?

13. What are the dimensions of a professional snooker table?

14. Toodles Galore is a character in which cartoon series?

15. Cape Breton Island is part of which Canadian province?

16. Who won *Celebrity MasterChef* in 2018?

17. *Said I Loved You…But I Lied* was a 1993 hit for which US singer?

18. The city of Lecce is in which European country?

19. What kind of creature is Bill in Disney's *Alice in Wonderland*?

20. The volcano Surt is found on which moon of the planet of Jupiter?

Answers to QUIZ 429 – Pot Luck

1	A1	11	Poseidon
2	Pádraig Harrington	12	Commodores
3	Darth Maul	13	Peter Benchley
4	12	14	Salamanders
5	Cilia	15	Inner Hebrides
6	Japan	16	Antarctica
7	Uruguay	17	Forcing
8	Milk jelly	18	Derrière
9	Promissory note	19	Madonna
10	Five	20	*Anna and the King*

1   "I Bianconeri" is the nickname of which Italian football club?

2   The Atlanta Hawks compete in what sport?

3   The Hive Stadium is in which London borough?

4   Derek Jeter (b.1974) is a former professional in which sport?

5   Galatasaray is a football club based in which European city?

6   How many players are there on a team in a match of Gaelic football?

7   Mario Balotelli signed for which British club in 2014?

8   Who took over the captaincy of the All Blacks Rugby Union team in 2016, announcing his retirement in 2019?

9   In feet, how wide is the goal in ice hockey?

10   Scoring a field goal earns how many points in American football?

11   The Currie Cup is a Rugby Union competition that takes place in which country?

12   Who won the 2019 PFA Player of the Year award?

13   Former footballer Carlos Valderama won 111 caps for which nation?

14   Location of the 2008 Ryder Cup, Valhalla Golf Course is in which US state?

15   What is the name of the annual award given to the Premier League goalkeeper who has kept the most clean sheets?

16   Harold Larwood (d.1995) played which sport for England?

17   As at the end of 2018, which team held the world record time for the men's 4x100m relay, set in 2012?

18   Who clinched the winning point in 2008 for the US to regain the Ryder Cup?

19   Which nation won the most medals at the 2018 World Rowing Championships?

20   What is the length of a rugby league pitch, in metres?

Easy

Medium

Hard

Answers to QUIZ 430 – Radio

1	1960s (1964)	11	The Selecter
2	Rev Kate Bottley	12	*Brain of Britain*
3	Scala	13	NASA
4	*Superstar*	14	1960s (1967)
5	*Pablo Honey*	15	William Joyce
6	Radio Rock	16	*The Archers*
7	Radio Luxembourg	17	*The Spirit of Radio* (Rush)
8	Peri Gilpin	18	*Desert Island Discs*
9	Hans Zimmer	19	WWII
10	Gary Cole	20	Simon Mayo

1   Biblically, Levi was a son of Jacob and whom?

2   Which of these Brad Pitt films was released first, *Fight Club*, *Meet Joe Black*, or *Twelve Monkeys*?

3   Which Netflix series centres around the character of Prairie Johnson?

4   The village of Rosemarkie lies on which Scottish peninsula?

5   What term for an inflatable boat is also used in astrology?

6   Who played Petyr "Littlefinger" Baelish in *Game of Thrones*?

7   The Broncos are the NFL team based in what city?

8   What does the French word *frappe* mean?

9   What is the name for a baby squirrel?

10   Who released the 1981 single *Coming to America*?

11   The town of Sandy in Bedfordshire houses the headquarters of which conservation organisation?

12   Which company manufactures the Duster car model?

13   In Greek mythology, who was the father of Ariadne?

14   Which Oscar-winning 1930 film was based on a novel by German novelist Erich Remarque?

15   What type of animal is Muriel in *Animal Farm* by George Orwell?

16   In which month does The Great North Run annually take place?

17   In the Southern Hemisphere, on what date are racehorses' birthdays celebrated?

18   *Matchmaker, Matchmaker* is a song from which musical?

19   Marlborough College is situated in which English county?

20   Which film was based on Sir Noël Coward's one-act play *Still Life*?

Answers to QUIZ 431 – Pot Luck

1	1960s (1968)	11	*The Firebird*
2	Three	12	Spain
3	Hexham	13	12ft x 6ft
4	Melbourne	14	*Tom and Jerry*
5	1920s (1927)	15	Nova Scotia
6	Dmitri	16	John Partridge
7	Six	17	Michael Bolton
8	Lugano	18	Italy
9	Count Dooku	19	Lizard
10	Ralph Fiennes	20	Io

Easy

1 *Hotter than July* was a 1980 album by which singer/songwriter?

2 Which group had a 1982 hit with *Instinction*?

3 Who released the 1987 single *Criticize*?

4 Which band had 1980s hits with *Always* and *Secret Lovers*?

5 *Tears are Not Enough* was the 1981 debut single by which pop band?

6 What was the title of Black Slate's only UK top ten hit?

7 Singer Gloria Estefan was born in which country?

8 Who had a 1985 hit with *Trapped*?

9 In which year did the Eurythmics have a hit with *Would I Lie to You*?

10 Which French musician released the 1982 album *The Concerts in China*?

11 *Word Up!* was a 1986 hit for which American funk band?

Medium

12 Mark King was the bass player with which 1980s band?

13 *Undercover* was a 1983 album by which band?

14 *Almaz* was a 1986 hit for which female US singer?

15 Which group's only no.1 album was *Colour by Numbers* (1983)?

16 Which Irish group sang the theme song to the 1982 TV series *Harry's Game*?

17 *You're Lying* and *Intuition* were 1980s hits for which band?

18 Joanne Catherall has been a member of which group since 1980?

19 *Seven and the Ragged Tiger* was a 1983 album by which band?

20 Which group released the 1983 live album *Oil on Canvas*?

Hard

QUIZ 435 – Pot Luck

ANSWERS ON PAGE 437

1 Who was the Greek goddess of domestic life?

2 In which county is the parliamentary constituency of Bassetlaw?

3 Which species of pheasant, native to Taiwan, shares its name with an operetta by Gilbert and Sullivan?

4 For which film did James Cagney win the Best Actor Oscar?

5 In which athletics event did Moses Kiptanui win three World Championship gold medals?

6 Annet and St Agnes are part of which island group?

7 Who played Florence Johnson in the TV series *Citizen Smith*?

8 What is a phormium?

9 *Run For Home* was a 1978 single by which rock band?

10 Puy lentils are produced in which European country?

11 Hydra is a moon that orbits which body?

12 Whose fourth solo album, released in 1989, was entitled *...But Seriously*?

13 In which decade did Florida join the United States?

14 Who played the steel mill owner in the 1983 film *Flashdance*?

15 In what year did tennis player Juan Martin Del Potro win the US Open?

16 The stately home of Haddon Hall is one of the country seats of which Duke?

17 In what decade was John le Carré born?

18 The Battle of Flodden Field took place in what year?

19 For what do the letters "EF" stand in UNICEF?

20 Who plays Maia Rindell in the TV series *The Good Fight*?

Easy / Medium / Hard

Answers to QUIZ 433 – Pot Luck

1	Leah	11	RSPB
2	*Twelve Monkeys*	12	Dacia
3	*The OA*	13	King Minos
4	The Black Isle	14	*All Quiet on the Western Front*
5	Zodiac	15	Goat
6	Aidan Gillen	16	September
7	Denver	17	August 1
8	Strike	18	*Fiddler on the Roof*
9	Kit(ten)	19	Wiltshire
10	Neil Diamond	20	*Brief Encounter*

Easy

1   Austin, Minnesota, is the location of a museum dedicated to what brand of tinned food?

2   In which city is Carnegie Mellon University located?

3   The flag of which US state still features the Union Jack?

4   Which US president is enshrined in the Wrestling Hall of Fame having had over 300 matches and only one defeat?

5   The US annexation of which area led to war with Mexico in 1846?

6   How is the chaparral rooster, the state bird of New Mexico, better known?

7   In what decade did Alaska join the United States?

8   What is the state capital of New Hampshire?

9   Lower East Side is an area in which New York City borough?

10 Who lost the 2012 US election to Barack Obama?

11 In what year was Woodrow Wilson elected US President?

12 Which is the first of the US Triple Crown races to be run in the calendar year?

13 Thomas Jefferson and John Adams both died on the same day, on what anniversary of the signing of the Declaration of Independence?

Medium

14 In which state is Crater Lake?

15 The airport with the code OKC can be found in which state?

16 Of which state was Ronald Reagan governor from 1967 to 1975?

17 Nantucket island is in which state?

18 Hell's Kitchen, also known as Clinton, is an area of which city?

19 In which decade was Yellowstone Park, the first national park, created?

20 By population, Jacksonville is the largest city in which state?

Hard

Answers to QUIZ 434 – 1980s Music

1	Stevie Wonder	11	Cameo
2	Spandau Ballet	12	Level 42
3	Alexander O'Neal	13	The Rolling Stones
4	Atlantic Starr	14	Randy Crawford
5	ABC	15	Culture Club
6	*Amigo* (1980)	16	Clannad
7	Cuba	17	Linx
8	Colonel Abrams	18	The Human League
9	1985	19	Duran Duran
10	Jean-Michel Jarre	20	Japan

1 Who played Salieri in the 1984 film *Amadeus*?

2 Which Californian city hosts the annual Rose Bowl American football game?

3 In which city is the TV series *River City* set?

4 Which river is known as Hafron in Welsh?

5 Who was presented with the 2018 BBC Sports Personality Lifetime award?

6 *A Good Catch* (2015) and *The Newcomer* (2019) are novels written by which TV presenter?

7 What is the decimal equivalent of the hexadecimal number 51?

8 Which word follows Widnes to give the name of their rugby league team?

9 Cardinal is a shade of which colour?

10 What is the name of Derbyshire's limited-overs cricket team?

11 Who played Siegfried Farnon in the TV series *All Creatures Great and Small*?

12 Which film won the Best Picture Oscar first, *An American in Paris*, *Casablanca* or *The Lost Weekend*?

13 Glycogen is converted by the body into which substance?

14 Whitburn and Seaburn are parts of which English city?

15 The town of Wisbech is in which English county?

16 In which European city is the statue complex featuring the Seven Chieftains of the Magyars?

17 The album *Hysteria* was a release by which rock band?

18 How many sharps are there in the key signature of a piece played in B Major?

19 What is the internet country code for the Republic of Ireland?

20 In which English county is the plateau known as the Long Mynd?

Easy

Medium

Hard

Answers to QUIZ 435 – Pot Luck

1	Hestia	11	Pluto
2	Nottinghamshire	12	Phil Collins
3	Mikado (pheasant)	13	1840s (1845)
4	*Yankee Doodle Dandy*	14	Michael Nouri
5	3000m steeplechase	15	2009
6	Isles of Scilly	16	Duke of Rutland
7	Hilda Braid	17	1930s (1931)
8	A plant (herbaceous perennial)	18	1513
9	Lindisfarne	19	Emergency Fund
10	France	20	Rose Leslie

1   *Notorious* was a 1986 album by which group?

2   *Barbie Girl* was an international hit by Aqua who hailed from which country?

3   Billy Corgan is the lead vocalist with which 1990s band?

4   What was the title of Bob Dylan's 1977 Grammy-award winning album?

5   Christina Aguilera released *Genie in a Bottle* in which decade?

6   *Cherish* was a 1972 album by which American singer?

7   Which former member of the Libertines formed the band Dirty Pretty Things?

8   *Ghost in the Machine* was a 1981 hit album for which band?

9   Shirley Manson is the lead singer with which band?

10   What was the title of Pixie Lott's second solo album?

11   The Followill family are members of which US band?

12   *Wanted on Voyage* was a 2014 album by which singer?

13   Who had a no.1 hit single with the theme to the 1985 film *St Elmo's Fire*?

14   Which group released the 1979 single *The Diary of Horace Wimp*?

15   Neil Hannon is the frontman of which group from Northern Ireland?

16   From which country do the 1990s band Savage Garden come from?

17   Kelton was the middle name of which legendary singer/songwriter?

18   *Music for the Masses* was a 1987 album by which group?

19   Which group had a 1972 hit with *Hold Your Head Up*?

20   *break up with your girlfriend, i'm bored* was a 2019 single by which singer?

Answers to QUIZ 436 – The USA

1	Spam®	11	1912
2	Pittsburgh	12	Kentucky Derby
3	Hawaii	13	50th anniversary
4	Abraham Lincoln	14	Oregon
5	Texas	15	Oklahoma (Will Rogers Airport)
6	Roadrunner	16	California
7	1950s (1959)	17	Massachusetts
8	Concord	18	New York City
9	Manhattan	19	1870s (1872)
10	Mitt Romney	20	Florida

1   The Leicester Tigers rugby union team play home games at which stadium?

2   "When the moon is in the seventh house" is the opening line of which song from the musical *Hair*?

3   Who directed the 1964 film *Doctor Strangelove*?

4   Royal Portrush golf club is in which county of Northern Ireland?

5   Which singer vowed to *Save the Best for Last* in 1992?

6   Which compound has the chemical formula C_6H_6?

7   What is the maximum squad size for a game of ice hockey?

8   According to Chinese acupunctural belief, which two letters represent life force energy?

9   Which fictional detective featured in the 1892 short story *The Adventure of the Copper Beeches*?

10   In which range of mountains does Mount Elbrus lie?

11   Nationwide Building Society has its headquarters in which English town?

12   Which character did Roger Lloyd Pack play in the film *Harry Potter and the Goblet of Fire*?

13   Whose account is the shortest of the four New Testament gospels?

14   At which racecourse did AP McCoy achieve his 4000th win?

15   What is the five-letter nickname of the ballet dancer Mikhail Baryshnikov?

16   For what does the "S" of ACAS stand?

17   What type of creature is a quetzal?

18   On which island is Loch Scavaig?

19   What is the meaning of the word isotonic?

20   Thanet is an administrative area in which English county?

1   What is the full name of the building material usually referred to as MDF?

2   What is the meaning of the abbreviation *viz*?

3   RAI is the home broadcaster of what Eurovision nation?

4   How many guys are named Moe in the title of the musical?

5   What nationality is the singer and rapper Psy?

6   What kind of animal can be referred to as a teg when young?

7   For what do the letters PSV stand in the football team name PSV Eindhoven?

8   For what does the "C" stand in FCA, the body that regulates financial services?

9   Who became the SNP's Leader in the House of Commons in 2017?

10 The 2019 PGA golf championship was played at Bethpage Black Course in which US state?

11 Which rank is immediately above flying officer in the RAF?

12 The East Lyn and West Lyn rivers rise in which UK national park?

13 Who played Lisbeth Salander in the 2018 film *The Girl in the Spider's Web*?

14 Nintendo® released the Wii™ to replace which video games console?

15 What was the title of XTC's highest-charting single, released in 1982?

16 In relation to home safety, for what do the initials RCD stand?

17 "Where are those happy days, they seem so hard to find" are the opening lines to which 1975 song?

18 What does the "P" stand for in the initials VPN?

19 In which decade did the first meeting of the TUC take place in England?

20 BKK is the airport code for the main airport in which city?

Answers to QUIZ 438 – Pop Music

1	Duran Duran	11	Kings of Leon
2	Denmark	12	George Ezra
3	The Smashing Pumpkins	13	John Parr
4	*Time Out of Mind*	14	The Electric Light Orchestra
5	1990s (1999)	15	The Divine Comedy
6	David Cassidy	16	Australia
7	Carl Barât	17	Roy Orbison
8	The Police	18	Depeche Mode
9	Garbage	19	Argent
10	*Young Foolish Happy*	20	Ariana Grande

ANSWERS ON PAGE 443

1   "Everyday is so wonderful" is a lyric from which song?

2   In what year was David Nalbandian runner-up at Wimbledon?

3   For which film did Clark Gable win his only Best Actor Oscar?

4   What kind of creature is Rango in the 2011 film of the same name?

5   The Sir Joseph Banks Conservatory is located in which English city?

6   What type of creature is a kagu?

7   Germany, Austria-Hungary and which other nation were the members of the 1882 Triple Alliance?

8   What is the title of the track by Pitbull and Jennifer Lopez that was selected as the official song for the 2014 FIFA World Cup?

9   In which decade did Disneyland open in California?

10 Where is Shakespeare's *The Comedy of Errors* set?

11 Who wrote the autobiography *Seven Pillars of Wisdom*, published in 1926?

12 Louis Van Gaal managed which football club between 2009 and 2011?

13 What is the literal English translation of the word *meerschaum*?

14 Which two colours feature on the flag of Ukraine?

15 The Crow's Nest can be found at which golf course?

16 What is the airport code for San Francisco International Airport?

17 Which comedian had a cameo role as a Greek customs officer in the film *Mamma Mia! Here We Go Again*?

18 The town of Uttoxeter lies in which English county?

19 What is the tallest fence on the Grand National course?

20 Which two countries did Michael Portillo explore on TV using *Appleton's Guide Books*?

Easy

Medium

Hard

Answers to QUIZ 439 – Pot Luck

1	Welford Road	11	Swindon
2	*The Age of Aquarius*	12	Barty Crouch Snr
3	Stanley Kubrick	13	Mark
4	County Antrim	14	Towcester
5	Vanessa Williams	15	Misha
6	Benzene	16	Service
7	20	17	A bird (of tropical America)
8	Qi	18	Skye
9	Sherlock Holmes	19	Having equal tension
10	Caucasus Mountains	20	Kent

1 What vegetable was being eaten in the title of an 1885 painting by Vincent Van Gogh?

2 The Sea Organ, designed by Nikola Bašić, is an art installation in which European country?

3 *Three Studies of Lucian Freud* sold for $142 million in 2013. Who was the artist?

4 The Frans Hals museum is located in which Netherlands city?

5 Which artist had the nickname "Little Dyer" owing to his father's occupation?

6 *Les Parapluies* is a famous work by which artist?

7 What fruit features in front of a man's face in the Magritte painting *Le Fils de L'homme*?

8 In what decade was Pablo Picasso born?

9 What was the first name of the artist Kandinsky?

10 In which European city is the Pergamon Museum?

11 How many *Campbell's Soup Cans* feature in the famous 1962 work by Andy Warhol?

12 Which artist was at the time chief assistant to Rubens?

13 In which Italian city was the sculptor Donatello (1374-1466) born?

14 *Sunday Afternoon on the Island of La Grande Jatte* is a famous work by which artist?

15 Which annual prize did video artist Charlotte Prodger win in 2018?

16 Edward Hopper painted a famous picture in 1929 that shares a name with which dish?

17 The Barber Institute of Fine Arts is located in which UK city?

18 In which year was the Tate Modern opened in London?

19 Willy Lott's cottage famously appears in which work of 1821?

20 *Venus of Urbino* is a famous 1530s work by which artist?

Answers to QUIZ 440 – Three Letters

1	Medium-density fibreboard	11	Flight lieutenant
2	In other words	12	Exmoor
3	Italy	13	Claire Foy
4	Five	14	GameCube™
5	South Korean	15	*Senses Working Overtime*
6	Sheep	16	Residual Current Device
7	Philips Sport Vereniging	17	*SOS* (Abba)
8	Conduct	18	Private
9	Ian Blackford	19	1860s (1968)
10	New York	20	Bangkok

1 What two six-letter words that differ by one letter mean "centre" and "an animal's shelter"?

2 What does an etymologist study?

3 In which Irish county is Mizen Head situated?

4 What was the first name of Oliver Cromwell's son, who became Lord Protector of the Commonwealth in 1658?

5 In which month of 1971 did the UK introduce decimalisation?

6 *Crystal* and *Landslide* are tracks on which group's self-titled 1975 album?

7 What is the nickname of Argentinian golfer Angel Cabrera?

8 Which university won the women's Boat Race in 2019?

9 Who was the Greek god of music and poetry, amongst other things?

10 Tamarins belong to which family of animals?

11 Which author wrote the novel *Night and Day* (1919) and the short story *Monday or Tuesday* (1921)?

12 Closed in 2014, in which US city was the Roseland Ballroom?

13 Which Italian football club signed the Portuguese player Luis Figo in 2005?

14 Who starred as Wing Commander Guy Gibson in the 1950s film *The Dam Busters*?

15 Who released the 1983 single *Waterfront*?

16 Which city is home to the silk factory Lombe's Mill?

17 For which 1992 film did Gene Hackman win his second Oscar, for Best Actor in a Supporting Role?

18 The first Super Bowl took place in which decade?

19 The *Secret Policeman's Ball* series of benefit shows have raised money for which charity?

20 In which AE Housman poem does he reflect on "blue remembered hills"?

Answers to QUIZ 441 – Pot Luck

1 *Beautiful* (Christina Aguilera)
2 2002
3 *It Happened One Night* (1934)
4 Chameleon
5 Lincoln
6 A bird (native to New Caledonia)
7 Italy
8 *We Are One (Ole Ola)*
9 1950s (1955)
10 Ephesus
11 TE Lawrence
12 Bayern Munich
13 Sea foam
14 Blue and yellow
15 Augusta (Georgia, USA)
16 SFO
17 Omid Djalili
18 Staffordshire
19 The Chair
20 The USA and Canada

1. Dr John D Dorian was the main character in which medical drama?
2. In which year was *Men Behaving Badly* first broadcast?
3. Angel Batista was a leading character in which US crime series?
4. In which borough of New York was *Friends* set?
5. How many series did *Last of the Summer Wine* run for?
6. Miles Chapman and Mark O'Sullivan play the title characters in which comedy series?
7. Billy Mitchell first appeared in *EastEnders* in which decade?
8. Which series starring Kristen Bell is set in the afterlife?
9. John Lacey was the main character in which 1980s sitcom?
10. What is cartoon character Bart Simpson's middle name?

11. Kyle MacLachlan played Orson Hodge in which US series?
12. *Suspect Behaviour* was a spin-off from which major crime drama?
13. Damon Beesley and Iain Morris co-wrote which sitcom, originally aired in 2008?
14. Kimball Cho and Grace Van Pelt were characters in which series?
15. Who played the title role in the 1989-90 TV series *The Manageress*?
16. Basil Makepeace was a recurring character in which 1990s sitcom?
17. In which decade was *Grand Designs* first broadcast?
18. What is the name of the company featured in *dinnerladies*?
19. Hiro Nakamura was a character in which sci-fi series?
20. Which member of Take That appeared as a presenter on the 2019 series *Mission Ignition*?

Answers to QUIZ 442 – Art

1	Potato	11	32
2	Croatia	12	Van Dyck
3	Francis Bacon	13	Florence
4	Haarlem	14	Seurat
5	Tintoretto	15	Turner Prize
6	Renoir	16	*Chop Suey*
7	An apple	17	Birmingham
8	1880s (1881)	18	2000
9	Wassily	19	*The Hay Wain*
10	Berlin	20	Titian

1 What was the name of Robert de Niro's character in the 1982 film *King of Comedy*?

2 Giuseppe Meazza (d.1979) played for 13 years at which Italian football club, scoring 241 goals in total?

3 Which ballet is subtitled *The Girl with the Enamel Eyes*?

4 Who had a hit with *Breakfast at Tiffany's* in 1996?

5 Chief Crazy Horse belonged to which Native American tribe?

6 Which vegetable is also known as turnip cabbage?

7 The town of Aylsham lies in which English county?

8 Which 1975 musical film featured the characters of Brad and Janet?

9 Occitanie is an administrative region of which European country?

10 Which writer appears on all notes issued by the Bank of Scotland?

11 In which TV series was Deputy Enos Strate often referred to as a "dipstick"?

12 The lotus is the national flower of which Asian country?

13 Who wrote the 1984 novel *The Wasp Factory*?

14 "Cetti's" and "willow" can precede what word in the name of birds?

15 Who sang *Through the Fire* (1984)?

16 The Catskill Mountains are part of which larger range?

17 Who created the characters of Snoopy and Woodstock?

18 Which US state is referred to as "The Potato State"?

19 In which season is the Ladbroke's Trophy run?

20 What substances are broken down in the body by the enzyme lipase?

Easy

Medium

Hard

Answers to QUIZ 443 – Pot Luck

1	Kernel and kennel	11	Virginia Woolf
2	Word origins	12	New York
3	County Cork	13	Inter Milan
4	Richard	14	Richard Todd
5	February (15th)	15	Simple Minds
6	Fleetwood Mac	16	Derby
7	The Duck	17	*Unforgiven*
8	Cambridge	18	1960s (1967)
9	Apollo	19	Amnesty International
10	Monkeys	20	*A Shropshire Lad*

Easy

1 What is the SI unit of electrical conductance?

2 Anaemia is caused by a deficiency of what?

3 Atlas is a moon of which planet?

4 What is the chemical formula for salt?

5 Which element comes between iron and nickel in the periodic table?

6 Ishtar Terra is the northern continent on which planet?

7 In which year was Mir, the world's first permanent manned space station launched?

8 Which chemical element, used in medicine, has the atomic number 83?

9 What does a marigraph record?

10 Hypermetropia is the medical name given to a condition affecting which part of the body?

11 What does a selenologist study?

12 *Articulatio humeri* is the Latin name for which joint?

13 What was the title of Stephen Hawking's 2013 memoir?

14 Which branch of physics deals with the application of computers and numerical methods to physical systems?

15 Which scientist said "Life is like riding a bicycle. To keep your balance, you must keep moving"?

16 What nationality was the scientist James Joule, after whom the unit of energy was named?

17 *Mariner 4* was the first spacecraft to fly by which planet?

18 What is the SI unit of electrical capacitance, named after a British scientist?

19 What is the science of defining and naming group of organisms?

20 With whom did Paul Dirac share the 1933 Nobel Prize in Physics?

Medium
Hard

Answers to QUIZ 444 – Television

1	Scrubs	11	Desperate Houswives
2	1992	12	Criminal Minds
3	Dexter	13	The Inbetweeners
4	Manhattan	14	The Mentalist
5	31	15	Cherie Lunghi
6	Lee and Dean	16	Waiting for God
7	1990s (1998)	17	1990s (1999)
8	The Good Place	18	HWD Components
9	Dear John	19	Heroes
10	Jojo	20	Howard Donald

1 The "Ship of the Fens" is found in which UK city?

2 Who beat Terry Christian to win *Celebrity Big Brother* in 2009?

3 Which actor's debut single was a cover of *Love Don't Live Here Any More* in 1985?

4 Rosie Fortescue can be found on which UK reality show?

5 Who had a hit in 1983 with *Come Back and Stay*?

6 What is the atomic number of boron?

7 Frenchman Jean Alesi made his Formula 1 debut in which decade?

8 Lake Maracaibo lies in which South American country?

9 In what year did Chile host the FIFA World Cup?

10 What name is given to the female reproductive organ of a flowering plant?

11 Bodhisattva is a term in which religion?

12 Who sang *I Can Help* in 1974?

13 Who was the first winner of the Rugby League Man of Steel award?

14 What word for a document detailing a ship's particulars can also mean "obvious"?

15 In which decade was James Callaghan (Baron Callaghan of Cardiff) Chancellor of the Exchequer?

16 What type of animal is the title creature of the 1950 film *Harvey*?

17 Who wrote the 1945 novel *Cannery Row*?

18 What do Americans usually call a bunker on a golf course?

19 In September 2017, what did Bibiana Steinhaus become the first woman to do?

20 Javine represented the UK in the Eurovision Song Contest in 2005 with which song?

Easy

Medium

Hard

Answers to QUIZ 445 – Pot Luck

1	Rupert Pupkin	11	*The Dukes of Hazzard*
2	Inter Milan	12	India
3	*Coppélia*	13	Iain Banks
4	Deep Blue Something	14	Warbler
5	Sioux (Oglala)	15	Chaka Khan
6	Kohlrabi	16	The Appalachians
7	Norfolk	17	Charles Schulz
8	*The Rocky Horror Picture Show*	18	Idaho
9	France	19	Winter
10	Sir Walter Scott	20	Fats

Easy

1   Who wrote the *Amores* collection of Roman poetry?

2   What female name preceded *a Fragment of a Confession* in the title of the first published work by Robert Browning?

3   What name is given to the principal form of division in epic poetry?

4   TS Eliot's conversion to Anglicanism inspired him to write a poem about which religious day?

5   In which country was Dame Carol Ann Duffy born?

6   Which poet is referred to in his native country as *il Somme Poeta* (The Supreme Poet)?

7   How many lines are there in a clerihew?

8   Which Romantic poet wrote his first collection entitled *An Evening Walk* in 1793?

9   Byron's epic poem *Don Juan* begins in which Spanish city?

10   Which famous 19th-century poem begins with the line "On either side the river lie, long fields of barley and of rye"?

11   What age was Percy Bysshe Shelley when he died in 1822?

Medium

12   Which member of the Rossetti family produced the poem *Remember*?

13   In the title of a Matthew Arnold poem, which US city precedes *Beach*?

14   Which poet has a bridge named after him which crosses the Delaware River?

15   "The Myth of Amherst" was a nickname given to which poet during her lifetime?

16   What term is given to a group of eight lines of verse?

17   Which English poet lived in a cottage in Higher Bockhampton?

18   Which city was William Blake describing in the poem that begins "I wander through each charter'd street"?

19   John Keats died of tuberculosis whilst visiting which country?

20   Who wrote the 1945 poem *Fern Hill*?

Hard

Answers to QUIZ 446 – Science

1	Siemens	11	The Moon
2	Red blood cells	12	Shoulder joint
3	Saturn	13	*My Brief History*
4	NaCl	14	Computational physics
5	Cobalt	15	Albert Einstein
6	Venus	16	English
7	1986	17	Mars
8	Bismuth	18	Farad (Michael Faraday)
9	Tide levels	19	Taxonomy
10	Eye	20	Erwin Schrödinger

1 René Higuita, the famously eccentric goalkeeper, played for which national football team?

2 Ken Barlow first appeared in *Coronation Street* in what year?

3 The Belmont Stakes is run in which US state?

4 Rhydian Roberts was runner-up to which *The X Factor* winner?

5 Tewkesbury is in which English county?

6 Which car was initially to be called the Ford Consul 325?

7 Logan airport serves which US city?

8 What term is given to the situation where inflation is high but prices and employment are not increasing?

9 Gabriel Oak is a character in which Thomas Hardy novel?

10 In which sport would you find a running back?

11 The British Overseas Territory of Anguilla lies in which sea?

12 Who wrote the play *Outside Edge*, adapted for television in the 1990s?

13 What type of creature is a small Apollo?

14 Matthew Kelly and Henry Kelly were original presenters of which 1980s show featuring practical jokes?

15 Which two five-letter words that differ by one letter describe a hand tool and a verb meaning "predict"?

16 What nationality is 1997 Wimbledon winner Martina Hingis?

17 Who captained the winning team in the 1974 FIFA World Cup?

18 The Wilis in the ballet *Giselle* typically dress in which colour?

19 Who wrote the 1985 novel *Oranges Are Not the Only Fruit*, which was adapted for television in 1990?

20 Which Irish county is known as "the Garden of Ireland"?

Answers to QUIZ 447 – Pot Luck

1	Ely (the cathedral)	11	Buddhism
2	Ulrika Jonsson	12	Billy Swan
3	Jimmy Nail	13	David Ward
4	*Made in Chelsea*	14	Manifest
5	Paul Young	15	1960s (1964-67)
6	5	16	A rabbit
7	1980s (1989)	17	John Steinbeck
8	Venezuela	18	Sand trap
9	1962	19	Referee a Bundesliga match
10	Carpel	20	*Touch My Fire*

1   What number is represented by the Roman numerals XCVII?

2   The Seven Mile Bridge can be found in which US state?

3   How many hours are there in March?

4   In hexadecimal, what number does the letter E represent?

5   What is the cube root of 343?

6   In imperial measurement, how many yards are in three chains?

7   What number of points do the values of the coloured balls in snooker add up to?

8   An atomic number indicates the number of which particles in an element?

9   What is the next highest prime number after 59?

10   What is the traditional gift for a 20th anniversary in the UK?

11   *Dreizehn* is the German word for which number?

12   What colour is the number 14 slot on a roulette wheel?

13   How many tiles are used in a game of mah-jong?

14   How many minutes are there in a standard day?

15   In the title of the play by Aeschylus, how many were there against Thebes?

16   How many ounces are there in five pounds?

17   What is a fifth of 675?

18   How many square yards are there in an acre?

19   Which fictional character had his shop at 186 Fleet Street?

20   "Buckle my Shoe" is a traditional bingo call for which number?

Answers to QUIZ 448 – Poets and Poetry

1	Ovid	11	29
2	Pauline	12	Christina
3	Canto	13	*Dover*
4	Ash Wednesday	14	Walt Whitman
5	Scotland	15	Emily Dickinson
6	Dante	16	Octave
7	Four	17	Thomas Hardy
8	William Wordsworth	18	London
9	Seville	19	Italy
10	*The Lady of Shalott*	20	Dylan Thomas

ANSWERS ON PAGE **453**

1   What names are the four players in a game of contract bridge given?

2   The London Stock Exchange moved its headquarters to which London square in 2004?

3   How many years did Nikita Khrushchev serve as first secretary of the Communist Party?

4   Which educational establishment was originally described as "the University of the Air"?

5   Tom Traddles is a character in which Dickens novel?

6   What nationality is racing driver Juan Pablo Montoya?

7   The computer-illiterate character Jen Barber featured in which sitcom?

8   Who married the American writer Joy Davidman in 1956?

9   "The Gateway to the World" is the motto of which British city?

10   How many seats did the Brexit Party win in the 2019 European elections?

11   At which course did Tiger Woods win his first Open Championship in 2000?

12   The annual East of England Show takes place in which city?

13   The noisy scrub-bird is native to which country?

14   Which actress starred as Bernadette Hogan in the 1995 film *Circle of Friends?*

15   What nationality is former athlete Lasse Virén?

16   Malpensa airport serves which European city?

17   Which Irish city was made the 2005 European Capital of Culture?

18   Suzanne Shaw was a winner on which reality show in 2008?

19   What nationality is author Patricia Cornwell (b.1956)?

20   SP is the postcode for which English city?

Easy

Medium

Hard

Answers to QUIZ 449 – Pot Luck

1	Colombia	11	Caribbean
2	1960	12	Richard Harris
3	New York	13	A butterfly
4	Leon Jackson	14	*Game for a Laugh*
5	Gloucestershire	15	Auger and augur
6	Ford Cortina	16	Swiss
7	Boston	17	Franz Beckenbauer
8	Stagflation	18	White
9	*Far from the Madding Crowd*	19	Jeanette Winterson
10	American football	20	County Wicklow

1. With four titles, which county was the most successful Benson & Hedges Cup participant?

2. Blue and which other colour are the main colours of Hampshire CCC?

3. The Parks is the name of which university's cricket ground?

4. Which animal's head features on the 2019 logo of Durham Cricket?

5. John Minshull is credited with the first recorded century, scoring 107 runs, in which decade?

6. Cricket at the 1900 Summer Olympics took place between Britain and which other nation?

7. In what decade did the West Indies acquire their test cricket status?

8. The first World Cup was organised by England in which year?

9. What was the first name of Wisden, creator of the famous almanack?

10. The Cricket Hall of Fame was launched in which year by the ICC?

11. With which county did batsman Jack Hobbs spend his whole career?

12. The first Twenty20 men's international took place in which year?

13. In which country is the Pukekura Park cricket ground?

14. At how many different London locations has Lord's cricket ground been situated?

15. Joe Root was born in which North of England city?

16. Which initials represent India's governing body?

17. Which team won the first edition of the IPL under the captaincy of Shane Warne?

18. In which city are the headquarters of the International Cricket Council (ICC)?

19. What name joins Duckworth and Stern in the name of the rain-interrupted scoring system?

20. Who was the first cricketer to reach 10,000 runs in test cricket?

Answers to QUIZ 450 – Numbers

1	97	11	13
2	Florida	12	Red
3	744	13	144
4	15	14	1440
5	Seven	15	Seven
6	66	16	80
7	27	17	135
8	Protons	18	4840
9	61	19	Sweeney Todd
10	China	20	32

1   Which actress co-starred with Sir Michael Palin in the 1984 film *A Private Function*?

2   The town of Jedburgh lies in which administrative region?

3   What was the first feature-length animated movie to be Oscar-nominated for Best Picture?

4   How many member countries in total are there on the UN Security Council?

5   Who wrote, produced and directed the 1925 film *The Gold Rush*?

6   Who was the legendary brother of Horsa?

7   What currency unit is used in Algeria?

8   In which English county is the town of Grays?

9   Who wrote the novels *Spy Hook* (1988), *Spy Line* (1989) and *Spy Sinker* (1990)?

10 What term is given to the eight historical ceremonial counties of Wales?

11 What nationality is racing driver Pastor Maldonado?

12 *Hear My Song* is particularly associated with which singer (d.1999)?

13 Which decimal coin, no longer in use, featured an image of St Edward's crown?

14 The town of Gillingham lies in which English county?

15 Which writer created the fictional pirate song *Dead Man's Chest*?

16 What type of drink is associated with Buckfast Abbey?

17 *Cosi Fan Tutti Frutti* was a 1985 album by which band?

18 The name Hesperus is given to what star - a synonym for Venus?

19 Who was asked not to "take your love to town" in the lyrics of a 1960s song?

20 The company Avast specialises in what type of product?

Easy

Medium

Hard

Answers to QUIZ 451 – Pot Luck

1	North, South, East and West	11	St Andrews
2	Paternoster Square	12	Peterborough
3	11	13	Australia
4	Open University	14	Minnie Driver
5	*David Copperfield*	15	Finnish
6	Colombian	16	Milan
7	*The IT Crowd*	17	Cork
8	CS Lewis	18	*Dancing on Ice*
9	Southampton	19	American
10	29	20	Salisbury

1   How many major schools is Zen divided into?

2   Who is the Hindu god of wisdom?

3   How many scriptural Vedas are there?

4   Which religion has a name meaning "Way of the Gods"?

5   In 2003, UNESCO celebrated 3000 years of which religion?

6   Gunasthana is a central 14-stage path in which religion?

7   How did Paul escape Damascus in the New Testament?

8   In which century did the first Sikh Guru emerge?

9   The Baha'I religion was founded in which century?

10 Buddhism's Noble Path has how many steps?

11 How many times does a Jewish man pray on the Sabbath?

12 Mohini is the female incarnation of which Hindu god?

13 In which century did the Jewish Enlightenment arise?

14 How many sons did Jacob have in the Old Testament?

15 *Chardi Kala*, or optimistic resilience, is a part of which religion?

16 In what book of the Bible are we told "the love of money is the root of all evil"?

17 Parvati is the wife of which god in Hinduism?

18 How many books are there in the New Testament?

19 Which book is between Judges and Samuel 1 in the Old Testament?

20 What word is given to the ideal truth, as set forth in the teachings of Buddha?

Answers to QUIZ 452 – Cricket

1	Lancashire	11	Surrey
2	Gold	12	2005
3	Oxford	13	New Zealand
4	Lion's head	14	Three
5	1760s (1769)	15	Sheffield
6	France	16	BCCI
7	1920s (1928)	17	Rajasthan Royals
8	1975	18	Dubai
9	John	19	Lewis
10	2009	20	Sunil Gavaskar

QUIZ 455 – Pot Luck

1   Santa Cruz was the first city to be founded in which country?

2   In metres, how long is the balance beam in gymnastics?

3   *The Old Home Guard* is a song from which Disney film?

4   Matt Di Angelo was runner-up to which fellow competitor on *Strictly Come Dancing*?

5   Who captained the USA team to victory in the 2008 Ryder cup ending a streak of three European victories?

6   *Cocos nucifera* is the Latin name given to what?

7   Who plays the title role in the 2016 TV series McGyver?

8   In croquet, one side plays with black and blue balls. What two colours does the other side use?

9   In what decade was Lord Byron born?

10   "Little Barrel" was the nickname given to which Italian artist?

11   What name is given to someone who studies shells of molluscs?

12   In which 1985 film did Cher portray Rusty Dennis, mother of a son called Rocky?

13   Who recorded the 1967 song *Ode to Billie Joe*?

14   In which English county is the town of Glossop?

15   What sport does Xander Schauffele (b.1993) play?

16   In which country were Lanchester and Napier cars manufactured?

17   Who directed the 1971 film *The Last Picture Show*?

18   The girl group Precious represented the UK in the Eurovision Song Contest in which decade?

19   Which US TV series centred around Mike and Hope Steadman?

20   The town of Sidmouth is in which English county?

Easy

Medium

Hard

Answers to QUIZ 453 – Pot Luck

1	Dame Maggie Smith	11	Venezuelan
2	Scottish Borders	12	Josef Locke
3	*Beauty and the Beast*	13	$\frac{1}{2}$p
4	15	14	Kent
5	Sir Charlie Chaplin	15	Robert Louis Stevenson
6	Hengist	16	Tonic wine
7	Dinar	17	Squeeze
8	Essex	18	Evening Star
9	Len Deighton	19	Ruby
10	Preserved counties	20	Cyber security

Easy

1 Who starred as James Conrad in the 2017 film *Kong: Skull Island*?

2 In which country was Island Records founded?

3 A cay is a low island composed of sand and what other substance?

4 Which of the Channel Islands lies furthest north?

5 "You do something to me that I can't explain" is a lyric from which 1983 song?

6 The Isle of Purbeck is a peninsula in which English county?

7 Which is the largest island of Japan?

8 The TV series *Island Medics* is based in which group of islands?

9 The nature reserve of Ramsey Island lies off the coast of which country?

10 *Island Girl* was a 1975 single by which singer/songwriter?

11 Eel Pie Island lies in which major English river?

12 In which Shakespeare play does the phrase "This royal throne of kings, this sceptred isle" appear?

Medium

13 The isle of Bute lies in which body of water?

14 What was the prefix of the title of Bill Bryson's *More Notes from a Small Island* (2015)?

15 Which island refers to itself in its own language as Ellan Vannin?

16 Norfolk Island belongs to which country?

17 Which island off the coast of England is also known as Holy Island?

18 SY are the international car registration letters for which island group?

19 Who directed the 2010 film *Shutter Island*?

20 The plane featured in the TV series *Lost* belonged to which fictional airline?

Hard

Answers to QUIZ 454 – Religion

1	Two (Theravāda and Mahāyāna)	11	Four
2	Ganesh	12	Vishnu
3	Four	13	18th century
4	Shinto	14	12
5	Zoroastrianism	15	Sikhism
6	Jainism	16	Timothy I
7	In a basket	17	Shiva
8	15th century (1469)	18	27
9	19th century	19	Ruth
10	Eight	20	Dharma

1   The sphincter of Oddi is in what part of the digestive system?

2   How old was Bear Grylls when he was appointed Chief Scout in 2009?

3   Which group did Terry Hall form immediately after leaving The Specials?

4   What is a tyro?

5   In which winter sport is a calculation point used?

6   The Sandanistas are a political party in which country?

7   *Fawlty Towers* was first broadcast in which year?

8   In which county is the parliamentary constituency of Filton and Bradley Stoke?

9   What is the minimum age a horse must be to run in the Grand National?

10 In April 2019, who set a new record for the fastest goal in the Premier League's history, 7.69 seconds after kick-off?

11 Herne Bay is a seaside town located in which English county?

12 Who directed the 1985 film *Out of Africa*, for which he won the Best Director Oscar?

13 Who was the 25th president of the USA, from 1897 until his assassination?

14 "May I have your attention, please?" is the opening line to which 2000 song?

15 In which decade did Rudolf Nureyev die?

16 *Telephone Line* was a 1977 single taken from which ELO album?

17 The writer Isabel Allende was born in which country?

18 *Vitis vinifera* is a Latin name for which fruit?

19 In what year was Julius Caesar assassinated?

20 Hyperion is a moon of which planet?

Easy

Medium

Hard

Answers to QUIZ 455 – Pot Luck

1	Colombia	11	Conchologist
2	Five metres	12	*Mask*
3	*Bedknobs and Broomsticks*	13	Bobbie Gentry
4	Alesha Dixon	14	Derbyshire
5	Paul Azinger	15	Golf
6	Coconut tree	16	England
7	Lucas Till	17	Peter Bogdanovich
8	Red and yellow	18	1990s (1999)
9	1780s (1788)	19	*thirtysomething*
10	Botticelli	20	Devon

1   Bob Parr is head of the family, in which series of animated films?

2   Who provided the speaking voice for Esmeralda in the 1996 film *The Hunchback of Notre Dame?*

3   Flik is the leading character in which 1998 film?

4   Madame Medusa is a villainous treasure huntress in which 1977 film?

5   Mr Ping, Po's father, is what kind of animal in *Kung Fu Panda?*

6   Dairy cows named Maggie, Mrs Caloway and Grace are leading characters in which film?

7   Emperor Kuzco is a leading character in which 2000 film?

8   How many puppies does Perdita first give birth to in *One Hundred and One Dalmatians?*

9   On what was the 2002 film *The Country Bears* based?

10 In *Toy Story*, what was the name of the TV show of which Woody was the star?

11 Who directed the live-action 2015 film *Cinderella?*

12 *Love is a Song* features in which 1942 film?

13 Jafar is the villain in which 1992 film?

14 Jim Hawkins is the leading character in which 2002 animated film?

15 Bolt, in the title of the 2008 film, was voiced by which actor?

16 *Mulan* is set in which country?

17 Nestor, Raul, Rinaldo and Lombardo are all characters in which film?

18 Norman Babcock is the leading character in which animated film?

19 *Scamp's Adventure* was a 2001 follow-up to which film?

20 Princess Merida of Dunbroch is the central character in which film?

Answers to QUIZ 456 – Islands

1	Tom Hiddleston	11	River Thames
2	Jamaica	12	Richard II
3	Coral	13	Firth of Clyde
4	Alderney	14	*The Road to Little Dribbling*
5	*Islands in the Stream*	15	Isle of Man
6	Dorset	16	Australia
7	Honshu	17	Lindisfarne
8	Shetland Islands	18	The Seychelles
9	Wales	19	Martin Scorsese
10	Sir Elton John	20	Oceanic Airlines

1   Who was the Greek goddess of peace?

2   The Erie Canal is a waterway in which US state?

3   How many Oscars did the 1954 film *On the Waterfront* win?

4   Anthony Edwards played Dr Mark Greene in which US TV series?

5   Who released the 1993 album *Ten Summoner's Tales*?

6   East-Sussex born Christopher Lloyd (d.2006) was a well-known name in which profession?

7   What was the minimum age at which women were allowed to vote in the UK in 1918?

8   In which English county is the large village of Yaxley?

9   Who did US actress Nancy Davis (d.2016) marry in 1952?

10   Walter Hartright and Laura Fairlie are main characters in which 1859 novel?

11   In which game might you see a Catalan Opening?

12   Who played Sailor Ripley in the 1990 film *Wild at Heart*?

13   *The Old Military Canal* is a song from which 1963 musical?

14   When was the first Argentina GP held in Moto GP?

15   Which group had a hit with *One Love* in 1990?

16   The camel spin is a move in which sport?

17   The ski resort of Grandvalira lies in which European state?

18   Who had a 1977 hit with *Don't Cry for Me Argentina*?

19   The Dodgers are a baseball team from which US city?

20   Old Catton and Taverham are areas in which English city?

Easy

Medium

Hard

Answers to QUIZ 457 – Pot Luck

1	Duodenum	11	Kent
2	35	12	Sydney Pollack
3	Fun Boy Three	13	William McKinley
4	A novice or learner	14	*The Real Slim Shady* by Eminem
5	Ski jumping	15	1990s (1993)
6	Nicaragua	16	*A New World Record*
7	1975	17	Chile
8	Gloucestershire	18	Grape (or grape vine)
9	Seven	19	44 BC
10	Shane Long	20	Saturn

1   What is a gewgaw?

2   What two words that sound the same but are spelt differently mean "coarse" and "a frilly collar"?

3   Which trade takes its name for the Latin word for the metal lead?

4   If something is described as viscid, what property does it have?

5   Which area of Wales is known as *Ynys Môn* in Welsh?

6   What is the English meaning of the German word *Reich*?

7   Of what is chionophobia a fear?

8   What is the meaning of the name Dublin?

9   What does a pomologist study?

10   The word "chutney" originates from which language?

11   What five-letter word can mean both to cook and to steal?

12   What is the English meaning of the name of the political party Fianna Fáil?

13   By what term is the meditative practice of *shinrin-yoku* known in English?

14   How many feet should a millipede have, according to the translation of its name?

15   What is meant by the Latin term *ex libris*?

16   What should you do if you are told to "haud your wheesht" in Scotland?

17   Known as a crash barrier in the UK, what is it called in the US?

18   What is the meaning of the word "winsome"?

19   What name is given to the scientific study of language?

20   From which language does the word "manifesto" originate?

Answers to QUIZ 458 – Disney Films

1	*The Incredibles*	11	Sir Kenneth Branagh
2	Demi Moore	12	*Bambi*
3	*A Bug's Life*	13	Aladdin
4	*The Rescuers*	14	*Treasure Planet*
5	(Chinese) goose	15	John Travolta
6	*Home on the Range*	16	China
7	*The Emperor's New Groove*	17	*Happy Feet*
8	15	18	*ParaNorman*
9	A theme park attraction	19	*Lady and the Tramp*
10	*Woody's Round-up*	20	*Brave*

1   Who won the Golden Ball Award at the 2014 FIFA World Cup?

2   The University of Warwick is located near which UK city?

3   In which year did the Ceefax service cease?

4   Which group had a 1990 hit with *I've Been Thinking About You*?

5   The town of Corsham lies in which English county?

6   William Golding's *Lord of the Flies* was published in which decade?

7   *No Milk Today* was a 1966 song by which British group?

8   Iapetus is the third-largest moon of which planet?

9   Lake Van lies in which country?

10 Motorcycle racer Giacomo Agostini won how many 350cc and 500cc World Championships in total from 1968 to 1975?

11 What sport do the Cleveland Indians play?

12 Which dynasty of emperors built the Colosseum in Rome?

13 On which Mediterranean island was the 1977 TV series *Who Pays the Ferryman?* set?

14 The town of North Walsham lies in which English county?

15 Who played Second Officer Lightoller in the 1958 film *A Night to Remember*?

16 David Byrne was a founder member of which US new wave band?

17 What nationality were the Scarlatti family of composers?

18 What does an isohel connect on a map?

19 Who was Leader of the House of Commons from 1998 to 2001?

20 Limburger cheese originated in which country?

Easy

Medium

Hard

Answers to QUIZ 459 – Pot Luck

1	Irene	11	Chess
2	New York	12	Nicolas Cage
3	Eight	13	*Half a Sixpence*
4	*ER*	14	2014
5	Sting	15	The Stone Roses
6	Gardening	16	Figure skating
7	30	17	Andorra
8	Cambridgeshire	18	Julie Covington
9	Ronald Reagan	19	Los Angeles
10	*The Woman in White*	20	Norwich

Easy

1. *Scheherezade* (1888) was an orchestral work by which composer?

2. Ludwig von Köchel catalogued which composer's works?

3. After which European capital is Haydn's 104th symphony named?

4. Georg Philipp Telemann was born in which country?

5. To the nearest ten, how many strings does a concert harp typically have?

6. In what country was Maurice Ravel born?

7. Who became presenter of Radio 3's *Composer of the Week* in 1999?

8. In what key is a piece of music that has three sharps as its key signature?

9. Which composer's seventh symphony is known as the *Leningrad* symphony?

10. In *The Carnival of the Animals* by Saint-Saëns, which instruments play the sound of the swan on the water?

11. Handel's *Water Music* was written in response to a request by which king?

12. In which coastal city was Edvard Grieg born?

13. What is meant by the musical instruction *ma non troppo*?

14. After which planet is Mozart's Symphony Number 41 named?

Medium

15. Who composed the music for the ballet *Spartacus*, part of which was used as the theme for the TV series *The Onedin Line*?

16. What nationality was the composer Carl Weber?

17. How many complete operas were composed by Giacomo Puccini?

18. The Bayreuth Festival celebrates the music of which composer?

19. In Holst's *The Planets* suite, how is Neptune described?

20. What is the nickname of Beethoven's Piano Concerto No.5?

Hard

Answers to QUIZ 460 – Words

1	A worthless trinket	11	Poach
2	Rough and ruff	12	Soldiers of destiny
3	Plumbing	13	Forest bathing
4	Stickiness	14	1000
5	Isle of Anglesey	15	From the books of
6	Empire	16	Be quiet
7	Snow	17	Guardrail
8	Black or dark pool	18	Attractive or charming
9	Fruit	19	Linguistics
10	Hindi	20	Italian

1   Who wrote the novella *Sally Bowles* (1937)?

2   Haematite is the chief source of which metal?

3   The Malabar Coast is part of which country?

4   What is the meaning of the Latin phrase *inter alia*?

5   In which decade was the first Dakar Rally?

6   Gurdwaras are religious building for followers of which religion?

7   What type of creature is a mandrill?

8   Who scored Spain's winner in the 2010 FIFA World Cup final?

9   *2:00 AM Paradise Café* was a 1984 album by which singer?

10 As at the end of 2018, for which film had Harrison Ford received his only Oscar nomination?

11 Which UK prime minister created the post of Minister for Women, now Minister for Women and Equalities?

12 Who provided the voice of the title character in the 2007 film *Beowulf*?

13 The Shiant Isles lie off the coast of which country?

14 Who wrote the song *I Get a Kick Out of You*?

15 Damien Hirst was born in which decade?

16 In Greek mythology, who was the mother of Oedipus?

17 From which US state does the band ZZ Top hail?

18 Who wrote the 1980 sci-fi novel *The Restaurant at the End of the Universe*?

19 The Valley is the home ground of which London football club?

20 Who wrote the story *The Ant and The Grasshopper*?

Answers to QUIZ 461 – Pot Luck

1	Lionel Messi	11	Baseball
2	Coventry	12	Flavian dynasty
3	2012	13	Crete
4	Londonbeat	14	Norfolk
5	Wiltshire	15	Kenneth More
6	1950s (1954)	16	Talking Heads
7	Herman's Hermits	17	Italian
8	Saturn	18	Areas of equal sunshine
9	Turkey	19	Dame Margaret Beckett
10	15	20	Belgium

Easy

1 What type of ship was the *Pilot*, built by the Russians in 1864?

2 Anton Chekhov died in which decade?

3 Ramón Mercader was the assassin of which famous Russian figure?

4 Due to boycotts, how many nations actually competed in the 1980 Olympic Games?

5 Graphene, invented in Russia, is an allotrope of which element?

6 Grigory Potemkin was a favourite of which Russian ruler?

7 Boris Yeltsin resigned his post as president in which year?

8 How many houses are there in the Federal Assembly of the Russian Federation?

9 How old was Rasputin when he was assassinated in 1916?

10 Igor Sikorsky was the first to invent and build an aircraft with how many engines?

11 The Gulag government agency was established in which decade?

12 In which gymnastics discipline did Svetlana Boginskaya (b.1973) win three Olympic gold medals?

13 The 1905 Russian Revolution began in which month?

Medium

14 Credited with painting the first purely abstract works, which Russian used bright colours in works such as *The Blue Rider* (1903)?

15 "Socialism in One Country" was a chief policy of whom?

16 What was the motto of the 2014 Winter Olympics in Russia?

17 Russia is divided into how many federal districts?

18 Made mainly from cabbage, what type of food is shchi?

19 Composer Alexander Borodin lived and died during which century?

20 For how many years did the Soviet Union rule Russia?

Hard

Answers to QUIZ 462 – Classical Music

1	Rimsky-Korsakov	11	George I
2	Mozart	12	Bergen
3	London	13	But not too much
4	Germany	14	Jupiter
5	50 (usually 46 or 47)	15	Khachaturian
6	France	16	German
7	Donald Macleod	17	12
8	A	18	Wagner
9	Shostakovich	19	The Mystic
10	Piano (two) and cello	20	Emperor

1   Who recorded the song *Boo'd Up*, which was named as the Best R&B Song at the 2019 Grammy Awards?

2   Which Italian won the 2014 Tour de France?

3   How many countries border Bangladesh?

4   The town of Chester-le-Street lies in which English county?

5   Which was published first, Darwin's *On the Origin of Species* or the Periodic Table?

6   The Eos car model is made by which company?

7   The trade union Solidarity was founded in which year?

8   Who had a 1982 hit with *State of Independence*?

9   How was the sea described in Coleridge's *Kubla Khan*?

10 Who played the title character in the 1995 film *Rob Roy*?

11 Which painter completed 12 murals for Manchester Town Hall shortly before his death?

12 What is the earliest date on which Easter Sunday can occur?

13 In 1971, who sailed single-handed round the world in a boat named *British Steel*?

14 *Can't Get Enough* (1974) was the debut single of which group?

15 The Chilterns are composed mostly of what substance?

16 In which decade was the women's marathon first included in the Olympic Games?

17 What term describes muscle strength training that is performed in a static position?

18 Grassholm Island is off the coast of which country?

19 In which decade was Sunderland made a city?

20 The name of the Fortran programming language was derived from which two words?

Answers to QUIZ 463 – Pot Luck

1	Christopher Isherwood	11	Tony Blair
2	Iron	12	Ray Winstone
3	India	13	Scotland
4	Amongst other things	14	Cole Porter
5	1970s (1978)	15	1960s (1965)
6	Sikhism	16	Jocasta
7	A monkey	17	Texas
8	Andrés Iniesta	18	Douglas Adams
9	Barry Manilow	19	Charlton Athletic
10	*Witness*	20	Aesop

1   Which designer said "Fashion changes, but style endures"?

2   In 2019, the V&A museum in London held an exhibition of clothes from which French fashion house?

3   Which fashion house has designed the on-field kit for AC Milan since 2004?

4   In what year did Victoria Beckham launch her eponymous fashion label?

5   Diane von Fürstenberg is best known for which style of dress?

6   Which designer founded the Fashion and Textile Museum in London in 2003?

7   What name is given to the tight-fitting dress that appears to be made from thin strips of cloth joined together?

8   In the 1980s, Gianni Versace launched the perfume *Blonde*, dedicated to whom?

9   Who introduced the "bubble dress" in 1954?

10 Which fashion designer designed the Team GB kit for the 2012 and 2016 Summer Olympic Games?

11 London Fashion week takes place in which two months?

12 What was the name of the wealthy fashion magazine owner played by Alan Dale in the TV series *Ugly Betty*?

13 The *Per Una* label was created by which fashion designer for Marks and Spencer?

14 In which building is the Bath Fashion Museum housed?

15 What nationality was designer Hugo Boss?

16 Which former model and TV presenter launched her eponymous fashion line in May 2017?

17 Who presented the 2018 documentary *Fashion's Dirty Secrets*?

18 A crew-neck sweater has what shape neckline?

19 Which designer introduced the modern pencil skirt in 1954?

20 Mary Louise Booth (d.1889) was the first editor of which fashion magazine?

Answers to QUIZ 464 – Russia

1	Icebreaker	11	1920s (1923)
2	1900s (1904)	12	Floor exercise
3	Trotsky	13	January
4	80	14	Kandinsky
5	Carbon	15	Stalin
6	Catherine the Great	16	Hot Cool Yours
7	1999	17	Eight
8	Two	18	Soup
9	47	19	19th century (1833-87)
10	Four	20	70 (1922-91)

1 Helen Schlegel is a character in which 1910 novel?

2 Which district of South Devon is noted for its cliff railway and model village?

3 Odin's Revenge is a feature of which American golf course?

4 Which small African country has the internet code .ls?

5 In which decade did *The English Patient* win the Best Picture Oscar?

6 Which singer featured on Mark Ronson's best-selling single *Uptown Funk*?

7 Which 1980 film starring Jamie Lee Curtis was set in the fictional town of Antonio Bay?

8 "This was never the way I planned Not my intention" is a lyric from which song?

9 Which band backed Lloyd Cole?

10 In which decade was the first power station built at Battersea?

11 Damon, Graham, and which other driver named Hill were Formula 1 world champions?

12 Swiss Cottage lies on which London Underground line?

13 Which English football club plays home games at Ewood Park?

14 What nationality is former cricketer Javed Miandad (b.1957)?

15 The medieval village of Lavenham is in which English county?

16 By population, which is the second-largest city in Poland?

17 What is an overpass usually called in the UK?

18 Madonna's *Beautiful Stranger* (1999) was a single from the soundtrack to a film in which series?

19 What is the official language of Mali?

20 Which 1987 song by Hue and Cry was their highest-charting single in the UK?

Answers to QUIZ 465 – Pot Luck

1	Ella Mai	11	Ford Madox Brown
2	Vincenzo Nibali	12	March 22
3	Two (India and Myanmar/Burma)	13	Sir Chay Blyth
4	County Durham	14	Bad Company
5	*Origins of Species*	15	Chalk
6	Volkswagen	16	1980s (1984)
7	1980	17	Isometric
8	Donna Summer	18	Wales
9	Sunless	19	1990s (1992)
10	Liam Neeson	20	Formula Translation

1   Gustav I of Sweden ruled in what century?

2   Which George became King of Great Britain and Ireland in 1760?

3   Who abdicated as King of Spain in 2014?

4   Which two buildings are linked by Edinburgh's Royal Mile?

5   How many kings of Scotland were called Malcolm?

6   Who directed the 2001 film *The Royal Tenenbaums*?

7   Which king died in 1702 after his horse stumbled on a molehill?

8   Who was the longest-reigning of the French kings?

9   The First English Civil War took place during the reign of which monarch?

10 In which year did King George V celebrate his Silver Jubilee?

11 *Royal Engagement* was the subtitle to which 2004 film sequel?

12 A library dedicated to what type of writing has been located at the Royal Festival Hall since 1988?

13 For how many years did William the Conqueror rule Britain?

14 What is the name of the Royal Family's official residence in Northern Ireland?

15 The 1980s TV series *King's Royal* was set in which country?

16 Following the death of General Franco, Spain re-established a monarchy in which year?

17 Prince Philip's original title was Prince of Greece and which other country?

18 In 1284, which king granted a Royal Charter to Lyme Regis?

19 The Royal Engineers are based in which English county?

20 Who was the mother of the first Princess Royal?

Easy

Medium

Hard

Answers to QUIZ 466 – Fashion

1	Coco Chanel	11	February and September
2	Christian Dior	12	Bradford Meade
3	Dolce & Gabanna	13	George Davies
4	2008	14	Assembly Rooms
5	Wrap dress	15	German
6	Dame Zandra Rhodes	16	Alexa Chung
7	Bandage dress	17	Stacey Dooley
8	His sister, Donatella Versace	18	Round
9	Pierre Cardin	19	Christian Dior
10	Stella McCartney	20	*Harper's Bazaar*

1 In 1901, who received the first Nobel Prize in Physics?

2 What type of creature is a parr?

3 The 1950s-1960s Interceptor sports car was manufactured by which English company?

4 Which 1983 film starring Dame Julie Walters is based on a stage play by Willy Russell?

5 Who was head coach of the England netball team from 2015 to 2019?

6 Lee Kuan Yew (d.2015) was the first prime minister of which Asian republic?

7 Which US actor played Ishmael Chambers in the 1999 film *Snow Falling on Cedars*?

8 Anniesland is an area of which Scottish city?

9 What term is given to the stalk and leaves at the base of a strawberry?

10 Which fruit juice is the main ingredient of a Salty Dog cocktail?

11 Which bird, extinct in Britain since the 19th century, was reintroduced to Salisbury Plain in 2004?

12 *Sei* is the Italian for which number?

13 *By the Sleepy Lagoon* is the theme music for which long-running radio programme?

14 Who won the women's US Open tennis championship in 2018 and the Australian Open in 2019?

15 Which US singer/songwriter wrote the song *Leaving on a Jet Plane*?

16 Which ride at the Alton Towers theme park shares its name with the title of a 2013 Tom Cruise film?

17 Scientist Dr Giles Yeo and surgeon Gabriel Weston appear regularly on which health-related TV series?

18 Who played Prince Vultan in the 1980 film *Flash Gordon*?

19 What do the prefixes "aber" and "inver" mean in Welsh and Scottish place names?

20 Rally driver Esapekka Lappi was born in which country?

Easy

Medium

Hard

Answers to QUIZ 467 – Pot Luck

1	*Howards End*	11	Phil (1961)
2	Babbacombe	12	Jubilee Line
3	Valhalla	13	Blackburn Rovers FC
4	Lesotho	14	Pakistani
5	1990s (1996)	15	Suffolk
6	Bruno Mars	16	Kraków
7	*The Fog*	17	Flyover
8	*I Kissed a Girl* (Katy Perry)	18	*Austin Powers*
9	The Commotions	19	French
10	1930s	20	*Labour of Love*

Easy

1. The character of William Guppy appears in which novel by Charles Dickens?
2. For which 2004 film did Jamie Foxx win an Oscar?
3. With which fish is the village of Findon, or Finnan, particularly associated?
4. Who wrote the 1994 short story collection *12 Red Herrings*?
5. Who played Susie Salmon in the 2009 film *The Lovely Bones*?
6. In which decade did Little Richard have a hit with *Good Golly, Miss Molly*?
7. The rock band Papa Roach was formed in which country?
8. Whose alter-ego is Ant-Man, played by Paul Rudd on screen?
9. Who wrote the 1953 novel *Fahrenheit 451*?
10. Which river provided the title of a top twenty single for The Piranhas in 1982?
11. The Florida Marlins play which sport?

Medium

12. Who wrote the 1947 opera *Albert Herring*?
13. Who played the title character in the 2017 film *Molly's Game*?
14. Which ventriloquist was associated with the puppets Titch and Quackers?
15. The character of Inspector Monkfish appeared in which comedy sketch series?
16. What name is given to the serrated part of a blade at the front of an ice skate?
17. Sardines are a particular feature of which 1982 farce by playwright Michael Frayn?
18. Which 1960s children's TV series centred around the organisation WASP?
19. Julian Bream is primarily associated with which musical instrument?
20. Which cartoonist created the character of Captain Haddock?

Hard

Answers to QUIZ 468 – Royal

1	16th century	11	*The Princess Diaries*
2	George III	12	Poetry
3	King Juan Carlos	13	23
4	Edinburgh Castle and Holyrood Palace	14	Hillsborough Castle
5	Four	15	Scotland
6	Wes Anderson	16	1975
7	William III (William of Orange)	17	Denmark
8	Louis XIV (72 years)	18	Edward I
9	Charles I	19	Kent (Chatham)
10	1935	20	Henrietta Maria

ANSWERS ON PAGE **473**

1   Under what title was *The Good Life* shown in the US?

2   What nationality was Simon Bolivar?

3   What was Elvis Presley's last single of the 1950s?

4   In which decade was Friends of the Earth founded?

5   How many nations took part in Rugby League's first World Cup?

6   Who wrote *Blue Remembered Hills*, originally for television and later adapted for the stage?

7   Tara Street railway station lies in which European capital city?

8   In which century was the ear trumpet, an early form of hearing aid, first used?

9   Native to Africa, what is the more common name of the brindled gnu?

10 Nathan Chen became World Champion in which sport in March 2019?

11 Who played Kim Boggs in the 1990 film *Edward Scissorhands*?

12 In 2016, Charlotte Moore became the first person to hold what post within the BBC?

13 What does an entomologist study?

14 The CY Young Award is given to players of what sport?

15 Who sang the 1980 song *Talk of the Town*?

16 Morley and Pudsey are areas in which British city?

17 What is a crocosmia?

18 How much did a copy of the the Highway Code cost when it was first introduced?

19 Who painted the famous 1830 work *Liberty Leading the People*?

20 The Gulf of Bothnia lies in which sea?

Easy

Medium

Answers to QUIZ 469 – Pot Luck

1	Wilhelm Röntgen	11	Great bustard
2	A (young) fish	12	Six
3	Jensen	13	*Desert Island Discs*
4	*Educating Rita*	14	Naomi Osaka
5	Tracey Neville	15	John Denver
6	Singapore	16	Oblivion
7	Ethan Hawke	17	*Trust Me, I'm a Doctor*
8	Glasgow	18	Brian Blessed
9	Hull	19	River mouth
10	Grapefuit juice	20	Finland

Hard

1. Which tree has the Latin name *taxus baccata*?

2. How many species of rhinoceros are there still extant?

3. The Roswell Pits nature reserve is located in which UK county?

4. Amber comes from the resin of which plant or tree?

5. In which century did the great auk become extinct?

6. Which US state gives its name to a species of condor?

7. Which plant is also known as Ramsons?

8. To which family of animals does the pademelon belong?

9. Which British bird can be green, lesser-spotted or greater-spotted?

10. What name is given to the steeply sloped area that forms the edge of a continent?

11. In meteorological terms, what is a supercell?

12. The Great Bear Lake is the largest lake to lie entirely within which country?

13. The name of which plant, used to make a herbal tea, takes its name from the Greek for "earth apple"?

14. What is a female walrus called?

15. For what natural feature is Aysgarth in the Yorkshire Dales noted?

16. What is the main constituent of natural gas?

17. On what do sundew plants feed?

18. What name is given to the muscular stomach of a bird?

19. What shape are ammonite fossils?

20. The Dingle Peninsula is part of which Irish county?

Answers to QUIZ 470 – Fish

1	*Bleak House*	11	Baseball
2	*Ray*	12	Benjamin Britten (Baron Britten)
3	Haddock (Finnan Haddie)	13	Jessica Chastain
4	Jeffrey Archer	14	Ray Alan
5	Saoirse Ronan	15	*The Fast Show*
6	1950s (released as a single in 1958)	16	Toe pick
7	USA (California)	17	*Noises Off*
8	Scott Lang	18	*Stingray*
9	Ray Bradbury	19	Guitar (classical)
10	Zambesi	20	Hergé

1   Bromine belongs to which group of chemical elements?

2   What type of animal is the cartoon character Kipper, created by Mick Inkpen?

3   What is the London railway terminus of the West Anglia Main Line?

4   In which city was George Bernard Shaw born?

5   The Bodhi tree is a central aspect of which religion?

6   Who won the 2019 Football Writer's Association Women's Player of the Year award?

7   Mark Wahlberg and Christian Bale starred in which 2010 boxing film?

8   Who directed the 2009 film *Looking for Eric*?

9   Which character in Sir Terry Pratchett's *Discworld* series of novels was made from sapient pearwood?

10   How many stars are there on the flag of New Zealand?

11   What is the six-letter mathematical term for a variable quantity that has force and direction?

12   What name is given to the study of the physical features of an area?

13   In which decade was the first World Snooker Championship held?

14   Which Latin phrase did Alfred, Lord Tennyson use as the title of an 1850 poem?

15   In which Scottish town is the Glen Scotia distillery based?

16   Which group released the 2005 single *City of Blinding Lights*?

17   The National Slate Museum is situated close to which village in North Wales, the terminus of a narrow-gauge railway?

18   How is a plant defined if it can survive outdoors but not in a severe frost?

19   What is the name of Sir Charlie Chaplin's 1952 film about ballet?

20   Zutano and hass are varieties of which fruit?

Easy

Medium

Hard

Answers to QUIZ 471 – Pot Luck

1	*Good Neighbors*	11	Winona Ryder
2	Venezuelan	12	Director of Content
3	*A Big Hunk O' Love*	13	Insects
4	1960s (1969)	14	Baseball
5	Four (Australia, France, Great Britain, New Zealand)	15	The Pretenders
		16	Leeds
6	Dennis Potter	17	(Small flowering) plant
7	Dublin	18	1 penny
8	17th century	19	Eugène Delacroix
9	Wildebeest	20	The Baltic Sea
10	Figure skating		

1   In which sport is the minimum ski length the height of the skier less 4cm?

2   Who was captain of the winning European team at the 2004 Ryder Cup?

3   Bruce McLaren, the runner-up in the 1960 Formula 1 Championship, was born in which country?

4   How far apart, in feet, are the inner edges of the upright goalposts in football?

5   When were the first Commonwealth Games held?

6   What nationality was the tennis champion Suzanne Lenglen (d.1938)?

7   The sport of pelota purépecha, which is similar to hockey, originated in which country?

8   Cutback, floater, and top-turn are terms used in which extreme sport?

9   How many different fences are there on the Grand National course?

10   Which country won the now discontinued Baseball World Cup more than any other?

11   What animal features on top of the Calcutta Cup trophy?

12   Who scored a hat trick in a famous 2014 Champions League clash when Manchester City defeated Bayern Munich 3-2?

13   In which sport is the "Petersen turn" a feature?

14   Which form of cycle racing has a name from the Japanese for "racing cycle"?

15   How many feathers are there on a shuttlecock?

16   Which golfer has the nickname *El Niño*?

17   On a tennis court, how many feet away from the service line is the net?

18   In which year did boxer Lennox Lewis win an Olympic gold medal?

19   How many times did Sir Stirling Moss finish second in the Formula 1 World Championship?

20   As at 2019, how many different Olympic snowboarding disciplines were there?

Easy

Medium

Hard

Answers to QUIZ 472 – Natural World

1	Yew	11	A thunderstorm
2	Five	12	Canada
3	Cambridgeshire (Ely)	13	Camomile
4	Pine tree	14	Cow
5	19th century (c.1852)	15	Waterfall
6	California	16	Methane
7	Wild garlic	17	Insects
8	Marsupials	18	Gizzard
9	Woodpecker	19	Spiral
10	Continental shelf	20	County Kerry

ANSWERS ON PAGE 477

1. Who voiced Ralph in the 2012 film *Wreck-It Ralph*?

2. *Hold My Girl* was a 2018 single by which singer?

3. The 2018 film *At Eternity's Gate* featured Willem Dafoe as which artist?

4. Which symphony by Haydn is known as the *Military*?

5. Sanatana Dharma is another name for which religion?

6. The TV series *House* first aired in what decade?

7. Which playwright co-wrote the screenplay for the film *Shakespeare in Love*?

8. The site of the ancient city of Palmyra lies in which modern-day Middle Eastern country?

9. In which Shakespeare play do the Antipholus and Dromio twins appear?

10. The Cape Farewell Archipelago lies off the coast of which island?

11. Which long-distance footpath passes the cascade of Cauldron Snout?

12. Which band recorded the 1981 album *Dare*?

13. Lea and Barton are districts of which British city?

14. How many daughters did Jacob have in the Old Testament?

15. In which city was the US TV series *Dexter* set?

16. Which organisation runs the campaign Greening Grey Britain?

17. From which country does the plant the tomatillo originate?

18. Who was appointed interim leader of the Change UK political party when it was first formed?

19. Which actress co-starred with Ashton Kutcher in the 2011 film *No Strings Attached*?

20. In which month of the year is the Earth closest to the Sun?

Easy

Medium

Hard

Answers to QUIZ 473 – Pot Luck

1	Halogens	11	Vector
2	Dog	12	Topography
3	Liverpool Street	13	1920s (1927)
4	Dublin	14	*In Memoriam*
5	Buddhism	15	Campbeltown
6	Nikita Parris	16	U2
7	*The Fighter*	17	Llanberis
8	Ken Loach	18	Half-hardy
9	The Luggage	19	*Limelight*
10	Four	20	Avocado

Easy

1   How is singer-songwriter Henry Olusegun Adeola Samuel better known?

2   Composer Charles Villiers Stanford (d.1924) was born in which country?

3   Carlo Mastrangelo was a member of which 1950s American singing group?

4   Which composer's Violin Sonata No.9 is referred to by the name *Kreutzer*?

5   What word completes the title of the Prokofiev work, *The Love for Three ___*?

6   Which vocalist has sung with both Deep Purple and Black Sabbath?

7   *Isle of the Dead* is a 1908 tone-poem written by which composer?

8   Which American composer wrote the music for the 1987 work *Nixon in China*?

9   Which band's albums included *Murmur* (1983) and *Reckoning* (1984)?

10 *Fantasia on a Theme by Thomas Tallis* (1910) was written by which British composer?

11 Itzhak Perlman was a virtuoso on which instrument?

12 Who released his debut album *Greetings from Asbury Park, NJ* in 1973?

13 The Manaus Opera House (Teatro Amazonas) can be found in which country?

14 Which band, minus their lead singer, were once known as The Vendors?

Medium

15 What type of instrument is a shakuhachi?

16 Which band had their only UK top ten hit with *Turning Japanese* (1980)?

17 What was the first name of Mark Knopfler's brother, who was a member of Dire Straits?

18 Hayley Williams is the vocalist with which American rock band?

19 The composer Albert Ketelby was born in which English city?

20 Who released the 2019 album *Gold in a Brass Age*?

Hard

Answers to QUIZ 474 – Sport

1	Biathlon	11	An elephant
2	Bernhard Langer	12	Sergio Aguero
3	New Zealand	13	Bobsleigh
4	24 feet	14	Keirin
5	1930	15	16
6	French	16	Sergio García
7	Mexico	17	21 feet
8	Surfing	18	1988
9	16	19	Four times
10	Cuba	20	Five

1 In which decade did India play their first test match?

2 Batata harra is a spiced form of what vegetable?

3 Intermediate cuneiform bones can be found on which part of the body?

4 The Royal National College for the Blind is located in which UK city?

5 Which company produces the *Street Fighter* video game series?

6 Medically, what is an erythrocyte?

7 Who provided the voice of Henry J Waternoose III in the 2001 film *Monsters, Inc.*?

8 Mount Nebo lies in which Middle Eastern country?

9 Which famous rock band once went by the name of Tea Set?

10 *The King of Barataria* is the subtitle of which Gilbert and Sullivan opera?

11 Which religious order of monks lives by the Vinaya code?

12 Who joined Pompey and Caesar in ancient Rome's First Triumvirate?

13 In what decade was the San Francisco Ballet founded?

14 Sitophobia is the fear of what?

15 "By the Rivers of Babylon" is the first line of which psalm?

16 Who created the TV series *Unforgotten*?

17 Which artist painted *Three Studies for a Portrait of George Dyer* which sold for $45 million in 2014?

18 What type of creature is a houting?

19 Ben Jonson's *The Alchemist* is set in which city?

20 Moritz von Jacobi was responsible for what transport innovation in 1838?

Easy

Medium

Hard

Answers to QUIZ 475 – Pot Luck

1	John C Reilly	11	The Pennine Way
2	George Ezra	12	The Human League
3	Vincent van Gogh	13	Preston
4	100th	14	One (Dinah)
5	Hinduism	15	Miami
6	2000s (2004)	16	The Royal Horticultural Society
7	Sir Tom Stoppard	17	Mexico
8	Syria	18	Heidi Allen
9	*The Comedy of Errors*	19	Natalie Portman
10	Greenland	20	January

1. Which national football team has the nickname "Los Cafeteros"?

2. Which English club won the 1981 European Cup?

3. In which year did the first African Nations Cup take place?

4. Újpest play in the top division in which country?

5. For which club was Kevin Moran playing when he became the first man to be sent off in an FA Cup Final?

6. In 1991 Filippo Inzaghi made his professional debut with which Italian club?

7. Which famous Norwegian team are known as the Troll Children?

8. Which Spanish football club plays its home games at the Nuevo Carlos Tartiere?

9. Juan Ramón López Caro managed which club between 2005 and 2006?

10. England defender Lucy Bronze signed for which club side in 2017?

11. In which decade was the Doncaster women's football club founded?

12. Who was voted the PFA Young Player of the Year in 1991-92 and 1992-93?

13. Who was manager of Liverpool FC when they won the European Cup in 1984?

14. Which nation won the first Asian Nations Cup in 1956?

15. Which Dutch club was founded in 1908 as Wilhelmina?

16. As at the end of 2018, which was the only country to have won the FIFA Women's World Cup three times?

17. Tottenham Hotspur played their first Premier League match in their new stadium against which side in April 2019?

18. In which country is the Estádio Nacional Mané Garrincha stadium?

19. Which East European club was founded during military operations in WWI?

20. "Flying Donkeys" is a nickname of which Serie A club?

Answers to QUIZ 476 – Music

1	Seal	11	Violin
2	Ireland	12	Bruce Springsteen
3	The Belmonts	13	Brazil
4	Beethoven	14	Slade
5	*Oranges*	15	A flute (made of bamboo)
6	Ian Gillan	16	The Vapors
7	Rachmaninov	17	David
8	John Adams	18	Paramore
9	REM	19	Birmingham
10	Vaughan Williams	20	David Gray

1   What is the capital of the Seychelles?

2   *Kingdom of the Sun* was the original title of which 2000 Disney film?

3   In which country is the Manuel Antonio National Park?

4   What sport is played using a sliotar?

5   Who was the frontman of rock band My Chemical Romance?

6   What was the second name of composer Carl Weber (d.1826)?

7   Mysophobia is the fear of what?

8   Who directed the 1973 film *The Way We Were*?

9   "As I remember Adam, it was upon this fashion" is the opening line in which Shakespeare play?

10 In the name of EM Forster, for what does the "M" stand?

11 The ancient Greek colony of Kepoi was a key region in which culture?

12 Which English city is home to a cathedral founded in AD 597 by St Augustine?

13 In what year did Picasso paint *Guernica*?

14 What sort of dish is *khao tom* in Thai cuisine?

15 ERT is the home broadcaster of what Eurovision nation?

16 In 1997, who became the first female Leader of the House of Commons?

17 A former champion, which British Formula 1 driver was runner-up three times in succession in the 1960s?

18 "By Virtue and Industry" is the motto of which UK city?

19 Which US statesman said "Honesty is the first chapter in the book of wisdom"?

20 Who played President Allison Taylor in the TV series *24*?

Answers to QUIZ 477 – Pot Luck

1	1930s (1932)	11	Buddhism
2	Potato	12	Crassus
3	The foot	13	1930s (1933)
4	Hereford	14	Eating
5	Capcom	15	Psalm 137
6	Red blood cell	16	Chris Lang
7	James Coburn	17	Francis Bacon
8	Jordan	18	A (virtually extinct) fish
9	Pink Floyd	19	London
10	*The Gondoliers*	20	The electric boat

1   Which Inca symbol is widely regarded as their equivalent of the tree of life in other mythologies?

2   The *Kalevala* is an epic poem of folklore and mythology from which country?

3   Epona was the Roman goddess who protected which animal?

4   In Greek mythology, who changed Callisto into a bear?

5   What word is given to the theory that gods arose from the deification of historical heroes?

6   Marduk was the chief god worshipped by which people?

7   Who was the Norse god of poetry?

8   Who were Balder's parents in Norse mythology?

9   In Japanese mythology, what does the goddess Amaterasu represent?

10 The Morrígan is a figure associated with war in the mythology of which country?

11 Of what was Hephaestus the Greek god?

12 In Egyptian mythology, who killed Osiris?

13 The Grootslang was a legendary cave-dwelling creature in which country?

14 Who was the Greek goddess of the sea?

15 In the legend of the Lambton Worm, what type of mythical creature is the "worm"?

16 Who was the Roman equivalent of the Greek god Pan?

17 What was Polyphemus in Greek mythology?

18 Antillia, known as "The Isle of the Seven Cities", was a mythical island in which body of water?

19 The *Mabinogion* is a collection of stories written in which language?

20 In Ancient Rome, what name was given to a priest who served a particular god?

Answers to QUIZ 478 –Football

1	Colombia	11	1960s (1969)
2	Liverpool	12	Ryan Giggs
3	1957	13	Joe Fagan
4	Hungary	14	South Korea
5	Manchester United	15	Feyenoord
6	Piacenza	16	USA
7	Rosenborg	17	Crystal Palace
8	Real Oviedo	18	Brazil (Brasilia)
9	Real Madrid	19	Legia Warsaw
10	Lyon (Olympique Lyonnais)	20	ChievoVerona

1   "How use doth breed a habit in a man" is a phrase from which Shakespeare play?

2   Valeri Karpin managed which Russian football club between 2012 and 2014?

3   *(Mama) He Treats Your Daughter Mean* was a 1953 US hit for which singer?

4   Of what is gnosiology the study?

5   Pius X was appointed pope in what decade?

6   *The Fudge Family in Paris* (1818) is a verse novel by which author?

7   Who was known as "the Grand Old Man" of English cricket?

8   The Animals were formed in the 1960s which English city?

9   In what year was Beethoven born?

10   *Wagashi* is the traditional Japanese name for what?

11   In which TV series did the character of musician Marvin Suggs first appear?

12   *Are You Experienced* was a 1967 album by which band?

13   Who wrote the 1902 work *Garden Cities of To-Morrow?*

14   In which country was religious reformer John Calvin born?

15   What name did the Germans give to the winter of 1916-17 due to food shortages?

16   What is the first name of Sir Michael Caine's character in *Educating Rita* (1983)?

17   *Quiddities: An Intermittently Philosophical Dictionary* was a work by which US philosopher?

18   What is the currency unit of the Solomon Islands?

19   To which family of plants does the hibiscus belong?

20   What was the name of Daryl Hannah's character in the 1982 film *Blade Runner?*

Easy

Medium

Hard

1 Who played Queenie in the series *Making Out*?

2 The title characters of which US sitcom had the surnames DeFazio and Feeney?

3 Which 1990s series followed the Demeter city police on the planet Altor?

4 Nicky Rasmussen, played by Esben Smed Jensen, was a character in which Danish series?

5 Who performed the theme music to *Father Ted*?

6 Isaac Hempstead-Jones played which character in *Game of Thrones*?

7 Who appeared in *Downton Abbey* as Harold Levinson, Cora's younger brother?

8 Which city was *The 10th Kingdom* in the 2000 fantasy mini-series?

9 In which decade was the current affairs programme *Nationwide* first broadcast?

10 The Channel 5 series *Family Affairs* was set in which fictional London borough?

11 Shona Spurtle was an Air Scotia employee in which sitcom?

12 What was Arkwright's first name in *Open All Hours*?

13 *Humans* is an English-language remake of the series *Real Humans*, broadcast in which language?

14 Nicholas Young and Peter Vaughan-Clarke were original cast members of which sci-fi series first broadcast in the 1970s?

15 Journalist Nicolò Zito is a regular character in which crime-fighting series?

16 *Jason King*, featuring Peter Wyngarde in the title role, was a spin-off from which series?

17 Which documentary series won the BAFTA award for Best Factual Series in 2018?

18 The phrase "Damn it, Jerry!" is associated with which US sitcom?

19 What was the name of Daniel Dae-Kim's character in the TV series *Lost*?

20 Splasher and Neptina were friends of which cartoon character?

Answers to QUIZ 480 – Myth and Legend

1	Chakana (or Inca cross)	11	Fire
2	Finland	12	Set (or Seth)
3	Horses (also asses and mules)	13	South Africa
4	Hera	14	Amphitrite
5	Euhemerism	15	A dragon
6	Babylonians	16	Faunus
7	Bragi	17	A cyclops
8	Odin and Frigg	18	The Atlantic Ocean
9	Sun	19	Welsh
10	Ireland	20	Flamen

1   In the group Crosby, Stills, Nash & Young, what was the first name of Nash?

2   In which US city would you find the Padres baseball team?

3   What cabinet post in the British Government did Edward Grey hold at the outbreak of WWI?

4   What type of creature is a krait?

5   Which animal's name derives from a Latin word meaning "spirit of the dead"?

6   In what decade was John Keats born?

7   *Zensai* in Japanese cuisine are what part of a meal?

8   What was the birth name of Dame Nellie Melba?

9   Who voiced the character of Rapunzel in the animated film *Tangled*?

10 Who was the first woman to hold the post of Lord Mayor of London (1983-84)?

11 *For The Russian People* is the political newspaper of which party?

12 What does a heortologist study?

13 Abolished in 2000, for what did the initials MIRAS stand?

14 In what decade did Juan Perón win his first presidential election?

15 Sanssouci was the summer palace of which king?

16 In 1957, who won the Wimbledon women's singles title against her doubles partner Darlene Hard, with whom she also won the women's doubles title?

17 Tarot, played by Michael MacKenzie, was the main character in which 1970s TV series?

18 What term is given to the balance of light and shade in a piece of art?

19 Of what is algophobia a fear?

20 What was the name of the first balloon to cross the Pacific, a feat achieved in 1981?

Easy

Medium

Hard

Answers to QUIZ 481 – Pot Luck

1	*The Two Gentlemen of Verona*	11	*The Muppet Show*
2	Spartak Moscow	12	The Jimi Hendrix Experience
3	Ruth Brown	13	Sir Ebenezer Howard
4	The philosophy of knowledge	14	France
5	1900s (1903)	15	Turnip Winter
6	Thomas Moore	16	Frank
7	Pelham Warner	17	Willard Van Orman Quine
8	Newcastle-upon-Tyne	18	Solomon Islands dollar
9	1770	19	Mallow (*Malvaceae*)
10	Sweets	20	Pris

1   What is a crosier on a plant?

2   What seven-letter term beginning with "g" is given to soft hail or particles of snow?

3   How is the Taiwan blue pheasant also known, named after the naturalist who first described the species?

4   What is the popular name of the lizardfish *Harpadon nehereus*, native to the Arabian and South China seas?

5   Native to New Zealand, what type of animal is a tuatara?

6   Which birds of the genus *Numenius* have long, down-curved bills and brown plumage?

7   The wisent is a species of which large animal?

8   What is the common name of the plant *macrocystis pyrifera*?

9   To what family of animals does the zorilla belong?

10 What type of marine creature is a luth?

11 In what environment would you find a barchan?

12 What is aposematic colouring intended to do?

13 A grig is a small fish of what species?

14 What type of creature is a shrill carder?

15 What is the name of the vertically rotating column of air in a thunderstorm that can turn into a tornado?

16 At nearly 5000m tall, what is the highest mountain in Venezuela?

17 What natural feature may be described as leucocratic or mesocratic?

18 Which bird has nicknames including "thick knee" and "wailing heath chicken"?

19 A limacologist studies what type of small creatures?

20 Which is the world's second-deepest lake?

Answers to QUIZ 482 – Television

1	Margi Clarke	11	*The High Life*
2	Laverne and Shirley	12	Albert
3	*Space Precinct*	13	Sweden
4	*Follow the Money*	14	*The Tomorrow People*
5	The Divine Comedy	15	*Inspector Montalbano*
6	Bran Stark	16	*Department S*
7	Paul Giamatti	17	*Ambulance*
8	New York City	18	*Parks and Recreation*
9	1960s (1969)	19	Jin-Soo Kwon
10	Charnham	20	*Marine Boy*

1 What is the capital of Sierra Leone?

2 In what decade did Rembrandt paint *The Night Watch*?

3 The 1972 debut album of which German band was entitled *Lonesome Crow*?

4 Lewis, an aspiring young inventor at an orphanage, is the lead character in which 2007 film?

5 Panama gained independence in 1903 from which country?

6 What was the Roman name for the city of Paris?

7 What was the name of the famous "marathon" runner who delivered news of a Greek victory?

8 On which mount did Moses discover "the burning bush"?

9 The walls of Jaipur were painted pink in 1876 for the state visit of which future king?

10 *The Mysterious Stranger* was the much worked-on final novel by which US author?

11 As at the end of 2018, how many laws of cricket were there?

12 "Now say Chatillon, what would France with us" is the opening line of which Shakespeare play?

13 Castries is the capital of which island country?

14 Who released the album *Listen* in 2014?

15 What material might be measured in SWG?

16 In the 2007 film *Juno*, what is the surname of the title character?

17 Emperor Atahualpa died and was buried in which Inca settlement, the site of a famous battle?

18 In which sport do Lilah Fear and Lewis Gibson compete for the UK?

19 Who played Sheriff Jack Carter in the TV series *Eureka* (aired in the UK as *A Town Called Eureka*)?

20 Kenzo Tange designed which record breaking tower in Tokyo, completed in 1994?

Easy

Medium

Hard

Answers to QUIZ 483 – Pot Luck

1	Graham	11	LDPR (Liberal Democratic Party of Russia)
2	San Diego	12	Religious festivals
3	Foreign Secretary	13	Mortgage Interest Relief at Source
4	A snake	14	1940s (1946)
5	Lemur	15	Frederick the Great, King of Prussia
6	1790s (1795)	16	Althea Gibson
7	Starter	17	*Ace of Wands*
8	Helen Porter Mitchell	18	Chiaroscuro
9	Mandy Moore	19	Pain
10	Mary Donaldson (Lady Donaldson of Lymington)	20	*Double Eagle V*

1   What was the full name of the title character in the 1941 film *Citizen Kane*?

2   Which US inventor (d.1901) was involved in a legal battle with Alexander Graham Bell over the invention of the telephone?

3   In which English resort town was novelist and poet Thomas Love Peacock (d.1866) born?

4   How was Henry John Temple (d.1865) better known?

5   The New York Guggenheim Museum building, designed by Frank Lloyd Wright opened in which decade?

6   In which decade was John Maynard Keynes' *The General Theory of Employment, Interest and Money* published?

7   Under what name did William Sydney Porter write a series of short stories?

8   Who played Kate Reddy in the 2011 film *I Don't Know How She Does It*?

9   How was Agnes Gonxha Bojaxhiu (d.1997) better known?

10   Martin Luther King Jr was born in which US state capital?

11   Which author created the fictional land called Pellucidar?

12   What stage name was adopted by Ellas Otha Bates (d.2008)?

13   The catalogue of works by Johann Sebastian Bach is known as the BWV. For what do these initials stand?

14   Who was the 27th US President?

15   Andrew Bonar Law was first elected as an MP in a constituency in which UK city?

16   What pen-name did Louisa May Alcott use early in her career?

17   Who wrote the 19th-century poems *Looking-Glass River* and *The Lamplighter*?

18   Alfred Arnold Cocozza was the real name of which 1950s singer?

19   Who plays Beth Pearson in the TV series *This is Us*?

20   What was the name of Haley Joel Osment's character in the 2001 film *AI: Artificial Intelligence*?

Answers to QUIZ 484 – Natural World

1	Coiled young leaf on a fern	11	Desert (sand dune)
2	Graupel	12	Warn off predators
3	Swinhoe's pheasant	13	An eel
4	Bombay duck	14	A bee
5	Reptile (lizard)	15	Mesocyclone
6	Curlews	16	Pico Bolívar
7	A bison	17	Igneous rock
8	Giant kelp	18	Stone curlew
9	Mustelids	19	Slugs
10	A turtle (leatherback sea turtle)	20	Lake Tanganyika

1 Which Chinese city has become the world's first to have an entire fleet of buses powered by electricity?

2 Which adjective describes long-legged wading birds?

3 In what decade was the ICC founded?

4 Gapper, homer and frozen rope are all terms you might hear in which sport?

5 Who painted *The Arnolfini Portrait* (1434)?

6 Caerleon was the original settlement of which Welsh city?

7 What is the dish *geng* in Chinese cuisine?

8 Ivan Elmanov invented which system of transport in 1820?

9 In which year were Led Zeppelin formed?

10 Richard Stilgoe and Sir Trevor McDonald have both served as president of which county cricket club?

11 Lepidolite is a main ore of which element?

12 By area, what was the smallest UK parliamentary constituency in 2019?

13 *Earthly Powers* was a 1980 novel by which author?

14 Who made history in 2003 by becoming the first woman to compete on the men's PGA tour since 1945?

15 Which singer said "The best revenge is massive success"?

16 Pontefract is famous for its liquorice. But which other English town has a historic liquorice industry?

17 What is the literal meaning of the word "pharaoh"?

18 In what decade was the US writer Walt Whitman born?

19 Who had a 1998 hit with *Crush*?

20 Winter, Hail, Ice and Frost all appear in which ballet choreographed by Marius Petipa?

Answers to QUIZ 485 – Pot Luck

1	Freetown	11	42
2	1640s (1642)	12	*King John*
3	Scorpions	13	St Lucia
4	*Meet the Robinsons*	14	David Guetta
5	Colombia	15	Wire (Standard Wire Gauge)
6	Lutetia	16	MacGuff
7	Pheidippides	17	Cajamarca
8	Horeb	18	Ice dancing
9	Edward VII	19	Colin Ferguson
10	Mark Twain	20	Shinjuku Park Tower

1 Hans Lippershey (d.1619) was a key figure in the development of which scientific instrument?

2 What type of machine is a cyclotron?

3 Anatomically, naevus is more commonly known by what name?

4 What does a manometer compare?

5 How are the elements with the atomic numbers 89 to 103 known?

6 Cubital refers to which body part?

7 Who was the first Japanese Nobel laureate, receiving the Nobel Prize in Physics in 1949?

8 Which derived SI unit of magnetic flux is equal to a flux of one weber in one square metre?

9 How many zeros follow the "1" in a British septillion?

10 Which scientist said "An investment in knowledge pays the best interest"?

11 Who discovered the now dwarf planet Pluto?

12 The metal cobalt takes its name from the German for what mythical creature?

13 Kyphosis affects which part of the human body?

14 Which chemical element has the symbol Tc?

15 In physics, the muon is classified as what type of particle?

16 Which is the heaviest member of the halogen group of elements?

17 What do the initials IUPAC stand for in the name of a scientific body?

18 Norman Lockyer named which element after being key to its discovery?

19 What does the protein myoglobin provide to muscles?

20 Which chemical term takes its name for the Greek for "same place"?

Answers to QUIZ 486 – Three Names

1	Charles Foster Kane	11	Edgar Rice Burroughs
2	Elisha Gray	12	Bo Diddley
3	Weymouth	13	*Bach-Werke-Verzeichnis*
4	Lord Palmerston (Third Viscount Palmerston)	14	William Howard Taft
5	1930s (1937)	15	Glasgow (Blackfriars and Hutchesontown)
6	1930s (1936)	16	AM Barnard
7	O Henry	17	Robert Louis Stevenson
8	Sarah Jessica Parker	18	Mario Lanza
9	Mother Teresa	19	Susan Kelechi Watson
10	Atlanta	20	David

1 In which decade did Sergei Rachmaninov die?

2 *The Grand Babylon Hotel* (1902) is a novel by which author?

3 Which museum, established in 1929, stands at 11 West 53rd Street in New York City?

4 Nick Banks was the drummer in which 1990s band?

5 *The Condor and the Cows* (1949) was a travel diary written by which author?

6 What is a more common name for a scintillating scotoma?

7 Off which Asian country would you find the Amami Islands?

8 Which popular game, issued in 1996, did Satoshi Tajiri create?

9 The MacRobertson International Shield is an event in which sport?

10 Pissaro belonged to which artistic school?

11 Who directed *Bumblebee*, the 2018 film in the Transformers series?

12 In which country does the Nilgiri Mountain Railway run?

13 Which European country's parliament is called the Sabor?

14 Peter the Great became ruler of Russia in what decade?

15 The World Economic Forum holds an annual meeting in January in which Swiss town?

16 Who was the first Roman emperor to be killed in battle?

17 The Irish town of Avoca was a main location for the filming of which 1990s TV series?

18 In which Paralympic sport have Menna Fitzpatrick and Jennifer Kehoe won medals?

19 Pindar was a famous Greek figure in what field?

20 In the Old Testament, Job (as Jobab) was once the ruler of which kingdom?

Answers to QUIZ 487 – Pot Luck

1	Shenzhen	11	Lithium
2	Grallatorial	12	Islington North
3	1900 (1909)	13	Anthony Burgess
4	Baseball	14	Annika Sörenstam
5	Jan van Eyck	15	Frank Sinatra
6	Newport	16	Worksop
7	Soup	17	Great house
8	Monorail	18	1810s (1819)
9	1968	19	Jennifer Paige
10	Surrey	20	*The Seasons*

Easy

1 How many stars are on the flag of the Central African Republic?

2 In which country is the River Lena?

3 Lhotse Mountain, the fourth highest mountain in the world, is at the border of which two countries?

4 The Thar Desert forms a border between which two countries?

5 What is the currency unit of Lebanon?

6 Which US state is known as "The Equality State"?

7 In what modern-day country is the city which the Romans referred to as Turicum?

8 What is the capital of the Pacific republic of Kiribati?

9 Which Indian city is known as "the Blue City"?

10 The thoroughfare Omotesandō is found in which capital city?

Medium

11 To the nearest hundred feet, how high is Angel Falls?

12 Trieste is the capital of which Italian region?

13 In which Asian country is the Bogda Peak?

14 Klerksdorp is the largest city in which South African province?

15 The O'Higgins/San Martín lake lies in which two countries?

16 The Icelandic krona was formerly divided into 100 units called what?

17 In which country would you find the sacred Buddhist Jogyesa Temple?

18 What name is given to a native of Havana?

19 In which US state is Tacoma airport located?

20 Which of the Indian states is listed last alphabetically?

Hard

Answers to QUIZ 488 – Science

1	Telescope	11	Clyde Tombaugh (in 1930)
2	A particle accelerator	12	Goblin
3	Birthmark	13	Spine
4	Pressures of gas or liquids	14	Technetium
5	Actinides	15	Lepton
6	Forearm or elbow	16	Astatine
7	Hideki Yukawa	17	International Union of Pure and Applied Chemistry
8	Tesla		
9	42	18	Helium
10	Benjamin Franklin	19	Oxygen
		20	Isotope

1   Which male figure skater won all the major championships in the 2001-02 season?

2   The pula is the unit of currency in which African country?

3   Who is the patron saint of librarians?

4   In which year did the civil defence force the Royal Observer Corps cease operations?

5   *Milvus milvus* is the taxonomical name for which British bird of prey?

6   What word completes the title of a famous Frida Kahlo work, *What the ___ Gave Me?*

7   Joanna was the wife of whom in the Bible?

8   What is the capital of the US state of Pennsylvania?

9   In which north of England town was the band Elbow formed?

10   "Los Rojiblancos" is the nickname of which Spanish football club?

11   For which household object did Thomas Saint invent the first design in 1790?

12   What is another name for the animal called a milu?

13   *The Girl at the Lion d'Or* was the second novel by whom?

14   In which European city is Hradčany Castle located?

15   What does an apiologist study?

16   Huskisson Street was the main setting for which sitcom?

17   What nationality was the inventor Joseph Bramah (d.1814)?

18   Billy Midwinter became the first cricketer to do what?

19   Which character from Shakespeare has a daughter called Lavinia?

20   In Thai cuisine, what type of dish is congee?

Answers to QUIZ 489 – Pot Luck

1	1940s (1943)	11	Travis Knight
2	Arnold Bennett	12	India (Tamil Nadu)
3	Museum of Modern Art	13	Croatia
4	Pulp	14	1680s (1682)
5	Christopher Isherwood	15	Davos
6	Visual migraine	16	Decius
7	Japan	17	*Ballykissangel*
8	Pokémon™	18	Alpine skiing
9	Croquet	19	Poetry
10	Impressionism	20	Edom

1   Petrichor is the characteristic smell of what?

2   Taken from ancient Greek theatre, what was the original meaning of the word "tragedy"?

3   What does a paroemiographer collect?

4   What is the collective noun for a group of wombats?

5   What is a morpheme?

6   In which decade did Samuel Johnson publish *A Dictionary of the English Language*?

7   What does the culinary term "fouetté" mean?

8   CLAP EARTH'S ADULTS is an anagram of the name of which famous building?

9   What does the medical term singultus mean?

10 Of what is sphragistics the study?

11 What word can mean both a unit of work and an area in a desert?

12 Estragon is another name for which herb?

13 What is an apophthegm?

14 From which language is the verb "bluff" derived?

15 Grammatically, what term is given to an adjective placed after the word it modifies?

16 What is the name given to the sound made by a cork being pulled from a bottle of wine?

17 The noun "puggle" was added to the *Oxford English Dictionary* in 2019. What is a puggle?

18 What, on ancient buildings, was a vallum?

19 "Tattie-bogle" is a Scottish word meaning what in English?

20 Which slang word meaning a home is also used for a pole supporting a sail?

Answers to QUIZ 490 – Geography

1	One	11	3,200 (3,213) feet
2	Russia	12	Friuli–Venezia Giulia
3	Nepal and China	13	China
4	India and Pakistan	14	North West Province
5	The Lebanese pound	15	Chile and Argentina
6	Wyoming	16	Aurar
7	Switzerland (Zurich)	17	South Korea
8	Ambo, Tarawa	18	Habanero
9	Jodphur	19	Washington
10	Tokyo	20	West Bengal

1 What is classified by the Köppen system?

2 Who was the losing finalist in the women's singles at the 2019 French Open tennis tournament?

3 Simon Kuznets (d.1985) was a leading figure in which field?

4 Whose 1905 *Woman with a Hat* painting depicts his wife, Amélie?

5 Plato was born in what century?

6 What type of creature is a powan?

7 *Memento Mori* (1959) and *The Driver's Seat* (1970) are works by which author?

8 Which British athlete won a gold medal in the 3000m steeplechase in the 1956 Olympic Games after being disqualified then reinstated?

9 Which two architects designed London's National Theatre complex?

10 Which 2008 TV series was set in the fictional Cornish village of Polnarren?

11 In what decade did Russian Alexander Sablukov invent the centrifugal fan?

12 *The Stone Book Quartet*, published in the late 1970s, was written by which author?

13 Whose 2006 debut album was entitled *Who Needs Action When You Got Words*?

14 Which Asian capital city is nicknamed "the Special City"?

15 In which 1982 film did Steve Martin play private investigator Rigby Reardon?

16 Paul Woessner was a multiple-time World Champion in what kind of racing?

17 What was Sir John Mills' real first name?

18 Who was the god of the west wind, in Greek mythology?

19 In what decade was composer Ralph Vaughan Williams born?

20 Steve Took was a member of which rock band?

Easy

Medium

Hard

Answers to QUIZ 491 – Pot Luck

1	Alexei Yagudin	11	Sewing machine
2	Botswana	12	Père David's deer
3	St Jerome	13	Sebastian Faulks
4	1995	14	Prague
5	Red kite	15	Bees
6	*Water*	16	*The Liver Birds*
7	Chuza	17	English
8	Harrisburg	18	Play for two nations in a test match
9	Bury		England and Australia
10	Atlético Madrid	19	*Titus Andronicus*
		20	(Rice) porridge

Easy

1. Gudrun and Ursula Brangwen are the leading characters in which 1969 film?

2. Ted Lewis' novel *Jack's Return Home* formed the basis of what film?

3. *The Hunger Games: Catching Fire* director Francis Lawrence found fame directing what type of film?

4. Which 1949 film was released in the USA under the name *Tight Little Island*?

5. Who directed *The Empire Strikes Back*?

6. In which 2002 film did Steve Coogan portray Tony Wilson, founder of Factory Records?

7. Which artist's life was portrayed in the 1956 film *Lust for Life*?

8. The fictional setting of Bandrika features in which 1939 film?

9. For which 1954 film did Grace Kelly win the Best Actress Oscar?

10. What was the name of the character played by Peter Sellers in *I'm All Right Jack*?

11. Mickey Rooney provided the voice of which character in *The Fox and the Hound*?

12. What is Tom Hanks's occupation in the 1985 film *The Man with One Red Shoe*?

13. The 1945 film *The Corn is Green* was set in which country?

14. Gelsomina is the central character in which 1954 Italian film?

15. Which composer wrote the music for the animated film *The Incredibles* and its sequel?

16. Who directed the 1994 film *Quiz Show*?

17. Which was the first film studio to be given an Honorary Academy Award (then known as the Special Award)?

18. In the 1966 classic *Alfie*, what is Alfie's surname?

19. Which 2012 animated film is set in the small town of Blithe Hollow?

20. Which singer starred in the 1970 film *Performance*?

Medium

Hard

Answers to QUIZ 492 – Words

1	Rain	11	Erg
2	Goat song	12	Tarragon
3	Proverbs	13	A concise saying
4	A wisdom	14	Dutch
5	The smallest grammatical unit of a language	15	Postpositive
6	1750s (1755)	16	Cloop
7	Whipped	17	A dog (a cross between a pug and a beagle)
8	St Paul's Cathedral	18	A Roman rampart or earthwork
9	Hiccup	19	Scarecrow
10	Seals (those attached to documents)	20	Gaff

1 Which fruit was known to the ancients as "the Fruit of the Gods"?

2 Who was the first Canadian to win a golfing major?

3 Sy Berger, who died in 2014, was associated with the creation of which collectable craze?

4 Who played Field Marshal Zhukov in the 2017 film *The Death of Stalin*?

5 In ancient Greece, what was a hoplite?

6 Nicky Wire plays bass for which rock band?

7 For how many years did Boris Godunov rule Russia?

8 Valerie Martin won the Orange Prize for Fiction for which 2003 work?

9 Playwright Samuel Beckett was born in which decade?

10 US painter John James Audubon was known for his depictions of which creatures?

11 What 1950s dance did US musician Chuck Willis popularise?

12 The word "pardine" describes which animal?

13 In which German city was Wagner born?

14 The briard breed of dog originated in which European country?

15 Threave Gardens is located in which Scottish region?

16 In what decade was Zenko Suzuki a Japanese prime minister?

17 Inventor Sir Humphry Davy was born in which English county?

18 What type of land animal is a dibatag?

19 In which city is Turffontein Racecourse?

20 Mike Shepherd and Kristin Sims investigate crimes in which New Zealand TV series?

Easy

Medium

Hard

Answers to QUIZ 493 – Pot Luck

1	Climate	11	1830s (1832)
2	Marketa Vondrousova	12	Alan Garner
3	Economics	13	Plan B
4	Henri Matisse	14	Seoul
5	5th century BC (c.427)	15	*Dead Men Don't Wear Plaid*
6	A fish	16	Hot Air Balloon
7	Dame Muriel Spark	17	Lewis
8	Chris Brasher	18	Zephyrus
9	Sir Denys Lasdun and Peter Softley	19	1870s (1872)
10	*Echo Beach*	20	T Rex

ANSWERS ON PAGE 498

1 Poet Robert Frost was born in which US state?

2 What was the middle name of author Anthony Powell?

3 *Grimus* was the 1975 debut novel by which writer?

4 *The Triumph of Life* (1822) is an unfinished piece by which poet?

5 Mr Allworthy is a country gentleman featuring in which 1749 comic novel?

6 *Mr Norris Changes Trains* was a key work by which author?

7 Who wrote the 1833 novella *Green Dwarf: A Tale of the Perfect Tense* under the name Lord Charles Albert Florian Wellesley?

8 Constance and Sophia Barnes feature in which novel of 1908?

9 Who created the character of Inspector Karen Pirie?

10 *Darkness Visible* (1979) was a James Tait Black Memorial prize-winning book by which author?

11 *Notes From Underground* (1864) was a literary work by which author?

12 Who wrote the 2019 novel *Machines Like Me*?

13 Published posthumously in 1924, *Billy Budd, Sailor* was written by which author?

14 What word completes the title of a work by John Galt (d.1839), *Annals of the ___*?

15 What was the real first name of Dame Iris Murdoch?

16 Isobel Fairfax is the main character in which novel by Kate Atkinson?

17 In which decade was Samuel Richardson's novel *Clarissa, or, the History of a Young Lady* published?

18 Who wrote the 1912 comic novel *The Crock of Gold*?

19 Ian McEwan's 2016 novel *Nutshell* was inspired by which Shakespeare play?

20 Who was awarded the Nobel Prize for Literature in 1948 for his services to poetry?

Answers to QUIZ 494 – Film

1	*Women in Love*	11	Tod
2	*Get Carter*	12	Violinist
3	Music videos	13	Wales
4	*Whisky Galore!*	14	*La Strada*
5	Irvin Kershner	15	Michael Giacchino
6	*24 Hour Party People*	16	Robert Redford
7	Vincent Van Gogh	17	Warner Bros
8	*The Lady Vanishes*	18	Elkins
9	*The Country Girl*	19	*ParaNorman*
10	Fred Kite	20	Sir Mick Jagger

1 The Sloe Fair takes place in which South of England city?

2 In which country is Changi Airport located?

3 An 1869 Leon Minkus ballet was named after which literary character?

4 "*Merz*", coined by Kurt Schwitters, is another name for which style of art?

5 Which poet was born at Cockermouth, Cumberland in 1770?

6 Of what is a hypsophobe afraid?

7 What type of creature is a twaite shad?

8 Dominika Egorova is the main character in which 2018 film?

9 Which British rock band released the 1995 album *Afraid of Sunlight*?

10 In which city was actor and singer John Barrowman born?

11 The Laysan duck, also known as the Laysan teal, is native to which group of islands?

12 Frank Pembleton and Tim Bayliss were fictional detectives in which American TV series?

13 *Oliang* is a Thai drink of what type?

14 The Nuggets are the NBA team from which city?

15 How is the glenohumeral joint better known?

16 In cricket, what score is represented by a double-Nelson?

17 What is the capital of the Pacific state of Tuvalu?

18 Which bird also has the name "awl-bird"?

19 In the Old Testament, what was the name of the sister of Moses?

20 Who reached no.1 in 2018 with *Sweet but Psycho*?

Easy

Medium

Hard

Answers to QUIZ 495 – Pot Luck

1	Persimmon	11	The stroll
2	Mike Weir (2003 Masters)	12	The leopard
3	Baseball cards	13	Leipzig
4	Jason Isaacs	14	France
5	Soldier	15	Dumfries and Galloway
6	Manic Street Preachers	16	1980s (1980-82)
7	17 (Feb 1598 to April 1605)	17	Cornwall
8	*Property*	18	A gazelle
9	1900s (1906)	19	Johannesburg
10	Birds	20	*The Brokenwood Mysteries*

Easy

1 During which battle of 1918 did the Austro-Hungarian empire collapse as a political entity?

2 What was the first dynasty in Chinese history?

3 What title was held by Edmund, the father of Henry VII?

4 An attack on La Guaria in 1739 was the opening battle in which war?

5 How many million dollars did the US pay France for "The Louisiana Purchase"?

6 In what year did Mary II, Queen of England, Scotland and Ireland, die?

7 Who was the commander of the British Fleet at the Battle of Jutland?

8 The title "The King's Beloved Sister" was given to which historical figure?

9 Which was the first organisation to be awarded the Nobel Peace Prize?

10 Who was King of Spain in 1931 when the Spanish monarchy was abolished?

11 The English Star Chamber court of law was abolished in which decade?

12 What series of Roman wars ended in 290 BC?

13 What was the name of the ship used as a floating exhibition hall for the Festival of Britain?

Medium

14 Representatives from how many countries attended the 1945 meeting in San Francisco that produced the charter of the United Nations?

15 In which century did Alfred the Great become the first king of a united England?

16 In 1901, Emil Adolf von Behring became the first recipient of which Nobel Prize?

17 Which battle took place from July 1 to July 3, 1863?

18 Magnus III of Norway was given what nickname?

19 What was the capital of Japan immediately before Kyoto?

20 The Zand Dynasty was founded in Iran during which century?

Hard

Answers to QUIZ 496 – Literature

1	California	11	Fyodor Dostoyevsky
2	Dymoke	12	Ian McEwan
3	Salman Rushdie	13	Herman Melville
4	Shelley	14	*Parish*
5	*Tom Jones* (Henry Fielding)	15	Jean
6	Christopher Isherwood	16	*Human Croquet*
7	Charlotte Brontë	17	1740s (1748)
8	*The Old Wives' Tales* (Arnold Bennett)	18	James Stephens
9	Val McDermid	19	*Hamlet*
10	William Golding	20	TS Eliot

ANSWERS ON PAGE 251

1   What is the capital of Equatorial Guinea?

2   *Lawdy Miss Clawdy* (1962) was the first single to be released by whom?

3   For what team did Juan Manuel Fangio win the last of his Formula 1 World Championships?

4   Nic Pizzolatto is the award-winning writer of which TV series first broadcast in 2014?

5   Which German territory did New Zealand seize in October 1914?

6   *The Celestial Omnibus* (1911) is a collection of short stories by which author?

7   Lake Ladoga lies in which country?

8   Hector Campora was elected president of which South American country in 1973?

9   Which play won the Best Play at the 2019 Tony Awards?

10 The songs *Only You Can Rock Me* and *Arbory Hill* appear on which 1978 UFO album?

11 *Toum* is a Lebanese sauce with what flavour?

12 The Bowman's capsule can be found in which part of the human body?

13 Which French artist was nicknamed "Le Douanier", because of his previous occupation as a customs officer?

14 *The Birthday Boys* (1991) was a novel by which writer?

15 ORF is the public broadcasting service of which European country?

16 After whom is the Scottish town of Helensburgh named?

17 "Our remedies oft in ourselves do lie" is a quote from which Shakespeare play?

18 Which European football club was once known as Lutnia Debiec?

19 Which actress provided the voice of Esmeralda in the 1996 Disney film *The Hunchback of Notre Dame*?

20 Lucerne is another name for which perennial flowering plant?

Easy

Medium

Hard

Answers to QUIZ 497 – Pot Luck

1	Chichester	11	Hawaiian Islands
2	Singapore	12	*Homicide: Life on the Street*
3	Don Quixote	13	(Iced) Coffee
4	Dada	14	Denver
5	William Wordsworth	15	The shoulder joint
6	Heights	16	222
7	A fish	17	Vaiaku, Funafuti
8	*Red Sparrow*	18	Avocet
9	Marillion	19	Miriam
10	Glasgow	20	Ava Max

Easy

1 Who played Tony in the 1961 film *West Side Story*?

2 The 1931 play *Green Grow the Lilacs* by Lynn Rigg was the basis for which musical?

3 In which 1996 musical does the character of Angel Dumott Schunard appear?

4 Who wrote the lyrics for the English version of *Les Misérables*?

5 *They Call the Wind Maria* is a song from which musical?

6 Which 1964 musical, set in 1905, was written by Jerry Bock, Sheldon Harnick and Joseph Stein?

7 Who choreographed *Cats* and *The Phantom of the Opera*?

8 Which musical was written and directed by Anthony Newley, who also starred in the original 1961 West End production?

9 In the 1972 film *Cabaret*, what was the name of Michael York's character?

10 What is the name of the man murdered by Roxie Hart in *Chicago*?

11 *A Dream is a Wish Your Heart makes* features in which Disney film?

12 Princeton and Kate are the main characters in which stage musical first performed in 2003?

Medium

13 In which year did *The Lion King* open at the Lyceum Theatre in London?

14 Who wrote and directed the 2016 film *La La Land*?

15 Which musical was the first musical to win the Best Picture Oscar?

16 *Waitress* opened at the Adelphi Theatre in London's West End in 2019 with which former *American Idol* contestant in the title role?

17 Which 1980 film musical was the last film to feature Gene Kelly?

18 *The Beautiful and Damned* (2003) was a musical about which author?

19 Who wrote the music for *Funny Girl*?

20 Bill Snibson is the main character in which 1937 musical?

Hard

Answers to QUIZ 498 – History

1	Vittorio Veneto	11	1640s (1641)
2	Xia	12	Samnite Wars
3	First Earl of Richmond	13	*HMS Campania*
4	The War of Jenkins' Ear	14	50
5	$11 million	15	Ninth (886 AD)
6	1694	16	Physiology or medicine
7	First Earl Jellicoe	17	Gettysburg
8	Anne of Cleves	18	Magnus Barefoot
9	Institute of International Law (1904)	19	Nara
10	Alfonso XIII	20	18th century (1751)